D0881083

School of American Research
Advanced Seminar Series

DOUGLAS W. SCHWARTZ, GENERAL EDITOR

SCHOOL OF AMERICAN RESEARCH
ADVANCED SEMINAR SERIES

Reconstructing Prehistoric Pueblo Societies
New Perspectives on the Pueblos
Structure and Process in Latin America
The Classic Maya Collapse
Methods and Theories of Anthropological Genetics
Sixteenth-Century Mexico
Ancient Civilization and Trade
Photography in Archaeological Research
Meaning in Anthropology
The Valley of Mexico
Demographic Anthropology
The Origins of Maya Civilization
Explanation of Prehistoric Change

# Explanation of Prehistoric Change

Advanced Seminars are made possible
by a gift in recognition of
PHILIP L. SHULTZ
for his efforts on behalf of
the School of American Research

# EXPLANATION OF
# PREHISTORIC CHANGE

EDITED BY
JAMES N. HILL

A SCHOOL OF AMERICAN RESEARCH BOOK

UNIVERSITY OF NEW MEXICO PRESS•Albuquerque

GN
358
E9

**Library of Congress Cataloging in Publication Data**

Main entry under title:
Explanation of prehistoric change.

(School of American Research advanced seminar series)
Papers from a seminar held in Santa Fe, Apr. 2-8, 1970.
"A School of American Research book."
Bibliography: p. xxx
Includes index.
1. Social change—Congresses.  2. Man, Pre-historic—Congresses.  I. Hill, James N., 1934-
II. Series: Santa Fe, N.M. School of American Research.  Advanced seminar series.
GN358.E9    301.24    76-57541
ISBN 0-8263-0451-6

# Foreword

The purpose of the seminar from which this volume grew was to formulate a coherent theoretical and methodological framework for explaining sociocultural stability and change. The framework was to be based in general systems theory, with support from biological ecology and evolutionary explanations. This aim was superbly accomplished by the seminar, and its results are now translated into this volume by leading the reader through the same steps taken by the participants themselves. The book moves carefully through a presentation of such fundamental concepts and their background as change, process, measurement, scientific explanation, prediction, systems theory, and computer simulation. But because of its organization and method of presentation, this seminar volume is also an opportunity for the reader to obtain an insider's view into the complex alternative opinions on major issues in contemporary archaeology. As such, it is an important document in the history of the discipline, since the chapters and the selected transcript of the discussion clearly chronicle the growing solidification of this new paradigm. Thus this volume is that rare combination in science: a substantive contribution and a case study in the intellectual dynamics of the discipline.

In the first three chapters, James N. Hill and Fred Plog deal elegantly with past models of change, process, systems theory, the nature of acceptable scientific explanation, and new views of stability and change through an integrated and general systems theory approach. The following five chapters (by Arthur A. Saxe, Richard I. Ford, Michael A. Glassow, Henry T. Wright, and William T. Sanders), each an important contribution to the theoretical and methodological discussion, also use the developing theoretical framework with data from Hawaii, the Midwest, the Southwest, Iran, and the Valley of Mexico. Plog then employs Saxe's Hawaiian material to introduce the potentials of computer simulation for explaining change. The last two chapters provide an opportunity to reassess the whole approach. First, Melvin L. Perlman evaluates two central ideas that cross-cut all the papers: the nature of explanation and the systematic approach to stability and change. Then an edited transcript of the seminar discussion ranges widely over the major issues confronted by the participants and captures both the heat and the light of the sessions.

If it is reasonable to assume that the future contribution of archaeology depends in part on our increased understanding of the processes of stability and change, then this volume represents a major step toward making that contribution possible.

Douglas W. Schwartz  
School of American Research

# Preface

The eighth in a series of advanced seminars sponsored by the School of American Research was held April 2–8, 1970, in Santa Fe, New Mexico. The topic of the seminar was the explanation of prehistoric organizational change.

Nine scholars participated: Richard I. Ford (Museum of Anthropology, University of Michigan); Michael A. Glassow (Department of Anthropology, University of California, Santa Barbara); James N. Hill (Department of Anthropology, University of California, Los Angeles); Melvin L. Perlman (Department of Sociology, Brock University, St. Catherine's, Ontario); Fred Plog (Arizona State University, Tempe); William T. Sanders (Department of Anthropology, Pennsylvania State University); Arthur A. Saxe (Department of Sociology and Anthropology, Ohio University); William T. Stuart (Division of Anthropology, University of Maryland); and Henry T. Wright (Museum of Anthropology, University of Michigan).

I served as chairman of the seminar. Melvin L. Perlman was the discussant and Lewis R. Binford served as an informal discussant for one day of the seminar.

Seven papers were prepared and circulated in advance of the seminar to communicate information and serve as a basis for the discussions. These papers were revised after the discussions and are presented in this volume, together with a statement by the discussant Perlman, edited portions of the taped discussions themselves, and my introduction. The additional paper by Fred Plog (on simulating the precontact Hawaiian system) was written at the request of the participants, and is an outgrowth of seminar discussion on this topic.

The purpose of the seminar was to learn and communicate as much as we could about methods and theories for explaining change in human sociocultural systems—with emphasis on data from prehistoric systems. It is an understatement to say that anthropologists have long been interested in explaining change, and that they have frequently attempted with varying success to so do. It is perhaps a cliché to point out that archaeologists, in particular, are in a very special position with regard to their potential for being able to explain change. Yet at the same time, it is evident that most of our explanations have been inadequate in one way or another—especially in light of the fact that we do not yet adequately understand what change is, how to measure it, or what an acceptable scientific explanation of it is.

The fundamental questions raised at the seminar were: What is change? What is stability? How does each occur? Why does each occur? Can we predict when changes will occur, and something about their probable nature and direction? What is a good explanation? What is a good explanation of change? Can we measure and explain change using prehistoric data? How should we go about it? How might computer simulation be useful?

The answers that came forth were indeed interesting. Some were not surprising, but others were both surprising and exciting. I have never before participated in such a stimulating intellectual exchange. While the degree of agreement among us was phenomenal, there were also a number of fundamental disagreements. While not all of these were satisfactorily resolved, I believe that the seminar has yielded a genuinely new (if not yet complete) synthetic approach to explaining change— whenever and wherever it may occur, or may have occurred in the past. In this sense, this book should be useful (or at least provocative) to other social scientists attempting to deal with change, as well as to anthropologists and anthropological archaeologists.

At the same time, it is clear that we have barely scratched the surface—and some of our ideas and formulations will be demonstrated to be inadequate. Moreover, the systemic and ecological approach to explaining change presented in this volume is a general one; it is at present far too general and in need of refinements, especially with regard to making it operational with substantive data. While we have presented some substantive explanations of change, we have by no means succeeded in achieving fully adequate definitions and measurements of our concepts, dimensions, and variables; and we have only just begun to learn the requirements and potential of simulating aspects of sociocultural systems on the computer. In short, we think we now have a much better understanding than we did about what change is and how we must go about trying to explain it—but there is a long way to go. The future promises exciting and rapid increases in knowledge with regard to explaining change. And the future of archaeology as a social science depends on increases in such knowledge.

The participants in this seminar are indebted to Douglas W. Schwartz, Director, and to the members of the Board of Directors, of the School of American Research, and to the community of Santa Fe. They provided us with both the opportunity and encouragement to participate in a most rewarding seminar. It was a unique opportunity, usually unavailable elsewhere, to get together in face-to-face discussion without interruption for an extended period of time, and with all of the facilities necessary to permit a continuous flow of intellectual productivity. Any scientific value this volume may have is in large part to the credit of the School of American Research.

We are also particularly grateful to Mrs. Douglas Schwartz for her generous hospitality, and to Mrs. Albert Schroeder for taking care of all of us with patience and enthusiasm. Finally, I am personally grateful to Janet D. Orcutt (UCLA) for many hours of editorial assistance.

James N. Hill

# Contents

Foreword
DOUGLAS W. SCHWARTZ, GENERAL EDITOR — vii

Preface
JAMES N. HILL — ix

1. Introduction
   JAMES N. HILL — 1

2. Explaining Change
   FRED PLOG — 17

3. Systems Theory and the Explanation of Change
   JAMES N. HILL — 59

4. On the Origin of Evolutionary Processes: State Formation
   in the Sandwich Islands
   ARTHUR A. SAXE — 105

5. Evolutionary Ecology and the Evolution of Human
   Ecosystems: A Case Study from the Midwestern U.S.A.
   RICHARD I. FORD — 153

6. Population Aggregation and Systemic Change:
   Examples from the American Southwest
   MICHAEL A. GLASSOW — 185

7. Toward an Explanation of the Origin of the State
   HENRY T. WRIGHT — 215

8. Resource Utilization and Political Evolution in the
   Teotihuacan Valley
   WILLIAM T. SANDERS — 231

xiii

# Contents

9. Systems Theory and Simulation: The Case of
   Hawaiian Warfare and Redistribution
   FRED PLOG                                                        259

10. Discussion
    JAMES N. HILL, ED.                                              271

11. Comments on Explanation, and on Stability and Change
    MELVIN L. PERLMAN                                              319

References                                                         335

Index                                                              353

# 1
# Introduction

## JAMES N. HILL

*Department of Anthropology*
*University of California*
*Los Angeles*

The papers and discussion presented in this volume are the result of a number of years of growing concern, on my part and that of the other seminar participants, over how to describe and explain change in what are variously referred to as social, cultural, or sociocultural systems (which I refer to here as "societal" systems, even though the term does not avoid all of the vague, loaded, and unoperational connotations of other terms). It is evident that while anthropologists and other social scientists have had a long-standing interest in explaining change (and have come up with some interesting results as well), we do not yet adequately understand either how to describe and measure change or how to explain it adequately in scientific terms. As scientists, we are not only interested in explaining varability within and among contemporaneous societal systems, but also we are interested in explaining both change and stability in such systems—or at least in those aspects of substantive societal systems that involve specific aspects of human behavior that we believe are in need of explanation.

The essential question is, Why and how did observed societal forms get to be the way they are (either today or in the past)? An extension of this question is, Can we predict future changes in these forms? The former question, at least, is precisely the one asked by Charles Darwin, Alfred Russell Wallace, and others with regard to biological forms; and it is the question that ultimately led to the modern synthetic theory of evolution. It is clear that we are in need of a coherent body of theory on *societal* evolution and we hope that this volume is a beginning in that direction.

A brief evaluation of past theoretical constructs (general explanations) of change is presented by Fred Plog (chapter 2). He tends to emphasize the elements of usefulness in these approaches, however, rather than focusing a great deal of attention on their inadequacies for our purposes; and this permits me the opportunity of focusing on the latter here, by way of introducing and justifying the seminar and its results. I make no attempt to cover all of the past approaches that might be relevant, but I do think it is important to point specifically to some of the fundamental inadequacies of at least a few of the most prominent published frameworks for explaining change—the ones that have been specifically labeled "evolutionism." The following statements, then, are viewed as supplementary to Plog's historical efforts; they do not include consideration of such explanatory models as "acculturation," "diffusionism," "behaviorism," and "growth" (see Plog, chapter 2).

I consider here only the paradigms of unilineal evolutionism, general evolutionism, multilinear evolutionism, and specific evolutionism ("neo-evolution" or "cultural ecology"). I do not intend, in doing this, to imply that the other paradigms Plog mentions are either more or less useful to us than these—they are not. I have chosen to review these four simply because they *do* claim evolution as their focus of attention.

Consider first the unilineal evolutionism of the nineteenth century (e.g., Morgan 1870, 1877; Tylor 1871, 1889, 1899). While it described general evolutionary stages, based on criteria of complexity, there was no satisfactory specification or detailing of the processes by which societies got from one stage to the next. "Progress" was, in a sense, inevitable for societies—or at least for some of them. In accounting for why some societies had evolved further than others (a process question), the answer was that some *races* had evolved further than others—they were more advanced on the evolutionary scale, and hence were more intelligent and capable of developing complex social institutions, technology, and so on. If this had been demonstrated to be the case, it would have been at least a useful partial general explanation of change. But since it was subsequently found not to be the case, the "explanation" is clearly inadequate.

In all fairness, of course, it should be pointed out that within the framework of then existing knowledge the explanation had to be considered reasonable—especially given the then believed "fact" that human biological evolution had occurred only very recently, and thus must have been very rapid. If the divergence of the races had occurred only in the last few thousand years, it stood to reason that some or all societal differences might be ascribed to racial differences. With the increased understanding of the mechanisms and great time involved in biological evolution, however, it became obvious that most societal differences had to be far more recent in origin than the divergence of racial types.

The more recent general evolutionism of Leslie White (1943, 1959) represents a major advance in societal evolutionary theory, yet it is also inadequate for our purposes. In fact, I would call it nonevolutionary, in the sense that it does not account for the *processes* through which evolutionary change occurs (as the biological theory of evolution clearly does). Essentially, his explanation for why some societies are more complex than others is that they are able to harness more energy per capita. So far so good; and the idea will probably be very useful to us. Although White explains why some societies are able to harness more energy than others (that is, because of more powerful and efficient technology), he does not specify the processes by which some societies obtain such technology in increasing amounts while others do not. The processes are simply unclear in his writings; and in the absence of processual mechanisms, it is inappropriate to label his ideas as a theory of evolution. To me, at least, the phrase "evolutionary theory" necessarily implies processual specification. While one can simply use the term evolution to refer to descriptions of evolutionary stages, there should in this case be no theoretical claims implied. Describing the course of evolution does not explain it—and the term "theory" always implies explanation.

The multilinear evolutionism of Julian Steward (1955a) also poses difficulties. It *does* become more specific in that it deals with accounting for variability in the adaptations of specific "culture types," or "levels of cultural integration," rather than dealing with general evolutionary stages. It is also more specific with regard to process in that it correlates specified "core" organizational attributes of the culture types with

3

specified general characteristics of the different types of physical environment and technology associated with each culture type. Steward is definitely explanatory; he does, at least at a general level, account for why it is that his different culture types have different core organizational attributes—in terms of general differences in environment, technology, and exploitation of the environment. As an integral part of this, he emphasizes the fact that there are cross-cultural regularities in these processes of adaptation—hence the intraculture-type similarities in core attributes of organization.

Steward's contribution, like White's, was substantial. At the same time, however, it is inadequate in several respects. In the first place, it is still too general; it accounts for cross-cultural similarities in only a few very general attributes, and does not account for many other aspects of intra- and intersocietal variability that are of interest. Related to this, his emphasis on explaining similarities virtually ignores accounting for differences in societies within his culture types. Third, he is usually not very specific concerning the precise determinant variables and processes involved; and he says little or nothing about the causal efficacy of feedback relationships between cultural systems and their environments. Much of his work, and that of his followers, has involved more the correlation of societal attributes with techno-environmental characteristics than the specific explanation of such correlations.

Also important is the fact that Steward's multilineal evolutionism is largely nonevolutionary in nature. His *Theory of Culture Change* (1955a) is devoted largely to accounting for why it is that there is variability among kinds of societal organization—not why or how they change from one form into another (evolution). In that sense his work is more "functional" than evolutionary. To be sure, some of his works are indeed evolutionary (*cf.* especially Steward 1937, 1949), but even in these instances his explanations are too simplistic. He emphasizes univariate rather than systemic causal determinacy, subscribing to population growth and/or large-scale irrigation as prime movers.

In short, while he (and his followers) have contributed a great deal to our thinking concerning the processes of societal evolution, he has not presented a coherent theoretical construct that will adequately account for both stability and change—especially in terms of accounting for why certain aspects of *individual* societal systems may remain relatively stable, while others are changing. The specific processes of stability and change are missing. Moreover, he offers no theoretical paradigm by which one might be able to predict the nature, direction, and timing of change.

There are, of course, a number of anthropological studies (largely post–1960) that have overcome some of the difficulties of multilinear evolutionism. These can be included under the labels specific evolutionism, neo-evolutionism, or cultural ecology. This approach is associated with such names as Marshall Sahlins, Elman Service, Andrew Vayda, Anthony Leeds, Clifford Geertz, Roy Rappaport, Marvin Harris, and others. It focuses on individual societal systems and aspects of such systems, and accounts for their maintenance in terms of systemic relationships among sets of specific societal components or measurable variables. Rappaport's work (1967) is a notable example.

This approach is a form of structural-functionalism. The basic emphasis is to show in some detail how the specific systemic components of a society interrelate with one another and "function" to regulate the system in such a way that it can continue to operate in the face of environmental variability. In short, aspects of a societal system serve (or "function") as homeostats to maintain stability or equilibrium.

Many of the studies emanating from this general approach focus on describing the interrelationships among substantive components of the societal system (that is, social groups and institutions), and on pointing to the functions they perform in maintaining systemic equilibrium. Other studies are more refined in a processual sense, and describe societal systems in terms of sets of interacting *variables* rather than as sets of interacting components (Rappaport 1967). But in either case, this approach focuses on describing *how* societal systems operate as subsystems within an ecosystem.

In this sense, such studies are clearly systemic, processual, and explanatory. They are systemic in that multivariate interdeterminacy is considered, including the importance of both internal and external feedback loops. They are processual in that they describe how specific regulatory mechanisms operate in the face of specific and measurable environmental variability. And they are explanatory in the sense that the behavior of the various components and variables of the system is accounted for (predicted) in terms of the behavior of other components and variables of the system and its environment.

The approach is clearly a useful one, and superior to the approaches previously considered—at least in its specification of process. It appears

5

obvious that before we can explain change in societal systems, we must be able to describe the operation of our systems—and the cultural ecology approach is well on its way to being able to do this acceptably.

Unfortunately, however, the approach suffers from being non-evolutionary; it will not, by itself, explain change. It is, for the most part, focused on describing societies as they are, rather than on discovering the processes through which they arrived at their current states, or the processes that might be promoting change. In fact, it appears that most modern social theory, as well as practice, is concerned primarily with the processes of equilibrium (cf. Sahlins and Service 1960; Buckley 1967:1–40). The emphasis is on describing societal organizations, correlating these organizations with their environments, and pointing out the ways in which they seem to be well "adapted" to their environments.

It is clear that theoretical constructs emphasizing the maintenance of stability will not be very useful, by themselves, in accounting for change. However, I argue in my own contribution to this volume (chapter 3) that the processes of systemic stability are an integral *part* of the processes of change.

The primary point that should be reemphasized here is that apparently none of the general approaches that call themselves (or have been called) evolutionary actually explicate the processes of evolution—at least not sufficiently. While we have a number of descriptions of change in the literature, the precise processes by which it occurs, and the means by which it might be predicted, are not specified.

I emphasize that my intent is *not* to imply that none of these so-called evolutionary approaches have important elements of usefulness to us in our quest for an integrated theory of societal evolution. As Plog points out, these as well as other approaches do contain useful elements; part of the trick is to separate the wheat from the chaff, and to integrate these useful elements (together with other relevant elements) into a coherent theory. Even the rightfully maligned culture historical or diffusionist approach (cf. Binford 1962, 1968a, 1968b, 1972; Flannery 1967) has some usefulness, as I point out in my own chapter (3). Nonetheless, a completely satisfactory evolutionary theory has not yet been developed—here or anywhere else.

The need for further investigations into the processes of societal stability and change is evident. The purpose of the seminar was not to sit down together and devise an a priori body of theory which we could claim

6

to be sufficient and useful as is, although general theoretical propositions are certainly proposed in the following chapters. At least of equal importance was the goal of doing what we could toward learning how to go about building an appropriate body of theory. In this sense, much of the material that follows is methodological rather than theoretical. Nonetheless, my feeling is that the following chapters, taken as a whole (and including the discussion), represent a remarkably coherent theoretical and methodological framework for explaining stability and change, its insufficiencies and lack of refinement notwithstanding.

In essence, our general framework is based in general systems theory, although it also includes the tenets of biological ecology, the theory of evolution, locational analysis, and other elements as well. While the approach is general, it is also ultimately testable against empirical data. And while we have done what we could to carry out some limited testing in these papers, the primary focus thus far is not on testing. That, however, is certainly the next step—and the idea that the testing will involve computer simulation is agreed upon.

It is worth noting that while the title of the seminar was "Explanation of Prehistoric Organizational Change," I have deleted the term "organizational" from the title of this volume. The reason for doing this is important by way of introducing what follows. The difficulty is that this term would perhaps have implied that we are concerned only with explaining change in things that are commonly understood as "organizational" (such as organization of residences, tasks, sodalities, statuses, and so on), and not in nonorganizational entities (for example, projectile points or house structures). Actually, this is not the case; our general approach is designed to explain change in any aspect of societal systems, whether it be a system or subsystem, or simply a physical and nonsystemically organized component of such a system.

The initial idea that we were dealing with "organizational" change as opposed to some other kind of change (to be defined) would have been a false distinction. The reason for this is, of course, that system components (entities) that are not themselves internally systemically articulated and regulated (as systems or subsystems) are nevertheless parts of such systems. As such, variability and change in them can only be explained by reference to variability and change in the systems of which they are a part. To give an example, changes in the forms of projectile points cannot be explained by reference to the projectile points themselves—they cannot cause themselves to change. They change only when activities surrounding their manufacture or use change (as when the nature of the hunting or warfare subsystems changes).

In this sense, then, everything we study is either a component or subsystem of some other system—a point that Arthur Saxe makes quite forcefully (chapter 4). Thus, explaining change is *always* explaining *organizational* change—systems, by definition, are organized. Plog and Wright (chapters 2 and 7) reinforce this idea by pointing out that the explanation of any given phenomenon lies in placing it within a context of interacting variables, and that within such a context the behavior of the phenomenon can be predicted by the behavior of these other variables.

Thus it is not surprising that at the seminar there was very little concern expressed for the definition of the term *organization*. Since we took a systems point of view from the outset, the discussion (and concern) was phrased in terms of What is a system? and What is systemic change? rather than What is organization? and What is organizational change? The term *organization* is understood once an understanding of the nature of systems is achieved. And that is indeed a major topic of consideration in this volume.

I might also point out that while the seminar title implied a concern for explaining change in aspects of cultures, social organizations, and so on, there was no discussion about what a culture or social organization might be, definitionally or otherwise. It was simply understood that definitions would constitute irrelevant academics—these concepts are not in need of definition. If we can describe and explain both stability and change in measurable aspects of societal systems, that is enough. Whether or not we call the results studies of "culture" or something else is unimportant—and this is reflected in the varied usages of such general labels throughout the volume.

Finally, I almost decided to delete the term *prehistoric* from the title, since it is in some sense irrelevant. Change is change, and understanding its processes is independent of the temporal loci of our data. Even though the intent of the seminar was to lay a groundwork for explaining societal changes that occurred in prehistoric times, our discussion was by no means restricted to prehistoric data and the relevance of our work should not be so restricted. At the same time, to delete the word *prehistoric* would have been misleading because most of our examples make use of prehistoric data. And we do indeed share the belief that archaeologists are in a very special position with regard to explaining change.

The seminar papers are presented as chapters in this volume (chapters 2 through 8). The primary rationale underlying their order of presentation is based on the relative degree to which each emphasizes either method-theory statements or substantive contributions. While virtually all of the chapters deal in one way or another with important methodological or theoretical concerns, I have tried to place the ones focusing exclusively on method and theory first, following these with those dealing with both kinds of contributions. Related to this, the ordering represents an attempt to lead the reader through the fundamental concepts and principles of our general approach before exposing him to substantive examples with the hope that the substantive cases can be better understood in their appropriate contexts. I have not been a slave to such an ordering, however. Even though Wright's contribution is primarily methodological, I have placed it near the end, immediately before Sanders's work, simply because both are concerned specifically with explaining the evolution of the state.

Plog's paper (chapter 2) deals, first of all, with the nature of acceptable scientific explanation. He proposes that in order to have a good explanation we must be concerned with the nature of our formal, logical model of explanation, the nature of our substantive explanation, and the operational procedures required for an acceptable explanation. He then defines "change," and discusses four general approaches to explaining change that have been employed by anthropologists in the past. He argues that all of these "paradigms" have been and are useful, but none are adequate in themselves, and none of them are mutually exclusive. Finally, he presents his own model of the nature, description, and explanation of change, which in turn is composed of three non–mutually exclusive models of change which he believes should all be used in explaining any given situation of change, whether in societal systems, small groups, or individuals.

It is perhaps noteworthy that Plog's contribution is the only one emphasizing the importance of employing several explanatory models concurrently. At the same time, I see nothing in his work that conflicts significantly with the views presented by the other authors—his concern is simply somewhat more broadly gauged, and it provides a good context for what follows.

9

My own contribution (chapter 3) attempts to describe and develop an integrated general systems approach to explaining both stability and change. I provide a discussion of fundamental systems concepts, including the nature of regulation and change in living systems. I then evaluate the previously published systems approaches of James G. Miller, Walter Buckley, and Magoroh Maruyama, concluding that there are probably no published systems approaches suitable for our purposes. Following this, I present a modified approach that I believe *is* useful, providing hypothetical examples to illustrate my points. I then specify my view of the operational requirements necessary in explaining change, including the place of systems simulation. I also consider the problems of measurement faced by archaeologists attempting to explain change; and I conclude by evaluating the usefulness of general systems theory for our purposes.

Saxe's chapter (4) begins with a consideration of the nature and behavior of living systems, emphasizing the processes of both stability and change (morphostasis and morphogenesis), and how they operate together as evolutionary processes. His focus, however, is on the *origin* of evolutionary processes; and he argues that change is never initiated by factors internal to a given system, but rather is initiated (caused) by external factors—namely, long-term matter-energy interrelationships with at least one other system. He concludes that "a system in adaptive equilibrium will remain in adaptive equilibrium unless the equilibrium is disturbed by some extrasystemic force." He makes a good case for the idea that "an evolutionist explanation involves a functionalist explanation at a superordinate systemic level."

Saxe then provides a demonstration of the usefulness of his model of the change process using protohistoric and early historic data from the Hawaiian Islands. In fact, he rather convincingly explains the origin of the state in Hawaii following the arrival of Captain Cook in 1778 (or, the evolution from "chiefdom" to "state"). His explanation accounts for why it was that this organizational change was inevitable, given the extrasystemic inputs that occurred—and why it could not have happened in the absence of such inputs. His explanation is, in a general sense, relevant to explaining the origin of the state anywhere—past, present, or future; and it explains the many such transformations that occurred elsewhere in the world following European contact. This, in my view, is one of the very few cases in which an anthropologist has offered and partially tested an acceptable processual explanation of change. Saxe's two appendices provide many of the data necessary to document his case.

Ford's contribution (chapter 5) also considers briefly the nature and processes of living systems. But he then focuses on the *ecosystem* as his system of interest, and argues the importance of considering societal evolution within the context of the evolution of the ecosystem (the latter can be equated with Saxe's "superordinate system"). He presents a processual model of both ecosystemic regulation and evolution, emphasizing successional change in such systems. In short, his model attempts to explain the evolution of ecosystems.

He then shows how man, at all levels of sociocultural complexity, is an integral part of his ecosystem; and he presents a series of hypotheses on how human organization (at different levels of complexity) should articulate with and respond to the ecosystem and its evolution as well as how human organization can serve to help regulate and partially determine the evolution of the ecosystem. He then applies his model to the prehistoric American Middle West, and attempts both to predict the nature of ecosystemic and societal evolution that ought to have occurred from Paleo-Indian to historic times, and to test his explanatory hypotheses against currently available data.

It is a most provocative presentation. Ford offers not only a general explanatory model for organizational change in the Midwest, but also one that is applicable to numerous other areas of the world as well—particularly during immediate post-Pleistocene times. He courageously makes predictions about sociocultural evolution that can be tested, and from which further, more specific propositions can be generated.

Glassow (chapter 6) relates the principles of systems theory (and locational analysis) to the specific problem of explaining variability and change in the spatial patterning of population aggregations—notably households. The basic idea is that the spatial distributions of households (and other system components) can be explained because they tend to be located optimally in terms of the frequency and costs of matter-energy and information flows among them, and between them and their environments.

After considering some of the kinds of statistics required for describing spatial distributions, and developing his own modifications of them, he turns to his own prehistoric data from northwestern New Mexico to test two hypotheses designed to account for changes that occurred in the spatial locations and clustering of households during the Basket Maker II–III periods. He then turns to data from the entire northern Southwest, and tests a series of hypotheses designed to explain the rapid increase in site size and household aggregation that occurred during the same time period.

Given that his test results are interesting, though not as satisfying as he wished, he concludes that a systemic explanatory model, involving a number of articulated hypotheses, is far superior to testing a series of individual hypotheses one by one. He then develops and partially tests a most interesting general systemic model which may account for a whole variety of Basket Maker II–III changes, including the shift to dependence on agriculture, changes in site location and aggregation, and the evolution of aspects of societal organization and integration.

It is interesting that while Glassow does not use Ford's terminology, his explanation of Basket Maker II–III social organizational changes is fundamentally the same as Ford's explanation of social organizational changes in the Midwest during Mississippian times. In both cases, the idea is that as groups of people become increasingly dependent upon agriculture, they become specialized agriculturalists without the possibility of reverting to substantial hunting and gathering, even in times of crop failure. Thus, because their crop success is dependent on their monitoring and responding to the vagaries of the environment, they are forced to undergo fundamental organizational changes that will permit them effectively to monitor both predictable and unpredictable environmental variation; and they are forced to develop adequate organizational and technological means for damping these environmental effects. In short, the societal system must undergo irreversible change—evolution. The essential nature of this kind of explanation is presumably widely applicable to accounting for a variety of changes in societal systems.

Wright's contribution (chapter 7), like those of Sanders and Saxe, is concerned with the systemic processes accounting for the general kind of societal complexity known as the state. He focuses specifically on the nature of research strategies that might be useful in this regard, given the probability that an acceptable explanation must necessarily be multivariate and systemic. The paper deals with the practical problems encountered in building an explanatory theory.

He first presents a four-category typology of past theories of the evolution of the state, and derives from this a series of four generalizations concerning the similarities among all four types of explanations. These are then used to isolate the major determinants (multiple variables) that can be presumed to have some determining efficacy with regard to the evolution of the state. He proposes that a good explanation must take account of these multiple variables, and must account for both growth and stability.

In presenting his views on how one might develop an appropriate theoretical model to account for the state, he discusses the nature of systems, the nature of operational explanation, the nature of a useful theoretical model, and the usefulness of simulation modeling. He then turns to his past and current work in southwestern Iran to exemplify his own strategies. He concludes, as Glassow also does, that it is much more desirable and useful to develop an a priori theoretical model to explain change, and deduce related hypotheses from it (to test) than it is to try to test the effects of various possible determinants one at a time in the absence of their theoretical articulation. In fact, hypothesis testing and theory development must go hand in hand.

While Wright's contribution is concerned with methods (strategy) for explaining the state, Sanders's work (chapter 8) is a substantive example of it. He describes and explains the evolution of the city and state of Teotihuacan in highland Mexico, attempting to account for why it developed where and when it did. After describing the area and its resources, and presenting an account of the successional changes that occurred in the area during prehistoric times (Early Formative through Historic), he offers and defends an explanatory model he feels is very similar to Karl Wittfogel's explanation of the origin of states. In essence, he explains it as a result of increasing population in the Valley, which resulted in increasing intensification of agricultural techniques and competition for critical resources (especially spring-fed irrigation water). An increasing population placed a premium on centralized managerial tasks for coordinating and managing the water resources, external competition, and trade networks. Eventually the city became large and powerful enough to control outlying areas, and to exploit them for critical resources necessary to support increasing craft specialization and class stratification within the city.

While Sanders phrases his explanatory model in ecological-successional terms, it is clearly a systemic model as well. It includes the interrelationships of several major variables, including population size and growth rates, intensification of agriculture, increasing centralized control and power monopoly, increasing population, and expansion of trade and control over hinterlands.

It is interesting to note that Sanders appears to rely heavily in his explanation on population growth as a prime mover. In comparison, the reader will note Wright's explicit emphasis on the importance of multiple variable determinacy. In spite of this apparent difference in viewpoint, it is important to point out that all of the seminar participants recognize the importance of multiple variable feedback determinacy—but at the same time, some tend to regard certain variables as more "determinant" than others. In fact, most of the papers (especially those of Hill, Ford, and Glassow) appear to regard population growth as, in some sense, a prime mover—even though rationally most of us would admit, I think, that systemic explanations do not necessarily (or even often) involve prime movers. The determination of the relative importance of specific kinds of variables in an explanation is a matter for empirical demonstration in the cases at hand.

Chapter 9, Plog's second contribution, represents a statement concerning the subject the seminar was taking up during the last day or so—computer simulation. As the seminar progressed, it became evident to us that computer simulation clearly has a major role to play in both developing and testing explanations of systemic change (and stability). While there was little we could do in the time available toward developing a simulation model of an empirical case involving change, we were nonetheless able to use Saxe's Hawaiian data (chapter 4) in an effort at setting forth the bare outlines of what a simulation model might look like.

Our view was that this was "icing on the cake," since we had already accomplished as much as we had set out to accomplish at the seminar—realistically, at least. And, indeed, this simulation attempt can be considered as no more than "icing," in that no claim is made to have produced more than the rudimentary outlines of a simulation. With more time, I'm sure we could have done more in this direction—and at this moment others (as well as ourselves) are actively pursuing this direction with some success. Nonetheless, we feel that it is important to present our tentative starts in the direction of computer simulation, since this effort may be found useful to those who are doing similar work. At the very least, we think we are pointing in the right direction. All of us are grateful to both Plog and Saxe for their contributions, and we look forward to a future seminar in which we can put more fully into practice the ideas that came forth at the conclusion of our meeting.

It is noteworthy that Plog's second contribution does not deal in detail with the usage of computer simulation in dealing with *change* in societal systems. Obviously, we must learn how to simulate equilibrium or steady-state situations before we can satisfactorily begin to use simulation in studying change. As far as I know, there have thus far been no successful attempts at explaining change using simulation modeling. While my own chapter (3) sets forth some of the procedures I believe will be necessary to do this, we have yet to see it done using empirical data. The problems such an endeavor presents, while not insurmountable, do indeed represent a challenge—as should be evident from a careful reading of this book.

Chapter 11, by Perlman, is a contribution of a somewhat different nature than the others. As one of the two discussants, his task was to evaluate the other papers, as well as the entire research effort represented by the seminar. Thus, even though he makes method-theory kinds of observations, his is the least formal paper in the volume.

The selection of Perlman as a discussant was indeed fortunate, since his views were in many respects quite different from those of the other participants; and he forced us to consider issues which we might not otherwise have discussed critically. This is clearly reflected in both the discussion (chapter 11) and his own contribution.

Since it was not possible for him to consider all of the papers and issues individually, he has chosen to comment on the two most important issues: (1) the nature of explanation, and (2) the nature of systemic stability and change. In both instances his views are clearly at odds with those of the other contributors. In considering the nature of explanation, for example, he contends that logico-deductive models are inappropriate for the study of complex systems, and that a "pattern" or "systems" type of explanation should be used instead. And in dealing with the nature of societal stability and change, he proposes that belief systems, ideologies, and system "goals" are extremely important. In fact, in his view the primary "process" involved is the "goal" of minimizing "disturbance" within a system. His notion of the nature of societal systems also differs from that of the other participants, though it is important to point out that he appears to be thinking primarily of substantive, on-the-ground systems rather than of systems as sets of variables related by equations.

In any event, many of Perlman's differences in viewpoint highlight major issues in the social sciences; and these issues inevitably arise whenever there is a confrontation between materialist and idealist philosophies (cf. Harris 1968). It is most unfortunate that the other discussant (Stuart) was not able to contribute his evaluative comments, as his views would have provided the contrasting strict materialist perspective.

Chapter 10 consists of edited portions of the taped seminar discussion. It is important because it deals directly with the pros and cons of many of the major issues surrounding the explanation of change. The other chapters do not, for the most part, do this; they instead provide coherent sets of ideas and data from the viewpoints of their respective authors. It is only in chapter 10 that one can really begin to see the force of the argumentation, the reasoning behind it, the degree of consensus, and so on.

It is my belief that, taken together, both the individual contributions and the discussion present many of the elements of an internally coherent approach to explaining stability and change, even though it may still be somewhat loosely articulated. It is, of course, largely a systems *theoretic* rather than a systems *analytic* approach—and we must certainly increase our sophistication in employing systems analysis techniques with our data. But the two "approaches" are not in opposition, for we must also continue to refine and modify the general theoretical framework within which we understand the nature and processes of change. And as archaeologists and others increase our capabilities for analyzing systems, the result should be a concomitant increase in our understanding of systemic processes—and hence advances in the development of theory.

2

# Explaining Change

FRED PLOG

*Department of Anthropology*
*Arizona State University*
*Tempe*

This chapter describes one approach to explaining changes in man's culture and behavior. It specifically deals with two questions: What is explanation? How would an investigator formulate an explanation of cultural or behavioral change? In answering the first question, I will not focus on specific laws, statistics, or operational procedures. I assume that any investigator is capable of acquiring these as appropriate to one's research. The discussion instead will consider the relationship between laws, operational techniques, and research designs. It will be argued that too heavy an emphasis on explanation in its formal, operational, or substantive contexts produces incomplete explanations.

The second half of the chapter concerns a model for the study of cultural and behavioral change. The model directs the attention of investigators to patterns of temporal variability rather than the spatial variability that has been basic to most anthropological studies of change. The model is also a synthetic one: it seeks to provide theoretical and analytical devices that facilitate transitions from investigations focused on individuals to ones focused on social aggregates. In fact, it seeks to make both foci necessary for the successful explanation of any given case of change.

## THE NATURE OF EXPLANATION

The anthropologist's subject is behavioral and cultural variability—the similarities and differences in behavior at specific temporal and spatial loci. Its object is to explain these similarities and differences. *Explanation* is a term that is used frequently by anthropologists in discussing their objectives. But one rarely finds a consistent meaning in such usages. Moreover, the problem is not unique to anthropology.

Our disagreement over the meaning of explanation is a reflection of similar disagreement on the parts of epistemologists and philosophers of science. Viewed from different philosophical perspectives, explanation can have very different meanings. Yet all definitions of explanation are attempts to provide models for knowing and knowing that one knows. Much of the variation in definitions of explanation is the product of varying emphases that different authors place on three components of the knowledge process: (1) the problem of constructing valid arguments; (2) the problem of constructing arguments that account for observed variability; (3) the problem of insuring that the observed variability in both topic and causal variables is indeed observed and not a product of bias in techniques of data collection or analysis. (I have not included discovery in this list. While this topic is critically important, I know of no really successful attempts to explain or even to define this phenomenon.) Within the context of these varying emphases, it is possible to define a number of diametrically opposed schools: deductivists versus inductivists; formalists versus substantivists; argumentivists versus correlationists; and so on. It will be argued that explanation which fails to place equal emphasis on all three components, explanation that fails to include deductive and inductive arguments, formal and correlational techniques, is incomplete.

### The Formal Component: Constructing Valid Arguments

Philosophers concerned with the formal component of explanation are defining the classes of statements of which an argument is composed and analyzing the logical relationships that must exist between those classes of statements in order that an argument be deemed valid. Investigators concerned with the formal component of explanation are anxious to make sure that their arguments are logically valid.

The model of explanation in this formal context that I have found most useful is the Hempel-Oppenheim or deductive-nomological model. In this model, an explanation is an argument that fits a phenomenon "into a pattern of uniformities and shows that its occurrence was to be expected given specified laws and pertinent particular circumstances" (Hempel 1966:50). Three classes of statements are used in constructing the argument: (1) statements about the phenomenon under investigation; (2) statements about pertinent particular circumstances; and (3) statements of laws. The last two types of statements are called the explanans, "the class of those sentences that are adduced to account for the phenomenon" (Hempel 1966:51). The explanandum is a sentence describing the phenomenon under investigation.

An explanation in this model looks like this:

$$L_1, L_2, \ldots \ldots L_n \qquad \text{General Laws}$$

$$C_1, C_2, \ldots \ldots C_n \qquad \text{Statements of antecedent conditions}$$

Logical
Deduction _____

$$D \qquad \qquad \text{Description of the empirical phenomenon to be explained}$$

Having built such a skeleton, one turns to linkages, relationships that must exist between the propositions if they are to be considered valid. Philosophers have specified that the propositions must share certain terms. Moreover, the order of the terms in the proposition is critical—denying the first term (antecedent) or affirming the second (consequent) produces invalid arguments. We need pursue this definition of explanation no further. The formal rules of explanation are available in any logic book and should serve as continual checks on our reasoning.

A primary question that arises from this model of explanation concerns the term *law*. It seems pointless to engage in the old debate over the existence of anthropological (behavioral and cultural) laws. Explicitly and implicitly, behavioral scientists use such laws. A more important question concerns the sources of such laws, or at least statements that are worth testing because they might be laws. James G. Miller's "Living Systems: Cross-Level Hypotheses" (1965c) and *Human Behavior: An Inventory of Scientific Findings* by Bernard Berelson and Gary A. Steiner (1964) are excellent sources of such propositions. The ultimate source is, of course, the mind of the investigator attempting to create the knowledge. Norwood Hanson (1965) has written a provocative discussion of the discovery process.

## The Substantive Component:
## Accounting for Observed Variation

Explanation in substantive terms means decomposing and accounting for variability in some phenomenon under investigation. Anthropologists deal with variation in behavior and cultural processes at different spatial loci at a single point in time, variation in culture and behavior at different points in time at a single spatial locus, and variations in culture and behavior at different points (usually parallel) at multiple spatial loci. In dealing with spatial phenomena, it is argued that the phenomenon under study has some patterned spatial distribution. In dealing with temporal phenomena, the variable forms a trace or trajectory over time. Explaining variability means developing the ability to predict or retrodict the spatial patterns or the shape of the trace, whichever is relevant.

The process of explaining substantively involves placing a phenomenon in a system of antecedent and intervening phenomena, placing a variable in a system of antecedent or intervening variables. These act and interact to cause the topic phenomenon to vary as it does. One might, for example, be interested in explaining changes in the population of a community over time. The topic variable might be the actual population at some series of points in time, or increments of populations per unit of time, or any of the various measures of rates of population change. Having chosen one or a number of measures as topic variables, the investigator compiles a list of phenomena in the social and natural environments of the community that are viewed as potential determinants of population change, and measurement instruments are developed for each of them. All other variables held constant, the relationship between each antecedent or intervening variable and the topic variable is considered. So are interaction effects. Statistics such as the partial correlation coefficient are used to tell the investigator in a reasonably precise fashion the percentage of the variability that a particular antecedent variable accounts for. The multiple correlation coefficient tells the investigator the percentage of variation in a topic variable that the entire system of variables under investigation accounts for. It is rarely possible to account for 100 percent of the variability in behavioral phenomena, but correlational techniques provide an investigator with a measure of his success in reaching this goal.

Simulation models provide an even more significant approach to substantive explanation. The simplest of these is the linear regression model in which the equation $y = a + bx$ is used to define the relationship between topic and antecedent variables. Multiple regression techniques allow for the analysis of a number of variables and permit the investigator to control for intervening variables and interaction effects. By specifying a series of variables and defining the relationship between them, in a statistical or formal simulation model, the investigator is able to generate a trace for population change that very closely resembles the one that was observed.

Ideas concerning appropriate topic, antecedent, and intervening variables are not acquired by accident. Thomas Kuhn has discussed paradigms in the history of science and argued that for any discipline at any point in time, there is a set of topic phenomena that are considered appropriate ones, as well as a notion of appropriate antecedent and intervening phenomena (1962).

This discussion of substantive variation in no way implies that correlational analyses, simulation models, or predictive devices are the be all and end all of explanation. Arguments without predictive or correlative power are fatuous ones, but so are correlations or predictions without arguments.

### The Operational Component: Finding Variation and Keeping It Observed

The operational component of explanation goes furthest in coming to grips with the whole activity or process of explaining, of doing research. Operational explanation is testing particular arguments or models. Operational definitions of explanation specify the classes of activities that constitute research and the way in which these activities should be ordered if an explanation is the desired product of the research. On the one hand they specify a set of procedures to be used in identifying patterns of variation that may not be directly observable. On the other, they attempt to insure that the variability with which an investigator works is in fact observed and not a product of bias in the techniques of observation or analysis that he uses. The operational definition of explanation that I have found most useful specifies the following activities: formulation of a problem; formulation of hypotheses; putting the hypotheses into operation; collection of data; analysis; testing; and evaluation.

*Problem formulation:* At this first stage in the research process, a problem that is to be its subject is formulated in such a way that data and/or solutions to the problem are suggested. That is, statements like I am interested in culture change or I am interested in southwestern prehistory are replaced by at least relatively precise questions—Why did horticulturalists living on the Colorado Plateau at about A.D. 700 begin to adopt water control techniques? Formulating the problem should always involve an extensive review of the literature pertaining to the problem. It is often the case, and has too often been the case in the past, that the problem centered on a set of data—a site that an archaeologist had been told to dig, a population that an ethnographer had been sent to study. I assume that anthropology is beyond the point where problems focused primarily on data collection are likely to be productive. None of anthropology's subdisciplines is lacking in either already collected data or research situations. To select a research site and to claim to be interested in all of the variability that can be observed there is naive and results in the rambling monographs that have been the bane of the discipline. Data sets and research settings must be selected with a problem in mind.

*Formulation of hypotheses:* Hypotheses are statements of relationship between two or more variables that are potential but unproven laws. They are the basic ingredients of the arguments that investigators formulate before they begin fieldwork. Good multivariate arguments and models must be based upon clear statements of bivariate relationships in an "if-then" format. "Arguments of relevance" providing some preliminary evidence of the probable validity of the hypotheses should be included. In short, this stage in the research process should involve a transition from high- to middle- to low-level theory. Placing the formulations of problems and hypotheses at the beginning of the research process is based upon the argument that rigorous research is founded on both a problem and one or more sets of hypotheses, potential solutions to the problem.

*Putting the hypotheses into operation:* The kinds of operational procedures that an investigator will use will vary with his problem and field setting. There are, however, important steps that must be taken in making any set of arguments operational. (1) Test implications of the arguments must be identified. The investigator should specify particular states and conditions or patterns in collectable data that he should find if the arguments he is proposing are valid ones. Any worthwhile argument should have observable implications, and it is to these implications that the investigator should direct his attention. (2) The data that must be collected in the field to determine whether the predicted states, conditions, and patterns are present should be specified. (3) Measurement devices for converting raw data to variables should be identified and their efficacy demonstrated. Raw field data are bundles of attributes, some of which are relevant to the investigator, and some of which are not. Devices for observing and measuring those specific attributes of behavior that are relevant to the test implications must be specified. (4) A technique for insuring that there is no bias, or at least that there is a statable bias, in the data that an investigator collects must be developed. The investigator must know the relationship between the sample of behavior that he observes and the behavioral universe. This concern need not imply random sampling. It is my impression that for most anthropological problems random sampling is useful only within a factorial design, a design stratified by antecedent variables.

*Collection of data:* All the activities that are to be performed in the field have now been specified. Additional aspects of the field situation have been discussed at length for all of anthropology's subdisciplines.

*Analysis:* The analytical procedures that are to be used in processing field data should have been specified in putting the hypotheses into operation. At this stage in the research, relevant attributes of the data are measured and the variables to be used in the analysis created.

*Testing:* Similarly, the testing procedures were specified in making the hypotheses operational. At this stage, those tests are carried out. It is worth emphasizing that the ultimate test of a particular argument or model is its ability to replicate the patterned variation of the topic phenomenon.

*Evaluation:* The results of the tests are examined, conclusions reached, and further research implications specified. Whether results are positive or negative, it is important to reconsider the entire research design and ask whether the results may be an artifact of the procedures used or whether they inhere in the data and theory.

This author and a number of others have argued that it is important to follow these steps in the order listed. Research is a process that is

23

characterized by feedback—the reformulation of arguments and models while research is under way, the redefinition of variables, and so on. Especially when a given investigator works on a single problem for many years, this retooling will be ubiquitous. However, at any stage in the research process, it is desirable to stick with a basic set of procedures. A precise record of reformulations and modifications of a research design is one of an investigator's most valuable tools in seeking and finding new directions.

### Summary

Research must be formally, substantively, and operationally complete if it is to result in explanations of observed variation. It is possible to formulate elegant arguments that are substantively meaningless. It is possible to make trivial hypotheses operational. It is possible to account for 98 percent of the variation in some phenomenon without understanding its behavior one whit. It is impossible to explain rigorously and to acquire understanding without being concerned with all three components of explanation.

## EXPLAINING ORGANIZATIONAL CHANGE

The focus of this seminar has been organizational change. For me, the critical component of the concept *organizational change* is the term *organization*. Organization refers to the components of a system and the interaction between the components. In this sense, human behavior at all levels—individual, group, and societal—is organized. Change refers specifically to change over time at a minimum of one spatial locus. While it is possible that studies of change might involve more than a single such locus, to be legitimate studies of change they must involve records of change over time at each locus.

We may make this definition somewhat more specific by noting that not all changes in time are organizational changes. Some systems are characterized by seasonal or multiannual cycles in which they take on varying poses. These changes are a regular part of the system's adaptation to its existing environment. In referring to organizational change, an investigator specifies a focus on irregular temporal variability, or non-cyclical variability—on changes in the components of a system or the patterns of interaction between components.

24

*Paradigms in the Study of Change*

Let us first examine the approaches that anthropologists have been and are taking to the study of change. Thomas Kuhn has created a very useful device for such tasks. He has discussed the history of science in terms of paradigms—"accepted examples of scientific practice—examples which include law, theory, application, and instrumentation together—[that] provide models from which spring particular coherent traditions of scientific research" (Kuhn 1962:10). Paradigms are "sufficiently unprecedented to attract an enduring group of adherents away from competing models of scientific activity. Simultaneously . . . [they] are sufficiently open-ended to leave all sorts of problems for the redefined group of practitioners to resolve" (ibid.).

In a strong sense, a paradigm supplies a problem and the laws, theories, and operational devices necessary to attempt a solution to it. In a weaker sense, it is a statement of a problem and a suggestion as to how that problem might be solved. Anthropology is in what Kuhn would call a preparadigm stage. We usually have many competing paradigms with overlapping and equally vigorous constituencies. While anthropology's paradigms are paradigms only in the weak sense of the word, Kuhn's model provides a convenient framework for investigating different approaches to change.

What changes do we seek to explain and how do we seek to explain them? This question is not a new one; anthropologists have already given many different answers to it. These answers can be organized in terms of four paradigms that have dominated our studies of change: evolutionism, cultural ecology, acculturation, and behaviorism. (I omit diffusionism from this consideration because of its explanatory poverty in every sense of the term. This is not to deny that diffusion occurs; historical patterns of interaction are important. However, they are the data of change, not explanations for it.)

Evolutionism is associated with the works of Tylor, Morgan, Childe, White, Sahlins, Service, Carneiro, and Naroll. I have relied heavily on the discussion of Sahlins and Service (1960), Harris (1968), and Service (1971) in describing this approach. The discussion of ecological approaches to change is based upon Julian Steward's *Theory of Culture Change* (1955a), Geertz's application of these ideas in *Agricultural Involution* (1963), Adams's use of them in *The Evolution of Urban Society* (1966), and again, Harris's *The Rise of Anthropological Theory* (1968). Sahlins

25

and Service have attempted to reconcile what I have labeled evolutionism and ecology by referring to the former as general evolution and the latter as specific evolution, and examining important aspects of their interdependence. While there is no doubt that these two approaches are not mutually exclusive, most investigators tend to be following one set of ideas or another in any given investigation. Evolutionism usually refers to specific cultures only as examples, while ecology typically uses more general evolutionary principles only insofar as they are needed to gain insight into particular patterns of change. Acculturational studies are principally associated with British and American functionalism, and represent attempts on the parts of these schools to deal with change. A number of the more important works of this paradigm are collected in Bohannan and Plog's *Beyond the Frontier* (1968). *Modernization Among Peasants,* by Everett Rogers (1969), is the most comprehensive, albeit still incomplete, application of the behaviorist paradigm. Anthropological practitioners of this approach are few, including most notably Ted Graves and his students in their studies of Navajo migrants to Denver (1966, 1967, 1970) and William B. Rodgers's studies of change in the Out Island Bahamas (1966, 1969, 1971).

No complete historical survey of the development of these paradigms will be attempted. I leave this task to others who have greater talents as historians. The paradigms will be compared with respect to five questions concerning the approaches to change taken by practitioners of each. These questions are as follows: What data are used by students of change? What variability is investigated? How is the variability measured? What does the investigator seek to explain? What classes of variables are related in laws or lawlike statements or explanations of change? These questions are of course attempts to come to grips with basic elements of Kuhn's definition of paradigm.

*Evolutionism:* Leslie White has been the leading figure in developing modern evolutionary approaches to the study of change. A single proposition has served as the focus of White's research and that of many of his students: "Other factors remaining constant, culture evolves as the amount of energy harnessed per capita per year is increased, or as the efficiency of the means of putting the energy to work is increased" (White 1959:368–69). The propositions in this law of evolution are ultimately vague. It has been in part the attempt to define these concepts that has produced the more insightful works of the evolutionists. Energy harness has been approached by creating typologies of food-procurement systems and measuring protein and caloric intake. Culture has been defined in terms of typologies that pigeonholed different kinds of cultural systems on the basis of their organization and in terms of scales of increasing organizational complexity. Unfortunately, some of evolutionism's most basic typologies have failed to separate measures of energy harness and "culture evolves," thus rendering legitimate tests of White's proposition academic. In any case, the concept of some directional progress along a scale of complexity has been crucial to the investigations of modern evolutionists.

The data employed by investigators taking this approach have come from all cultural systems in all times and places. The methodology of the approach has been a combination of broadly historical and archaeological syntheses and cross-cultural studies. Sequences of change in particular societies are important only to the extent that they serve to illustrate the evolution of culture—culture meaning the culture of the whole earth. And, it is the evolution of the totality that is of principal concern to the evolutionist (Service 1971:13). He seeks to describe and explain the processes that underlie the continued evolution of the human population that inhabits this planet. The propositions that evolutionists formulate relate the energy base to other cultural variables, and changes in the energy base to changes in the physical and social environments of the societies in which particular evolutionary advances occur. It should be clear from the preceding that evolutionism is concerned with adaptive processes, but only insofar as is required to understand the evolution of the whole. White has at times claimed that the laws of evolution need not have any relevance for the prediction or retrodiction of particular events in particular societies.

*Cultural ecology:* As stated earlier, it is possible to argue that cultural ecology and evolutionism are a single approach. Both place a heavy emphasis on the material conditions of life. Nevertheless, in that evolutionists have looked at all cultures and ecologists at particular ones, different theoretical and analytical tools have developed. While this discussion emphasizes the uniqueness of the two approaches, no absolutist position should be implied.

Julian Steward has rather neatly described ecological studies in terms of three foci:

> the interrelationship of exploitative or productive technology and environment. . . . the behavior patterns involved in the exploitation of a particular area by means of a particular technology.

. . . the extent to which the behavior patterns entailed in exploit-
ting the environment affect other aspects of culture. (Steward 1955a:
40–41)

Cultural ecologists find it convenient to describe populations as cultural
systems emphasizing the interrelatedness of environment, subsistence
behavior, and institutions, and institutions and behavior in general.

Steward has also characterized the strategy of the ecologist in
attempting to find laws of cultural process. (1) There must be a typology
of cultures, patterns, and institutions. (2) Causal interrelationships of
types must be established in sequential or synchronic terms, or both.
(3) There must be a formulation of the independent recurrence of synchronic and/or sequential interrelationships of cultural phenomena in a
scientific statement of cause and effect, regularities, or laws.
(ibid.:180–81).

The focus of study in most ecological investigations of change is a
specific cultural system, or a few cultural systems at the same level of
integration or in relatively similar habitats. *Levels of integration* refers to
categories that have usually been created to include a reference to both
an organizational typology and a habitat (forest hunting band). The
sequence of levels (adaptive process) in one or more regions is defined and
then compared to another observed elsewhere. Similarities in the
sequences are the source of regularities or laws. Successions of change in
the culture core and social organization of these systems are associated
with changes in these systems' social and natural environments, and it is
these relationships that the laws describe.

*Acculturation:* Acculturational studies have been by and large non-
materalist and nonevolutionist. These studies have been based on the
concepts of British functionalism and structural-functionalism, and
represent attempts on the parts of investigators associated with these
schools to deal with the effects of Western capitalism on native
populations. The data used in such studies are generally drawn from a
single cultural system, a number of systems in the same area, or a number
of systems responding to the same contact pressures. Acculturationists
attempt to explain why particular cultural responses to contact are
observed in particular situations, and why these responses vary from
situation to situation. Broom, Siegel, and Watson's statement (1953) on
acculturation is an excellent description of this approach. While it would
be difficult to argue that any single piece of research follows this design,

most acculturational analyses are following some subset of the procedures in it.

The different responses of populations to contact situations are seen by acculturationists in terms of a typology of "processes" or, more accurately, outcomes: cultural creativity; cultural disintegration; reactive adaptation; progressive adjustment (fusion, assimilation); and stabilized pluralism. More than one of these outcomes may be present at different times in any given contact situation.

The differential occurrence of these processes is explained in terms of attributes of the two social systems involved in the contact, the contact situation itself, and the specific mediating roles that govern the interaction between the two systems. Relevant attributes of the cultural system include the boundary-maintaining mechanisms, the flexibility and rigidity of the systems, and the nature of homeostatic mechanisms in them. Boundary-maintaining devices are all those mechanisms that serve to limit the participation of individuals in a particular society. Flexibility and rigidity are described in terms of the precision of articulation of system components and the permissible range of behavioral variation in the population. Homeostasis is evaluated principally in terms of the societies' ability to respond to change in general.

The acculturational paradigm is exceedingly weak in its treatment of the natural environment and material variables. The "contact situation" is defined in ecological and demographic terms. But, the authors of the 1953 statement seem to have had a poor notion of how these topics should be studied, and the investigation of them in field situations has been insubstantial.

The particular roles that arose to carry interaction between the two cultural systems vary both with the socioeconomic backgrounds of the individuals involved in the contact situation and with the nature of the two systems. The role network is seen as a powerful intervening variable.

In summary, acculturationists sought to describe the kinds of changes that occurred in terms of the nature of the cultural systems, the contact situation, and intercultural role networks. While the notion of a search for regularity is represented in this paradigm, the notion of laws and the search for laws is less well represented here than in any of the other approaches.

*Behaviorism:* Behaviorism is somewhat simpler and more eclectic than the other approaches. It has generally been used in investigating changes within a single society, although similar studies have been carried on in different cultures, providing some basis for generalization. The situations in which such studies are carried out are not necessarily contact situations or ones where evolutionary change is occurring. Behaviorism focuses on longitudinal variability in the behavior of some collectivity as measured by the summed behavior of the individuals in that collectivity. Very routine items of behavior—drinking, the adoption of innovations, employment—under routine circumstances are basic to this paradigm. The investigator focuses on changes in the frequency of performance of these behaviors over time.

Three general categories are used in formulating the propositions that explain changes in behavior. The first is the biological, social, and cultural background of the individuals being studied. It is recognized that past experience is one important determinant of present behavior. Second, the behaviorists consider the models for behavior that individuals carry in their heads. Attitudes toward the world and notions of the appropriateness of particular patterns of behavior will affect the behavior that the individual exhibits. Finally, the behaviorists study situational determinants of behavior in both general and specific senses. At the general level, the status of the individual in the population is viewed as an important variable. More specifically, it is argued that the concrete situation in which the behavior is observed is an important determinant.

Laws are a focus in this approach, laws that relate the determinants of behavior to the performance of discrete acts. Behaviorists tend to be very quantitatively and statistically oriented in this pursuit.

### Concepts in the Study of Change

Each of these paradigms has produced contributions to the anthropology of change and each has created difficulties for investigators of change. Rather than offering a critique of each paradigm, I want to discuss the way that anthropologists conceptualize change. And rather than presenting this critique as a list of negativisms, I will try to defend a series of statements about change that are not represented in the existing paradigms, and that I find fundamental to any such study.

*The study of change is the study of diachronic or longitudinal variation in behavior and culture.* Perhaps the greatest obstacle that anthropologists have encountered in their attempts to study change is their concept of time. Anthropology has been first and foremost a

30

synchronic discipline. The similarities and differences that we have sought to explain have been similarities and differences in human behavior and culture at different spatial loci. Studies of variation in the organization of and behavior in particular social systems as these systems changed over time have been rare. Even those anthropologists who have identified culture change as their particular concern have used synchronic data more often than diachronic data. And, while theories of change, such as evolutionism, invoke an inferred pattern of change over time, this set of theories was invented to explain the diverse forms that culture and behavior take in their spatial dimension.

There is certainly every reason to be concerned with synchronic or spatial variability in culture and behavior. But, if we are to understand and explain change, our research must focus on change. Processes always have a temporal dimension. (In fact, most definitions of the term *processes* refer to changes-in-time.) Cause-and-effect relationships have temporal concomitants, and are usually discussed in terms of preceding events. But, processes and cause and effect are in most cases discussed and investigated using synchronic data.

Can processes and cause-and-effect relationships be inferred from an examination of synchronic data? The answers that anthropologists have given to this question have been equivocal at best. For example, we find Marvin Harris, in a critique of British social anthropology, observing that "without recourse to diachronic data, the whole question of degrees of functional adaptiveness is shut out. . . ." (1968:536). In a parallel critique of Murdockian cross-cultural studies he observes: "None of the studies have concerned themselves with time structured data and as a result they merely show probabilities of association between elements which as far as the statistical methods are concerned may be indifferently regarded as either dependent or independent" (1968:618). However, in examining the work of evolutionists, to whom Harris feels a great deal more kinship, he concludes that:

> It is unquestionable that contemporary primitives exhibit techno-environmental, techno-economic, social organizational and ideological adaptations that are both structurally and chronologically distinctive of preliterate and pre-state societies. (1968:155)

What he is saying is that synchronic data are usable for his studies of change, but not anyone else's. In fairness, Harris is no more inconsistent on this score than most of us. In fact, he presents as strong a case for a heavier reliance on diachronic data and techniques as has appeared in a major historical-theoretical volume to date. But as long as we continue to offer apologies and defenses for data that we know are inadequate to some purposes for which we attempt to use them, our results, our understanding of cause and effect, and our understanding of process will suffer. If diachronic data are necessary to the study of processes, and if we wish to explicate processes, we must begin to focus our investigations on these data rather than continuing to seek synchronic data first and foremost, to infer change from such data, and to defend with tortuous and tenuous arguments the inferences that we have made.

Some may be dubious about the fact that change cannot be inferred from synchronic data. I offer two examples as evidence why such inferences should not, and probably cannot, be made. Figure 2.1 shows the classic spatial pattern that is supposed to result from the diffusion of a trait from a center of innovation. Anthropologists, and especially archaeologists, have attempted to force their data into distributional patterns such as this one on the assumption that they were buying an understanding of "diffusionary processes." The diffusionist model involves a number of assumptions about change—that a trait originates at a center and spreads from it, and that it will be both more abundant and more varied in form at the original center.

These assumptions do substantial violence to reality, and even greater violence to logically possible models which demonstrate the spread of a trait in a region. For example, we can think of a number of different ways in which each of the zones shown in Figure 2.1 might have been generated by temporal processes. Over three time periods, Zone A might have changed from a light to a moderate to a heavy representation of the trait as the model implies. Zones B and C might have followed a similar pattern. (This temporal process is represented in Figure 2.2, path 3.) But, there are other possibilities. It might have had a widespread distribution in the region, been adopted at A and B, and then been adopted to an even greater extent in A (Figure 2.2, path 2). The trait may have had a relatively widespread distribution in Zone A and B, been subject to rapid adoption at A, and then spread to B and C (Figure 2.2, path 1). When different alternative paths or trajectories that could, over two preceding time periods, have produced the spatial distribution shown in Figure 2.1 are summed, the total is over 4,000. Given the very limited alternatives that this simple model allows, there are over 4,000 event sequences that could underlie the spatial patterning. How can an anthropologist pretend to understand or explain change without knowing which of these event

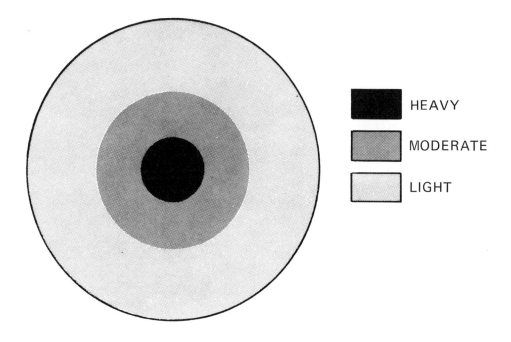

Figure 2.1 A diffusionary model of the spread of a trait from some point of origin.

sequences is being investigated? For some problems in anthropology, it may be possible to ignore or assume temporal processes, but certainly not when one claims to be studying change.

This argument is not limited to diffusionist models; it is equally problematic in other paradigms. For example, Carneiro, Naroll, and a number of other investigators have used scaling devices to arrange societies in order of increasing complexity of organization or culture. In the cases of some of these investigators, it has been argued that the scale represents a historical sequence: societies higher on the scale are further along some evolutionary trajectory than ones lower on the scale, and traits that occur in all societies are functional prerequisites for those that occur in only a few. Using devices and assumptions such as these, cross-sectional and cross-cultural data are used in inferring evolutionary sequences. Is this activity defensible?

In Figure 2.3, one such scale is illustrated. Three societies (A, B, C) have been arranged in order of increasing organizational complexity on the basis of three organizational attributes (1, 2, 3). Having constructed such a scale, can the investigator have any confidence that he is dealing with a

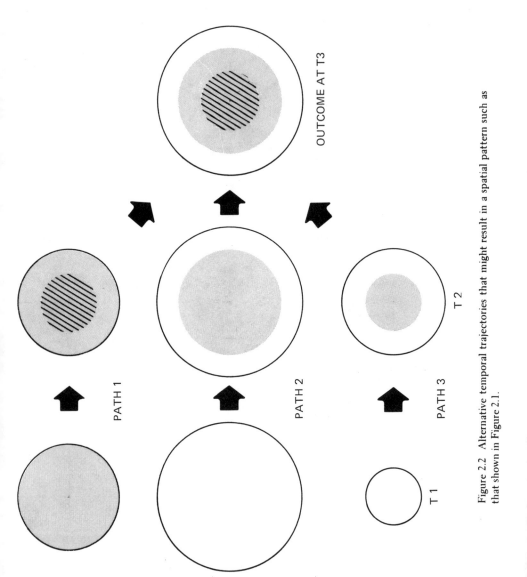

Figure 2.2 Alternative temporal trajectories that might result in a spatial pattern such as that shown in Figure 2.1.

Societies

| A | B | C |   | A |
|---|---|---|---|---|
|   |   |   |   | t |
|   |   | X | 3 | t |
|   |   |   |   | r |
|   |   |   |   | i |
|   | X | X | 2 | b |
|   |   |   |   | u |
|   |   |   |   | t |
| X | X | X | 1 | e |
|   |   |   |   | s |

Figure 2.3   Three societies (A, B, C) arranged in an evolutionary sequence on the basis of the traits (1, 2, 3) they possess.

historical process? That society C is further along some evolutionary trajectory than B, and B is further along than A? That trait 3 is a functional prerequisite for 2 and 1, and that 2 is a prerequisite for 1? Obviously, he cannot.

Suppose that we examined the efficacy of such a scale by examining the conditions that characterized the societies at two preceding time periods. The points at which the observations were made would be $t_3$, $t_2$, and $t_1$. We can ask, for example, how many different sequences of change there are that result in a situation at $t_3$ that is the same as the observed: A having one trait, B two, and C all three traits. In answering this question, we are not concerned with which particular traits were present in the earlier time intervals, only with how many traits were present. The possible sequences of change that produce a pattern in which society C has all three traits are shown in Figure 2.4. There are 16 such sequences. Similarly, there are 16 sequences of change over three time periods that result in society B having 2 traits, and 16 sequences that result in society A having only one. There are, then, a total of 4,096 sequences that might have resulted in the pattern observed at $t_3$. And, in arriving at this number we were not concerned with which particular trait (1, 2, or 3) was present, but only with how many were present. If the concern is with particular traits (replacing the x's in Figure 2.4 with 1's, 2's, and 3's) there are 260,144 sequences of change that produce the pattern observed at $t_3$.

```
                    X                       X
                    X          X            X
        -   X   X          X    -   X

                    X                       X
                    X          X            X
        -   -   X          X   X   X

                    X                       X
            X   X          X   X   X
        -   X   X          X   X   X

            X   X              X   X
            X   X          X   X   X
        -   X   X          X   X   X

                    X          X            X
                    X          X            X
        X   -   X          X    -   X

                    X          X            X
                    X          X            X
        X   X   X          X   X   X

                    X          X            X
            X   X          X   X   X
        X   X   X          X   X   X

            X   X          X   X   X
            X   X          X   X   X
        X   X   X          X   X   X

        t¹  t²  t³         t¹  t²  t³
```

Figure 2.4  Sixteen sequences of change in the occurrence of three traits in a single society that result in that society possessing all three traits in the last of three stages.

Obviously, some of these sequences of change are more probable than others. Probably, there is a positive correlation between the scale and the most probable sequence. But, what is explaining change if it is not showing why different sequences are characterized by different probabilities, and why one particular sequence, rather than near or equiprobable alternatives, was the one that occurred? If one claims to be interested in change, he cannot assume a sequence of change; he must know what that sequence looks like. When we assume a sequence of change, we are in large part assuming the conclusions that might have been derived from the study.

The particular fallacy of such scaling techniques is assuming that societies are simple trait-acquiring mechanisms. At any point in time, every society is in the process of acquiring, maintaining, and losing traits. It makes no sense to assume that only one of these processes is operative.

Moreover, the number of traits, number of societies, and number of time periods are quite small relative to the normal kinds of problems that anthropologists tackle.

Scaling techniques are not the only ones that anthropologists have used in attempting to build a diachronic dimension into synchronic data. Rodgers (1969) has summarized a number of the approaches that have been used: reconstruction, cross-sectional analysis, controlled comparison, and restudy.

Reconstructions are based on verbal information, the recollections of informants concerning earlier conditions or events in their society. It is surprising that some anthropologists who are normally careful with the distinction between verbal and nonverbal behavior use this technique as if they were describing real behavior. As Boulding has argued, the stuff of history is the image, images of images, and even images of images of images (1968). The anthropologist has no independent check on the informant's reconstruction, and every reason to believe that it represents a selective and probably conventionalized account of the past.

Cross-sectional analyses have an apparently legitimate temporal dimension—some individuals in the sample are biologically older than others. And when older and younger individuals exhibit different patterns of behavior or different responses to a questionnaire, it is certainly the case that some of these differences are due to biological aging. But the more important question is, What percentage of them? Undoubtedly there are differences between the behavior of an eighty-year-old man and a teenager that can be traced to biological age alone. But one cannot ignore differences in the social and natural environments in which the individuals were reared, nor those in which they currently live. Especially in the case of studies of change, one cannot make assumptions about the proportion of this variation that is a product of aging.

Similar problems characterize controlled comparisons (Rodgers 1966, 1967; Eggan 1954). Two societies or communities with a known difference in their exposure to some change agent (for example, Western capitalism) may be compared and differences in their responses noted. But this approach has two problems. First, potential variation in all other social and natural environmental variables should be held constant, and the investigator can rarely accomplish this task. Second, in some extreme cases, users of this approach come close to seeing time as a cause of change. Time is a concept, an abstraction; it does not cause anything to happen; it is a dimension in which events occur. While exposure may be a crude index of the extent of the forces that have affected an individual, group, or population, it does not necessarily get at the processes of change that are, or should be, the principal focus of studies of change.

Restudies involve a single natural laboratory that is studied at at least two points in time (Redfield 1930; Lewis 1951; Mead 1956). In this fashion, they do hold spatial variation constant and focus on changes in time. However, two points are not sufficient for the definition of a sequence of change. Two points are sufficient to define a straight line, but they do not necessarily do so; lines that connect them can be drawn in many different shapes. While restudies legitimately examine change, before and after pictures are rarely precise enough to allow the explication, much less the explanation, of processes of change.

All of the approaches discussed in the preceding pages make assumptions about change—too many assumptions. If an investigator is not primarily interested in change, he may certainly make such assumptions. But for those anthropologists who regard cultural and behavioral change as a primary topic of concern, to make such assumptions is to assume the patterns of variation in the topic phenomenon and, all too frequently, to assume conclusions.

*Tools appropriate to the study of synchronic variation are not necessarily appropriate to the study of diachronic variation.* If synchronic studies are the ethnographer's forte, diachronic studies are the ethnohistorian's and the archaeologist's. Yet even studies by the last two kinds of anthropologists are significantly handicapped by the predominance of synchronic concepts and tools in the discipline. Let us examine the case of archaeology in some detail.

During the last decade, a number of archaeologists have argued that the archaeological record is a more appropriate basis for the study of temporal than spatial variability. It is exceedingly difficult to establish with any high degree of probability that a particular group of sites was contemporaneously occupied. It is somewhat less difficult a task to arrange the same sites, allowing for substantial overlap, in a probable temporal sequence that permits the construction of a record of longitudinal variation. Even when the problems of establishing contemporaneity can be solved, almost all spatial or synchronic variability that existed prehistorically can be examined in far greater detail employing modern data. The study of temporal variation is and has been a logical choice for the archaeologist.

However, even the archaeologist has by and large approached change with a set of tools attuned to the investigation of synchronic phenomena. While proclaiming their interest in processes and change, many archaeologists have continued to force their data into traditional archaeological molds—stages, phases, and a host of other chronological units. The use of such units has a devastating effect on analyses of change. Chronologies are most successful when the temporal units that archaeologists define bound periods of relative stability. In this fashion, variability within units is minimized and that between units is accentuated.

However, one of two fates befalls periods of change in chronologies created in this fashion: they are either forced onto the boundaries between units (the lines between the boxes in a regional sequence), or they are allowed to fall half in one unit and half in another. This problem is particularly acute since periods of change tend to be of shorter duration than periods of stability, and therefore are in the first place more difficult to observe in any detail. The more successful the chronology, the less insight offered into the processes of change in the sequence under consideration. (This argument is true of typologies created for anthropologists in describing any historical sequence.)

Other disciplines have not succeeded in understanding and explaining processes of change in time by describing a series of macro steady states and then comparing and contrasting them. Lewin (1935) has contrasted Aristotelian and Galilean modes of thought in physics and argued that the fundamental change that underlay Newtonian physics was the shift from a focus on categorical measures of physical phenomena to a focus on continuous ones. Similarly, advances of Newtonian physics were predicated upon the development of calculus, a technique that permitted the investigator to shrink time and rates of change into increasingly smaller units. The history of the natural sciences has involved a progression from the study of change with categorical concepts that most of us are using now to the use of precise and continuously measured variables at smaller time intervals. In our case, it is unlikely that we will succeed in using the diachronic data that we have until we begin to employ the dynamic tools that are appropriate to these data.

*Sensitivity to the periodicity of change facilitates longitudinal studies.* Behavior can be studied at different levels. This fact should be evident from a simple comparison of the paradigms studied earlier. A change that the evolutionists characterize as the evolution of culture, the ecologist may study as a shift in the level of integration of the society in question, the acculturationist as a case of contact between societies, and the behaviorist as a shift in the frequency of particular items of behavior. Any given behavioral event can be studied and will be differentially defined from each of these perspectives.

In short, social scientists study behavior at different levels—some study whole societies, others groups, and others individuals. Unfortunately, arguments have arisen as to which of these levels is the proper domain of science or particular sciences. Schools focusing on these different levels have their profane vocabularies for other schools that approach the situation differently: to study the individual is reductionism, to study whole societies is oversimplification, and so on. In studying change, it is essential that we learn to observe temporal variation at all levels and to develop some facility in moving from one level to another.

Before considering the importance of examining behavior at more than one level, let us distinguish between behavior, the phenomenon, and behaving, the act. Whatever the level of behavior at which a given research project is directed, the unit of observation *is* the individual. This point seems to be one on which both materialistically and behaviorally oriented anthropologists are in agreement:

> We see whole bio-organisms, regularly, effortlessly, and infallibly. We do not see whole sociocultural organisms. These, and all of their parts including social structure, must be constructed through a process of logico-empirical abstraction out of the material furnished by the observation of the behavior of specific human beings. (Harris 1968:527)

Harris's recognition of this point and his discussion of it in *The Nature of Cultural Things* (1964) has not penetrated the ecological and evolutionary literature nearly so completely as some of his other thoughts. Many ecologists pay lip service to the concepts of intrapopulation variability and the individual as the behaving organism. But they have not developed techniques for doing ecology that refer to, precisely measure, and then infer cultural processes from individual behavior.

By far the most sophisticated set of operational devices for measuring differences in individual behavior is associated with the behaviorist paradigm. However, practitioners of this approach have been rather unsuccessful in creating the logico-empirical devices required to infer social structural and group variables from the observation of individual behavior. To the extent that group-level variables have been employed, they have been employed principally to explain the behavior of individuals. The fact that individuals are the *behavers* does not imply that studies of *behavior* must all be studies of individuals; it does imply that studies of behavior at all levels must have some empirical roots in observations or measures of behaving individuals. And it does imply that social scientists should prefer models and approaches that emphasize multilevel studies of behavior.

Studying behavior at multiple levels is of particular importance in dealing with diachronic variation. It is, of course, the case that one ethnographer has neither the time nor the funds to replicate the study of a whole society at one-year intervals for thirty or forty years. To the extent that these kinds of data are necessary, the demise of the one-man system of anthropological fieldwork is implied. With a research team visiting a field site over a period of years, detailed records of change could be obtained.

But we need not sit back and await the day when funding necessary for the collection of such data is available. There are data available to us now if we will spend some time in thinking about the periodicity of change at different levels of behavior. It is quite clear that change at the level of the known behavioral universe has a period of decades, centuries, and millennia. The archaeological record and historical data should provide the information necessary for operationalizing variables for the study of change at this very high level of abstraction. At the other extreme, changes in the behavior of individuals have periods measured in minutes, hours, days, months, and years. By concentrating on studies of individuals and changes in their behavior the investigator can reasonably expect to collect longitudinal data in the course of one or a few field seasons.

Small groups and populations, the units to which most anthropological attention has been directed, represent the most difficult problem. Periodicity of change in these groups is seasonal, annual, and decadic. This strikes the human life cycle in such a way that it is not likely that a single anthropologist will collect detailed records of change for units of this size. That is, of course, no reason why populations should not be studied. The suggestion is simply that this level of behavior is a difficult one that is more amenable to studies by groups of anthropologists than by individuals.

A good deal of the preceding discussion is based on my assumptions about the study of change. The distinction between short- and long-term change and its potential importance for diachronic analyses has been left largely unexamined. We really know precious little about the periodicity of behavioral and cultural change. If we spend more time thinking about this phenomenon, we may find readier sources of diachronic data than we have envisioned. Basic to such a search, however, is the conviction that valid and complementary conclusions may be derived by examining behavior at different levels.

*It is necessary to be reasonable in evaluating approaches to the study of change, and in trying to formulate new ones.* This point seems like a trivial one, but I think it is not. In the first place, there are many silly arguments in the literature about the appropriateness of particular models of change. There are conflict models, equilibrium models, short-term models, long-term models, and so on. That so many different models exist is not surprising; that they are regarded as mutually exclusive is. Change is ubiquitous, and investigators who seek to emphasize only one concomitant of change are playing blind man and elephant.

An analogy should clarify this point. The earth is spinning on its own axis at a rapid rate, moving around the sun at a more rapid rate, and moving through space at a more rapid rate still. Everywhere there is motion. But this motion is patterned, and it is the patterns in the motion that the physical scientists study—that they create laws to explain. In the same way, change is ubiquitous; it is everywhere. And focusing on differences in its particular manifestations is a silly endeavor. Our attention should be focused on the patterns that persist despite the motion.

Anthropologists are unreasonable in discussing change in a second sense. It is sometimes implied that diachronic studies are a panacea. Some writers have suggested that if temporal sequences of events were available, cause-effect relationships would be immediately observable. For anyone who has worked with longitudinal data, the problem in such statements is obvious. Variables spend a lot more time fluctuating than they spend in arranging themselves in a neat little $a \rightarrow b$ models. This should surprise nobody. Feedback was discovered decades ago; minute changes in one variable lead to changes in another that reinforce or counteract changes in the first, leading to further changes in the second, then pushing a third variable over some threshold, and so on. The world is complex, and diachronic analyses do not promise to remove that complexity.

In that regard, I wish to emphasize that I nowhere in this chapter argue that the proper study of anthropology is diachronic variability. I only argue that the proper study of anthropologists who claim to be interested in change is change—diachronic variability. We must not assume sequences of change. We must observe them and then explain them.

### *Summary*

I have developed a number of ideas that describe an approach to the study of change. It is convenient to summarize these ideas by returning to the questions that were asked concerning each of the paradigms of change, and answering those questions again.

What data are to be used? The data should describe at least one behavioral system at as many points in time as are required to characterize the pattern of variation under study. It is, of course, possible that a study may also involve more than one spatial locus. But the sequence of change in time for each such locus must be measured.

What variability is investigated? Variability in the culture and behavior of individuals, groups, and communities is appropriate to the study of change.

How is the variability measured? It has been argued that in every society the individual is the behaving unit. Therefore, no matter which level of behavior—individual, group, or community—an investigator finds interesting and appropriate for his studies, some measure of the incidence of different acts or activities must be employed. The use of artifacts of behavior in prehistoric and ethnographic situations is included within this definition. It should not be inferred from the preceding that characterizing variation in a group or community is a simple matter of summing individual behaviors. Inference implies more than addition. The measures of behavior appropriate to the study of change are usually continuous rather than categorical.

What does the investigator seek to explain? He seeks to explain why the behavior of individuals, groups, or societies changes from $t_1$ to $t_n$. Moreover, he attempts to show why the observed sequence of change occurred, rather than other equiprobable or nearly equiprobable alternatives.

What classes of variables and phenomena are related in laws or lawlike statements? Laws relate changes in behavioral phenomena at all levels to patterns and changes in the social and natural environment in which the behavior occurs.

## MODELS IN THE STUDY OF CHANGE

The preceding paragraph demands a consideration of the conceptual framework in which cultural and behavioral phenomena and their social and natural environments can be studied. I will discuss three models that meet this need. Behavioral phenomena will be considered in terms of strategies, systems, and dimensions. Environments will be characterized as either stable or changing. Let us begin with a definition of these terms. (1) A *strategy* is some combination of two or more acts, all of which result in the acquisition of the same natural or social resources. (2) A *system* is two or more groups linked by exchanges of social or natural resources such that a change in one group leads to changes in the others. (3) A *dimension* of behavior is a fundamental continuum along which behavioral systems vary. (4) Natural and social environments are *stable* when changes do not exceed limits that are expected by the population adapting to them. (5) Environments are *changing* when a change occurs that exceeds previously established limits. In order to understand the whole range of changes that are occurring in a population, it is necessary to examine each of the defined behavioral phenomena under stable and changing environmental conditions.

### Behavioral Strategies Under
### Stable Environmental Conditions

Anthropologists are frequently concerned with the fashion in which individuals and groups accomplish particular ends. How do they acquire the food resources required for survival? How do they maintain equitable relationships between individuals? Alternatively, we are concerned with the whys and wherefores of some particular item of behavior. Why do men give food to their mothers' brothers? Why do men in the society hunt rabbits? In asking such questions, we are implicitly or explicitly sensitive to other ways of behaving and other ways of accomplishing a given end as they exist within that society or within other societies. It is the particular mixture of such alternatives that given individuals (or groups of them) practice that I have referred to as a strategy.

Let us take as an example the subsistence practices of a population. At worst, we characterize a society basically as hunting-gathering or agricultural. At best, we may say that the subsistence is derived seventy percent from the practice of agriculture and thirty percent from the practice of hunting and gathering. We should recognize that any individual in the population we are studying practices some combination of the two, and that the precise combination varies from individual to individual. At the community level, we also find variation in the average mix of the population of the communities as aggregates.

Thus, we may represent behavior that acquires some desired resources—in this case subsistence resources—along a continuum—in this case from hunting-gathering to agriculture. The variation along this continuum can be represented by a curve (Figure 2.5). (We will use a normal curve as a matter of convention. No argument is made that all such distributions are normal ones.) Having represented behavioral variation in this fashion, we may begin to ask questions about the shape of the curve. Why does it have a given shape? Why does the mode occur at a particular point on the continuum? Why does it have the extant range of variation?

Answering these questions would force us to refer to processes—or linked series of events. It is argued that two processes underlie the shape of such a curve for a particular aggregate of individuals: variety generation and selection.

Variety is continually generated in every human population. This variety exists in two forms. On the one hand, individuals know how to accomplish a given task in ways that are different from the ones they are actually practicing. On the other, there are individuals in the population who are accomplishing the end in different ways. That is to say, variety exists both in the minds of individuals who know of alternative behaviors but are not practicing them, and by the actual practice of such strategies by deviant individuals within the population. This variety has a number of potential sources, including contact with other populations, mislearning, invention, and boredom. All of these act to generate variety within a population—to push the curve describing variation outward.

It is important to remember that one cannot predict what new item of behavior will be introduced into a society at a succeeding time period simply by looking at that society. Variety generation is analogous to mutation in this regard. We can, however, make predictions about the rates of variety generation, diffusion, and innovation.

Clearly, variety generation cannot be the only process that is operating in a system. If it were, the curve for most populations would tend to become infinitely broad or flat, because the generation of variety tends to push the curve outward. The process that limits the generation of variety

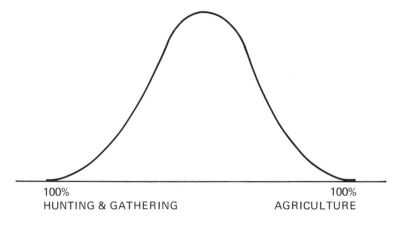

100%                                 100%
HUNTING & GATHERING               AGRICULTURE

Figure 2.5 A possible pattern of variation in the subsistence strategies practiced by the members of a single population, assuming that agriculture and hunting-gathering are the possible alternative.

is referred to as selection. Selection produces both limits to the variety and a modal pattern of behavior.

Selective pressures emanate from the environment of the population. In speaking of selective pressures, we are typically arguing that the pattern of variation in behavior will closely reflect the variation in the environment under stable conditions. A number of investigators in anthropology and the social sciences have argued that the modal pattern of behavior can be viewed in this regard. Sahlins and Service, for example, have argued that "the cultural system that is most effective in the exploitation of a given environment will spread at the expense of less effective systems" (1960:75). Homans has observed that "when a response is followed by a reward, the frequence or probability of recurrence of the behavior increases" (1967:36–37). Sahlins and Service are discussing populations and Homans is discussing individuals. But all are arguing that there will be some strategy of behavior that will be most common because it most effectively secures the social and natural resources or rewards of a given environment.

It is important that we carry the discussion of selection beyond this point, however, because selection is the cause not only of modal behavior, but also of limits. Behavior that never acquires any of the resources or rewards of a given situation will be dropped from the population's repertoire. Behavior that meets even infrequently occurring environmen-

46

tal conditions will be retained, although in small quantities. Similarly, some variety will be created when resources necessary to practice the most desirable strategy are not available, and alternatives must be sought.

To this point, the discussion of selection has been a very abstract one. But it need not be left so. It is possible to specify both conscious and unconscious (or mechanical) behavior that we can associate with selection. At the mechanical level, those individuals within a population who are practicing inappropriate strategies will die or their offspring will die. Similarly, those individuals who are practicing appropriate strategies will survive and will produce more viable offspring. At a conscious level, people are imitators; and if an individual notices that someone down the road is acquiring more of a set of resources than he, he is likely to modify his behavior in that direction. And, it may be desirable for the population as a whole to support individuals who in average years do poorly in securing necessary resources, but who are very productive in years when the environmental variable is tending toward its limit. Such individuals may represent the margin of survival for the population in difficult years.

Clearly, the curve for any population is a product of both variety-generating and selective pressures. If only variety generation occurred, the curve would tend toward total flatness. If only selection occurred, the curve would tend toward total height, with no range at all. Neither occurs in nature; variability described by some curve is the typical case. The interaction of the two processes is illustrated in Figure 2.6.

### Behavioral Strategies Under
### Changing Environmental Conditions

Processes of variety generation and selection continue to operate under changing environmental conditions. In dealing with such situations, the investigator must determine whether a given population or a given strategy is likely to survive the change that has occurred. It should be recalled that changing environment refers to a shift in both the mode of the environmental variable and its limits.

The most significant proposition put forth for making such a prediction is Sahlins and Service's law of evolutionary potential: "The more specialized and adapted a form in a given evolutionary stage, the smaller is its potential for passing to the next stage" (1960:97). This proposition suffers from the evolutionary jargon in which it is couched. We may

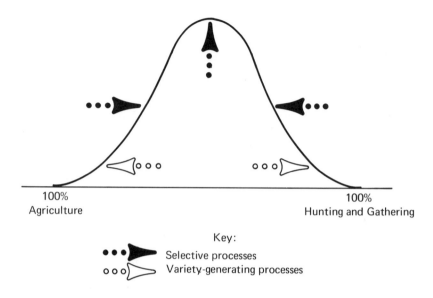

100%
Agriculture

100%
Hunting and Gathering

Key:

Selective processes
Variety-generating processes

Figure 2.6 The action of variety-generating and selective processes. Variety-generating processes would tend to produce a flatter and broader curve while selective pressures would produce a narrower and higher one.

restate it to cover a broader range of behavior as follows: The more specialized a population in acquiring some resource, the lower the probability that the strategy will survive a change in some conditioning environmental variable; the less specialized, the greater the probability. The vast literature in the social sciences concerning the crucial role of marginal individuals in periods of change becomes relevant when the proposition is formulated in this fashion. It is the presence of deviant individuals and of different behavioral strategies that is important when environmental change occurs.

We may see the validity of this proposition by returning to the model of varying strategies used in considering the case of stable environments. If a specialized population experiences an environmental change, it may not possess any individuals practicing strategies that are appropriate to the changed conditions. If a diverse population experiences a shift, there is a much higher probability that at least some individuals in the population will already be practicing an appropriate strategy. Their success under the new conditions will be evident, as will the appropriate direction for behavioral modification.

Some qualifications must be put on such a model. First, the number of individuals in the populations under consideration is a relevant factor. If a highly varied population consists of only four individuals, it is not likely that the population, even given its variety, is going to survive. If a more specialized population consists of thousands of individuals, it will more probably survive. The larger population lessens the risk of experimentation that follows a change.

The question of experimentation is itself an important one. There is some evidence to show that under stress conditions, experimentation increases. It is not evident at this point whether experimentation is increasing, or alternatives that had been already known are brought into practice. In any case, it is necessary to investigate the differential creativity of populations in responding to changes as a potentially important intervening variable.

In summary, we can surely say at this point that the probability of a population's continuing to practice a given strategy in the face of environmental change is directly proportional to both its size and variation. Figure 2.7 illustrates the concepts used in studying strategies under changing conditions. Line x marks the point in time when an environmental shift occurs.

### Behavioral Systems Under Stable Environmental Conditions

The discussion of behavioral systems under stable and changing environments will be a limited one. Two chapters in this volume (3, 4) deal with these topics. Nevertheless, several crucial points can be made.

At a minimal level, a system can be defined as two or more behavioral strategies linked to each other in such a way that a change in one is likely to produce a change in the other. In treating strategies in this fashion, one strategy would be just that, and the second would be treated as the environment. Alternatively, the strategies could be treated as each other's environments, and the emphasis would be on the interaction of the two. Thus, rather than dealing with a subsistence strategy, one could characterize a subsistence system composed of the following strategies: land allocation, land use, storage, production, and distribution. Moreover, subsistence strategies are related to other strategies in the system. Strategies associated with socialization, reproduction, and organization, to mention only a few, could be included. In short, it becomes both difficult and unreasonable to view a complex set of events in a society as a composite of strategies. Similarly, approaching a problem in terms of

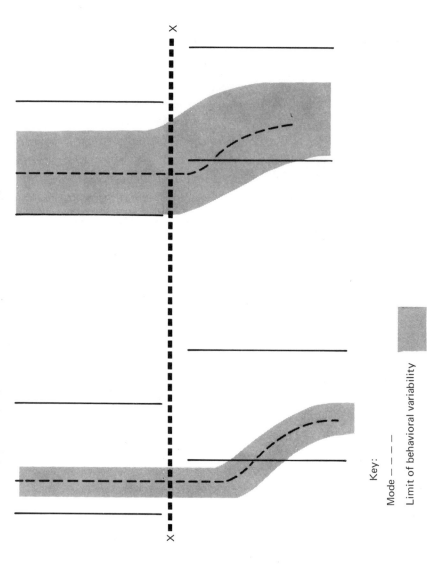

Key:

Mode – – – –

▓ Limit of behavioral variability

Time

Figure 2.7 Variation in the limits and modal strategies over time. One would expect relatively independent changes in the modal pattern and the extent of variation around that pattern. At the same time, specific environmental variables should limit the variation that occurs.

strategies assumes that the behavior of individuals is additive. It is difficult to work with the concept of social structure if such a concept is maintained.

For both of these reasons, it becomes convenient to deal with a society in terms of the less rigorous definition of a system given at the outset of the discussion of models of change. This definition puts the emphasis on institutionalized relationships between groups within a society.

It is characteristic in anthropological literature to see a system discussed in analogy with a thermostat. This model is appropriate to only a very limited subset of systemic behavior. When the environment must be characterized in very amorphous terms, and the information that populations receive from their environments must be similarly treated, this model is appropriate. But many problems can be treated in terms of a far more bounded model of a system, which I will call the exchange model. This model is shown in Figure 2.8. In this model, two groups, A and B, each possess a stock of some resource. These stocks are linked by an exchange channel that may be either unidirectional or bidirectional. This channel has a regulator. In response to some signal from either A or B, or both, goods flow from one stock to another. (Clearly, we could construct a model that involved more groups and more exchange channels.) Thus, we could imagine that A and B possessed goods that they exchanged when one group's stock fell below some minimum. Or, we might characterize an exchange of wives or information (reinforcement, affect, and so forth).

Figure 2.8   A systemic model of exchange.

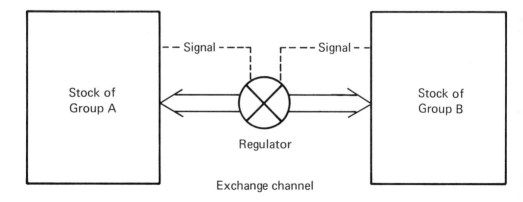

The crucial condition that must characterize such a system under stable environmental conditions is homeostasis. Again, homeostasis has been rigorously defined elsewhere in this volume. In simple terms, homeostatic conditions exist when the signal and the response are negatively correlated: a positive signal calls forth a negative flow, and a negative signal calls forth a positive flow. Thus, in the illustration, a decrease in the stock of B would result in an increase in the flow. An increase in the stock would result in a decrease of the flow, or even a reverse flow. Under these conditions, a constant level of a resource can be maintained in a stock.

Changes are occurring constantly in such situations. But the changes are deviation-countering changes. A deviation from an initial state evokes a response that returns the system to its original state.

*Behavioral Systems Under*
*Changing Environmental Conditions*

The preceding discussion presumed that the system's environment was characterized by normal fluctuations that did not exceed some limit or threshold. But, there are conditions under which a change is so great that the response fails to restore the initial equilibrium. These conditions are called morphogenic conditions, and the changes associated with them are called deviation-amplifying changes. Acting as was desirable in the past creates problems rather than effecting a solution.

For some systems, our knowledge of deviation amplification is substantial. MacArthur and Connell have discussed the operation of population-regulating systems (1966). Their analysis suggests that if the line corresponding to the ratio between a change in population and the existing population $(dp/P)$ is greater than 63 degrees, equilibrium will never be restored. Every reaction will be an overreaction, until an entirely new equilibrium is established.

Changes in a system's environment that exceed established limits of variation are usually characterized as stress. It is not possible to predict on the basis of examining system components and interaction when a stress will occur. That is, stress is an exogenous event. However, when stress occurs, changes will probably be deviation-amplifying rather than deviation-countering ones, and either the system will be replaced by a new one or the population will cease to exist.

The similarities between the approach taken in characterizing systems and that taken in characterizing strategies should be clear. The consideration of change under stable conditions focused on the mechanisms that limit fluctuations in behavior. The discussion of changing environments focused on the responses to conditions when expectable patterns of environmental variation were exceeded.

### Behavioral Dimensions Under
### Stable Environmental Conditions

Just as one must ultimately provide for working with complex patterns of behavior rather than simple strategies, he must confront the task of comparing patterns of change in several societies. It is logically possible to do so by building a complete systemic model of whole cultural systems. While such an approach is logically possible, it is not a feasible one in most research.

It is for this reason that I introduced the concept of behavioral dimensions. These are fundamental characteristics of behavioral systems. I have argued previously that behavior at this macrosystemic level can be understood in terms of four such dimensions: population, differentiation, integration, and energy (Plog 1969). Why are the four characteristics important, and why do I call them dimensions rather than variables?

If one asks what characteristics can be described for any cultural or behavioral system, the answer is size, number of components, interaction of components, and flow of resources between them. (It is assumed that such pathways necessarily imply the flow of information, even if they do not evidence an actual flow of goods and services.) Variation in the size of a system can be measured by reference to the number of individuals participating in it (population). Variation in the number of components can be measured by reference to a count of the number of different groups in the system (differentiation). Integration is a measure of the strength of the ties between component groups. Finally, the magnitude of the material flow between system components is quantified in terms of energy.

Most of the variables that social scientists study are specific measures of one of these dimensions. There are many measures of the population dimension that we employ—size, density, potential, fertility, fecundity, and so on. Variables such as specialization, role homogeneity/heterogeneity, class, and caste are measures of differentiation. Studies of organization, command, extent of group participation, ethical codes, as well as those of attitudinal and psychological configurations in cultures are studies of integration. Energy is measured by variables such as caloric intake/output, GNP, community product, output per capita, and so forth.

It must be remembered that the preceding paragraph attempts to define a basis for comparing societies at the most abstract level. There is no implication intended that for some purposes caste and class, for example, are not very different phenomena. There will be many circumstances in which an investigator will wish to preserve distinctions between variables that I have combined under a single dimension. My suggestion is simply that at this level of abstraction these variables tend to share a single datum. (A criticism of those social scientists who employ shotgun multivariate analyses of hundreds of variables and pretend surprise when some prove to be highly correlated is definitely implied. The correlations are a mechanical product of the shared datum.)

Ultimately, this list of dimensions is not a surprising one: such concepts are the stock-in-trade of evolutionary studies. I suggest more than that these variables should be used in drawing up a list of societies and comparing and contrasting them. These dimensions have determinate and causal connections with each other. Moreover, these connections differ under stable and changing environments. Let us first look at a stable environmental situation.

There are a very large number of causal models that could be formed using these four dimensions. Four of these receive primary support in the literature of the social sciences. (1) The relationship between population and energy is well known: all other things being equal, population is some direction function of available resources (energy). This argument does not imply that population will rise to carrying capacity—only that it will be some function of it. (2) The link between population and differentiation is discussed throughout the ecological literature in both the natural and social sciences. Population increases with all other variables held constant tend to be met by the specialization of the population. There is an implicit intervening variable in this relationship—competition. With resources held constant, and a change in population, an increase in population leads to an increase in competition. Competition is removed by turning to a somewhat more finely differentiated model of resource acquisition, greater specialization. (3) A typical Durkheimian argument would lead one to conclude that an increase in differentiation leads to increasing integration, because the interdependence of organisms on each other increases. This seems an unwarranted generalization based on the case of Western industrial capitalism. In the absence of an overarching organizational structure, such as the one that provides an available supply of linkages, the immediate effect of increasing differentiation is to decrease integration. Increasing differentiation is, by definition, disintegrative; the number of components increases with no necessary relationship between the new components and existing ones. (4) Increases in integration are positively correlated with increases in energy. An increase in the organizational efficiency of a society will result in an increase in the available resources, even if production is held constant, because waste in the system will be reduced. Moreover, the organization of larger numbers of individuals at discrete spatial loci permits economies of scale and decreases waste in the sense of foregone economies.

These causal connections are combined in Figure 2.9. This model is subject to one characteristic of all simulation models: if there is an uneven number of negative connections, the system can cycle and cycle with no change in the relationship between the dimensions or in their magnitude. Fluctuations will occur ad infinitum, but change will not. Using a model like this one renders academic all of the arguments over prime movers. The limits on change are a function more of the relationships between the components of the model than of the components themselves.

Observing such a system, there is no way of predicting what the next change in its environment will be, or of predicting which dimension will be affected. Population, differentiation, integration, or energy might be the first dimension to change. One cannot predict exogenous events on the basis of endogenous evidence. But one can predict how the system will respond, given a change in any one of the dimensions.

In the case of this model, any change that can occur will be countered. The table at the bottom of Figure 2.9 shows why. Let us assume that an exogenous event causes a population increase. This causes differentiation to increase, integration to decrease, and energy to decrease. In turn, population decreases, differentiation decreases, integration increases, and energy increases. Thus, after two cycles of the model all changes are canceled.

Admittedly, this is a very simple model. It does not speak to the issue of how many cycles are required before a change is completely damped. Similarly, the pluses and minuses should be replaced by precise coefficients. Unless these coefficients are equal, some change will occur

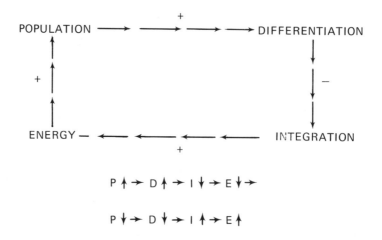

Figure 2.9 A model of the relationship between population, differentiation, energy, and integration. Given the postulated sequence of changes, a steady-state relationship between the variables would be maintained.

secularly because of the unequal effects of the initial change on the different dimensions. The importance of the model is the suggestion that there are fundamental characteristics of all social aggregates that can be modeled as a dynamic equilibrium. The model is essentially a deviation-countering one.

### Behavioral Dimensions Under
### Changing Environmental Conditions

The only way to upset the equilibrium of such a model is to change the number of negative linkages so that they are either nonexistent or of an even, rather than an odd, number. These conditions are typically met when an environmental change of great magnitude occurs that short-circuits the system by affecting more than one dimension simultaneously. Such changes may have either positive or negative effects. The adoption of an innovation like irrigation has independent and immediate effects on every dimension save population. The adoption of a subsistence strategy such as sedentary domestication has immediate effects on every dimension. Thus, it is not surprising that we tend to associate major evolutionary changes with significant technological innovations. These have the greatest potential for simultaneously affecting all of the dimensions. But so do a series of nontechnological innovations—the organizational patterns of urbanism, for example.

Given that an innovation has occurred that short-circuits the negative link, the system behaves as a deviation-amplifying rather than a deviation-countering one.

### Summary

The implication of these three models of change taken as a totality should be clear. Any given change can be viewed microscopically as a strategy, systemically, or macroscopically in terms of a dimensional model. I think that there is more to be gained examining the change from each of these stances than by employing any one of them exclusively.

The discussion of these models has been quite abstract. For its abstractness, I apologize. But at this point, an empirical analysis would look very tacked on—which is precisely what it would be. I have, though, attempted to summarize a consistent theoretical position behind the diverse and more empirically oriented studies that I have done or begun to do in the last few years. I regard the lack of empiricism in this chapter as a detriment only to the extent that I fail to continue to use and test these models in succeeding years. The models can be used in deriving both lawlike propositions and test implications. In that respect they show the road to further research and testing, even if they are ultimately abandoned. Whatever inadequacies the models may prove to contain, I am convinced that it is such models that promise the best hope of a compromise between that research which is too theoretical to be of utility in accounting for observed variation, and that which is too empirical to offer meaningful insights into human nature and behavior. If the models are inadequate, their test implications and the means for disproving them are clear.

3

# Systems Theory and the Explanation of Change

JAMES N. HILL

*Department of Anthropology*
*University of California*
*Los Angeles*

## INTRODUCTION

Explaining variability and change in human behavior is the primary goal of the social sciences, yet we expend a great deal of research effort that is of dubious value in this regard. We create typologies, generate trait lists, get statistical correlations, devise hypothetical evolutionary sequences, and so forth; but we too rarely formulate and test hypotheses that actually purport to *explain* observed spatial and temporal variability (Binford 1968a, 1968b; Fritz and Plog 1970; Watson, LeBlanc and Redman 1971).

One reason for this is that we often do not ask specific research questions that demand explanatory answers (Hill 1972:77–79). Second, we have not adequately learned how to formulate and test our proposed explanations. Beyond this, there is widespread uncertainty over what constitutes an acceptable scientific explanation (cf. Weingartner 1968; Fritz and Plog 1970; Watson, LeBlanc and Redman 1971; Tuggle, Townsend and Riley 1972).

In the context of explaining change there is yet another important difficulty—namely, misunderstanding what change is. It seems axiomatic that in order to explain change in human (or cultural) behavior we must know something about what constitutes change. I deal, in this chapter, solely with this and related questions. I hope to contribute to our understanding of the nature and processes of change, as well as to the development of a general theoretical framework (Kuhn 1962) within which we can account for change in human behavior—especially changes in those things commonly called "cultural."

There are at least two general requirements for such a framework. In the first place, it must be able to account for *both* change and stability. These appear to be two sides of the coin in that the same general kinds of processes probably account for both (Argyris 1959:123; Buckley 1968b; Perlman, n.d.). And second, it is evident that such an approach must be suited to accounting for cultural stability and change anywhere in the world, and at any time; it must thus be useful in accounting for both prehistoric and contemporary change. The fact that prehistoric data are often quite different from data gathered by ethnographers should not mislead us into thinking that the nature of our explanations must be different—and it is for this reason that my subsequent discussion is not oriented solely to archaeological concerns.

Since it is my belief that general systems theory (GST) can provide us with some useful outlines for a general explanation of stability and change, I devote much of this chapter to a critical evaluation of its usefulness. I do this in the context of evaluating the usefulness of three of the major general systems approaches that have already been published—and I conclude that there are probably no published systems frameworks that are wholly suited to the purpose of explaining stability and change in cultural systems. I follow this with a presentation of what I think is a more useful approach for our purposes;[1] and I present a sketchy example of how this approach can be employed. I also attempt to deal with some of the inevitable problems of measurement that must be faced in dealing with change.

I make no pretense to covering the concepts or voluminous literature of GST in any comprehensive way, although I present in the following section a few of the basic concepts that are required in understanding the discussions that follow. For an introduction to the subject, see especially Bertalanffy (1950, 1951, 1956, 1962, 1968); Ashby (1956a, b; 1962); Mesarovic (1964); Young (1964); James G. Miller (1965a-c); Buckley

(1967, 1968a), and the publications *General Systems* and *Behavioral Science*. More or less successful applications of systems theory in anthropology include Sahlins (1958); Vayda (1961a, b); Vayda, Leeds, and Smith (1961); Service (1962); Geertz (1963); Coe and Flannery (1964); Cohen (1964); Leeds (1965); Rappaport (1967); Alland (1967); Flannery (1968). Discussions and arguments concerning the usefulness of GST in the social sciences are found in Boulding (1956); Argyris (1959); Cadwallader (1959); Rapoport and Horvath (1959); Mesarovic (1963); James G. Miller (1965a-c); Clarke (1968:43–130); Hole and Heizer (1969:Ch. 17); and Perlman (n.d.).

### SOME BASIC SYSTEMS CONCEPTS

What is a system? There are many definitions of "system" in the literature (*cf.* Bertalanffy 1956; Hall and Fagen 1956:84; Ashby 1962; Ackoff 1964; Easton 1956), but the one by James G. Miller (1965a:200–201) seems reasonably acceptable.

> A system is a set of units with relationships among them (Bertalanffy, 1956). The word "set" implies that the units have common properties. The state of each unit is constrained by, conditioned by, or dependent on the state of other units. The units are coupled. Moreover, there is at least one measure of the sum of its units which is larger than the sum of that measure of its units.

This definition would apply to a pyramidal-shaped stack of tennis balls as well as to societies. It could also apply to an abstract system, such as a mathematical model, although I am not considering such systems at this point.

Many different kinds of systems are considered in the literature, but there is no need to consider them here. It is worth noting, however, that human societal systems are generally considered to be "living systems." As such, they are relatively "open," in that they have inputs, throughputs, and outputs of matter-energy and information; and they are "self-regulating" or "adaptive" in nature, since they (like organisms) can modify their behavior in response to environmental variation (Miller 1965a).

All living systems are presumed to be composed of "subsystems" (which are themselves systems in their own right), and to be part of a larger system, the "suprasystem." Each subsystem is presumed to carry on one or more activities or tasks for a given system; and each subsystem is articulated with and responsive to others in the system. Further, each subsystem is made up of "components," which are the material (matter-energy) units composing the subsystems—although components can be subsystems in themselves (Miller 1965a, b; Bertalanffy 1968; and others).

Another characteristic of living systems is that they are presumed to have "boundaries" that separate the systems from their environments, and across which flow matter-energy and information in exchange with the environment or suprasystem (Khailov 1954; Simon 1965). And these boundaries are presumed to have discrete, clear demarcations, such that what is within a system can be differentiated from things outside of it.

The "environment" of a system or subsystem is generally considered to be anything outside of that system; and the "effective environment" constitutes those things in the "total" environment with which a system has matter-energy relationships.

A particularly important characteristic of living systems is, as indicated above, the feature of "self-regulation" (Ashby 1956b; Ashby's articles in Buckley 1968a and Cadwallader 1959). This is the idea that systems can respond to variation and stress in their environments in such ways as to prevent collapse and maintain equilibrium or steady-state (cf. Shalins and Service 1960:45–68; James G. Miller 1965a:225–26; Buckley 1967:8–40). The systemic mechanisms that respond to environmental variation are called "homeostatic mechanisms." In organisms, these adjustment mechanisms are usually automatic, and come into play whenever a system is threatened by stress (Cannon 1932). For example, under threat of attack, an organism's adrenaline flows more rapidly than usual—a system-maintaining response.

Societies can also be thought of as having homeostatic mechanisms, though they may be less automatic than those at the level of the individual organism. Just as in organisms, it is the case that societies have critical limits or tolerance ranges with regard to both inputs and outputs; and when environmental variation threatens to force departure from tolerance ranges, the homeostats can come into play to maintain system equilibrium. As the biologist Ralph Gerard says:

> The vast bulk of the functioning of any enduring system is as displacement-correcting responses. Here is the negative feedback of engineering or the adaptive or self-regulating or homeostatic response of physiology. (1957; in Buckley 1968a:55–56)

These regulatory mechanisms involve the flow of "information." Information coordinates the activities of the components within a system, and the system with its environment. The information is considered to flow in "loops," called negative feedback loops. The idea is that as a system is confronted with a stress situation, information about the stress is acted upon by the system such that one or more of the system's homeostatic mechanisms is invoked to cope with the stress. Information about the results of this action (or, the effects of the system response on the environment) is then fed back to the system, and it constitutes new information to which the system may respond further if necessary (Miller 1965a:226–28). Excellent discussions of this negative feedback process are given in Deutsch (1948–49); Wiener (1954); Vickers (1959b); Haberstroh (1960); Hardin (1963); Miller (1965a:227–29); and Buckley (1967:52–58).

There are a number of examples of this process already reported in the anthropological literature. This kind of deviation-counteracting account of cultural systems often goes under the name of "functionalism." For examples, see Sahlins (1961); Vayda (1961a, b); Vayda, Leeds and Smith (1961); Leeds (1963, 1965); Rappaport (1967).

One of the clearest examples is that by Leeds (1965). Leeds examines the social organization of the Chukchi reindeer herders of Siberia, and explains large portions of it as results of adaptations that function to maintain reindeer herds at optimum size. To summarize, Leeds shows that as the size of a given herd decreases (for various reasons), and as it approaches the lower limit for optimum herd size, certain alliances and other institutional rearrangements are made which either add animals to the herd or permit the herd to join another herd. On the other hand, when a herd begins to get too large for optimum mobility and local grazing resources, another set of social rearrangements comes into play. It is also notable that *people* are sometimes redistributed by various institutionalized means, so that small herds will be managed by an optimum number of people, and large herds get more herding assistance.

There are also other homeostatic mechanisms involved. For example, as herd size gets too large (approaches tolerance limits), there is an increase in the theft of animals, trading them to others, and giving them as gifts at weddings and other rituals. As herds become too small, people turn increasingly to hunting wild reindeer.

It should be clear that these kinds of adjustment processes serve, when effective, to *maintain* the cultural system in steady state; they are equilibrial processes. However, this kind of process will not, by itself, account for cultural change—and the reason should be obvious. Homeostatic mechanisms are, by definition, reversible. That is, they come into operation in response to variations in system inputs or outputs that are threatening to depart from tolerance range; but they become inoperative again after the homeostats have restored the system to its normal range of operation. In short, homeostatic mechanisms are behavioral responses that serve to prevent change or collapse. In fact, the whole point of Leeds's study, and other functionalist studies, is to demonstrate the complex ways in which societies maintain their stability.

This is not to deny the importance of equilibrial processes in situations of cultural change; I think they are a part, but only part, of the change process. The term "change," like the term "evolution," refers primarily to irreversible change, in my view (see p. 93 below). Change should be considered to occur only when the homeostatic mechanisms of a system fail to work adequately. In this situation, a system must either collapse or undergo change (Maruyama 1963). One of these alternatives must occur whenever a system cannot maintain itself as it is. This is where the concept "positive feedback" comes in. I will, however, reserve further discussion of this to my consideration of the "Maruyama Framework," since Maruyama (1963) has dealt with this in some detail.

It is interesting to note that most systems theorists, other than Maruyama, have not really come to grips with systemic change. The literature has been more concerned with classifying systems into "types," and with making generalizations about how the different kinds of systems operate in equilibrium. This is true with regard to systems theoretical discussions of human society as well, as will become apparent in considering "The Miller Framework" (James G. Miller 1965a-c).

I now consider the general systems approaches of James G. Miller (1965a-c), Walter Buckley (1967, 1968b) and Magoroh Maruyama (1963). In each case I present first the author's conception of what a societal system is, and my evaluation of the usefulness of his ideas. Then, making similar evaluations, I present his ideas on how a societal system operates (system equilibrial processes); this is followed by a description and evaluation of what change is considered to be, and how the author accounts for it.

## THE MILLER FRAMEWORK

Miller's definition of "system" has already been given (p. 61 supra). His work deals with all living systems, including societies; and he gives societal examples for each of his points. While his work is heuristically useful, I think it presents certain difficulties when it is applied analytically in the study of societies. The main reason for this seems to lie in the fact that he was thinking more in terms of individual organisms than he was of populations or societies.

Miller views the universe as being made up of systems, each of which has "subsystems" within it, and each of which is included in a larger system, or "suprasystem" (1965a:211–14, 218–22). I see a major difficulty with his views of the concept "subsystem," and I deal with this first.

In his article, "Living Systems: Structure and Process" (1965b), he outlines the essential subsystems that a system should have. For him, each subsystem carries out an operation, task, or process for the system, much as the circulatory system in an organism circulates nutrients to the body.

> The totality of all the structures in a system which carry out a particular process is a *subsystem*. A subsystem, thus, is identified by the process it carries out [read "function"]. It exists in one or more identifiable structural units of the system. These specific, local distinguishable structural units are called *components* or *members* or *parts*. (1965a:218)

I think this is a useful definition; and I think Miller's list of proposed subsystems (1965b; Table 1) is a good one, in that it seems to include most or all of the essential kinds of systemic tasks or processes required by a living system—though at a very general level.

The difficulty comes in applying his list of subsystems to actual research in human societies. He lists, for example, such matter-energy processing subsystems as the following: Ingestor, Distributor, Decomposer, Producer, Storage, Extruder, Motor, and Supportive; and he implies that every living system has only one of each of these (and one each of the other subsystems as well). While it may be reasonably easy to think of individual organisms as having single subsystems for each of these processes, it seems likely that human societies may have many and varied subsystems that contribute to each process. There is often not just one "Extruder" subsystem, for example; wastes are removed by dumping garbage, disposing of sewage, exiling individuals, and even burying people. These activities would often not constitute a single extruder "subsystem"; and they may often not be articulated as a subsystem, in that little, if any, matter-energy or information would flow among them (cf. Miller 1965b:363). Thus, in a practical sense, we gain little by thinking of such activities as belonging to a single subsystem.

The same kind of comment can be made with regard to all of Miller's "subsystems." To try actually to isolate and describe *the* "Boundary" subsystem of a society, or *the* "Decider," or *the* "Output Transducer" would often be fruitless when considering whole societies—there are many, and often nonarticulated, subsystems in societies that carry out different aspects of each of the general subsystem processes Miller discusses.

Thus, while Miller's understanding of "subsystem" is heuristically useful, it is analytically weak. It does serve to point up the fact thaat there are various kinds of system-maintaining activities that are carried out by societies; but at an operational level, it may frequently be impossible to demonstrate that all of the activities performed by one of Miller's subsystems are actually integrated as systems in themselves. While this may sometimes be the case, it is certainly something that would need to be demonstrated empirically.

Miller's conception of how systems operate (maintain equilibrium) is reasonable, at least in general outline. His discussion of the processes of systemic regulation is virtually the same as my earlier discussion of negative feedback processes (Miller 1965a:224–29); and I would, in essence, agree that,

> Each level of system maintains in steady states its own particular sorts of variables related to matter-energy and information process-ing. (1965b:363)

I also think we can agree that the kinds of variables he lists (1965b:363) are reasonably representative of the general kinds of variables that are crit-ical to societal systems, and which tend to be maintained in steady state.

At the same time, however, I think his conception of systemic self-regulation is needlessly teleological. He resorts frequently to the idea that a system's steady state is determined by system "goals." To him, a system pursues both internal *goals* and external *purposes;* they are conscious, and sought actively by each system (1965a:231–32). While he tries to avoid teleology by saying that it is the maintenance of certain critical variables in equilibrium that constitutes the goals of a system (1965a:232), he fails to be convincing because he insists that the equilibrium range for each of the variables is determined by societal choice or preference (*cf.* 1965a:204, 1965b:358, 364, 375).

While it is certainly true that individuals, and even societies, can have goals and purposes, and make decisions with respect to them, it is equally evident that many system states and adaptive responses in societies are not conscious to many or most of the people involved—they are in no useful sense goal oriented. This has been amply demonstrated by anthropologists, notably in those situations in which they find informants agreeing on certain kinds of standards or goals, and then they determine statistically that the standards and goals are in fact not being maintained or achieved—in fact, something quite different may be occurring that few or no people are aware of (cf., for example, Meggitt 1965; Buchler and Selby 1968:76–81. See also my discussion, pp. 75–76).

A further reason I regard Miller's view as inadequate is that he exaggerates the importance of societal agreement on system goals (1965b:356, 370). He subscribes to a normative or consensus model, and does not seem to recognize that dissent, conflict, and other kinds of variability are commonplace in societal systems (Nadel 1953). It is this variability that the processes of selection act upon in adaptation and change, as will be seen. I think it may be *because* Miller ignores this variability that he ultimately says little about what change is and, specifically, how it occurs—it may also account for the fact that what he does say is somewhat vague and equivocal.

In some of his statements, he does not even seem to recognize that change can occur.

Inputs, internal processes, and outputs of different kinds of matter-energy constitute the matter-energy metabolism necessary to all systems. It is accomplished in such a way that *living systems at all levels combat entropy and maintain their steady states over time.* (1965b:344; italics mine)

When a system has exhausted all of its adjustment processes and is unable to maintain one or more of its critical variables within the proper range of stability . . . *it cannot survive.* Then, after a more or less rapid decline, its existence is terminated. (1965b:378; italics mine)

This seems to suggest that when a system's homeostats fail, the system must collapse rather than change. At other times, Miller clearly recognizes change, but seems to equate the processes involved with something vague called "history."

How have the various levels and types of living systems come to exist? Over time, systems with novel structures and processes appear at all levels as the result of cumulative evolutionary changes. *These are historical processes,* which are difficult to reverse or essentially irreversible. (1965b:369; italics mine)

While I would agree that evolution is irreversible, I am unhappy with his view that it is usually a gradual, cumulative historical process resulting from "accumulation in the system of residues or effects of past events." (1965a:209). Although he may be simply referring to the fact that past system structure can affect future adaptation and change (which is correct), his vagueness precludes understanding of the specific "historical" processes involved.

On occasion, however, he states the processes of change in a way much more acceptable to me.

> There is a *range of stability* for each of numerous variables in all living systems. . . . An input or output . . . which . . . forces the variables beyond the range of stability, constitutes a *stress* and produces a strain (or strains) within the system. (1965a:224)

> If such disturbances are prolonged, they may exhaust the adjustment processes which the system has available to cope with them. Some pathological states are corrected with little permanent damage to the system. . . . *Others bring about new, and often but not always a less desirable, steady state. This is historical change, irreversible process which produces a new structure.* (1965b:376; italics mine)

> Positive feedback alters variables and destroys their steady states. Thus it can initiate system changes. (1965a:227)

While I do not subscribe to everything in these statements, it is evident that Miller does sometimes recognize the importance of the breakdown of homeostatic mechanisms in explaining change; and he sees it as involving a positive feedback process, which I consider in detail later.

Nonetheless, a major impression one gets of Miller's work is that the most important processes of change are something altogether different. He argues in several places that change is brought about by changes in the "templates" of systems (or "charters" in societies) (1965a:224; 1965b:370–71). By "charters," he means not only written charters, but also, in the case of societies, norms, values, standards, beliefs, and so forth. As I already indicated, he strongly implies that these charters change in order for the system to achieve a "common purpose" (1965b:370); and they change by "consensus of a majority of the components" of the system (1965b:356). This hints strongly at a strict concept of goal-directed change; and it leaves the reader unsure whether Miller regards change as occurring primarily as a response to systemic stress (that is, breakdown of homeostats), or whether he would see change occurring simply because people decide they *want* to change in a certain direction.

My overall impression is that Miller's argument is the following: When a society's homeostatic mechanisms have failed to cope with a stress situation (a "historical" situation), the society may "decide," as a whole, to restructure itself in the direction of one or more of its a priori goals or purposes; and this is accomplished by gaining conscious "consensus" of a majority of the people. Thus the society "learns" how to achieve its long-term goals—and this is evolution.

While one reason for my objection to this teleological view of change has already been given, I present further argumentation later in connection with my discussion of Buckley's views.

The most important difficulty with Miller's view, however, is that it is really not evolutionary. The reason for this, as I indicated, is that he virtually ignores the processes of *selection*. Since selection must operate on a pool of variability, Miller's normative-consensual paradigm precludes it. If most of the individuals in societies have the same goals, and agree on these as well as on the means of attaining them, then there is no variability to be selected from in responding to stress. So, how could evolution occur at all in his framework?

Finally, Miller's view of the *sources* of change is ambiguous and leads to difficulties. While he sometimes suggests that change results from stresses impinging on a system from outside the system (environment), he just as frequently implies that change can be instigated from *within* the system. For example,

> *Steady states may be disturbed by malfunctioning of subsystems or components* or by unfavorable conditions in the environment or suprasystem. (1965b:376; italics mine)

> Some forms of internal matter-energy processing can alter a system's structure in an abnormal direction. . . . [For example] after an earthquake leveled much of Anchorage, Alaska in 1964, streets had to be reoriented inefficiently. (1965b:377)

This is an unfortunate example, since it should be clear that earthquakes are stochastic events exogenous to a system, not something internal to it. But the first quotation is more disturbing, because he implies that "malfunctioning of subsystems" can result from internal sources of stress. I fail to understand how a system can have internal sources of stress. There *must* be something external to the system, with which it is interacting, that causes a subsystem to malfunction in the first place. There is some confusion here on Miller's part, but I will defer discussion of it until I consider the "Buckley Framework," since Buckley is a stronger proponent of the idea that change can originate internally. (For a thorough criticism of this idea see Arthur Saxe's chapter 4 and "Seminar Discussion" in this volume.)

## THE BUCKLEY FRAMEWORK

Walter Buckley, a sociologist, has presented a detailed systems framework for societies (1967, 1968b), which is somewhat similar to the Miller approach, but is in some crucial senses quite different. Perhaps the biggest difference is that Buckley emphasizes the idea that societies are usually not in equilibrium, but are continuously changing—and his emphasis is on the change process itself. He calls his approach the "Complex Adaptive System Model," and contrasts it with two other kinds of systems models of society that he regards as less useful: the "Mechanical Equilibrium Model," and the "Organismic Homeostasis Model" (Buckley 1967:8–41).

In attacking the Homeostasis ("Morphostasis") model, he presents at least three major objections to it (1967:8–41):

1. It is similar to functionalist approaches, in that it emphasizes the maintenance of societal stability rather than accounting for change.
2. It is inappropriate because societies are in fact nearly always changing; they are rarely, if ever, in a state of "static" equilibrium.
3. It implies an unacceptable emphasis on intrasocietal cooperation, consensus, and order that does not really exist. There is, in fact, "distunction" and lack of consensus—and this is the variability upon which selection operates in societal evolution.

These points are all well-taken, at least in part. However, the first two points present some important difficulties that will become apparent as the discussion proceeds.

Buckley's view of what constitutes a system is in many ways like Miller's in that he regards systems as being made up of articulated subsystems and components, and having discrete boundaries (1967:5, 41–51). He also heavily emphasizes the importance of societal norms, values, beliefs, preferences, and so forth. In fact, he is really more interested in such things than he is in the matter-energy organization of a system (1967:172–76). He feels that social systems are much more important information processing systems than they are matter-energy processing systems. And to him, communication is the "predominant feature" of the "structure" of a social sytem (1967:48).

"Structure" is regarded as a snapshot view of a system at a single point in time; thus, structure is static and nonprocessual. To him, the structure of a system is made up of both people (individuals) and a set of norms, values, and so forth. The term "process" refers primarily to individuals interacting with one another (1967:18–23). It is the complex interaction among people, as they negotiate, bargain, and accommodate one another in the face of stress or tension situations (1968b:498). These tension situations arise from the fact that there is always some disagreement on the value of the prevailing norms or their interpretation (1967:161). The processes of bargaining or negotation serve to resolve these tensions, although they never do so completely.

Buckley's view of system self-regulation seems generally similar to that of Miller and other systems theorists, except that he is even more teleological than Miller in subscribing to the idea that social systems pursue "purposes" and "goals" (1967:69–70, 165). To him, homeostatic ("feedback") processes serve to adjust the system to its chosen goals when it begins to deviate from them.

> It is generally agreed among systems theorists that a basic principle underlying these purposive, or goal-seeking mechanisms is embodied in the concept "feedback." (1967:52)

> [The system] . . . is continually processing feedback information about its own state and its goal deviations. (1967:165)

Further, it is through the above mentioned processes of negotiation that the system evaluates its current state in relation to its goals. "Decisions" are then made to correct for any deviation (1967:69–70, 77, 129).

> Thus, decision making is seen as the exemplar, in the sociocultural system, of the general selective process occurring in every adaptive system, whereby variety is selectively organized and utilized for self-regulation and self-direction. (1967:79)

I have already pointed out my belief that much of societal behavior has little or nothing to do with "goal-seeking." Individuals more frequently

71

have goals and make decisions than do societies. And, of course, Buckley does view societal structure as an aggregate of individuals, so it is easy to see why he takes the teleological kind of view he does.

Beyond this, it seems to me that Buckley's view of societal systems as aggregates of interacting individuals virtually ignores the organizational aspects of such systems. He says very little about subsystems and how they might be organized or articulate with one another—he instead considers only the "sociocultural system" as a whole, and its components (individuals). While he expressly tries to get away from what he calls the "organismic" view of societies (1967:11–17), I don't think he succeeds. Thus, even though he is aiming at describing and explaining aspects of *societal* systems, he is really talking about aggregates of *individuals* and their decision-making processes. He thus appears to be mixing his systemic levels.

But what is most interesting is how he accounts for change. He sees little usefulness in homeostatic processes in accounting for either the operation of a social system, or change in such a system. While I can agree that such equilibrial processes cannot, by themselves, account for change (only stability), I feel that they must be considered an integral part of the change process. Buckley, however, views homeostatic and morphogenic processes as entirely separate and unrelated:

> Care must . . . be taken to distinguish . . . between self-regulation of a given system structure—which tends to maintain that structure in its essential form (as in homeostasis)—and self-direction (or control) of the system itself, which may imply frequent change of its particular structure (as in biological and sociocultural evolution). We have argued that *the latter represents the more characteristic feature of sociocultural systems.* . . . (1967:163–4; italics mine)

> . . . we might say that physical systems are typically equilibrial, physiological systems are typically homeostatic, and *psychological, sociocultural, or ecological systems are typically morphogenic.* From this view, our paradigm of the mechanisms underlying the complex system becomes a basic paradigm of the morphogenic process. . . . (1968b:511–12, Note 7; italics mine)

One reason that he downplays the importance of homeostatic processes is that he thinks that societies characteristically do not maintain equilibria; and second, he feels that morphogenic processes are adequate, in themselves, to account for both stability and change. He feels that social systems maintain stability *by* changing.

> As a fundamental principle, it can be stated that a condition for maintenance of a viable adaptive system may be a change in its particular structure. (1968b:510)

> In dealing with the sociocultural system . . . we jump to a new system level and need yet a new term to express *not only the structure-maintaining feature, but also the structure-elaborating and changing feature of the inherently unstable system,* i.e., a concept of morphogenesis. The notion of "steady state," now often used, approaches or allows for this conception if it is understood that the "state" that tends to remain steady is not to be identified with the particular structure of the system. That is, *in order to maintain a steady state the system may have to change its particular structure.* (1967:15; italics mine)

There is nothing wrong with this view, so long as when one is discussing "steady state," "maintenance of the system," and so forth, he is referring to the survival of a social system as a social system. Of course, a society may have to change in order to maintain viability, or survive. But what Buckley is doing is denying that social systems can often maintain a more or less stable equilibrium, through homeostatic processes, without actually changing. He seems not to be recognizing any difference at all between stability and change—change *is* stability!

It may be, of course, that he is correct in thinking that societies, as wholes, are never in stable equilibrium—but even if true, this does not mean that portions of societal systems cannot maintain equilibrium, while at the same time other parts or subsystems are changing. Of course, if one is regarding a society (as a whole) as his system of interest, then if part of it changes, the whole system is to some degree changed, by definition. But as I argue later, we will rarely be considering whole human societies as our systems of interest, since it is analytically impractical.

In any event, I think Buckley's equation of stability with change is misleading; it fails to recognize any real difference between the two. I think it is more useful to regard change as the *failure* of stability (homeostasis)—otherwise we would have no basis for knowing when a change has occurred. Presumably, there is a real difference between relatively stable and relatively changing aspects of societies; while some subsystems may be changing rapidly, others may remain in an equilibrial state for long periods.

But to continue, Buckley's views on the specific processes of morphogenesis require further comment. He makes use of the biological concept "selection"; and the basic idea is that change occurs through a trial-and-error process of selection for various individual viewpoints and selection against others; this is the process of negotiation for the resolution of conflicts or tensions discussed earlier.

> On the sociocultural level, social selection . . . occurs through the variety of processes usually studied under the headings of conflict, competition, accommodation, and such; power, authority and compliance; and collective behavior. . . .(1968b:495)

> There are the *selection processes* whereby the perceived variety, showing up as uncertainty, ambiguity, or conflict, is sorted and sifted in intraindividual and interpersonal interchanges. Communication networks and information flows can be seen as vehicles whereby tensions, intentions, and expectations are communicated as social pressures or interpersonal influences, and whereby selective responses are made whose sum total at any period contributes to the "institutional" order (or disorder) at that time. This *transactional process* of exchange, negotiation, or bargaining is thus inherently a morphogenic process out of which emerge relatively stable social and cultural structures; that is, definitions, expectations, motives, and purposes developing with (and outside) a given institutional framework act to reconstitute, elaborate, and change it by a complex of various levels of feedbacks. (1967:160)

> The selection processes continue such that some of the role matrices come to be established as more enduring organizations or institutions, the new frameworks within which the dynamic social process occurs. But they themselves, in turn, generate their own brand of variety and tension. . . . (1967:160–61)

This, then, is how change occurs in Buckley's view. The tensions and conflicts in societies lead to negotiated settlements which create new systemic structure and organization. The term "selection" refers simply to the fact that individuals make decisions and choices, and through the negotiation process some of these choices get more heavily selected for than others, and thus get institutionalized. While he occasionally talks about positive feedback processes (1968b:507–8), he is unclear as to how this works. Again, he is evidently considering individuals (organisms) as his systems of interest, and dealing with feedback among individuals rather than between a societal system and its environment. In fact, he evidently doesn't need any systems concepts and terminology in his approach. His is a straightforward and clear presentation of "interactionist" theory, which has been available for some time (Secord and Backman 1961; Turner 1962; Strauss *et al.* 1963).

A further aspect of his approach is that he regards social systems as not

74

only having goals, but as actually instituting purposeful change *because* of these goals (solely because the goals exist).

> [Compared to simpler systems, the sociocultural system has] . . . a greater elaboration of self-regulating substructures in order—not merely to restore a given equilibrium or homeostatic level—but to purposefully restructure the system without tearing up the lawn in the process. (1968b:496)

> The sociocultural system is the only natural adaptive system in which the over-all direction and control become largely a function of the self-direction and control inherent in the individual (including subgroup) units that make it up. (1967:182)

This is, of course, opposed to my own view—and that of most of the seminar participants—which is that societies tend to *resist* change. It is not that societies tend consciously to pursue change; rather, they change in the process of failing to maintain stability. After all, why would social systems direct themselves to institute change just for the sake of change? Surely social systems usually only change when they are under stress that cannot be coped with otherwise—not because they have a priori long-range goals, with people willing to forego stability and institute change to reach these goals.

Again, I am not arguing that individuals and social systems never have goals. I do think, however, that such goals must originate in response to stress, rather than occurring in a vacuum. A clear example of this is seen in contemporary city planning. City planners prepare plans or goals for development. These goals come about as a result of stress or perceived stress, however, such as overcrowding, traffic congestion, smog, and so forth. It is only when certain critical variables are approaching or exceeding their tolerance limits, or are perceived to be approaching them, that individuals or social systems establish goals—and these goals are simply statements concerning possible solutions to the stresses involved.

But perhaps the most fundamental difficulty with Buckley's approach is that it really fails to account for change, even though this is his primary interest. The major reason for this is that he regards the source of change as being primarily internal to the system (1967:128–129, 159–61, 163, 206–7; 1968b:507); and he is a much stronger proponent of this idea than Miller is.

> We have appealed to the principle that norms and values alone do not specify action, that it is the norms and values, plus the interactions of those differentially interpreting them, that generate the

social behaviors we are trying to explain. . . .in the case of society, some of the very rules and goals change as an emergent product of the ongoing interactions of the inevitable generation of "deviation." (1967:165)

With the transition from the higher primate social organization to the full-blown human, symbolically mediated, sociocultural system, the mapping of the subtle behavior, gestures, and intentions of the *individuals making up the effective social organization become increasingly central, and eventually equals or even overhadows, the mapping of the physical environment.* (1967:65; italics mine)

[Social structure is seen] . . . as a complex adaptive organization that may remain viable by readjusting to external conditions *and to its normal internal conflicts and deviations.* (1967:106; italics mine)

In the first place, this is illogical. Buckley is arguing, in essence, that a system can change itself! He is saying that tensions arise in the system, negotiations occur, changes are then made; and then new tensions arise, and the process begins again. This is a perpetual motion machine. As Saxe (in chapter 4 of this volume) attempts to demonstrate, no system can change itself; change can only be instigated by outside sources. If a system is in equilibrium, it will remain so unless inputs (or lack of inputs) from outside the system disturb the equilibrium. Of course, the individuals in a social system may consciously realize that change is necessary; but the reason the change is necessary lies in the relationship of the system with its environment.

Otherwise, why would change occur at all? In Buckley's approach, why would not the negotiation process eventually lead to stable equilibrium? Why do further "tensions" arise? Where do they come from? Buckley claims that they are inherent in the system—but this is no answer; it begs the question.

Buckley's view is only reasonable if he is referring to *individuals* as his systems of interest. If this is the case, individuals are adapting to their environments, and thus developing different viewpoints, conflicts, and so forth. Taking each individual's personality as a constant, these adaptive responses are the result of inputs *external* to each individual (the behavior of other people, and so forth). However, these individual adaptive situations are *internal* to the larger social system (which Buckley claims as his system of interest); hence they are a part of the ongoing matter-energy and information fluxes of the system, and cannot be employed as sources of change for the larger system. To account for

76

change in this system, we must look for sources external to it. If we needlessly insist on talking about "tensions" as causes, then we still must look outside the system to discover what is causing the tensions.

As an example, consider one of the examples Buckley uses in his effort to demonstrate that the source of change can be internal. He cites Ronald Cohen's study of the Kanuri of Nigeria (1964; In Buckley 1967:157–59). He says that the Kanuri political organization is changing itself (internally) because the people involved in it are interacting with the British colonial administration, and are changing their "roles" in response to the "role expectations" of the administrators. I would argue to the contrary. It should be clear that the source of change here is coming from outside the system (the native political system), since the colonial administrators are outside that particular system. They are outside of it, that is, if the native political system is the system of interest here. If it is, then the colonials are part of its environment. If, on the other hand, Buckley is viewing the colonial administrators as part of a larger system (including the native political subsystem), the interactions between the colonial and native subsystems (including the individuals involved) constitute matter-energy and information fluxes within the larger system, and cannot be used in accounting for change.

In my view, Buckley is mixing his systemic levels of interest. That is, he claims to be focusing on something called the "sociocultural system," yet he is really usually talking about individuals, and individual adaptive response. I feel that it is exceedingly important to precisely define one's system of interest, since it is only then that one can distinguish the internal from the external—the system from its environment.

Thus, while it may be that Buckley presents an adequate framework for how change sometimes occurs (that is, negotiation), he does not offer any framework for explaining *why* it occurs. In fact, he sometimes enters the realm of the mystical when he occasionally refers to change as simply being caused by goal preferences. While he says he is developing an approach that will explain change (evolution), he provides no explanation of how variability gets into a social system and maintained, nor why certain aspects of this variability are selected for, while others are selected against. An acceptable theory of evolution must answer these questions, as the theory of evolution in biology clearly does.

A final criticism of the Buckley framework is that it is inadequate as an explanation because it cannot predict when either change or stability would be expected to occur (*cf.* Hempel 1966:47–69). Presumably, change will occur when "tensions" reach some point. But at what point? He cannot predict. All he can say is,

> Although this complex of performances [negotiation, etc.] ordinarily maintains a society, it may also change it significantly, or even fail to maintain it. . . .(1967:153–54)

This is, of course, virtually meaningless; and he seems at one point to recognize it:

> given the relatively greater degree of freedom of internal structuring [of societies as compared to organisms] . . . and the *potentially* great speed with which restructuring may occur under certain conditions, it becomes difficult to predict the reactions of such a system to environmental changes or internal elaboration. (1968b:496)

The crucial phrase here is "restructuring may occur under certain conditions." But what are those conditions?

In a following section, I consider a general approach that does specify the general conditions under which change can be predicted to occur; but since this approach is based heavily on Maruyama's discussion of morphogenesis (1963), I must first present his views.

## THE MARUYAMA APPROACH

Maruyama (1963) does not deal with the structural nature of systems in detail, but he does consider the cybernetic processes of both stability and change, with emphasis on the latter. And it is his contribution to understanding change that is my focus here, since I think his approach (with at least one major modification) is suitable for our purposes.

Maruyama begins by pointing out what I have already pointed out—namely that homeostatic or deviation-counteracting processes are inadequate, in themselves, to account for change. Change can only be explained by considering both deviation-counteracting and deviation-amplifying processes.

> By focusing on the deviation-counteracting aspect of the mutual causal relationships . . . the cyberneticians paid less attention to the systems in which the mutual causal effects are deviation-amplifying. Such systems are ubiquitous: accumulation of capital in industry, evolution of organisms, *the rise of cultures* of various types. . . . (1963); In Buckley 1968a:304; italics mine)

He calls the study of deviation-counteracting processes "the first cybernetics," and the study of deviation-amplifying processes "the second cybernetics." And he coined the term "morphostasis" to refer to the former process, and the term "morphogenesis" to refer to the latter process (In Buckley 1968a:304). While deviation-counteracting processes involve "negative feedback," the deviation-amplifying processes involve "positive feedback" (Ibid., 304).

Morphogenic or positive feedback processes are sometimes said to be "circular causal systems" (Hutchinson 1948). The reason is that the feedback involved is circular and reinforcing. The process begins, according to Maruyama (1963), with a small deviation ("initial kick") in one of the critical variables of a system. Then, instead of being counteracted by a negative feedback process (homeostat), the deviation is amplified or made even stronger by its interaction with other variables. In other words, each variable affects the others in such a way as to increase the deviation in one direction rather than decreasing it as would be the case in homeostasis. Hence the term "positive feedback."

Maruyama gives a number of examples, one of which is as follows:

> Take, for example, weathering of rock. A small crack in a rock ["initial kick"] collects some water. The water freezes and makes the crack larger. A larger crack collects more water, which [freezes and] makes the crack still larger. (1963; In Buckley 1968a:305)

If such a process is carried on very long, it is called a "spiraling" or "runaway feedback" process; and if it is not eventually halted by negative feedback processes, it can lead to the destruction of the system. But, it can also lead to rapid evolutionary change, assuming only that the process *is* at some point halted.

It is easy to see that this kind of process goes on in societal systems, and that it will be useful in dealing with change. There is, however, an important difficulty with the approach as Maruyama presents it; and it is indicated by one of his major examples, which purports to show how the positive feedback process can lead to the growth of a city on a homogeneous plain:

> At the beginning, a large plain is entirely homogeneous as to its potential for agriculture [by Maruyama's stipulation]. *By chance an ambitious farmer opens a farm at a spot on it. This is the initial kick.* Several farmers follow the example and several farms are established. One of the farmers opens a tool shop. Then this tool shop becomes a meeting place of farmers. A food stand is established next to the tool shop. Gradually a village grows. The village facil-

itates the marketing of the agricultural products, and more farms flourish around the village. Increased agricultural activity necessitates development of industry in the village, and the village grows into a city. (1963; In Buckley 1968a:305; italics mine)

Aside from the fact that Maruyama's initial farmer locates himself by chance on a homeogenous plain (which seems unlikely in real life), the major difficulty lies in his "initial kick" idea. There is little reason to think that the "initial kick" of having one farmer settle on the plain is sufficient to account for more farmers arriving. Does one farmer lead to another without any additional causal factors involved? This is doubtful. I think that Maruyama has a strong tendency to ignore the effects of environment, and to think óf the deviation-amplifying process as something that begins and is carried on all by itself, in a vacuum so to speak. To him, all that is needed is an "initial kick," and everything goes from there. He puts it this way:

A small initial deviation, which is within the range of high probability, may develop into a deviation of very low probability (or more precisely, into a deviation which is very improbable within the framework of probabalistic unidirectional causality). (1963; In Buckley 1968a:306)

As in the case Maruyama's farmer, however, it seems evident that it takes more than just an "initial kick" to get such a process going and to maintain it. Thus, in his example more farmers would not come (nor would the initial one have come) unless the environment of the plain was such as to attract and support farmers. And the deviation-amplification would not continue until a city evolved unless the plain could support such a large number of people, and unless his earlier "village" had relationships with other areas and communities that led to the increasing growth of industry, and so on. In short, I would argue that for such a process to continue, a system would have to have continuing relationships with its environment. (See Saxe, chapter 4 this volume, for a detailed discussion of this problem.)

I think a major part of the reason that Maruyama relies on an initial arbitrary "kick" to get the morphogenic process moving is that he underemphasizes the importance of negative feedback or homeostatic processes. This is indicated by the fact that he does not seem to be concerned with the idea that negative feedback processes are operating between a system and its environment *prior* to the beginning of the positive feedback process that leads to change. What actually happens, I would argue, is that systems are continually being strained by deviations in inputs and outputs that threaten to cause the departure of critical variables from their tolerance ranges. When this occurs, the system's homeostatic mechanisms come into operation as adjustment processes to maintain equilibrium. In fact, there may be a whole series of homeostats that come into operation one after another (or together) until the system is re-equilibrated. However, such homeostats do not always work adequately—and, in fact, it is the positive feedback or morphogenic process that causes the homeostats to break down, thus leading to change (as will be clear in a subsequent example). Thus it is not just a matter of having an initial "kick"; it is evident that systems are continuously responding to their environments, and the morphogenic process originates out of this relationship. That is, there may be no "kick" at all, but rather a gradually developing disequilibrium between a system and its environment, as the two interact. Then, at some point (threshold), one or more critical variables may actually depart from their tolerance ranges, and the system will be forced either to change or collapse.

It is important to point out that Maruyama does invoke negative feedback processes at the *end* of a period of deviation-amplification—and this is correct; it is how the deviation-amplification gets terminated, if the system does not collapse.

> At one time, a random initial kick produces a deviation in a certain direction. Deviation-amplification takes over and this deviation is amplified consistently in the same direction. But this does not last very long. Soon, deviation-counteracting takes over, and the population becomes fixed at a certain point of deviation. After a while, another random initial kick produces a deviation in a new direction. Deviation-amplification takes over again and the population drifts consistently in this direction for a while. But soon, deviation-counteracting takes over and the population becomes fixed at a new point in the direction of deviation. Then another initial kick starts a deviation in a new direction. The process repeats itself with unpredictable drifts. (1963; In Buckley 1968a:308)

I am simply arguing here that deviation-counteracting processes are always occurring in the system, and that one cannot adequately deal with the processes of change without considering their operation prior to change, together with the factors that lead to their failure to equilibrate the system.

But, aside from the inadequacy of the "initial kick" idea (and his final mention of "unpredictable drifts," which I doubt is necessarily the case), this is a pretty good statement of how change occurs. And Maruyama clearly contributes by showing that both morphostatic and morphogenic processes operate together in a situation of change.

> A society or an organism contains many deviation-amplifying loops as well as deviation-counteracting loops, and an understanding of a society or an organism cannot be attained without studying both types of loops and the relationships between them. (1963; In Buckley 1968a:312)

Thus, it can be seen that change, as the term is used here, refers only to what happens when homeostatic mechanisms fail to maintain critical system variables within their operational tolerance limits. When change (rather than collapse) occurs, the system is a different system—we are not simply observing temporary fluxes in the normal equilibrium or steady state of a former system.

Before closing this section, I should point out that the deviation-amplification process can be relatively rapid or relatively slow; and runaway feedback need not be involved. For example, a system may undergo a deviation in one of its critical variables; its homeostats may fail to restore equilibrium; and new critical variables and homeostats may develop very quickly, without a continuation of the "vicious circle" kind of feedback. While I suspect that this is not very common, it is still, by definition, a positive feedback process, and the result is irreversible change in the system.

In any event, regardless of certain difficulties with Maruyama's approach, it appears to be the most usable one thus far published. Further, I feel that he makes an important contribution by inadvertently showing that systemic change need not be a conscious thing on the parts of the people involved, much less goal-directed. In the case of Maruyama's city, for example, the increase in the numbers of different kinds of specialists through time represents such a situation. It would not necessarily be the case that in a small village the people would have the conscious "goal" of adding craft specialists. It could happen unconsciously and inevitably. Once there is a specialist in the village, this almost inevitably leads to other specialists in some degree; the reason is that the specialist cannot support himself by growing his own crops and otherwise meeting his own needs, since he must devote a great deal of time to his specialty (such as plow repairing). His reliance on others to grow much of his food, obtain his firewood, and so forth, would tend to force certain farmers and wood collectors to devote more of their time to these tasks; and thus they would become more specialized. This, in turn, can necessitate further specialization on the parts of others. And all of this can be predicted, whether people are conscious of it or not. In short, the consequences of the deviation-amplification process can often be totally unanticipated by the people involved.

In the following section I make heavy use of the essentials of Maruyama's approach in developing what I think is the kind of systems framework we can use in describing and explaining societal change. I first describe the kind of systemic structure I think we can most profitably deal with; and I follow this with a consideration of what change is in the light of my proposed conception of "system." I then deal with the requirements we must meet if we are to explain change acceptably.

## A BETTER FRAMEWORK

Throughout this discussion I have already managed to present many ideas concerning what needs to be done to construct a more useful systems framework than the ones I have considered—and the basic ingredients have been presented. These ideas, however, must be drawn together into a coherent framework and refined so that they can be made operational in research.

### System Description

In the first place, it should already be clear that it will be virtually impossible to describe and account for change in whole substantive societal or "cultural" systems. Relatively complete description and measurement would be far too complex a task to undertake. There are nearly an infinite number of possible kinds of subsystems, components, and variables in "cultural" systems.[2]

I feel, then, that we must abstract from these substantive systems those aspects that are of interest to our specific problems. Thus, we should not be worried about trying to define *the* subsystems and components of societal systems, but should instead abstract sets of specific, measurable

83

*variables* that we think can be shown to articulate with one another as systems (that is, "formal" systems). As Rappaport says,

> The selection of variables is a product of hypotheses concerning possible interrelations among phenomena under investigation, and these, in turn, flow from the interests and theoretical conceptions of the analyst. (1967:5)

This is precisely what Rappaport did reasonably successfully in his study of the Tsembaga of highland New Guinea:

> In the functional and cybernetic analysis of the ecological relations of the Tsembaga that has been attempted here, variables have been abstracted from events or entities in the physical world and treated as components of an *analytic* system. . . . quantitative values must be assigned to all variables, and in the case of those variables that define the adequate functioning of the system their tolerable ranges of values must also be specified. (1967:230; italics mine)

Thus, to make research practicable, we must define an analytical system composed of variables, each of which has a tolerance range within which the system can operate, and which has at least one homeostatic mechanism that tends to keep these variables within their tolerance ranges when the system is in equilibrium. I can agree with Rappaport, then, that for practical purposes,

> a system is any set of specified variables in which a change in the value of one of the variables will result in a change in the value of at least one other variable. [And the system must be regulated.] A regulatory mechanism is one that maintains the values of one or more variables within a range or ranges that permit the continued existence of the system. (1967:4)

It is the set of articulated "dependent" and "independent" variables that I am considering a system here. In short, the system must include both the variable(s) being explained at any given moment (the dependent variable) and the variables suspected to be causing the dependent variable to vary in certain ways. Of course, in such a system each variable may be affecting the others as well (mutual causal relationships), so none of them are, in a sense, truly "independent" variables. They can be thought of in this way, however, if they are regarded in a given analysis as causal rather than being the variables that are being explained.

Let me present a hypothetical and highly simplified example of the kind of system I am referring to, simply to illustrate my points. Consider a human population that relies on hunting and gathering, and has as one of its primary critical resources a specific kind of amaranth seed. There are occasional periods in which these seeds are scarce, because of various environmental conditions; however, these periods of scarcity are compensated for by homeostatic processes—namely, in this case, by the increased gathering of other seeds that are usually not eaten in large quantities. This homeostat comes into operation whenever the availability of amaranth seeds falls below a certain level. The variables and their tolerance ranges are as follows:

1. Number of bushels of *seed* required per capita per year to sustain the population indefinitely. (We can presume that this represents *all* seeds providing the total per capita requirements of carbohydrates.)
   Tolerance Range = 9–15 bushels.
2. Per capita annual harvest of amaranth seeds (in number of bushels).
   Tolerance Range = 7–10 bushels.
3. Per capita annual harvest of "other" carbohydrate-yielding seeds (in number of bushels).
   Tolerance Range = 2–5 bushels.

In essence, this is saying that variable number 1 has a tolerance range of from 9 to 15 bushels per capita. That is, the population can survive on a minimum of 9 bushels per capita, and it can consume no more than the maximum of 15 bushels per capita. For variables numbers 2 and 3, the high end of each tolerance range indicates the total number of bushels per capita that can possibly be harvested, given the maximum availability of plants in the area in the best of times, and the technology used in harvesting them. The low end of each range represents the lowest number of bushels per capita of each kind of seed that is usually available.

Here is how it works. Since the population must have at least 9 bushels of all types of seed per capita to survive, and since amaranth seed is most easily available and easiest to process, the population harvests as many amaranth seeds as it can each year—and then it harvests enough of the "other" seeds to make up for any shortage. Thus, in a productive year they may harvest the maximum of 10 bushels per capita of amaranth, and not really need to gather any of the "other" seeds. On the other hand, in a relatively unproductive year yielding only 7 bushels of amaranth, the population will have to harvest at least 2 bushels of the "other" seeds in order to survive.

Thus, the homeostatic mechanism in this system is the alternative of gathering the "other" seeds when an insufficient quantity of amaranth is available. In terms of the concept "feedback," what is happening is that the population is exploiting amaranth seeds which it finds in its environment. Information may be fed back to the population to the effect that there are not enough such seeds available; the population responds by gathering increased amounts of the "other" seeds. If there are enough "other" seeds available to make up for the shortage in amaranth seeds, this information is fed back to the system, and no further system response is necessary.

The feedback loops involved can be seen in Figure 3.1. The solid arrows represent matter-energy transmissions (each type of seed) as the seeds flow through the system, from procurement to consumption. The dashed arrows represent information flows. In this diagram, the Procurement Component harvests amaranth and "other" seeds; the Sensor Component receives information concerning the availability of both amaranth and "other" seeds in the environment, and transmits this information to the Decider Component, which instructs the Regulator Component to regulate the input of seeds. If amaranth seeds become scarce, the Regulator transmits information back to the Procurement Component instructing it to terminate (or decrease) the harvesting of amaranth, and increase the harvesting of "other" seeds. This homeostat is triggered whenever the system receives information to the effect that less than 9 bushels of amaranth seeds are available for harvesting.

The triggering of the homeostat probably depends on a "cost function." That is, while it may still be possible to continue harvesting amaranth seeds (say at greater distances from the population), the relative cost of doing this becomes greater than the cost of switching to the "other" seeds. At this point the homeostat is triggered. I would, in fact, argue that homeostats are only triggered when they become "least-cost solutions" in a given situation, or when they are perceived as "least-cost" solutions.

This homeostatic mechanism regulates the system, keeping it in equilibrium. And the system could actually be simulated. That is, we can predict that if the amaranth harvest falls below 9 bushels by "x" amount, the harvest of "other" seeds will increase by "y" amount.

A real difficulty would arise, of course, if the population could only harvest, say, 6 bushels of amaranth seeds and 2 bushels of "other" seeds per capita. If this should for some reason happen, the homeostat would

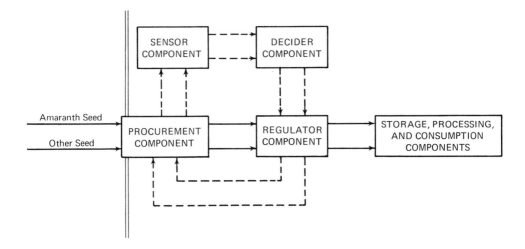

Figure 3.1 Illustration of a simple negative feedback system. Solid arrows represent matter-energy transmissions; dashed arrows represent information transmissions (feedback loops).

have failed, and the system would have either to collapse or to change. I deal with this situation further later in this chapter.

It is worth noting that Roy Rappaport's *Pigs for the Ancestors* (1967) provides an example of a description of the operation of an empirical system that is in some ways similar to this model. His simple system, constructed for the Tsembaga of New Guinea, shows how the ritual slaughter of pigs every 5 to 15 years acts as a homeostat, permitting the society to maintain its population size and dispersion, and regulating the use of relatively scarce land (among other things). I am here arguing that we must attempt to describe our systems much as he does, if we hope to make any practical use of systems theory.

One of the primary advantages of abstracting systems of variables from our substantive systems is that we can begin to determine the limits or tolerance ranges of critical variables in societies, and determine the thresholds at which they will be exceeded, thus leading to change. We would then be able to predict precisely when change could be expected to occur. As Rappaport indicates,

> In addition to designating limiting conditions or parameters, it may also become possible, when dimensions of phenomena are regarded as variables in a system, to discover the "system-destroying" levels of these variables. (1967:97)

Another point that should be evident in this discussion is that such

87

systems as this are not, strictly speaking, "cultural" systems. They are composed of articulated variables, some of which are part of what is usually considered to be "environment." Thus, in my example, the amaranth and "other" seeds are part of the *analytical* system, but they would not usually be considered part of a "cultural" system, at least until they had been harvested (although all of my system variables are part of an "ecosystem," of course). Thus, our systems will usually be composed of *both* societal and environmental variables. This is reasonable, since to try to separate culture from environment would lead to a situation in which the articulation between causal variables (environmental), and the aspect of a system being studied, would be severed!

Rappaport says the same thing in a somewhat different way:

> Culture has been regarded here not as itself a whole, but as part of the distinctive means by which a local population maintains itself in an ecosystem and by which a regional population maintains and coordinates its groups and distributes them over the available land. That which is regulated by the command patterns of belief and ritual does not consist merely of the interrelations of other components of culture, but also includes biological interactions among organisms not all of which are human. (1967:233)

This is a crucial point. Many anthropologists tend to try to study "culture," on the one hand, and environment on the other (see note 2). It is, of course, reasonable to isolate some subsystem or other *within* a cultural system, and explain aspects of it in terms of causal interrelations with other subsystems within the same overall system (that is, explaining aspects of social organization by reference to technological variables); but in this case, a specific subsystem would be the system of interest, and other intracultural variables would be external to it—or in its environment. The point is simply that our analytical systems will generally be constructed using variables from more than one subsystem within an ecosystem.

A final aspect to be mentioned concerning the description of systems is that it is inappropriate to view them as static structures or "snapshots" at given points in time—at least for most purposes. The static structure of a system tells us little about how the system operates. Even to describe a system it is necessary to include not only the variables involved in it, but also the operation of the homeostatic mechanisms as the values of the variables fluctuate. And this means we must include the time element in system description. It is necessary to describe all of the various states through which the system passes during its normal cycle of operation.

Most anthropologists, because of their brief visits to the field, do not have the time-depth necessary to describe a system in this way, much less to deal with change. There may be, for example, homeostats that only come into operation once every few years, because certain variables approach their tolerance limits only once in a number of years. Rappaport's study is a good example of this; he points out that it takes between 5 and 15 (or 20) years for a Tsembaga pig herd to get so large that the homeostats (pig slaughter and warfare) must come into operation. Thus, if he had visited this society in almost any other year than he did, he would not have observed the pig-slaughtering rituals. As it was, he had to rely on informant memory information to get a general idea of how the system operated throughout its normal cycling.

I would guess that there are many cases in which this cycling would take a great deal longer than 20 years. And to explain change in such a system (which Rappaport could not do), it can be presumed that a very great time-depth indeed—perhaps even hundreds of years—would often be needed. This, I feel, is where the future of archaeology lies.

## EXPLAINING SYSTEMIC CHANGE

I have already pointed out my belief that systemic change (morphogenesis) occurs only when the homeostats for one or more critical system variables fail to operate adequately, as a result of positive feedback processes that enhance rather than counteract the deviation. It is at this point that new system homeostats are selected for, and the system becomes qualitatively different. That is, it can be said that there has been change if there has been alteration in either the specific variables composing the system, or in the nature of the functional (mathematical) relations among them.

Consider my previous example of a simplified hunter-gatherer subsistence system. No change is considered to occur as long as,

1.  The number of bushels of seeds per capita required by the population remains the same.
2.  The availability (harvest) ranges of amaranth and "other" seed remain the same, per capita.
3.  The three variables are the only variables in the system.

4.  The mathematical equations describing the relationships among the variables remain the same. (That is, a specific variation in one variable will lead to the predicted variation in the others.)

The system would not necessarily be considered to have changed, for example, if the human population grew, thus requiring more seeds to be harvested. As long as there are enough amaranth and "other" seeds available, the required per capita harvest can be maintained—the system has the same variables and operates just as it had before population growth. (While there is, in this case, a quantitative shift in the absolute number of bushels required to feed the population, there has been no qualitative change in either the nature of the variables or their relationships).

The system would be considered to have changed, however, if for example, population increase created a situation in which not enough seeds could be harvested to maintain the population (and thus the harvesting of "other" seeds failed as a homeostat). If the system did not collapse, it would be forced to change qualitatively; for example, it might begin domesticating a suitable seed crop, institute birth control practices, and so forth. These, then, would be *new* homeostats that would enter the system—and any description of the new (changed) system would have to include these variables, as well as different mathematical equations to describe the interrelationships of all the variables in the new system.

This, it seems to me, is a clear definition of change. If we can make these ideas operational in empirical research, we will have a reasonably clear means by which we can identify change situations, and separate real change from other observations that may simply represent alterations in the normal homeostatic cycling of systems.

But how, specifically, can change be explained? There are a series of specific requirements that most of the seminar participants and I feel must be met in order to explain change successfully.

The first requirement is that we must be able to describe the operation of a given system of interest *prior* to the occurrence of change, and describe its operation *after* change has occurred (not to mention, for the moment, what goes on in between).

In describing the system at T-1 (or more precisely period 1) we must be able to simulate the operation of the system. That is, we must not only list the variables involved, but also show how they interact with one another to form a system. Thus we have to be able to show that variation in one variable affects the values of one or more other variables in the system—they are mathematical functions of one another. Beyond this, it is necessary to show how the homeostat(s) works in maintaining system equilibrium. We must have a satisfactory description of both the variables and the equilibratory mechanisms. And the system must be "workable" in the sense that if we were to simulate it, by computer or otherwise, we would be able to predict the magnitude of variation in each variable when the value of any one of them is varied to a specific amount. If it does not operate as a system, reequilibrating itself with variation in input or output, it cannot be considered a system.

Similarly, we must describe such a system for period 2 (that is, after change has occurred). All of the same information is needed in this case as for the system at period 1.

Further, we must be able to demonstrate why the system in period 1 could no longer operate as it did, and thus was forced to change. That is, in order to be predictive, we must know the tolerance ranges for each critical variable for each of the components in the system. And we must discover precisely what exogenous varability it was that caused a particular system variable to depart from its tolerance range—and why it was that the homeostatic mechanisms failed to perform adequately.

Finally, it is necessary to demonstrate that the "new" variables and homeostats (in period 2) did in fact reequilibrate the system, though in a different form. In short, it must be shown that the changed system represents a response that alleviated the previous stress on the system, but only by changing the system. An attempt should also be made to demonstrate that the changes in the system are essentially irreversible, and thus represent morphogenesis rather than the temporary and reversible adjustment processes of morphostasis.

In summary, I feel that the essential requirements for successfully explaining change are:

1. A functional (mathematical) description of the system and its homeostatic processes *prior* to change.
2. Isolation of the extrasystemic inputs promoting change, and demonstration of the failure of homeostatic mechanisms to cope with the inputs—and that change is thus a "least-cost" alternative.
3. Demonstration that "new" variables and homeostatic mechanisms have been selected for, which stabilize the system at a different level.
4. Determination of the fact that the change is essentially irreversible.

While I recognize that these requirements may sound idealistic for archaeologists at the moment, it is important to recognize the fact that if it is necessary to demonstrate these things in order to account for change, then it is equally necessary that we begin trying to do it. I think that even now we can at least approximate the kinds of measurements needed to explain change in relatively simple systems.

Turning back now to my hypothetical example of a hunting-and-gathering subsistence system, it is evident that I described the operation of the system in equilibrium, but did not attempt to explain change in any detail. Let us presume that this hypothetical system did change, and that it began to harvest increasing amounts of domesticated seed crops (corn, for example) at the expense of the former staple, amaranth. In terms of the just stated requirements for explaining change, what would be necessary for explaining this particular change?

I have already described the operation of that system in equilibrium, and have thus met the first requirement. The only homeostat I considered for the system was the alternative of adjusting for a deficiency in amaranth seeds by increasing the collection of the "other" kinds of seeds. Nonetheless it is a system; and I can predict, using the figures given previously, approximately how many bushels of the "other" seeds will have to be collected, given any specific amount of deficiency in amaranth seeds.

In meeting the second requirement, I might propose that the primary extrasystemic input promoting change was an increase in population size. I could propose that as population increased, a threshold was eventually reached at which there was not enough seed material of either type to support the population adequately, and that this caused the usual adjustment process to fail. I would, of course, have to demonstrate that the gathering of "other" seeds was insufficient to augment the per capita supply of amaranth seed, and that therefore the system would either have had to change or collapse.

As a part of doing this, I would have to try to demonstrate that there were no other regularly available homeostats (as an extant part of the system) that could feasibly have been employed to regulate the system short of necessitating change. While I am assuming, for the sake of simplicity in my example, that no other homeostats exist, this may not be the case in many empirical systems; and it could lead to difficulties in demonstrating that indeed all homeostats have been exhausted, and that in fact change was a necessary and "least-cost" solution.

In meeting the third requirement, I would have to demonstrate that the new system component (corn, in this case) did in fact provide increasingly sufficient amounts of food to support the increasing population, and that this increasing corn production resulted in an equilibrial situation.

And in meeting the fourth requirement, I would have to demonstrate that the change to domestic crops was essentially irreversible. The term "essentially irreversible" simply means that,

1.  The change is not reversible, in the same sense that a homeostatic mechanism is reversible—that is, it does not come into operation and out of operation periodically, as do homeostats.
2.  The change is not reversible, in that the system can probably never revert to precisely what it was prior to the change. (At least, this would be highly improbable, as it is in biological evolution.)

Thus I do not mean to imply, for example, that a society could not adopt agriculture and later revert to hunting and gathering (although this is improbable). I simply mean that once the system has changed, it is highly unlikely that it can ever again become precisely as it was prior to the change.

But why, in my example, did the system change through the addition of domesticated corn to the system? Why could there not have been a selection for a new homeostat that would simply regulate population size rather than increase the food supply—for example, infanticide, abortion, and so forth? Our ultimate goal is to be able to predict that under certain specifiable conditions a system will change in certain specifiable ways —and all I can say at the moment is that I would presume that the direction of change will be determined by the relative costs of available "alternatives." That is, there will be selection for the "least-cost" or optimal change. And in my example, I would clearly have to try to demonstrate that the particular change that did occur was such an optimal solution.

One of the important implications of this optimization idea is that systems really may not have many "choices" or "alternatives" in their responses—at least not if they are to survive in the long run. While this is not to say that systems have not and do not make inadequate responses, it does suggest that they cannot do this very frequently, or for long periods, if they are to survive. One of the important differences between societies and organisms is, of course, that there is some flexibility in the kinds of homeostats that can be employed—however, I would doubt that there is much flexibility in the long run, if a system is to survive. And in dealing with the long-term stability and change situations that archaeologists consider, I think we can presume that most of the established changes we observe were optimal changes (or nearly so), since they were evidently reasonably successful for a long period of time.

It is difficult, however, to demonstrate that a particular change was a least-cost or optimal response, and I do not want to underestimate this difficulty. Nonetheless, I think it will be necessary that we demonstrate this. Otherwise it will be difficult to make general predictive statements (laws) that specify directions of change, given specified conditions.

We should, I think, be able to do this by making use of computer simulation models of our analytical systems. On the assumption that we have, in a given case, already observed change in the archaeological record, I would propose that we do the following:

1. Simulate the system *before* change, such that it will function as a system (that is, such that the homeostats will regulate deviation in the values of the variables in it).
2. Determine the tolerance ranges (limits) of each of the critical variables in the system. (This can be done by altering the values of the various variables to the point where they exceed or depart from the limits at which the system will no longer operate—in this case, simulate.)
3. Generate specific hypotheses that suggest which system variables (in the prechange system) were the ones that exceeded their tolerance limits and led to the observed change, and what extra-systemic factors caused this deviation-amplification to occur.
4. Simulate the prechange system again, this time altering the values of each of the hypothesized change-causing variables in turn, such that one can observe precisely what happens to the system when the specific variables are (one at a time) forced beyond their tolerance limits. One might observe, in each case, which parts of the system collapse first, or last, and what happens to each variable of the system specifically. (This kind of simulation should serve as a tool for discovery, in that it should help refine one's hypotheses and generate better ones. These hypotheses can then be tested against the archaeological record.)
5. *Change* the system by plugging into it the *new* variables (homeostats) that constitute the actual, observed change in the system. It should simulate, in the sense that it should operate as an equilibrium system (if, in fact, it was so prehistorically).
6. Generate a list of possible alternative changes that might have been selected for in the system that might *also* have been in-

stituted in the empirical prehistoric case (that is, alternatives to the change that actually did occur).

7. Plug each of these "alternative" variables or homeostats into the simulation model one at a time (and then in various combinations) to determine whether or not they too could have led to a new equilibrium in the system (that is, whether or not the simulation will operate with these variables included, rather than the change that actually did occur). If any of these alternative changes is adequate, then one could presume that there could in fact have been alternatives that for some reason were not selected for.

8. The relative efficiency or "cost" of each such alternative might then be evaluated by comparing each of the simulations (with each of the alternative variables), to determine which one regulates the system best, or more quickly, or perhaps which one would support the largest population, or which one would cause the least disturbance in other defined subsystems in the society under study.

In some such way as this, it might be possible actually to demonstrate that the observed change either was or was not the optimal solution. And further, this kind of exercise might permit us to generate general hypotheses concerning what specific kinds of conditions can be expected to lead to what specific kinds of changes.

In any event, there are two additional points that should be made here. First, the kind of morphogenic or evolutionary approach described here does *not*, if it is correct, support the expectation that change is some sort of gradual, unidirectional continuum. The simple idea that change does not occur until a threshold of some kind is reached argues for the idea that for specified analytical systems change occurs relatively abruptly. That is, we can expect to observe relatively long periods of stability, punctuated by relatively brief periods of deviation-amplification and change, which are in turn followed by periods of stability.

This does not mean, of course, that within a given *societal* system there may not always be aspects of it that are changing. However, they do not all change at the same time, or at the same rates (Notterman and Trumbull 1950); and for any given *analytical* system, change will usually be found not to be continuous. This is, of course, a matter for empirical testing and demonstration rather than something that can be legislated by me, a priori. But I do think that the paradigm yields the expectation that change usually occurs relatively abruptly.

Second, this approach is clearly one that conforms to evolutionary theory. The concept of "selection" is an integral part of it. It is presumed that variablility exists in societies, and it is generally from this pool of variability that system responses are selected. In short, we do not always have to go outside the societal system to look for the sources of ideas, techniques, and so forth, that are adopted by the system in establishing a new equilibrium. The pool of possible responses may already be there within the system; I suspect this is often the case. Even in my example dealing with the beginning of agriculture, it might well be that the people already know about agriculture, and thus this information is already a part of the societal system (though perhaps not the analytical system of interest).

Therefore, the important problem in explaining change is not the problem of discovering a point of innovation or diffusion. It is rather, the question of why selection in societies occurs *for* some things and *against* others (and why rates of selection vary). Simply because something is invented or known about is no reason to think that it will be adopted. And, of course, anything that is adopted (selected for) must already be known about, whether it occurs within the society or in some other society.

In any event, I am arguing that when a system changes, selection for "new" variables or homeostats is generally made from a pool of existing variability. Once such selection has occurred, the new variable becomes a part of the analytical system being considered. Thus, in my example, the variability that existed in the societal system included not only Amaranth and "other" seeds, but also the knowledge of plant domestication. This only became a part of the analytical system of interest, however, at the point when the failure of the homeostat ("other" seeds) developed.

In this sense, the approach proposed here is very much like the selection process of biological evolution, except that it is not genes that are being selected for and against, and there is no mechanism of reproduction and gene-flow in the biological sense. While I think we can make use of other biological concepts such as "drift" or "founders effect" (see Binford 1963), I will not attempt this here.

In concluding this section, I want to point out that even though this is a very general framework for accounting for systemic change (and stability), I think it is, nonetheless, on the right track. It provides a general explanation of *any* change situation in societies—and while it is the specific refinements of it that will actually be most interesting and useful to us, it does appear to be a useful framework within which such refinements can be made.

Further, it is interesting to note that this approach sheds useful light on the concept of societal "adaptation." (For definitions of adaptation, see Lewin 1947; Sommerhof 1950; Pringle 1951; Russell 1959; and Marney and Smith 1964). Perhaps the most common idea is that adaptation refers to system responses that are *beneficial* in some way to the system, or responses that help adjust a system to its environment (Russell 1959). However, one is hard put to distinguish these responses that are advantageous to a system from those that are not. The approach proposed here regards "adaptation" as any system response, good or bad, appropriate or inappropriate, conscious or unconscious. This follows Lewin, Sommerhof, and Marney and Smith above.

In societies, adaptation should probably be regarded as the statistical result of cultural selection processes; and a good explanation is primarily one that explains the processes by which some system variability is selected for, and some is selected against. Thus it is the actual selection process we are after—and the effort has barely begun. It even seems likely that societies will select for increasing disorganization under certain conditions (Vickers 1959a, In Buckley 1968a:355).

### PROBLEMS OF MEASUREMENT

The most serious difficulties we have in both generating and testing explanations of change lie in our abilities to quantify or measure the specific system variables we are interested in. Some theoreticians are more optimistic than others in this regard (cf. Ashby 1962, In Buckley 1968a:118; Miller 1965b:361; Flannery 1967:120).

While I have already pointed to the fact that we cannot hope to measure whole cultural systems, we are going to have to be able to devise at least crude measurements of the nature, magnitude, and frequency of matter-energy transmissions within our analytical systems (much as Rappaport tried to do, 1967). It seems likely, however, that with the rapid development of techniques and data processing facilities, we will be able to solve many of these problems.

There is also the problem of measuring the effects of *past* systemic structure on the selection processes of systems. That past structure does affect the kinds of adaptations a system may make is well attested (cf.

97

Khailov 1954; Gerard 1957; G. A. Miller 1963; Buckley 1968b:495–96). It will be an exciting and useful pursuit, in fact, to attempt to discover the conditional probabilities concerning the kinds of organizational changes that can occur, given specific kinds of previous organizations.

It is possible that one of the most difficult problems of measurement may lie in the measurement of information transmissions (meaning "communication")—and this includes stored information. Just as systemic responses are affected by past structure, they are also affected by past adaptive "experiences" a system has had (cf. Deutsch 1948–49; Cadwallader 1959; Miller 1965a:224). And since system responses are conditioned by both past "experiences" and the stress situations of the moment, it may be necessary that we be able to measure them both.

The measurement of inputs, throughputs, and outputs of information would be equally difficult. The possible importance of doing so is indicated in Cadwallader's statement to the effect that in order to test cybernetic models and hypotheses, it will be necessary to quantify information (1959, In Buckley 1968a:439). However, the quantitative measurement of information in societies is as yet unoperational.

This difficulty might be the single most significant technical difficulty that archaeologists face—if, that is, there is no suitable way to explain change without doing it. As Buckley (1968b:497) says, "when the system ceases to operate, the links maintaining the sociocultural structure are no longer observable." At the same time, as Lewis Binford and others have pointed out, the physical or artifactual remains of systems can be used to discover how prehistoric systems operated (Binford 1962, 1968b); and it seems likely to me that we can even sometimes measure information linkages within and among systems. Since the organization of a societal system is in some sense a "map" of the environment it is coping with, and since organization can be measured by information, it should be possible to measure information by organization.

For example, we might presume that within archaeological sites doorways represent communication "channels," and that "nets" of rooms interconnected by doorways represent more frequent intercommunication than occurred between such units. We might also presume that adjacent units of any sort maintained more intercommunication than distant units; and in some cases there may even be roadways or trails remaining, from which we can infer communication linkages. Measurements of amounts and kinds of trade should be useful here, too. And we might presume that cultural units possessing great style similarities had more information exchange than occurred between units that are stylistically more dissimilar. Status symbols and other kinds of artifacts can also be used in inferring information channels.

I should add here, however, my own belief that archaeologists (and other anthropologists) probably will be able to test systems-cybernetic explanations of change without having to measure information, in the sense of communication, "decision-making," and so forth. We should be able to explain change by simply demonstrating that specific kinds of matter-energy input and output variables (and past structure) lead predictably to specific kinds of change. The fact that communication exchanges must often have accompanied these processes can be presumed, but it is not of critical importance to our explanations. I think Rappaport's study (1967) demonstrates this.

A further kind of difficulty in measurement comes in being sure that when we are describing and measuring change, we are really measuring *change*, and not something else. At least some of what we commonly observe archaeologically as change probably does not represent change at all—or at least not change in aspects of societal organization. We observe that artifacts, for example, change in style through time. But unless we are considering "artifact systems" as our systems of interest, we may not be dealing with societal organizational change at all. Organization might remain relatively stable, with its regular homeostatic adjustment processes, but specific artifacts can change in style without there being a true systemic change in the society manufacturing the artifacts. While changes in both style and uses of artifacts provide hints that organizational change is occurring, they are insufficient in themselves to demonstrate systemic change. I think this can only be done in the manner I have previously indicated.

The trick here, of course, is to be very careful to distinguish what is commonly called societal or "cultural" change from change in specific analytical systems of interest. This problem of mixing levels of system analysis is extremely common. We cannot demonstrate change in specific kinds of artifacts or tool-kits, and then infer on this basis that a whole societal system has changed (which we can then describe as a set of immutable phases or stages of culture). We must measure change in each analytical system of interest separately.

Another problem of measurement involves the scales of measurement we use. It should be clear, given my example, that interval-scale measurement of our variables is generally required if we are going to describe the operation of systems and simulate them. In this way, we can specify quantitatively the degree to which specific variables are critical to a system; we can specify their tolerance ranges and can predict the points at which homeostats will be activated, or when they will break down. In short, I feel we must usually use variables measured on an interval-scale if we are successfully to simulate systems. It may be that interval-scale measurement will often be difficult or impossible to obtain; and we may have to use ordinal-scale measurements at times—but even this ought to be better for most simulation purposes than using nominal categories.

The same is true with regard to measuring change. Change may occur slowly or rapidly. And in order to measure *rates* of change we must use something other than a nominal scale.

A final problem of measurement lies in the precise specification of concepts and entities. The concepts and entities we use in our hypotheses and descriptions of systems must be clearly specified and measurable, at least in principle (see White 1954). One of the most fundamental difficulties anthropologists have is in formulating their concepts so that they are usable in quantitative analysis (see note 2). Such concepts as "Band," "Tribe," "Chiefdom," and "State," for example, cannot have not been made adequately operational—we simply don't know how to measure such things. The reason for this is, of course, that they have not been established as empirical entities. I would argue that we should not usually try to establish a priori categorizations, and then proceed to try to fit our observations into them. We should attempt to *discover* what kinds of entities, processes, changes, and rates of changes actually occur—and only then apply taxonomic tags to them (White 1954:466). Entities of any kind that exist, and can thus be measured, can be regarded as phenomena usable in our system descriptions and explantions of change.

This does not mean that we cannot on occasion deduce measurable concepts, processes, and entities from theory, and then test their empirical validity against data. I am simply saying that we cannot expect to achieve adequate descriptions of systems and changes in systems unless we can measure the entities and processes involved in them. We certainly cannot satisfactorily explain change in something unless we know precisely what it is that has changed, and can measure the change quantitatively.

I would argue further that some of the changes we think we observe in the archaeological record—such as that from "Chiefdom" to "State" —may never be quantitatively measurable, and will remain unoper-

100

tional. In short, I think it may be fruitless to try to establish such concepts as "Chiefdom" and "State" as empirical entities. Whatever these entities are, it is agreed that they are complex; they are made up of a number of entities and processes, not all of which are found in any given society. Some societies have some of the characteristics of "Stateness," for example, while others have other characteristics. I argue that our research will be more operational if we specify those measurable attributes of what we call a "Chiefdom" or "State," and then proceed to explain changes in each of these attributes separately—that is, explain the development of writing systems, increasing internal differentiation, increasing specialization, increasing class stratification, and so on. The entities and processes involved in these things are certainly in many cases independent of one another, and can be accounted for separately. And such concepts are eminently more suitable to being made measurable than are such things as "Chiefdoms" and "States."

There are, of course, other kinds of measurement problems facing archaeologists than I have touched on here; and they may include many of the same difficulties faced by other anthropologists—the main difference being that the specific nature of the data differs. Currently we have difficulty measuring even such variables as population size, storage space, relative amounts and phasing of dietary inputs, and so forth. We are, however, making progress in the measurement of such variables.

## THE USEFULNESS OF SYSTEMS FRAMEWORKS

It seems obvious, given the preceding discussion and those of a number of other anthropologists, that systems theory provides us with concepts and ideas useful in accounting for societal stability and change. In concluding, however, a few additional evaluative and cautionary comments are in order.

First, it is evident that the general systems literature does not provide a theoretical panacea that we can simply take over unaltered. Even the few examples I have presented suggest that there are almost as many different views of systems and systems theory as there are theoreticians and practitioners. In developing the general framework proposed here, I have had to draw something from a number of systems theorists—and have tried to show that there are difficulties or pitfalls in simply "applying" published systems frameworks to human societies.

Beyond this, most of the systems literature does not deal with *change* in enough detail to be of much use. Systems research has been much more concerned with what systems are, how they can be described and classified, and how they are regulated. And further, since general systems theory is designed to be general, and to deal primarily with *similarities* among different kinds of systems, it provides very few useful ideas on how human social systems might differ from other kinds of living systems in terms of the processes of stability and change.

Systems theory, of course, does not provide us with many useful, specific, ready-made hypotheses that we can test directly in the field; nor does it tell us which data to collect. It does not provide us with the means of measuring our variables. (Even though Ashby feels it will [1962, In Buckley 1968a:118], I am sure that his statements do not yet apply to most aspects of societal systems.)

But systems theory does provide a general viewpoint or paradigm that is useful in organizing thought and research on societal stability and change—and it accounts not only for social group or populational behavior, but also for the behavior of individuals. Thus it is likely that all aspects of societal systems can be covered by a single, reasonably coherent framework—assuming only that we do not mix system levels in our analyses. We do not need an essentially different *kind* of general explanation for explaining stability and change in the behavior of individuals, groups, or societies; although in each case the specific kinds of variables that must be measured may be quite different.

I emphasize the fact that this "theory" accounts for both stability and change, so we do not need separate approaches for each (see Perlman n.d.:11–13). This does not mean, of course, that there are not other approaches that will be useful in our research. Many other paradigms may be helpful in dealing with one or another aspect of societal stability and change—and we need not settle on one as being the "best" or "better" than the others. In fact, in any given explanation, several approaches might usefully be employed in conjunction with one another. I do think, however, that systems theory may be a useful umbrella framework, under which other approaches will play their parts.

Further, it is worth pointing out that the systems literature already provides a number of stimulating hypotheses concerning stability and change which, though very general, are at least usable in terms of deducing more specific hypotheses that we can in fact test (see, for example, Miller 1965c). The testing of such hypotheses will be useful in theory-building. As Miller (1965a:202) points out,

> Science advances as the formal identity or isomorphism increases between a theoretical conceptual system and objective findings about concrete or abstracted systems.

Thus, by testing systems propositions we will either build confidence in the usefulness of systems theory, or lose confidence in it. In the process, we should be able to build useful middle-range theory.

In summary, I think systems theory provides (together with ecological theory and other viewpoints) a good course in how to *think* about societal organization, stability, and change, while at the same time providing some useful hypotheses that can be modified to suit our purposes.

However, we must be cautious and critical in dealing with this "theory." And we must, above all, be both specific in defining our systems of interest, and in isolating measurable variables. My success in drawing from systems theory a general framework for accounting for societal stability and change can be adequately judged only after it has been tested in a number of specific situations where change has occurred. And I again submit that archaeology, of all the sciences, is in the best position to do this.

### NOTES

1. Some of my discussion of this apparently most useful system approach is based on the discussion that occurred during the seminar. I am indebted to all of the seminar participants and discussants, but acknowledge the special counseling of Arthur A. Saxe, William Stuart, Michael A. Glassow, and Fred T. Plog.

2. In fact, I believe we can profitably do without the concept "culture," since it appears to be unoperational in analysis. Thus far, it has not been possible to describe and measure satisfactorily "cultures." While we can describe and measure specific aspects of what we call culture, there is no acceptable way to measure "culture" as some kind of whole. The reason for this is that "culture" has never been established as an empirical entity. One can presumably measure it if one first *defines* it in such a way that the concepts and entities in the definition are measurable. But the idea of devising an operational definition suitable for all our purposes is unrealistic. I feel that the concept "culture" has outlived its usefulness, and now serves as an important barrier to the accomplishment of specific, operational research. Instead of attempting to describe "cultures," "culture-change," and so forth, I believe it will be more productive to emphasize the solution of specific problems and the testing of hypotheses that are of interest to us. While these problems and hypotheses will presumably be concerned with describing and explaining aspects of human behavior, they may or may not involve concepts, entities (and data) that belong within the realm of traditional definitions and understandings of culture. (For an excellent discussion of the concept "culture" that is in some ways similar to this, see Leslie A. White 1954).

# On the Origin of Evolutionary Processes:
# State Formation in the Sandwich Islands,
# A Systemic Approach*

ARTHUR A. SAXE

*Department of Anthropology and Sociology*
*Ohio University*
*Athens*

*That which is above shall be brought down;*
*That which is below shall be lifted up;*
*The islands shall be united;*
*The walls shall stand upright.*
    (Old Hawaiian prophecy, quoted in Malo 1903:154)

## INTRODUCTION

When Captain James Cook of the British Royal Navy first landed in the Sandwich (later Hawaiian) Islands, his was apparently the first entourage of North Atlantic culture bearers to do so.[1] That day, the 19th of January, 1778, witnessed two events, the understanding of which is crucial to the argument presented in this paper.

---

*This chapter is published just as it was presented in 1970 to facilitate understanding the discussion that ensued. An updated version, perhaps more satisfying, would lose this historical perspective. The definitions and arguments presented here have nonetheless retained their utility.

The first event, ongoing as Cook first landed at Waimea on the island of Kauai (Fig. 4.1), was the *makahiki* season celebrated in honor of the god Lono (for whom Cook was initially mistaken). To understand this ceremony, which in its secular aspect involved the economics of redistribution, and the politics of ranked chiefdoms, is to understand the relatively stable ("morphostatic") systemic relations which prevailed prior to North Atlantic culture contact. This system, although changing in personnel and other details, was essentially a stable system and had been so for a number of generations. If this ongoing system were misunderstood, the effect of contact would be unintelligible.

The second event occurring on the 19th of January, 1778, was the arrival of Cook, harbinger of more and more intensive contacts with North Atlantic cultures. These contacts introduced factors which had a "deviation-amplifying" effect on parts of the system, resulting eventually in the appearance of a new, differently integrated, type of system. Without some such contact, the Hawaiian system would not have undergone evolution ("morphogenesis"). That, in fact, is the particular argument of this paper. The general question asked is, What initiates morphogenic processes in systems? The general answer is deceptively simple: always, extrasystemic variables! In order to make the argument more intelligible we shall first define the theoretical approach; next, sketch Hawaiian politics and economics prior to contact; then, sketch the nature of North Atlantic culture contacts; and finally, sketch the way the system dealt with these inputs, including the changes wrought sequentially.

## THEORETICAL CONCEPTS DEFINED

The approach we shall use to explain why sociocultural change occurred in the Hawaiian Islands is one labeled a "systemic" (sometimes "processual") approach. Basic to this approach is the concept of "system." Therefore it is important that this concept be clearly understood, lest the approach be rendered ineffectual.

A *system*, any system, whether it be organic, inorganic, or superorganic, possesses certain *qualities* which do or do not make it a system. In a phrase, *a system is a system if it exhibits systemic behavior*. There are a number of ways to define "systemic behavior," as I am sure other chapters in this volume will show. Different definitions are not necessarily in conflict with one another; they may merely focus on different aspects of

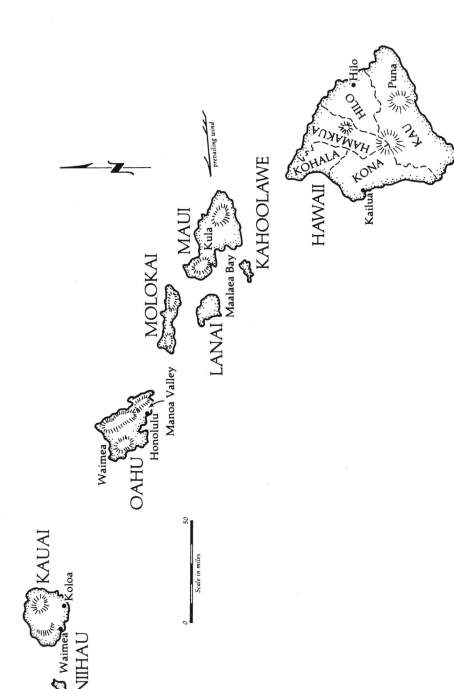

Figure 4.1  The Hawaiian Islands

the same thing. We shall present two definitions which do exactly that. The first focuses on what has traditionally been called "function," and the second on "structure." Each is the reciprocal of the other; each is the other side of the same coin, and therefore compatible.

A system consists of: (1) a set of elements so interrelated that changes in any one require changes of some sort in others; (2) a set of relationships between elements whose relations to one another are determined by their relationship to the whole.

The solar system is a classic example of a system. It consists of a set of elements which are the planets and the sun. Each planet's orbit around the sun is unique, yet no single orbit can be explained simply on the basis of attraction between that planet's mass, the sun's mass, and the distance between them.[2] The reason is as simple as it is profound: all the planets and the sun are *simultaneously attracting each other*. Naturally, not all elements are equal in attraction since they have different masses and at different times are at different distances from one another. In fact, if you would take snapshots of the solar system from out in space, each picture would be unique; the solar system would not look the same twice. Nevertheless, since the *relationships between the elements are regular and repetitive* (since it is, in other words, a *stable system*), the behavior of the solar system is predictable. It is these regularities in relationships that scientists look for when they look for "systems" or "processes." Indeed, since each event as it occurs in nature is unique (like a snapshot), scientists *must* look for systemic behavior or give up the search for order in the universe. The payoff in terms of the solar system occurred when "aberrant" behavior was noted on the parts of the known planets. This could be explained, with one theory, if another planet (yet unknown) was out there in such-and-such an orbit with such-and-such a mass. When the telescopes were trained on that point in the sky its existence was verified.

This example illustrates both definitions of "system." The relationship between two heavenly bodies in the solar system cannot be explained simply by examining their respective masses and distance from each other. *All* the planets and all the orbits must be considered to explain and predict the relationships between any two of them. This is what is meant when we say that "a system is a set of elements whose relations to one another are determined by their relationship to the whole."

This is also why *the whole (system) is greater than the sum of its parts*. The dynamics of interaction of a system are not derivable by simply looking at elements in isolation; it is the *organization of the elements* as a system that gives them properties they do not exhibit in isolation.

Hydrogen ($H_2$) and oxygen ($O_2$) behave very differently as gases than when organized into water molecules ($H_2O$). The properties of water are not derivable from its constituent parts. Sociocultural institutions also are composed of parts (for example, personality systems, as actors) but exhibit dynamics not derivable from them. It is for these reasons that A. L. Kroeber coined the term "superorganic." These organizations *sui generis* are often referred to as "emergents" or "emergent levels of organization."

The discovery of the last planet in our solar system also illustrates what might happen if a planet were to disappear; if, let's say, we were to vaporize the earth in a nuclear holocaust. What would happen? Obviously, all the other planets would have to rearrange their orbits and their distances from each other and from the sun.

Or, let us ask, what would we have to do to change the orbit of the earth? Obviously, we would have to change the other orbits of the other planets. This is what is meant when we say a system consists of a set of elements so interrelated that changes in any require changes in others.

This illustrates another characteristic of systems: *because they are systems they tend to be stable or conservative.* That is, since it is impossible to change just one part, and since the other parts "resist" change, systems may be characterized as conservative.[3] Furthermore, the more complex a system is, and the more different kinds of parts it has, the more stable it should be.

This property of systems underlies a prime environmental concern of today: if industrial society keeps simplifying the earth's ecosystem, we shall reach a point of instability in which a minor "trigger" may precipitate eco-catastrophe. The results would be disastrous to life as we know it.

So far, we have made the following points:

1. Defined and exemplified what a "system" is.
2. Discussed the uniqueness of events as they occur, the order lying in systemic (or "processual") behavior.
3. Noted the "emergent" properties of systems, the whole being unequal to the sum of its parts.
4. Discussed the "conservative" properties of systems.

Next, we shall attempt to clarify a semantic pitfall in the use of the term "system," a confusion widespread among our contemporaries.

## SYSTEMICS AND SYSTEMATICS

So far we have discussed what a system *is* in terms of systems theory. Unfortunately there is another traditional use of the term "system," which is quite different in meaning. Therefore, we shall now examine this semantic problem to point out what a system *is not*.

When a zoologist classifies life forms into species, and so forth, he is engaging in taxonomy also known as "systematics." He is, in other words, "behaving systematically," which means "behaving in an orderly manner." The end product of such systematic behavior on the part of the investigator is called "a system." A *"system" therefore, in this context, refers to the end product of orderly behavior on the part of the investigator.*

On the other hand, a "system" can also refer to the behavior of entities which (we assume) exist, whether we investigate them or not. When we speak of "systemic behavior" we are referring to the mutual and reciprocal relationships between elements that are related to each other by being related to the whole. A system, in this context, is the thing we study, not the way we study it.

To summarize:

1. "Systemic behavior" is behavior engaged in by the entity under study (for example, the solar system). It exists whether we study it or not. A "system" is the name for the entity that engages in systemic behavior.
2. "Systematic behavior" is behavior engaged in by the investigator when it is done in an orderly manner. A "system," in this sense, is what the investigator produces (such as a classification, taxonomy, contingency chart, and so forth).

Since it is useful for scientists to proceed in an orderly manner, and since the study of external reality (rather than introspective musings) is the goal of science, we may summarize as follows: *our aim as scientists is to study systemic behavior systematically.*

## SYSTEMIC APPROACHES: FUNCTIONALISM AND EVOLUTIONISM

Contrary to the make-believe world of fairy tales and detective stories, the facts never speak for themselves; they must be interpreted. Even the determination of what is a fact may be problematic.

Every thing or event, every occurrence, has an infinite number of attributes or facts. The tip of my pen may be described physically, chemically, socially, technologically, thermodynamically, and so forth, *ad infinitum*. What are the "real" facts? Well, that depends on the questions one asks about the pen tip—*always!* Facts are only facts when they are relevant to the answering of questions; facts become relevant when they are useful to testing a model (a series of notions) about what happened and why. It is the model that directs our attention to certain facts and not to others. People who claim to be "purely inductive" (that is, have no model other than that which "emerges" from the facts) are simply ignorant of what their models are and their very existence. Such naivete may lead one to become an unwitting victim of his own nonconscious (implicit) model. For this reason it is good practice to make models explicit. Overtly stated models are more amenable to criticism and revision.

A model is an intellectual tool in the same sense that an axe is a physical tool. An axe is more useful than a hammer in felling a tree because it is designed to deal with the natural properties encountered in the tree-felling process. Models, if they are to be useful, call our attention to properties or relationships encountered in the systems we are studying. Models, therefore, can also be more or less useful.

Two classes of models that have received notoriety in twentieth-century anthropology will be briefly discussed here. We shall discuss them here because both are systemic models and therefore potentially useful to us—but polemics have shrouded their potential utility. These models have been labeled "functionalist" and "evolutionist" (White 1945). Both are "systemic" models in that they are concerned with the systemic behavior of sociocultural systems. The basic difference lies in the types of questions each model asks about the systems being studied.

*Functionalist models* generally ask how a system operates, how the elements are interrelated or, in other words, they ask about systemic stability or maintenance. They tend to focus attention on those factors known as "deviation-counteracting mechanisms" (Buckley 1967).

*Evolutionist models* generally ask how a system came to be the way it is, or what would cause it to become a new system. In other words, they ask about systemic change (rather than systemic stability), and tend to focus attention on "deviation-amplifying mechanisms" (Buckley 1967). As such they tend to focus attention upon factors that may be quite different from those employed in a functionalist model; indeed, they may focus on factors completely outside the realm of consideration in a functionalist model.

White (1945:238) has defined evolutionism as functionalism through time. This definition is clearly inadequate when we observe, for example, Bohannan's study of witch-hunts among the Tiv (1958:1–12). He shows how periodically recurrent witch-hunts maintain the egalitarian nature of Tiv political life—that is, how they operate as "deviation-counteracting mechanisms." Bohannan has done "functionalism through time"; but functionalism, whether through time or not, remains functionalism. He has explained systemic stability, and evolution is systemic change. The different questions we must ask when doing each type of study make them different from each other.

Here, though, is where the issues have been shrouded in polemics. Simply because the two are different does not make one superior. Each has its place in answering the questions each was designed to answer. The intellectual danger lies in expecting one to do the work of the other.

What then do *we* mean by "systemic stability" and "systemic change"? Since we have discussed "systemic," let us now focus on "stability" and "change." There are, for our purposes here, two types of change: systemic and nonsystemic.

*Nonsystemic change* refers to events that may recur within the system, but when they recur they may do so in different forms. An example would be Bohannan's witch-hunts, cited above. Each witch-hunt is unique in the minds of the Tiv. And indeed, each is. There are different issues, different personnel, and so on. The witch-hunts do recur in changed form; but the important point is that they *recur*. Not only do they recur, but when they recur they result in the same thing: return of the system to an egalitarian condition. Thus, witch-hunts are like a steam valve in a heating system that opens whenever certain variables begin to exceed the limits of the system—and then they cease. They occur as a "function" (in the mathematical sense) of other parts of the system, and vice versa. Thus, "nonsystemic changes" may also be termed "functional alternations" of the system (which is perhaps more accurate than "repetitive" or "recurrent" changes). Functional alternations do not alter the basic systemic relationships between the elements that give the system whatever stability it has.

If American blacks were to achieve the same economic mobility available to other ethnic groups, this would surely be a change. However, as long as other ethnic groups are available to fill the economic slots currently filled by blacks and do so, the system has not changed one bit. What we would have witnessed would be "nonsystemic change," otherwise known as a "functional alternation."

For another example, we may return to the mechanical system we call the solar system, which is in a state of constant nonsystemic change. The earth and all the planets vary in their distances from one another and from the sun at different points in time. Snapshots at different points in time would show different structural configurations, yet the system is a stable one; the relationships expressed in terms of mass, velocity, and distance ("functional" relationships in the mathematical sense of the term) remain constant. This is what is meant by nonsystemic change. All systems exhibit nonsystemic change regularly. This is also why all events in the time-space continuum are unique.

Before moving on to systemic change, it is perhaps necessary to clarify the phrase "function, in the mathematical sense," since we have referred to it twice above.

The term "function" has at least two different sets of meanings as used in anthropology. These two sets of meanings do overlap semantically, but they are not identical and thus may be confused. The first meaning, "function, in the nonmathematical sense," answers the question "what is it *supposed* to do?" In this usage the word function refers to emic "oughts"; that is, value judgments as to its proper role. It is in this context that words like eufunctional or dysfunctional (doing or not doing what it is supposed to do) have any meaning. Such labels, since they imply good as opposed to bad or impaired behavior, indicate a bias on the part of the investigator. The eufunction label has tended to be applied to behavior that supports the status quo, dysfunction to behavior that does not. Value judgments, as we know, are incompatible with science. Furthermore, a disaster, as seen by an actor in a cultural system, may be a regulating mechanism (a homeostat) when viewed by a systemic analyst. Such dysfunctional events as epidemics or warfare may reflect alternate states of the same systemic processes that produce health or peace (functional alternations). Value judgments obscure such insights.

In summary, the nonmathematical use of the term function is incompatible with systemic science. This should become clearer as we discuss the second usage of the term.

The second meaning is contained in the formula: $Q f (Y)$, or $Q$ is a function of $Y$, where $Y=\dfrac{2x}{Q}$. Then $Q=\dfrac{2x}{Y}$; or $Q$ varies as twice $x$ divided by $Y$.

In words, a mathematical function $(f)$ is a statement of relationships among, in this case, the variables $Q$, $x$, and $Y$. This means that if the value of $x$ were to change, then the value of $Q$ or $Y$ or both would have to change. This sounds like systemic behavior, does it not? This is exactly why this sense of the term is closest to the meaning of "function" as used in systemic science or systems theory. Thus, functionalism is the study of reciprocal relationships between elements of an ongoing system. It seeks the sources of stability.

As long as the formula (and, of course, the system it represents) remains the same, we have systemic stability. The variability in the values of the variables represents functional alternation or nonsystemic change.

*Systemic change* refers to changes in the nature of the relationships between the elements and/or the nature of the elements themselves. In short, the initial system disappears and new systemic arrangements emerge. It is this type of event that we define as "evolution," and the study of it, "evolutionism."[4]

The value of distinguishing systemic from nonsystemic change is evident in the confusion generated where this distinction is not made. To wit:

> A social system, however, does not have any such fixed, normal structure which, if changed beyond narrow limits, leads necessarily to the system's "death." In contrast to an organismic system, social systems are characterized primarily by their propensity to *change their structure* during their culturally continuous "lifetime." (Buckley 1967:31)

What is meant by "change" here? If nonsystemic, then as already noted, solar systems *also* have a propensity to change their structure during their "lifetime." But if "change their structure" be interpreted to mean "systemic change," then it is just nonsense to say that when a given system goes out of existence it has not gone out of existence ("died") merely because its human actors have not died. Further, and somewhat irreverently, only a person who conceives of human society as distinct from culture could assert that social structural change can occur in the midst of cultural continuity, and offer no clarification. I suspect the author is confusing survival of a population with cultural continuity (since to sociologists culture tends to be in the actor's mind anyway). Our point is that confusion would diminish if "change" were consistently clarified. With some basic definitions and concepts now behind us, let us briefly examine the general systems approach that will carry us to the goal of this seminar: the explanation of sociocultural systemic change.

## TOWARD A GENERAL SYSTEMS APPROACH[5]

We, as scientists, make certain assumptions about nature which underlie the formulations of particular theories that attempt to explain nature.[6] For our present purposes there are four such basic assumptions:

1. Nature proceeds as events in continuous time-space.
2. Nature as a whole is a stable system consisting of interrelated subsystems.
3. Nature is not understandable directly; we must isolate and conceptualize segments of nature so as to make it intelligible.
4. Any level of systemic isolation is grounded in subordinate levels but has properties not derivable from these other levels (e.g., compounds and atoms).

Nature may be made intelligible in a number of ways. For our purposes we shall mention two. (1) The *"natural history"* approach attempts to make nature intelligible by isolating events in the time-space continuum and ordering them in terms of other events also in the time-space continuum. The relevance of the ordering must stem from the investigator's experience with the events themselves, or from the findings of *systemic* studies. The point to be made is that the events themselves are not self-explanatory. If they were there would be no need for other types of explanation. The time-space arrangment of the events merely relates what occurred, and does not tell why or how the sequence was as it was. The explanation of the arrangement must always be referred to another type of analysis, the *systemic.*

(2) The *"systemic approach"* attempts to make nature intelligible by isolating and conceptualizing nature as a system of interlocking subsystems. This approach makes it possible to deal with events, not with respect to their position in the time-space continuum (which necessarily makes each unique), but as repetitive events—that is, the results of the operation of a stable system. Thus we will be able to speak of the precontact Hawaiian system as a stable system regardless of its unique qualities at any given point in time (such as shifting personnel and political boundaries).

Because nature is considered to be a system of subsystems, any isolated system is considered to be a system of subsystems. This means that each element in that system is also isolatable as a system unto itself. Systems may be isolated (or "bounded") by defining their parameters on the basis of intersystemic relationships. This involves the determination of:

1. Whether the elements do actually articulate structurally and functionally.
2. Whether the system as isolated can be considered as an element of a system more broadly conceived.
3. Whether the elements of the isolated system can each be considered a subordinate system, or a closed system in its own right.

*Closed systems* are isolates in which factors impinging from outside the defined parameters are taken as a given and not considered relevant for the problem at hand.

*Open systems* are isolates in which factors impinging from outside the defined parameters are considered as relevant in the discussion of the problem at hand.[7]

The types of systems isolated depend upon the problem at hand. In addition to open/closed decisions, systems may be isolated on: (1) the basis of the stratification of nature—chemical isolate, atomic isolate, and so on; or (2) simply the basis of the interaction of two systems within one stratum—that is, dyadic relations between two personality systems and their many variants; or (3) any number of other ways suitable to the question at hand. At times, any of the above may be isolated with the addition of time-space continuum decisions. These dimensions focus our attention on systems as operative at a particular place and time in history.

## TOWARD EXPLAINING SOCIOCULTURAL SYSTEMIC CHANGE

In order to explain systemic change one must isolate the system under study as an *open system*. This is because *the processes that result in systemic change for all systems are and must be initiated by extrasystemic variables*. This is the argument of this paper. This proposition, in itself, is not new. The reasons for which it is proposed here, however, are if not new, at least different from those reasons which have been used to support it in the past.

116

First, *a system in a steady state will remain in a steady state unless disturbed by some extrasystemic force.*

All living systems (and this includes sociocultural systems) are essentially open systems. Open systems maintain themselves by a continuous inflow and outflow of matter and energy, a building up and breaking down of parts for replacement. When a system is "maintained constant in its mass relations in a continuous change of component material and energies, in which material continually enters from, and leaves into, the outside environment," we say it is in a "steady state" (Bertalanffy 1968:39, 121, and *passim*). The term "steady state" is preferred to the term "equilibrium" since "steady state" does not imply the *static* condition found in chemical equlibria or other nonliving systems that can be understood as closed systems.

A sociocultural system in an adaptive steady state should not undergo systemic change, therefore, unless its extrasystemic environment changes.

To say this is *not* to say that a "steady state" is a sweetness-and-light thing of consensus and conformity, either within the sociocultural system we are concerned with, or between it and its environment. The adaptive stability may consist of many things which emically viewed are "bad," "deviant," "in conflict," and so forth. The United States of America could not now continue to exist in its present form without the presence of certain levels of unemployment, warfare, ignorance, political repression, and so forth. I shall shortly note the endemic existence of warfare, assassination, expropriation, and so on, as part and parcel of the adaptive steady state present in the Sandwich Islands prior to European contact. The term "dysfunction," as noted above, is a nonsense term in a systemic approach.

To say this *is* to say that because the parts of a system are interrelated in various and complex ways, no one part can be altered without simultaneously effecting changes in other parts of the system. Thus, the cumulative effect of many deviation-counteracting devices being triggered tends to offset and countermand the change. It is for this reason that systems in equilibrium can be characterized as "conservative," "stable," or "steady state" systems.

To say this is also to say that "extrasystemic" is a *relational concept* and does not necessarily correspond to time-space correlates. Thus, for example, the initiation of malignant cell growth takes place within the organism, but the variables operative are "extrasystemic" (radiation, for example). Or, if a sudden climatic change were to occur and affect the USA, it does not mean that because the effects were felt within the borders of the USA that the climatic change is within the American system. Obviously, the factors controlling global weather changes experienced locally are extrasystemic to the USA.

Second, *if order is anywhere in the universe, then it must be everywhere in the universe: we cannot have a partially determinant universe.* As already stated, the systemic approach attempts to make nature intelligible by isolating and conceptualizing nature as a system of interlocking subsystems. This approach makes it possible to deal with events as repetitive events, as the results of the operation of a stable system. By giving the "triggers" of systemic change extrasystemic status we are not placed in the contradictory position of postulating "spontaneous mutations" as a source of variety within the system, while holding to determinant relations elsewhere. We can state quite simply that these "initiators" are a product of the operation of the system of which they are a part, but that for us they are the givens—the independent variables.

For example, we know that sociocultural systems had to make numerous adaptations during the Pleistocene in response to changing climates. To explain the cultural adaptations, however, one can take the climatic variations as a given, just as a paleoclimatologist concerned to explain the Pleistocene climatic system can take the geological mantle system (which according to one theory apparently triggered oceanographic and climatic changes) as a given. Given these factors, our job is then to explain the complex adaptive interrelations within and between the system and its relevant environment. It may well be, as I argued in 1962 (Saxe 1962) that all internal systemic change comes about precisely because that system (which is merely one element in a more inclusive system) is experiencing a nonsystemic change in the larger system of which it is a part.[8] If so, the "triggers" are rendered determinate and not fortuitous.

In conclusion, let me rhetorically ask, although all sociocultural systems produce conflict, discensus, and deviance, under what circumstances do these result in *systemic* change? I submit as an answer, only when extrasystemic variables act as deviation-amplifying, positive feedback mechanisms. It is this proposition that I shall try to illustrate using the Hawaiian Islands as a case in point.

Before that, however, let us tarry just a while longer on the intellectual issues raised by our proposition. First, a look at W. Buckley's position (author of the first book relating systems theory to sociocultural science), and then a look at M. Maruyama's position (formulator of the term "morphogenesis").

### Comments on Buckley

The terms "morphostasis" and "morphogenesis" correspond closely to the different implications of nonsystemic and systemic change as defined above. As Buckley summarizes them:

> morphostasis . . . refers to those processes in complex system-environment exchanges that tend to preserve or maintain a system's given form, organization, or state. Morphogenesis will refer to those processes which tend to elaborate or change a system's given form, structure, or state. (1967:58)

He also summarizes a "generalized paradigm of morphogenesis or evolution":

> the paradigm underlying the evolution of more and more complex adaptive systems *begins with the fact of a potentially changing environment* characterized by constrained variety and an adaptive system or organization whose persistence and elaboration to higher levels depends upon a successful mapping of some of the environmental variety and constraints into its own organization on at least a semipermanent basis. (Buckley 1967:63; italics mine)

Except for the implication that the processes always result in greater complexity (already criticized in footnote 4), the paradigm is quite congruent with mine: particularly where he says the process *begins* with a potentially changing environment. But in this "beginning" was merely a word. By the time Buckley recalls the morphogenic model for us some sixty pages later the environment has been demoted to second place:

> We recall that the model assumes an ongoing sytem of interacting components *with an internal source of tension,* the whole engaged in continuous transaction with its varying external and internal environment. . . .(1967:128; italics mine)

In fact, this is immediately followed by:

> The *internal source of dynamics for the ongoing process* is the continuous generation of varying degrees of "stress," or "strain," within and between the interacting components. . . .(1967:129; italics mine)

No more do we hear of extrasystemic variables, and never did we explore them. The chapter on "organization and its genesis," from which the above two quotes are taken, concludes with a plea for a "complex *adaptive* system model," but the nature of the environment (transactions with which determine adaptation) is left in limbo. Of the four features that "the newer model suggests that we focus on. . . ," all four are concerned with intrasystemic variables (Buckley 1967:159–60).

### Comments on Maruyama

Maruyama, in arguing for greater cybernetic concern with morphogenic processes (deviation-amplifying) such as evolution of living organisms, rise of cultures of various types, international conflicts, and so on, summarized the nature of these processes as follows:

> in short, all processes of mutual causal relationships that amplify an insignificant or *accidental* initial kick, build up deviation and diverge from the initial condition. (1963:164; quoted in Buckley 1967:59; italics mine)

And,

> The secret of the growth . . . is in the process of deviation-amplifying mutual positive feedback networks rather than in the initial condition or in the initial kick. This process, rather than the initial condition, has generated the complexly structured city. It is in this sense that the deviation-amplifying mutual causal process is called "morphogenesis." (1963:166; quoted in Buckley 1967:60–61)

Maruyama's argument, in calling our attention to morphogenesis, is a major contribution to systems thinking, but it is not necessary to his argument that the initial conditions be demoted almost to irrelevancy, or what is worse, to "chance." Morphogenesis remains a valid concept independent of the applicability of "equifinality" to urban development.

His hypothetical city development starts with a farmer settling at a chance location on a homogeneous plain. I seriously doubt that a farmer's settling decisions are ever random, just as I doubt that a plain can appear homogeneous to farmers as it does to city folk. But even if all this were possible, the eventual location of a city there, I would contend, has nothing to do with the initial decision of the farmer, since many other such farmers made similar decisions and cities did not evolve. The "initial kick" to urban development, I would argue, comes at the point that towns start to be built; and the "kickers" at that point will probably lie in such things as trade, the crossing of routes, the communication techno-logy available, and so on—all of which involve factors exotic to the initial subsistence farmer on his homogeneous plain.

Maruyama can be completely wrong on the nature of "initial kicks," and yet it does not affect his morphogenesis argument one bit. For this reason it would have been more accurate to state that the source of the initial kick is *irrelevant* to the argument, that he is not interested in it, and therefore it will be taken as a given (an independent variable), as something that does not have to be explained. We must be careful not to confuse our interest in and ignorance of the systems that produce these "givens" (climatic change to archaeologists, mutations to population geneticists) with the existential states themselves. Factors we are ignorant of often appear fortuitous.

In this paper we *are* interested in these "kickers," their source (systemically speaking), their nature relative to the system of focus, and how necessary they are to initiating morphogenic processes. We are interested in open system intersystemic relations. After all, once two systems have joined sufficiently for morphogenesis to have begun, will it continue if the contact is severed? Or is it necessary for a steady-state to develop, making the intersystemic relations stable while their respective structures change to accommodate the transactions? And furthermore, for purposes of this seminar, we would be doing paleosocial anthropology a disservice if we did not at least attempt to answer the question, where do we look for the source of social change—intra- or extrasystemically? With questions such as these in mind, we now turn to the ancient Hawaiian situation.

## THE SITUATION IN THE SANDWICH ISLANDS

The points to be made are as follows:

1. The Hawaiian Islands (as the Sandwich Islands were later known) had at contact a stable ecosociocultural sytem operating. Earlier morphogenesis had come to an end and morphostasis ensued.
2. From the time of contact on, the Hawaiian system selected for foreign inputs in Hawaiian terms, and the foreigners dealt with the Hawaiian situation selectively in terms of their "needs." Morphogenesis began, eventually resulting in the transformation

of a complex chiefdom into a full blown state society—not, however, as a simple reaction to contact (the "kicker"), but rather as a result of intensive and continuous exchanges of energy, artifacts, personnel, and information over a period of time.

As noted in the introduction to this paper, the two events occurring on the 19th of January, 1778, crucial to understanding the arguments presented, were the celebration of the Makahiki and the landing of Cook on the islands. The two appendices attached to the end of this paper provide useful documentation. The first appendix briefly describes the aboriginal Hawaiian social organization, stressing those elements related to stratification; it is an excerpt from Sahlins (1958). In it may be found the Makahiki (p. 132), but also the political and economic arrangements of which the yearly collection/redistribution ritual represents but the apex. And since, as we are told, "The administrative hierarchy in sociopolitical regulation was the same as the hierarchy operative in economic processes," we also, by understanding the Makahiki, understand both. Sahlins also informs us how the patterns of divinity fit those of the economic and political areas. Thus, to understand the Makahiki, which is to understand ancient Hawaii, the reader is referred to Appendix I.

The second appendix presents a selected series of historical events occurring during those critical years under scrutiny here (1778–1827). It can serve as supplement and document for the more abstracted points to be made in this section of the paper. Cook's significance as harbinger of things to come is quite evident. In short, what the foreigners wanted from the Hawaiians (during our time period) was trade. At first they wanted ship's provisions (beginning in 1786): this trade increased in volume as Hawaii became a major stopover on the oriental trade routes, and for those involved in the Northwest Coast fur trade (after 1805). Sandalwood, used for perfume, became (after 1810) the bullion of world trade, and Hawaii was rich in sandalwood. After 1820 came the whaling ships, compounding all this commercial activity. By the time the first successful plantations were set up (1835–40) the old system was long dead. But we are at the end, and we should begin at the beginning.

Sahlins (1958) has cogently argued that the different degrees and different forms of stratification found among the Polynesian islanders developed as they did as adaptive responses to differing natural environmental conditions. Polynesia is a nice "laboratory" case because its people are historically related and because the insular conditions reduce the amount of adaptation necessary to "cultural environment" (relative to continental situations, of course). The high correlation between environmental diversity (through productivity) and social complexity (through stratification) is impressive. Logically, it could be that way only if these societies had sufficient time to fill out their respective niches and then *stabilize* at that level of complexity.

This appears to have been the case in the Hawaiian Islands. As may be seen in the first few pages of Appendix II, during the time of Cook's visits the Islands were divided among four paramount chiefs who periodically warred with one another, assassinated one another, abandoned one another, and so forth; and so did the lesser chiefs under them. The largest relatively permanent political unit achieved by any one paramount was one island and perhaps part of another—his own political unit often falling apart as he was overseas trying to incorporate others. In Appendix I, Sahlins tell us that:

> In Hawaii, rebellion, assassination, and migration into other domains were some of the mechanisms that limited the tyrannical power of high chiefs and the local stewards.

Unfortunately, since these things were characteristic of Polynesian political life he does not inform us of them.[9] What we are missing, then, is a picture of the morphostatic processes, the deviation-counteracting mechanisms that kept more complex political units from developing, that kept one paramount from uniting the islands, that kept one group from gaining a monopoly of force over others. This, I shall now try to sketch.

In the Hawaiian Islands we had a situation unusual in Polynesia; the lineage (conical clan, ramage) of highest rank, that from which came the paramount chiefs and all the other high chiefs (allii and konohiki), had no corporate estate in land which was theirs. Their estate lay in the political system of overrights, to which they were reappointed each time a new paramount chief was instituted. This arrangement underlay the conflict which was also responsible for the morphostasis.

Each time a new paramount chief took office, either by conquest or peaceful accession, the administrative overrights were taken from those who had them and given to those who were within ten degrees of consanguinity of the new paramount. His very close relatives who might have the rank to usurp his position were the exception; they got no overrights, but became part of his retinue. This meant that current chiefs could look forward to being demoted when a new paramount took over, or to having their estates removed from them if they fell into disfavor with the current paramount. In fact, in terms of the ranking system *each new accession guaranteed a demotion in rank, hence overrights, hence land, people, and status.* It is this situation which appears to underlie the ubiquitous interference with the "normal" course of succession. Men were not only protecting their positions, but also their posterity since the genealogies were reworked ("errors" were found) to correspond to political realities; that is, to whomever the victor in battle was, to whomever the successful assassinator was—in sum, to whomever the new paramount chief was. Thus, *conspiracy and alliance* were not only perennial but *existed at all levels of social organization.* Since each level of chief was interested in keeping his position he tried to be generous with his subordinates in order to keep them allied with him, and also to attract followers from the domains of other chiefs. The fact that *low status Hawaiians* were not permanently tied to a natal tract of land is related to this fact. Historical particulars of this system and how it operated to limit the extent of the chiefdoms may be found in Appendix II.

This type of system was not new to the eighteenth-century Hawaiian Islands. If we take the presence of a dominant ruling lineage whose estate consists of overrights (and hence attempts to aggrandize these overrights) as an indicator of this type of system, then its antiquity dates back to at least A.D. 1500.

Malo reports that Haho, forty-first king ("paramount chief" is the preferred term for accuracy here) was the founder of the Assembly of Chiefs to which admission was granted only to those who could prove their royal ancestry (1903:327).[10] This Assembly sounds similar to the *Hale Naua* or *Ualo Malie* which is said to have been instituted during the reign of King Kalakua (Malo 1903:263). The latter is described as the assembly in which the genealogists (in the presence of those already established as "royalty") determined membership by tracing closeness to the paramount back through ten ancestors (Malo 1903:253–54). Umi-a-Liloa, a paramount of Hawaii of about A.D. 1500, overthrew his half-brother (a "bad" chief) in concert with the former counselors of the paramount with a tale of how he was really the son of a paramount (Alexander 1891:96). Umi-a-Liloa was famous because he united all the districts of Hawaii (Kamakau 1961:1).

The abortive attempts to unite the Islands and thus aggrandize one's overrights were also not new to the eighteenth century. Alexander, reckoning time by generations of chiefs and "allowing thirty years on an average to a generation" (1891:99) places the beginning of interisland warfare near the end of the thirteenth century (1891:95) when Liloa was the Hawaiian paramount. Kuykendall and Day date the interisland fights for supremacy, including the tendency to form the four major chiefdoms occurring historically,[11] from the end of the period of long voyages, or the end of the fourteenth century (1948:6–7). Kalaunuiohua, the fifty-fourth paramount, is reported to have conquered all the islands but was then captured by the paramount of Kauai in alliance with the other paramounts he had beaten on the way to Kauai (Kuykendall and Day 1948:332). Defections, coups, and other such acts effectively rendered all attempts at interisland unification failures. Kamehameha I, the focal actor of this paper, experienced such acts as these, as I discuss later.

Thus the sociocultural system found operating in the eighteenth century by the North Atlantic culture bearers was already in operation sometime between A.D. 1300 and 1500, the date chosen depending on how conservative one is in estimating the length of a generation. Ruling lineages with the Assembly of Chiefs and/or the *Hale Naua* to verify access rights existed. Competition (often violent) for the paramountcy and its overrights existed. Wars carried out in the name of islandwide or interisland unity existed. Morphostasis (steady state) thus existed during at least three hundred years before North Atlantic culture contact.

It is noteworthy that the Makahiki ceremony is also tied into these morphostatic wars in that it was at this time that the chief announced his intention of war or peace by the type of temple and preparations he made with the vast redistributive system at his disposal. In addition, the chief traditionally had control over vast amounts of corvée to be used for enterprises of war or peace.

In summary, we have noted Sahlins's (1958) high correlation between adaptive diversity and types of social organization. We concluded that the process of adaptation was completed between A.D. 1300 and 1500, and that morphostasis ensued for the next three hundred years. Apparently it was impossible for more complex political units to evolve. Every time the threat of success appeared, it triggered the counteracting mechanisms of conspiracy, alliance, warfare, desertion, migration, and assassination. We have shown how these "triggers" were built into the political-economic-kinship relations.

What was it then, with the appearance of American and European foreigners, that resulted in all this being changed—and changed long before Hawaiians lost political control of their own islands?

Basically, what the chiefs wanted from the foreigners (and they did control contact with the foreigners) was a means of improving their armed might against other chiefs and occasional rebellions. The chiefs could control this contact because they were at the crucial nodes in the redistributive networks which were activated for purposes of provisioning ships.

During Cook's visit in 1779, the Hawaiians found out that these foreigners had weapons of iron, owned ships of great size and speed, and were mortal. When the provisioning trade started in 1786 each of the greater chiefs of the Islands carried on a provisioning trade of his own. Each held a monopoly of trade administration (as befits Polanyi's model of "administered trade"), and each traded mostly for goods that would enhance his political status.

Malo noted that the chiefs traditionally kept control (either through tabu or overrights) of the sources of wood used for weapons (1903:256, 265). These, together with goods used for rank insignia, and goods used in public works projects, were among the few classes of items collected by the chiefs but not redistributed back to the producers. When the provisioning started, the old right of these chiefs to tabu materials was extended to cover the weapons, foreign advisors, and ships coming into the system through the trade. Nonmartial items, such as mirrors, trinkets, and cloth were redistributed. It was only a matter of time before some chief achieved the ability to gain and hold a monopoly of force over the others.

Kamehameha was a chief of the island of Hawaii who in 1782 seized the paramountcy by treachery, although not without precedent since genealogically he was in the same position that Umi (the sixty-first paramount) had been in when his father died earlier in the same century. Kamehameha merely speeded up the process. Between 1786 and 1790 Kamehameha gained a trade advantage because of his favorable geographic location,[12] and because he had been able to gain advice on foreign ways through a high born chief who had shipped out with the British. He also captured one of the first American vessels to provision at Hawaii, as well as an American sailor, and other foreigners a little later. When, in 1792, Vancouver and his three ships sent by the British government wintered in the Islands, Vancouver recognized Kamehameha's superior position; though he preached peace, he cultivated Kamehameha's favor by supplying him with arms, a canoe rigging, and information on drill. By 1974 Kamehameha's main competitor, Kalanikupule, was regularly trying to use foreign vessels (either by arrangement or by capture) in his wars.[13] By 1795 Kamehameha had a large and well-equipped army and a fleet of large vessels to carry them between the Islands; with these he captured all the Islands except Kauai and Oahu. Once again, with success in sight, he was deserted by his closest ally, who went over to the enemy. But by this time things had changed, and the defection was not sufficient to countermand the new techniques and tools of warfare: "Kamehameha's artillery, served by foreigners, played an important part in the battle" (Kuykendall 1947:47). Oahu was his; Kauai never was defeated, but did agree to Kamehameha's hegemony a few years later. From 1796 until 1802 peace prevailed, during which time Kamehameha accumulated a squadron of small schooners, large double canoes, and a large supply of muskets, cannon, and ammunition. This process continued, increasing in magnitude as the trade became more intensive.

But what was happening on the internal economic side of things as this process accelerated? Taking the flow of goods and services up and down the redistributive network in the precontact period, we may characterize this as *relatively balanced redistribution*. With the exceptions previously noted, this meant that the goods that went up mostly came down, and the specialized produce that a Hawaiian contributed was returned, diversified in kind. However, as more and more of the goods and services were funneled off for purposes of external trade, less and less was being redistributed back down to the producers—since most of what the chiefs traded for was held by them as a monopoly of right. The economy was, in other words, experiencing progressively greater *imbalance* in the redistributive network.

The more manpower utilized to supply the Europeans' needs, the less the manpower available for the production of traditional Hawaiian needs. The more armaments, ships, and so forth, the more intense the warfare, the larger the armies, and the greater the logistic demands in the field. The more men in the field, the fewer the producers, and the greater the demand on the lessened production. The more armaments, ships, and so on one chief got, the more imperative it was for enemy chiefs to get more. What we have, then, is a "runaway" feedback system akin to a snowball rolling downhill: the larger it gets, the faster it gets larger. It is what Maruyama refers to as a "deviation-amplifying mutual positive feedback network."

127

As this imbalance in the redistributive economy grew, the populace and the lesser chiefs grew increasingly restive. But as the restiveness increased, so did the means of attaining a monopoly of force—the two being reciprocals. From the standpoint of the chiefs, as the means of force increased, so did the need to implement that monopoly of force. Here, then, is the background for the structural changes that Kamehameha instituted during this period. It explains why he was both *able* to institute these changes, and why he *had* to institute these changes.

Lacking a monopoly of force, a paramount chief was wise to exclude relatives within three degrees of consanguinity from having overrights. Although these peoples' interests lay closest together, under the traditional setup, these were also the people most likely to usurp and organize against the paramount, since they were his potential competitiors for that position. Without overrights they could not organize followings; and since they traveled with the king, unlike those who were given overrights, he could keep an eye on them. Under Kamehameha, with his newly achieved monopoly of force, this arrangement was altered.

As Kamehameha conquered the Islands he included *all* relatives within ten degrees of consanguinity in the overright distribution, giving the closest the most and thus bringing *de jure* rank into line with *de facto* political power. But not quite: since overright distribution was taken care of at each conquest the net result was to have each chief's holdings scattered over different islands. This made it difficult to build a significant, and consequently threatening, following. Furthermore, Kamehameha had all these high-ranking chiefs come live with him as previously only the closest relatives had done. To administer and rule the islands in residence, he appointed governors, who were loyal to him, directly responsible to him, and whose statuses placed them outside of the old ranking system.

Given the systemic changes triggered and subsidized by North Atlantic culture contact, Kamehameha had little choice but to institute the type of change he did. He had acquired the means of force, and a need to institute a monopoly of its use. If he had not done so, or had been less effective (or even less treacherous)—or if his army had been decimated by a volcanic eruption instead of Keoua's (see below, p. 140)—we would now be focusing upon some other person who would have been "responsible for" uniting the Islands and transforming a complex chiefdom into a state form of organization.

128

## CONCLUSIONS

At the time of Cook's contact, morphostatic processes held sway. Although I have emphasized those of conflict, those interested in nonconflict can easily find them in such emic accounts as Malo's *Hawaiian Antiquities* (1903). What triggered a new burst of morphogenesis was the appearance in the Hawaiian environment of a new resource (foreigners, foreign goods, and foreign ways). This resource enabled the Hawaiians to solve "problems" (of social control and peace, for example) that emerged under the traditional way of life, but which were unresolvable under the old setup. Little did anyone realize that dealing with this new resource in terms of old arrangements would trigger a sequence of events that would result in a new and different system.

The appearance of the foreigners did not simply trigger morphogenesis which then proceeded on its own. There were no systemic changes that occurred during the eight years after Cook's visit when the Islands were not contacted. The accelerating economic imbalance and other changes occurred only after 1786 when the two systems established permanent and intense (from the Hawaiian view) transactions. The foreigners sought certain goods and services and encouraged the currying of favor, special deals, and alliances for their own benefits. In other words, the environment was exceedingly active.

The model that fits this situation is one of steady-state, wherein two open systems, each for their own "goals," engage in transactions of an intense and relatively permanent nature. In the course of these transactions the less complex system undergoes a fairly rapid increase in complexity, while the more complex system, which has other alternatives and is already structured to incorporate areas like the Sandwich Islands, undergoes little change.

The insular anthropological laboratory of Polynesia has allowed us to control for extrasystemic cultural inputs in explaining evolutionary change. I hope this chapter will suggest ways to get at these inputs in continental situations where culture contact tends to be constant. The logic of systems theory argues for an open system model of systemic change with extrasystemic variables being crucial to explanation. The Hawaiian case has illustrated the approach. To the extent that the model called our attention to causal factors in Hawaiian evolution, the model itself is supported.

Finally, our discussion of what systems theory involves was designed to state simply and clearly what all too often is shrouded in esoteric verbiage. The future of scientific anthropology, and indeed of the earth, lies in systems-type thinking. It is to this end that this chapter is directed.

# APPENDIX I

## A Brief Description of Aboriginal Hawaiian Social Organization

Quoted from: Marshall D. Sahlins, *Social Stratification in Polynesia*. Seattle: University of Washington Press, 1958, pp. 13–22.

The stratification system of aboriginal Hawaii can be divided into three status levels.* The first consists of "high chiefs" (*alii*) and their families, i.e., chiefs of islands and major districts of an island and their "retinues" of close relatives. The paramount chief (*alii nui*) of an island, which was usually the autonomous political unit, and his principal advisor (*kalaimo-ku*) were the most powerful members of this status level. A second level consisted of local "stewards" (*konohiki*), persons of intermediate rank who administered the great domains into which a chiefdom was divided. Persons of this status were distant relatives of the paramount chief, or were men of high descent in their locales, or both. The "commoners" (*makaainana*) formed the bulk of the population. They were frequently distant, inferior relatives of the chiefs and stewards.

The term *kauwa*, often used simply to indicate derogation, perhaps refers to a fourth status level, an "outcaste" group. According to Malo, the status was inherited (Malo 1951:69). Bryan writes that it may have

---

*Throughout the text all frequently occurring terms are at first given in Polynesian transcription together with the English translation most frequently found in the sources. Thereafter, only the English language term will be used. Glottal stops are not indicated in the transcription of native terms because of frequent inconsistencies on this point in source materials. English terms are used to increase readability, but the author is merely following the usual translations or equivalents and cannot vouch for their accuracy.

been formed by those who broke tabus, by conquered peoples, or by remnants of an aboriginal stock (Bryan 1950:65). The economic and social significance of such a group is not recorded, but apparently they were few in number, were not a laboring class, did not act as servants, held land "given" them by their "masters," and were used for sacrificial offerings (Beckwith 1932:144).[14]

Priests and craftsmen were not placed on separate status levels. The status of a priest or a craftsman was determined by his inherited rank, and this might vary from high to low.

The use of the lands throughout an entire island was managed by the paramount chief through his principal advisor. Other high chiefs managed districts of the island, men of intermediate status managed tracts of the districts, the commoners held small subdivisions of these tracts. Each manager was subordinate to the higher manager within whose domain he held stewardship prerogatives (Malo 1951:56 and Wise 1933:88)[15] Thus, if a high chief declared a tabu on coconut harvesting in his district, his stewards controlling subdivisions of the district were obliged to honor the tabu. Each manager was considered the holder of the title to the land he managed. Prerogatives to the use of the sea within one and one-half miles from shore were held by the manager and the group bordering the sea.

The paramount chief had the right to redistribute all lands upon his accession, but in practice severe tenure changes only took place as a result of warfare (Wise 1933:82 and Dole 1892:6). Uusually, the larger stewardships were reallotted among the chief's close relatives (except the closest, for fear they might be tempted to revolt), but the tenure of commoners was rarely disturbed. The paramount chief could alienate the land of any manager and bestow it on someone else; he evidently did not appropriate it for himself. Anyone of higher status level could dispossess a commoner and replace him. Secreting "wealth," and failure of the woman of the household to produce mats were sufficient reasons for a commoner's dispossession (Malo 1951:74). Dispossession might also result from failure to contribute labor for irrigation-works construction, and from failure to make the household plot productive (Perry 1913:93–94). The frequency of dispossessions is not recorded.

The sytem of access to water used in irrigation was the same as that of access to land. The high chiefs and the local stewards supervised the allocation. The water allocated was proportional to the amount of labor supplied by any land manager in constructing the ditch, and to the acreage planted. Thus, the amount of water controlled by status levels was proportional to the amount of land controlled, and to the corresponding number of subordinate relatives. During the dry seasons, the high chiefs and men of local importance could adjust prearranged allotments. Any commoner who refused to contribute labor to the maintenance of ditches and dams could be deprived of water rights or lands (Perry 1913:94, Nakuina 1894:82, and Beckwith 1932:173).

The high chiefs and local leaders of intermediate status initiated large enterprises such as ditch construction and repair, and cleaning of ditches. They also engaged craftsmen. Through their role in the redistributive network they could subsidize such activities. Commoners usually could not. The local stewards, as supervisors of construction and maintenance of irrigation works, formed a "primitive bureaucracy." They also directly supervised the production of the households under them, and made sure that the land was cultivated (Handy 1933b:34).

Anyone of higher status could call upon those under him to contribute labor for communal enterprises. In this way, the command for labor for building irrigation works passed down the hierarchy of statuses to the commoner level, the major source of manpower (see Handy 1940:36–37 and Bennett 1931:*passim*).[16] Through the local stewards the paramount chief could also mobilize commoners and craftsmen for the production of houses, canoes, and religious structures for the chief. According to some sources, the demands for labor were fulfilled at regularized time intervals. It is unlikely that this was true before European contact; most probably, the demands occurred merely when necessary (Handy 1933:34). Malo states that a commoner could be put to death for refusing to comply with a demand for labor (Malo 1951:61). A refusal by a man of chiefly family to mobilize his labor force for the paramount chief was presumably tantamount to rebellion.

Although evidence is not entirely consistent, it appears that the high chiefs and their families did not engage in subsistence production (Malo 1951:58, Ellis 1825:93, and Handy 1933b:38).

The three status levels were the focal points of the collection of larger and larger amounts of surplus food and manufactured goods and of their redistribution. A collection by a high chief necessitated prior collection by local stewards from, in turn, the commoners. Distribution followed the same pattern. Most of the goods so collected reached the producers eventually, especially goods collected for feasts. Usually, a small share was taken out by high chiefs and local stewards in the process of collection.

The magnitude of collection activities can be judged by Kepelino's account of the giving of gifts to chiefs. On formal occasions, calabashes of taro pudding (*poi*) presented to high chiefs numbered "perhaps not below 20,000 and the pigs 40,000" (Beckwith 1932:148).[17] Dogs, chicken, bananas, sea slugs, fish, and other items were also presented.

Goods were passed up the social hierarchy in connection with religious ceremonies that required offerings, and for festivities associated with life-crisis rites in chiefly families. The same was true of occasions when local stewards or chiefly families engaged specialists, when war parties were organized by the chiefs, and when it was necessary to provide food for those engaged in communal labor. During Makahiki, the annual religious cycle of the god, Lono, there occurred mass ceremonial collections of goods involving entire islands. Most tabus on the use of land or its resources were placed by managers of the land so that it would be possible for goods to be amassed for purposes of redistribution. Such tabus were in the nature of conservation measures. This practice occurs generally in Polynesia.

Less regularized collections took the form of presents or gifts made to chiefly families and men of intermediate status by inferiors, whenever some item was plentiful. This was an obligation, but in no case was the amount of the obligation fixed; it probably varied with the current surplus. A high chief could seize foodstuffs from commoners if the latter did not contribute a "sufficient" amount (Ellis 1825:398). The high chiefs had large storehouses to hold accumulated goods in preparation for redistribution.

In Hawaii, and generally in Polynesia, certain choice foods were reserved for the consumption of the high chiefs. The difference in food consumption, however, could not have been marked because the commoners were prosperous (Malo 1951:62). Indeed, the obligation of the chiefs to redistribute accumulated food insured an adequate quantity for all. The paramount chief's counselors advised, "When the people brought presents of food to the king [i.e., paramount chief] . . . it was a wise thing for the king to invite all of the people to partake of the food, that they might not go away fasting." The storehouses controlled by the paramount chief were designed "as a means of keeping the people contented, so they would not desert the king [i.e., paramount chief]" (Malo 1951:194–95). This slight difference in food consumption was fairly constant throughout Polynesia along with the chiefly redistributive ethic, and will not be discussed in this comparative treatment.

The differences in the consumption of luxury goods are of greater comparative significance. Often these goods were distributed among members of the upper statuses exclusively, and therefore served as insignia of rank. The feathers of certain birds were used only by the paramount and other high chiefs as garment decorations. The high chiefs wore special cloaks and battle regalia, feather-covered helmets, whales' teeth, and other ornaments. They had staves of office with bearers to carry them. The quality of housing and the number of houses in one's establishment varied with rank.

The native social system of the Hawaiian Islands has gained notoriety for the marked social distinctions between statuses, and for the personal despotism and authority of chiefs. An extreme but not uncommon view is expressed by von den Steinen; "A developed kingly despotism is characteristic of Hawaii. The king is the sole ruler and possessor of power; his will is law." (". . . fur Hawaii ist charakteristisch eine ausgebild-ete Despotie des Konigs. . . . Der Konig ist der alleinige Herrscher und Machthaber. Sein Wille ist Gesetz.") (Steinen: 1926:156). Malo re-peatedly writes of the despotism of chiefs and of the life and death powers that the paramount chief held over those of low rank (Malo 1951:34, 53, 57, 61; see also Ellis 1825:402).

The administrative hierarchy in sociopolitical regulation was the same as the hierarchy operative in economic processes. Consequently, the various status levels exerted differing amounts of authority and power in the control of interpersonal affairs. The paramount chief probably consulted with other high chiefs to determine questions of peace and war. However, the decision evidently was made by the paramount chief and the *kalaimoku* before others were consulted (Malo 1951:96). Messengers were sent round the realm to inform the local stewards of the decision. They, in turn, mobilized the warriors. The assembled army was fed and led to battle by the high chiefs, but they did not necessarily lead in the actual battles.

According to Malo, chiefs did not adjudicate disputes (Malo 1951:58). But Ellis writes that the administrative structure formed the framework in which a hierarchy of chiefs acted as a series of courts of appeal to adjudicate disputes (Ellis 1825:402). Both Handy and Perry report that high chiefs and local stewards settled altercations over water rights (Handy 1940:34 and Perry 1913:95). Case records are lacking.

Generally, assault, murder, and theft were punished by the collective action of the supporters of the injured party. The higher the status, the larger the musterable support. Consequently, punishment varied according to the status of the parties. Within this framework, coercive force was applied by the chief in punishing those who infringed his rights, especially if the transgressors were low in status. According to Ellis, Handy, Malo, and others, people were slain by a high chief if they violated his economic or personal tabus, stole from him, or committed adultery with his wife (Ellis 1825:401–402, Handy 1933b:34 and Malo 1951:*passim*). Malo, who passed part of his life in aboriginal Hawaii, gives the impression that violent punishments were frequent, but he does not list specific cases. To take another example of the role played by status differentials, it is stated that anyone who discovered a man tampering with a dam could kill him on sight, but if the offender were of high rank, the killing caused considerable local "disturbance" (Perry 1913:95). Fornander records an instance of a man of unstated rank stealing a pig from a high chief of Oahu. The man was punished by being forced to roast and eat the pig until he was "nearly suffocated with food." He was told that if he repeated the offense "the law of the land . . . will punish you, viz., you will be sacrified as a malefactor. . . ." Fornander gives evidence that chiefs did resort to the use of human sacrifices as a means of eliminating those who fell from favor (Fornander 1880: II, 96, 269).

In Hawaii, rebellion, assassination, and migration into other domains were some of the mechanisms that limited the tryrannical power of high chiefs and the local stewards. Mechanisms of this sort which operated to inhibit tyranny were a constant feature of Polynesian political life and will not be considered in the comparative treatment of the islands.

The incest range was progressively narrowed toward the top of the social hierarchy; hence, dispersal of economic, social, and religious privileges was prevented. Care was taken to select the nearest possible relative as a wife for a high chief. Brother-sister, or brother-halfsister marriages were common among the paramounts.

The Polynesian tabus concerning approaching, touching, or otherwise violating the sanctified chiefly personage, were elaborate and rigidly enforced in Hawaii. Malo describes a number of such tabus that surrounded the paramount chief. The following is only a partial list: it was prohibited for a man's shadow to fall on the paramount's house, back, robe, or any possession; it was prohibited to pass through his door, climb his stockade, to put out in a racing canoe before him, to put on his robe or his bark cloth; it was required that one kneel while he ate, not appear in his presence with a wet bark cloth, or mud on one's head (Malo

1951:56–57). In general, the commoner could not touch anything used by the paramount chief. Even the ground the chief walked on became charged with mana and was avoided by others. In the presence of the paramount, all had to prostrate themselves on the ground in a posture of extreme humility and obeisance. A paramount chief was preceded by heralds who warned of his coming so that the people could prepare themselves. Honorific terms were used in addressing all high chiefs. It is difficult to determine whether this was a "chief's language," a social dialect, such as was found elsewhere, particularly in Samoa and Tonga.

Malo indicates that death was the usual punishment for a breach of the personal tabu of a chief, but Ellis reports that death would not result if the delinquent had powerful "friends," another illustration of the role played by status differentials in the application of sanctions (Ellis 1825:389). According to Kepelino's manuscript, many people, especially children, broke the requirement of prostrating oneself before the chief when "many of the chiefs traveled together." It became the function of the chief to spare the offender from the "executioner" who traveled with these parties (Beckwith 1932:138–40).

The paramount chief was the direct descendant of divinity. He had some priestly functions, including consecrating temples (heiau) and presiding over particular rites. Certain gods were worshiped only by high chiefs. Particularly spectacular ceremonial phenomena that distinguished high chiefs and their families from others were their life-crisis rites. There was a special cermony to promote the conception of children among those of high rank, and special birth ceremonies, including consecration of males in the temples. Circumcision rites were elaborated in proportion to rank. There were three forms of the ceremony. One was for high chiefs, one for lesser chiefs, and one for the others. During a high chief's sickness, an entire island was practically immobilized by tabus. No one was allowed to walk abroad, cook, or engage in other specified pursuits. The mourning ceremonies of chiefly families were presided over by high priests. Mutilations and other bizarre practices occurred that were absent at a commoner's death (Ellis 1825:51 and Malo 1951:100). A paramount chief's corpse was defleshed and deified. Chiefs were buried in a flexed, commoners in an extended, position. (Additional principal sources consulted on Hawaii; Pukui 1939:27–37; Bryan 1915; Emory 1933; Emerson 1895:101–11; Handy 1933c, d, e; Handy and Pukui 1950:170–90, 232–40; 1951:66–79, 187–222; 1952:243–82; and Hobbs 1931:26–33).

# APPENDIX II
## A Historical Sketch, 1778–1827

The primary source for Appendix II is Kuykendall (1947). This appendix is modified from an unpublished research paper by Gordon Black, Drexel Cochran, and Arthur Saxe, "The Origins of the State: The Hawaiian Islands" (1959).

### The Pre-Kamehameha Period, 1778–82

Captain Cook first went to Polynesia in 1768 to observe the transit of Venus across the sun from a vantage point in Tahiti. In 1777 he visited the Societies for the third time, and in December of that year he departed for the northwest coast of North America in search of a supposed "Northwest Passage" across the continent. On the morning of January 18, 1778, his two ships, the *Discovery* and the *Resolution*, came in sight of land. This later proved to be the islands of Oahu and Kauai. On the 19th of January, 1778, Cook landed at Waimea, Kauai, where he was greeted as the god Lono. Cook had arrived during the makahiki season, and Lono was the god of that season. The way that he sailed along the coast twice during that season with his sails resembling Lono's banners of *kapa*, may have suggested the progress of that god during the *makahiki* festival. While on Kauai, Cook traded iron for ships provisions; and during the exchange a native was shot by one of his men. This incident further contributed to his acceptance as a god. Everywhere that Cook went the Hawaiians treated him as a god and prostrated themselves before him. The legend of Lono's coming spread to the other islands and Cook was greeted as that god when he later visited several of them. After spending a fortnight on Kauai, Cook departed with his ships for North America and began his fruitless search for a northwest passage (Kuykendall and Day 1948:13–16).

In November of that year (1778) Cook returned to the Hawaiian Islands and sighted Maui and Molokai. The next day he anchored the *Discovery* near Molokai, and Kahekili, the paramount chief of that island, came aboard and presented him with a feather cloak. A few days later the *Resolution* anchored off the east end of Maui and entertained Kalaniopuu, paramount of Hawaii, who was at war with Kahekili. Among his retinue was a young chief named Kamehameha, who spent the night aboard ship. The two ships stayed in the Maui area for approximately two months and then toured the eastern and southern sides of Hawaii.

On January 17, 1779, the *Discovery* and *Resolution* anchored at Kealakekua Bay on the Kona coast of Hawaii, where they were met by an estimated 10,000 people. Cook went ashore and underwent a ceremony by which the priests acknowledged him as the god Lono. The next couple of weeks were spent in refitting and provisioning the ships for a return to the Arctic; and on January 25 Kalaniopuu again visited Cook. On this occasion Cook and he exchanged names and Cook was presented with several feather cloaks. Cook reciprocated with a presentation of several daggers and some trade trinkets. On that same day Cook left for a return to North America.

On February 11, the two ships suffered severe damage during a storm and were forced to return to Kealakekua. Shortly after, the cutter was stolen from the *Discovery* by a group of natives, and Cook went ashore to recover it. Kalaniopuu agreed to become Cook's prisoner until the cutter was returned, but then changed his mind and a battle resulted. During the fighting Cook was killed and his bones were divided among the chiefs. By February 21 the Europeans and natives had resolved their differences, and Cook's bones were returned and later buried in the waters of the bay. Both vessels then weighed anchor and never again returned to the islands that Cook had named for the Earl of Sandwich.

At the time of Cook's visits the Hawaiian Islands were divided into four chiefdoms:

1. Hawaii, under Kalaniopuu (who also controlled the Hana district of east Maui).
2. Maui (except Hana), and its three dependent islands, under Kahekili. He was at war with Kalaniopuu.
3. Oahu, under a distinguished old king named Peleioholani (who was also at war with Kahekili).
4. Kauai and Niihau, where the political scene was confused and shifting. By 1783, Kaeokulani, a half brother of Kahekili, emerged as the paramount chief.

The most important personages at the court of Hawaii at this time were: Kalaniopuu, the paramount; Kiwalao, his oldest son; Keoua, his youngest son; and Kamehameha, the king's nephew. Kamehameha was of nearly equal rank with his cousin Kiwalao, and was next in line to the kingship after him.

138

Kalaniopuu, from the very beginning of his reign, had made repeated attempts to defeat Kahekili and occupy Maui. Sometime in 1776(?) he made his last big attack and landed a large army on Maui, and defeated Kahekili (though it cost him a large number of troops), and he thereby achieved control over the Hana district.

1780—Kalaniopuu convened a council of chiefs and designated his son Kiwalao as the successor to the kingship, and gave Kamehameha the custody of Kukailimoku, the war god of the paramount chiefs.

1781(?)—As the last act as paramount, Kalaniopuu went to the south to put down a rebellion. The rebel chieftain was brought to Kau to be punished by sacrifice to the war god. The sacrifice was supposed to be made by Kiwalao, as his father's representative, but Kamehameha carried out the sentence as he supposed was his duty as custodian of the war god. This incident caused an estrangement between the two cousins, or further deepened an existent jealousy. It ultimately resulted in Kamehameha's withdrawal to his home in Kohala.

### Kamehameha I, 1782–1819

1782—Kalaniopuu died in Kau while Kamehameha was at the other end of the island. Kiwalao was under the influence of his uncle Keawemauhili, who saw this as an opportunity to gain power through the customary redistribution of lands following the death of a paramount. Since Keawemauhili was the chief of Hilo, the western chiefs feared that any such action would be at their expense. They formed an alliance to protect their own interests and persuaded Kamehameha to join them and become their leader. His closeness to the paramount, his fighting ability, and the identity of his interests with their own were sufficient reasons for his selection.

"Their fears were justified, and soon an open war broke out, in which the forces of Kamehameha won a victory at Mokuohai. Kiwalao was killed, and as a result the island was divided into three regions, with Kamehameha in control of Kohala, Kona, and Hamakua" (Kuykendall and Day 1948:24). Keoua, the younger brother of Kiwalao, held Kau and part of Puna, and Keawemauhili controlled Hilo and the adjacent parts of Hamakua and Puna. The chiefs that were loyal to Kamehameha in 1782 remained so for the rest of his life, and with them he went to war against his two rivals. Ten years of civil war followed in which

Kamehameha was pitted not only against his two rivals, but also against Kahekili, the chief of Maui, whom Keawemauhili had gained as an ally.

1786–90—A period of peace prevailed during which foreign trading ships began to make the Islands a rendezvous and a base of supplies. The chiefs took advantage of this intercourse to supply themselves with foreign weapons, and Kamehameha gained an advantage in this trade because of his territorial location. He also gained a valuable ally named Kaiana, a native of Kauai who had just returned to the Islands on a British trading vessel. Kaiana was an *alii* of high rank and a well-known warrior whose prestige was enhanced by his years of foreign travel.

During the winter of 1789–90 the first American vessels (the *Columbia* and the *Lady Washington*) entered the Islands. Early in 1790 the sloop *Fair American* was attacked by one of Kamehameha's chiefs and the crew was slaughtered except for one man, Isaac Davis. Both the sloop and Davis were turned over to Kamehameha, and a few weeks later he gained the services of another foreigner, John Young.

Kamehameha also gained Keawemauhili, chief of the Hilo district, as an ally during this time; and with that chief protecting his interests on Hawaii, Kamehameha launched an attack on Maui. Kahekili was residing on Oahu at that time, and his son Kalanikupule was no match for Kamehameha's forces. After taking Maui, Kamehameha went to Molokai to effect a reconciliation with Kalola. (Kalola was the mother of Kiwalao, the sister of Kahekili). While visiting Kalola, Kamehameha agreed to look after her granddaughter, Keopuolani (Kiwalao's daughter), who was an infant at this time. Kamehameha later married Keopuolani and she was the mother of the two princes who followed him on the throne.

Keoua, meanwhile, had taken advantage of Kamehameha's absence from Hawaii, invaded the Hilo district, and killed Keawemauhili. Kamehameha returned and soon drove the invaders back toward their homes in Kau. During the retreat, Kilauea erupted and wiped out approximately one third of Keoua's army. This made many of the islanders believe that the fire goddess (Pele) was on Kamehameha's side. Nevertheless, Keoua still owned nearly one half of the island of Hawaii.

On the advice of a renowned soothsayer of Kauai, Kamehameha built a large *heiau* in honor of the war god. Keoua was induced to the spot to be reconciled with Kamehameha; but to his surprise, a high chief of Kamehameha stuck a spear in him as he stepped ashore. This left Kamehameha free to carry on his war with Kahekili, who by this time was ruler not only of Maui, but Molokai as well.

140

1792—Vancouver arrived at the command of three ships sent by the British government to winter in the Islands. Vancouver recognized the superior position of Kamehameha and cultivated his friendship. He was, however, strongly opposed to the traffic in firearms and spent many hours talking with the chiefs about the advantage of peace. Indirectly, he did aid Kamehameha's military power by rigging a large canoe with full sail and a Union Jack for the masthead. He also left a supply of grenades and skyrockets with John Young to be used for protecting Kamehameha. Further, he taught the native troops how to drill as a body of soldiers. Vancouver also advised Kamehameha not to permit foreigners to settle in Hawaii, but did say that Young and Davis should stay because they were good men.

The real impact of Vancouver's visit was the defense alliance that he arranged between Great Britain and Kamehameha. The British government never took cognizance of the agreement until some years later, but from that time forward Kamehameha considered himself under the King of England.

1794—In the spring Kahekili, who at that time controlled the islands of Maui, Lanai, Molokai, and Oahu (and indirectly Kauai, through his brother Kaeokulani) died. At the time of Kahekili's death Kaeokilani was on Maui, and he took charge of all of the islands except Oahu, which was under the rule of Kahekili's son Kalanikupule. In the fall Kaeokulani left Maui for his home island of Kauai, and stopped over on the north coast of Oahu for a few days to rest up before attempting the crossing. He was opposed by the forces of Kalanikupule and some fighting resulted, but peace was restored. He then learned that some of his chiefs were plotting against him, and he diverted them by attempting to conquer Oahu. In the first encounter he was successful, but at this time three foreign vessels in the harbor of Honolulu put themselves at Kalanikupule's disposal. In the battle for Honolulu, Kaeokulani was killed and his forces defeated.

With success, Kalanikupule thought he could best Kamehameha, and he captured the two English vessels that had helped him (the *Jackall* and the *Prince Leeboo*), and killed the two captains. By January 12, 1795, he had the ships equipped for battle and was ready to attack Kamehameha, when the Britishers mutinied and drove off the native troops. Then the two ships went to Hawaii and notified Young and Davis of the occurrences, provisioned, and left the arms and ammunition that had belonged to Kalanikupule with Kamehameha.

At this point Kamehameha was ready. He had a large, well-equipped and trained army and a fleet of vessels large enough to transport it across the channels. Marshaling his forces he took Maui, then Molokai, then crossed to Oahu. Here Kamehameha suffered the only serious defection of his career. Kaiana deserted with part, or all, of his followers and went over to the enemy. The loss was serious but not fatal, and Kamehameha won a decisive victory. "Kamehameha's artillery, served by foreigners, played an important part in the battle" (Kuykendall 1947:47); Kaiana was killed in the battle; Kalanikupule was in the mountains for several months, captured, and sacrified to the war god.

1796—Kamehameha readied his fleet to attack Kauai which was in a very distracted political condition. Kaeokulani's death on Oahu led to a civil war between the two contenders, Keawe and Kaumualii. Kaewe won the battle but died shortly thereafter, and Kaumualii became the paramount (1797?) of Oahu.

Outside of one small revolt on Hawaii, led by Kaiana's brother, Kamehameha enjoyed a peaceful period from 1796–1802. During this time he had his artisans make large double canoes of a special type called *peleleu*, and had a squadron of small schooners built by his foreign carpenters. Through his trading, Kamehameha had accumulated a large supply of muskets, cannon, and ammunition.

1802—Kamehameha moved his fleet and army to Maui where they spent a year.

1803—They went on to Oahu.

Meanwhile, on Kauai, Kaumualii made preparations for defense. Some foreigners in his service were building a ship for him, and he planned to use it to escape to China if defeat was indicated.

In July of 1803 Kamehameha sent a message from Oahu to Kaumualii demanding that he acknowledge Kamehameha as his sovereign. The message was ignored.

1804—The invasion fleet was ready to launch for Kauai when an epidemic spread through the population. This ruined Kamehameha's army and killed two of his remaining original chiefs. The attack on Kauai was postponed.

1804–10—Kamehameha continued to prepare for an invasion of Kauai. He obtained a hundred-and-seventy-five-ton ship, the *Lelia Bird*, from an American trader, and had more than thirty sloops and schooners constructed.

During these six years Kamehameha also tried diplomacy. The sandalwood trade was getting started, and peace was desirable both to the

142

traders and the chiefs. Messages were exchanged, as were ambassadors, both native and foreign.

In 1805 Kamehameha again set a message to Kaumualii demanding that he acknowledge Kamehameha as king and pay him a yearly tribute. Kaumualii agreed but refused to go to Oahu to submit in person as Kamehameha desired.

*1810*—With an American trader assuming the role of mediator, he finally went to Honolulu, but only after leaving the American Captain's first mate as a hostage on Kauai. The two chiefs met and agreed on the status of a "tribute kingdom" for Kauai. Some chiefs plotted to posion Kaumaualii, but Isaac Davis foiled them by warning him. Davis himself was later poisoned for this act.

*1812*—Kamehameha left Oahu to return to Hawaii where for the last years of his life he resided in the Kona district. He fished, rebuilt *heiaus*, and set an example for his people by laboring on agricultural plots. The last six years of his life witnesses a lively growth in trade for the Islands.

*1817*—Kamehameha I had sent a ship of his own, under his own flag, to Canton loaded with sandalwood. Although the venture was a financial flop, he learned much about the trading activities of the foreigners.

*1819*—Kamehameha I died at Waimea, Hawaii.

But what had happened to the Hawaiian Islands? In theory, everything belonged to the king, Kamehameha I; but in practice he had to satisfy his supporters or run the risk of rebellion. "The usual procedure was for the king . . . to retain such lands as he desired . . . and to divide the rest among his great chiefs, who would hold them by a kind of revocable feudal tenure. The chiefs followed a similar course with the lands assigned to them; and thus the scale descended" (Kuykendall 1947:51). Contrary to Malo's description of not giving the best lands to the king's closest relatives for fear of revolt, Kamehameha entrusted the largest districts to his highest chiefs (Malo 1903:257).

As the islands fell successively to Kamehameha, he distributed portions of them to his followers. This resulted in a scattering about the islands of the holdings of a single chief. In the early part of his reign, Kamehameha kept his chiefs with him in a traveling court system. Each of these chiefs had a subchief who actually looked after the land. These subchiefs were called *konohikis*. Kamehameha exercised his power in whatever district he might be visiting, and involved himself in even the most minor problems.

Though Kamehameha used his five original chiefs as an advisory council, he never extended that function to the younger chiefs who ultimately replaced them. In this later period the authority of Kamehameha was absolute, and although he might ask the advice of the council, there was no assurance that he would accept it. As his Kalaimoki, Kamehameha had appointed a younger chief who became known as William Pitt, or Billy Pitt, and functioned as prime minister, treasurer, and main advisor to the king.

The one really new thing that Kamehameha initiated was the appointment of governors of the conquered islands based upon their executive ability and their loyalty to the king, rather than upon their chiefly rank. The only subordinate administrative officers were the tax collectors who collected produce for the support of the king, his retinue, and his armed forces. Coinage never gained acceptance as an exchange medium among natives during Kamehameha's reign, and only very little foreign currency was involved in market transactions.

Even though Kamehameha felt a strong bond with the British, he treated the ships of all nations accordingly. During the war of 1812, both British and American ships were welcomed to his islands. When the activities of the Russian commercial agent Scheffer began to threaten the sandalwood trade, the rest of the traders appealed to Kamehameha to end this threatened monopoly. Kamehameha ordered Kaumualii, on whose island the Russian agent resided, to expel him—which Kaumualii forcefully accomplished.

### Kamehamha II, 1819–25

"Behind the glamour with which the achievements of Kamehameha I have been surrounded, stands the hard fact that the kingdom was created by force and that it was held together by force" (Kuykendall 1947:61).

Many of the chiefs were unwilling to submit to his authority. There is some indication that an actual coalition was underway to divide up the kingdom upon his death. The manner in which he administered his kingdom was designed to eliminate the tendency towards usurpation that had been evidenced in the past.

Kamehameha I had named his son Liholiho as heir to the throne when the latter was five years old. He also made him the "caretaker of the gods" and gave him the kapu of the temples. Kamehameha I also charged that

144

the god Kukailaimoku be given to Kekuaokalani, a cousin of Liholiho, who was a brave chief that clung to the old gods and kapus.

*1819*—In May of that year, Kamehameha I died at Kailua, Hawaii. Immediately after his death the young king Liholiho went to Kohala until Kailua had been ritually purified. It was here that his conservative cousin (the Ku keeper, Kekuakalana) expressed concern at the possibility of mixed eating coming about. (More on this below.) A week later Liholiho returned; and during his installation ceremony (as king) the dowager queen Kaahumanu (one of Kamehameha I's wives, but not Kamehameha II's mother) informed him that it was the wish of Kamehameha I that the two of them rule together. Liholiho agreed and Kaahumanu became *Kuhina-nui* as Liholioho accepted the title of Kamehameha II. Kuhina-nui has been translated in various ways. One of these is "administrative assistant." In the constitution of 1840 the office is formally defined and the duties explained.

In November of that same year (1819), some of the chiefs of the territory incorporated by Kamehameha I still held hopes of regaining their titles. Since the "coronation" of Kamehameha II in May, the political affairs of the country had been quite unstable. Kekuaokalani (the Ku-keeper) was particularly hostile toward Kamehameha II, and openly talked of revolution. One of the principal grievances of the chiefs was the monopoly on the sandalwood trade held by Kamehameha II as a heritage from Kamehameha I, who had "established it." Kamehameha II was finally forced, seven months after his accession, to give these chiefs a share.

At the request of John Young, Louis de Freycinet, the captain of a French man-o'-war pledged his support to the young king in the event of open hostility. This pledge, made during a council of chiefs, probably served to curb any revolutionary zeal at that time.

The kapu "system" was also abolished in November. As the actual cause of this abolition, Kuykendall points to a number of events—Hawaiians observing the foreigners' violation of the kapus without harm, and the news that the kapu system had been abolished in the Society Islands. Kaahumanu herself had been known to eat bananas, a kapu food. The end of the kapu system was symbolized by Kamehameha II unexpectedly eating with some women during a large feast and thus initiating "free eating" (ai noa) as opposed to kapu eating (ai kapu).

Kekuaokalani looked upon this action as "a most heinous offense." He

145

gathered a large force (December) at Kaawaloa; at approximately the same time a revolt broke out in Kamakau. After a peace parley failed to settle grievances between the two, Kamehameha II directed his forces against those at Kaawaloa, first so as to "lay the axe at the root" of the tree. His cousin was killed and with his death the opposition (overt) to the abolition of the kapus was ended. Furthermore, Kamehameha II gained even greater acceptance as a result of the favorable way in which most of the chiefs responded to his call for aid during the battles. The formal religious services in the heiaus and the Makahiki celebration were discontinued. This "revolution did certainly weaken very greatly the power of the priests, (but) it did not altogether destroy their power; and the power of the chiefs was scarcely touched" (Kuykendall 1947:69–70).

Thus closes the year of 1819. At this very time when the Hawaiians were discarding their old religion, missionaries were on their way from the USA. Also, in October of this year, two whaleships, the harbingers of a vast fleet yet to come, had visited the islands. Kuykendall interestingly observes "That they came at nearly the same time is a striking coincidence; and it is still more remarkable that they came just when the Hawaiians themselves were preparing the way for a new order of things" (Kuykendall 1947:70).

1820—Although the defeat of Kekuaokalani ended all open resistance to Kamehameha II, the reports of foreigners during this period indicate a great deal of unrest and rumors of insurrection. A Russian played the role earlier played by de Freycinet; again protestations of loyalty to the king on the part of his chiefs resulted. Some of this unrest seemed to be fostered by certain American traders who were anxious to unload cargoes of arms. Some of the trouble may also have been caused by certain foreign powers "jockeying for power." It was said of Kamehameha II that he never was as forceful a king as his father had been. Nevertheless, he did continue the land tenure policy established earlier. In 1820 he directed that all foreigners to whom he had not given land be expelled from the islands. In this respect the foreigners held land rights on the same basis as the natives, that is, on tenure from the king. A document written in 1820 says:

> White men, who hold extensive lands, derive little benefit from them, unless they cultivate their ground themselves. A fare, precarious and coarse, is the portion of most foreigners who reside here; yet none, who have any sobriety or industry are in danger of starving (Kuydendall 1947:73).

146

At the end of 1820, Kamehameha II moved his capital from Kailua, Hawaii, to Honolulu, Oahu. This was on the advice of his prime minister, the *kalaimoku*. (This is a secular position not to be confused with the *Ku-kailaimoku* who is the high priest.) The purpose of this move was to centralize the government, to have a place to anchor the roving king, and most probably was also a reflection of the importance of the fine harbor located there. It is to be noted that this period and the years thereafter were the high marks in the sandalwood trade among other activities. It is reported that the king went about on horseback personally looking after the cutting of sandalwood.

*1821*—Kamehameha II sailed with a very small retinue to Kauai where it was rumored that Kaumualii was preparing to overthrow him. The paramount of Kauai, however, pledged to Kamehameha II the same allegiance he had given to his father. Kaumualii was then persuaded to return to Honolulu with the king where he was virtually held a prisoner. Kaahumanu, the kuhina-nui, took him for her husband. Later—a *short* time later—she also married his son, Kealiiahonuii.

Kamehameha II carried on the same policies initiated by his father in dealing with foreign nations, and regarded his domain as being under the protection of Great Britain. In 1823 it was decided in council that the king should go to England and discuss the relations between those two powers. In November the king, his favorite wife, a retinue, and a secretary-interpreter named John Rives left for England. Upon his departure, Kamehameha II directed that a nine-year-old brother should succeed him in case of death; that the same Kalanimoku continue as foreign minister; and that Kaahumanu should become regent as well as kuhina-nui.

Scarcely had the party been accorded a royal welcome in London before several of its members became stricken with measles. Both Kamehameha II and his wife (named Kamamalu) died. At his death, Boki, the governor of Oahu, took charge of the party and completed the interview with King George IV. Boki received the assurance that England would not try to add Hawaii to her empire, but that she would come to the aid of Hawaii if she was ever threatened by another foreign power. On the advice of councilors, George IV ordered that a ship of war carry the royal party and the remains of Kamehameha II and his wife back to Hawaii. The command of the ship was under orders to observe covertly both internal and external conditions in Hawaii, and to establish a protectorate if he deemed it necessary.

Up until 1830, furs, sandalwood, and whale oil were the basis of commercial enterprise in Hawaii. Of these only sandalwood was produced in the islands. From the first contact of foreigners until about 1805, the fur trade alone was responsible for the trade dealings with the islands. From 1805 until 1820, both fur and sandalwood shared in importance, although the sandalwood trade first became intensive in 1812. The whaling trade began in 1819.

Until his death, Kamehameha I maintained a monopoly on both pork and sandalwood. At one point, based on experience with European ways, he even instituted a system of tonnage, harbor, and pilot fees.

Sandalwood, as mentioned, did not really move until 1812, but was a medium of exchange by 1818. It was the standard of value, in terms of which trading deals were couched. Although Kamehameha I had a store of silver dollars, they were never in general circulation. It was not until 1823 that we find a foreigner writing to his home office and stating that money was becoming an object in trade.

Whereas we have already noted Kamehameha's monopoly of sandalwood, and the fact that in 1819 Kamehameha II was forced to give his chiefs a share of this trade, we may now note an observation of a visitor to the Islands in 1822: "the King and his Chiefs compose a united corps of peaceable merchants, whose principal object is to become rich by the pursuit of trade" (Kuykendall 1947:89).

The methods of collecting sandalwood are found in an early historical account which states that Kamehameha furnished food and clothing to the workers whom he ordered to the mountains to cut sandalwood. He also ordered his chiefs to get their people to cut the wood. A result of this intensive diversion of labor, especially after Kamehameha I's death, was famine and "oppression" to say nothing of the exploitation of the sandalwood which rapidly diminished in a few short years, and was exhausted by 1829.

The year 1819 was the year of Kamehameha II's coronation, the year of the abolition of the kapu system, and the year that Kamehameha "cut in" the chiefs on the sandalwood trade; it was also the year of a severe financial crisis in the USA which rendered it difficult for the American traders to procure specie for the China trade. As a result, the New England traders swarmed to Hawaii with all sorts of goods (from scissors to billiard tables) to trade directly for sandalwood. This trade reached a level of intensity previously unknown, one considers that the whalers were now flourishing. Many of the chiefs fell heavily into debt by accepting goods against future deliveries of sandalwood.

In 1826, American warships visited Hawaii to inquire after a debt of $200,000 owed by the Hawaiians to a number of American traders. This obligation was considered a national debt by the chiefs, and as a result the first written tax law in Hawaii was effected on December 27, 1826. It required every able-bodied man in the kingdom to deliver a half a picul of sandalwood to the proper authorities before September 1, 1827, or four Spanish silver dollars, or the equivalent in goods. Each woman was required to submit a mat or tapa worth one silver dollar.

It was also in 1826 that the first treaty with a foreign government was made—designed to safeguard American trading in the South Pacific. It provided for the protection of Americans in the event of war.

The 1820s saw the growth of the "diversification of trade" in Hawaii. "New commercial interests entered the field and forged rapidly to the front. Indeed it may be said that during the later years of the decade, the Hawaiian mercantile structure was being shifted to a new basis" (Kuykendall 1947:92). There developed a greater demand for supplies of domestic and foreign produce, both internally and externally. Locally, "the number of foreign residents increased and as contact with foreigners and the work of missionaries elevated the standard of living and diversified the wants of the natives" (Kuykendall 1947:94). Thus the trade was composed of two elements—local trade and the more general Pacific trade complex. The latter was foreshadowed in the provisioning trade begun in 1786, while the former was foreshadowed in the 1810s with a smattering of foreign trading houses set up in Honolulu.

In 1827, Boki, the governor of Oahu, opened a retail store on Oahu. He also attempted to run a sugar plantation on Oahu. Later, while attempting to repay a number of debts to British and American creditors, he even outfitted two ships to make an expedition to the New Hebrides in search of sandalwood. He failed.

Missionaries arrived in Hawaii in 1820. To the best of our knowledge, they were the first of their kind allowed in. They were evangelical and from the USA. Three principal means were to be used to convert the Hawaiians—preaching, teaching, and printing. Kamehameha II permitted them to stay at Kailua for one year; one half of them went on to Honolulu. Their main job was to convert the chiefs, for it was by their disposition that the missionaries were allowed to carry on. In 1824, at a large meeting in Honolulu, many of the high chiefs, including the queen regent and prime minister, were converted.

Two of the missionaries went with George Kaumualii to Kauai. Many more came from the States, and by 1840 they were ubiquitous. They built schools, devised a written alphabet, printed books, and simplified the dialect differences into a common interisland language.

During the reign of Kamehameha III (1825–54) the Hawaiian Islands saw the establishment of plantations, a constitution, and many other accoutrements of the nineteenth-century North Atlantic penetration.

## NOTES

1. Although controversy surrounding the first European contact does exist, the generally accepted view is that Cook was the first to arrive; the rare occurrences of iron he reported in use probably came from driftwood (Bradley 1942:2, n.). Even if this were not the case, it is true that the type of intensive interaction that resulted in systemic change did not occur until after Cook's visit. Indeed, European culture contact had no fundamental effect on the Hawaiian systems until intensive and regular exchanges of goods, services, information, and personnel were established.

2. Gravitational attraction varies inversely as the square of the distance between the masses.

3. In the case of the earth's orbit I may add "Thank God!"—or life would not be long in surviving.

4. Note the systemic change does not necessarily imply increasing complexity as a result. The course of negentrophic evolution (living systems) has indeed witnessed simplification, extinction being a case of ulimate simplification but also a bona fide example of systemic change.

5. Modified after Saxe (1962).

6. An assumption is a useful belief, but one that can be neither proven nor disproven.

7. What I am clearly implying is that "closedness" or "openness" are not integrally tied to a system being "entrophic" or "negentrophic" in behavior. If the universe is a system of subsystems then even the entrophic ones must be related to others at some level, and hence "open." The only "truly" closed system is the universe because we have defined it that way. I suspect the search for an "ontologically real" closed system is fruitless.

8. Despite fear of clouding the issues, let me restate this as: An evolutionist explanation involves a functionalist explanation at a superordinate systemic level; i.e., the "independent variables" (extrasystemic variables) are functional variations in a system more broadly conceived.

9. And for good reason: universals do not help us explain diversity.

10. When Kamehameha I became paramount chief his predecessors numbered well over sixty—that is, there were at least twenty paramounts post-Haho.

11. These consist of Hawaii, Maui, Oahu, and Kauai.

12. He controlled the lee side of the island of Hawaii, with its fine bays for European and American ships.

13. He had three foreign vessels help him resist an invasion of Oahu by his father's brother. When he appropriated the two English ships, the crews mutinied and carried his weapons to his main enemy, Kamehameha.

14. This information suggests to me that *kauwa* was not a class of people, but simply a derogatory term applied to sacrificial victims especially.

15. Chiefs gave a few tracts in perpetuity to warriors, priests, and others for services rendered. Another few tracts were set aside for chiefly families themselves.

16. Terrace developments were large (up to three by one miles); their construction involved a great expenditure of labor.

17. Kepelino's excellent account of the manner of collection, but not distribution, may be found in Beckwith (1932).

# Evolutionary Ecology and the Evolution of Human Ecosystems: A Case Study from the Midwestern U.S.A.

RICHARD I. FORD

*Museum of Anthropology*
*University of Michigan*
*Ann Arbor*

$A$rchaeologists wear many hats. Some prefer chronological studies, others espouse a humanistic orientation, many emphasize past life-ways, and a few seek solutions to contemporary social problems. Despite varied objectives and diverse methods, all archaeologists study change.

The archaeological record is littered with monuments of cultures that expired and remnants of those that succeeded. The more we dig, the more varied the remains appear, and it is precisely because archaeologists attempt to explain this variability that archaeology is a social science amenable to testing evolutionary principles.

Social science explores the many expressions of human behavior; archaeology exposes the patterns and structural consequences of this behavior in the past. At the same time archaeologists have an enviable ally that evades their behavioral-science colleagues: time. The diachronic depth open to the excavator can illuminate a wide latitude of normal systemic variability shaded from other investigators. We also are discovering that as social scientists committed to explicating how change occurs in the finite ways it does, we must derive answers not from the dissection of a complex system per se, but by returning to its simpler archaeological beginnings and detecting the rules that generated the final form we recognize today. This places a heavy burden on archaeology, but one it can happily support with the methods and theory now available.

Philosophers of science teach that social science should be nondisciplinary. The fragmentation of science into compartments for practical and historical reasons has yielded much knowledge about particular subjects at the expense of nomothetic formulations bridging several fields. So-called interdisciplinary studies fail this objective, too. More often than not they are a patchwork of individual disciplines cloaked by self-interest with only a thread joining the parts. Nineteenth- and twentieth-century philosophers did attempt to overcome the segmentation of science without complete success. From their ranks we rediscover Herbert Spencer, who championed evolution as the basis of unified science. For archaeologists the concepts of evolution drawn from the syntheses of systems theory and evolutionary ecology again offer a long neglected cohesive theory.

What passes for ecology, however, has a wider latitude than the goals of archaeologists. *Any* interest in plants, animals, or climate is so labeled. The net result is that the processual aspects of ecology are overshadowed by static descriptions of natural phenomena, leading skeptics to dismiss it altogether. They assert that obviously man living the simpler life of a hunter and gatherer or even that of a small-scale horticulturalist is closer to nature, and that therefore ecology (or environment) applies, but civilized man with his infinitely more intricate cultural surroundings somehow is exempt from ecological analysis. We intend to refute this opposition both with a logically deduced model and with archaeological data.

To understand the evolution of human ecosystems we first must build a theoretical model based on a synthetic theory from which testable hypotheses about specific behavior can be deduced. A theory then is a set of general assumptions stating the relationships between components or variables. Each variable is a measurable entity. Hypotheses about the interrelations of variables are derived from the theory, and are tested with empirical data by stating the conditions necessary for the functioning of one or more variables.

The theoretical statements can generate a systemic model composed of a number of testable hypotheses. A system is a set of interrelated variables

154

and a change in one results in a change in all others. Wright (chapter 7 in this volume) notes that this is accomplished by varying any variable through its full range of values. The model itself consists of statements about the conditions of variables and their interrelationships. As stated previously, theoretical tenets need not be sought from a single discipline. For explaining the processes by which variables and systems changed in the past. a general evolutionary model can borrow tested hypotheses from ecology, sociology, psychology, anthropology, engineering, and so forth.

Systems exist in nature but their complexity usually prevents us from "seeing" them in their entirety. Therefore, as scientists we partition nature and analyze an artificial system assumed to be representative of natural phenomena. One useful methodological tool in this regard is simulation. Plog, Hill, and Wright (chapters 2, 3, and 7) stress the importance of this technique for archaeology. Once the model is constructed, values for each variable can be given initially and the model "run." The successful operation of a model, however, does not mean that the model is tested: this must be done with independent data. But it is an invaluable procedure for comprehending the relations between variables, for generating new hypotheses, and for discovering the kinds of data archaeologists need to test them, which in turn will improve our initial theory.

Hill (chapter 3) has reviewed some of the various general systems models employed by social scientists, emphasized their deficiencies, and has presented a more inclusive model of his own. With this background available we can proceed directly to the theoretical ideas in systems theory applicable to evolution and to human ecosystems.

The systems we will examine are open and therefore living. They permit the entry of energy, matter, and information into their organization. As living systems they are characterized by four principles, first distinguished by Von Bertalanffy (1968), which have evolutionary implications, as we will show later in the paper.

Each living system is organized for self-preservation. It is the total order that is maintained and not simply one of the components. In these terms then an individual variable, or a combination composing a subsystem, function for the perpetuation of the whole; they are special-purpose systems. The larger system which they serve is a general-purpose system; its purpose is survival (Rappaport 1969).

Each living system is hierarchically arranged. The total system is composed of variables and subsystems of variables. These operate at different rates and times, and under different conditions. The biological world expresses this in its organism, population, and ecosystem hierarchy.

Living systems return to a particular state after disturbance. Each system is regulated, and when a variable exceeds its viable range, a mechanism detects this and triggers a corrective response. This returns the deviant variable to its acceptable range. Confronted with stress, every system has a number of regulatory mechanisms, or controls, to protect the constituted system. This systemic property to adjust behavior to environmental changes has also been called adaptive (Miller 1965a).

Each living system tends to develop toward a maximum organization. This property is more controversial than the others since it implies purposiveness and teleology (Ackoff and Emery 1972). Von Bertalanffy recognized this in the ontological development of an embryo wherein a few genetic instructions provided the code for a differentiated and complex adult form. From this example he hypothesized that all living systems develop according to a few rules into an organization of maximal differentiation of specialized parts that are the most complex in organizational structure. Using Ashby's term (1960:20), this is a trajectory for a system which implies that even when an earlier and less complex system is preserved from disruption, it is only an episode of recovery. The system contains a code commanding a more complex organization. The principle of maximal organization is basic to biological succession.

When a system is threatened by disruption, regulatory mechanisms are activated to correct deviation and to protect systemic integrity. Regulation is common to all systems and several types of controls are distinguishable. Variable independent regulation proceeds without reference to the value of a particular variable or subsystem. It may occur automatically at predictable time intervals. This variety is *time dependent* regulation which operates regardless of the condition of any variable, sometime correcting stress and sometimes not, depending upon random events in the environment. *Variable independent* regulation may operate when unpredictable events warrant action independent of homeostasis. The killing of twins, female infanticide, and prescriptive marriage rules are three common cultural practices that regulate local population size even though the population is not jeopardized. On the other hand, *variable dependent* regulation is responsive to the values of particular variables. These density dependent controls are truly cybernetic with reliance on feedback endogenous to the system. By this means their effectiveness is more dependable and their impact is more pervasive. The actual corrective mechanisms for safeguarding order are always fewer than the variables regulated. For example, the now classic case of ritual regulation that Rappaport (1967) describes for the Tsembaga simultaneously determines the amount of cultivated land, pig herd size, crop size, marriage rate, and intervillage alliances for collective activities. Each type of control can function independently or in concert.

Regulatory mechanisms in complex systems often are hierarchical. Thus, when a time dependent regulator fails to maintain the system, a density dependent control may back it up. Controls that are triggered by the irregularity of variables usually are less frequent, but most important, for system maintenance. To illustrate this process I have shown a hierarchy of regulatory mechanisms in operation for a Tewa pueblo in New Mexico (Ford 1968; 1972b). Each farmer is guided by variable independent religious prescripts to plant his corn in dispersed fields in order to raise four pure colors of corn. In a land with tremendous localized physical and biological environmental fluctuation, the farmer, by satisfying the gods' needs for unicolored corn in ceremonies, assures that grasshoppers, hail, or other natural calamities attacking one field may spare another and not divest him of his entire effort. However, losses do occur and differential consumption patterns may leave some households embarrassingly short in late winter and early spring before "mother earth is awake." During this period a series of time dependent rituals accompanied by food redistribution help to even village food consumption. On unpredictable occasions, though, conditions may worsen, prayers may not be answered, and the entire village population may be endangered. Perceiving their plight on a collective basis, the village elders may decide to move part or all of the village's population to a new location where land is plentiful and water abundant. By means of migration, a density dependent correction, the man/land ratio, soil productivity, and other variables are changed. If only one regulator were functioning, the system would soon expire.

The information component of the system coordinates the relations between the subsystems of variables. Information relates to communication of the status of each variable and the system's environment. It provides monitoring, the storage of corrective programs, and analysis of alternative responses.

In simplified form the information system detects (monitors) the value of a variable by comparing it with a reference value. If a variable has gone awry, then a stored effector program is activated to correct that variable. The mechanism that does the correcting is the regulator, but the total command and execution process is part of the information system. This process has several obvious implications. First, speed becomes critical. If adjustment is too slow, the system is endangered. On the other hand, too fast a response to every minor fluctuation can also have a price in expense, inefficient operation, and overspecialization. Adaptation is usually to long-run cycles or extreme perturbations and not short-run changes within a variable's range value. Second, there are qualitative differences between commands paralleling the hierarchical arrangement of variables within a system. Those emanating from low-ranking systems directly affect variables and contain high specificity of corrective information, while those from more inclusive levels are vague, more general, and low in specific programs for action (Rappaport 1971b:30). Third, reference values can cause internal confusion. They may be mistakenly set outside an appropriate range and the correction itself could change the system. As the number of levels increases, the problems in transmitting and interpreting information also increase with more possibility for errors to occur during homeostasis. Difficulties related to speed of transmission, types of rules, and reference values are not apparent in most biological systems, but as we will discuss, they become paramount in some human ecosystems.

Despite all efforts to the contrary, systems change. These are not changes within the normal value range of a variable, the dynamic aspect of a system we expect (even if anthropologists have missed it in the past!). Our primary concern is with changes that arise in either the structure of the system, or in its functional relations when a control mechanism fails to respond properly, or when the exogenous environment is altered to such a degree that the system cannot counteract it without reorganizing.

Reconstitution of a system may take several forms. The system may differentiate toward greater structural complexity and in so doing it may evolve. It may lose parts, becoming less complex and simpler in design. It may rearrange its internal organization to meet the selective pressures of the moment. Flannery (1972) following Rappaport (1969; 1971a) has discussed some of the mechanisms involved in this process. One control in a hierarchy may bypass a lower-level control thereby short-circuiting the operation of the latter; this mechanism he calls linearization (Flannery 1972:413). Similarly, a lower-level control may be promoted and assume the functional and structural position of a control higher in the suprastructure. Promotion (Flannery 1972:413) may result from solving a stressful situation by permitting an institution to become more self-serving. In either case the system's structural ability to confront future selective pressures is altered. If one level assumes simultaneous control over several other controls at a lower level, then systems with a high degree of integration often lose an ability to react to new and unusual disruptive forces because they cannot process the information rapidly enough and too much effort is expended preserving a maladapted organization. Therefore a system can become too specialized for coping with specific problems by means of a structure too ineffectual if conditions change.

Ironic as it sounds, evolution is basically a conservative process. Feedback mechanisms and efficiency of handling information are to maintain constancy and the status quo. It is precisely in the attempt to do this that systems change. Romer's Rule (Hockett and Ascher 1964:137) states in general terms that systems change so that vital components do not have to change. In an effort to preserve, new structures are created or new organizations are advanced. At the same time these changes may not confirm an advantage under new exigencies. Unless the selective forces are well-defined, all one knows is that the structure of system will condition its future constitution though not the form of its organization. Extinction and evolution both result from systems that changed through an attempt to stay the same.

The same principles that determine the structure, function, and changes in general systems apply to biological systems. It is necessary to discuss ecological systems in order to understand man's place in nature.

Ecology unravels the interdependency of biotic populations and their physical environment. These relations are dynamic with the measurable variables continually fluctuating in response to an everchanging environment. Ecologists distinguish several levels of interaction existing in nature. The lowest is the individual organism. Each has a genetic foundation that determines its form and partially guides its behavior. At the same time the organism is composed of special anatomical systems that maintain its existence. A group of organisms of a single species constitutes a population; those occupying a particular geographical area exchanging matter and energy with other populations make up an ecological population. Populations are structurally and functionally different from organisms, just as ecosystems are different from their individual populations. Ecological populations in an area form a community, and communities in conjunction with their abiotic physical environment constitute the ecosystem, the highest level of inclusiveness to concern us in this paper. Ecosystems can survive the loss of some populations but a population's existence depends upon the continued viability of its ecosystem. The ecosystem then must contend with the ever present challenges of its environment.

The concepts of energy flow and material exchanges within ecosystems enable us to understand, or at least to monitor, the interactions of the population variables and thereby to test certain system-specific hypotheses. Solar energy comes into the system and is converted to protoplasm through photosynthesis by plants. The living tissues of the plants possess the potential energy required by the primary consumers feeding upon them. These herbivores are consumed in turn by various carnivores and omnivores. By constructing the system as an energy pathway, physical laws are applicable to it. The first law of thermodynamics states that energy can be converted from one form to another and this is exactly what is observable between trophic exchanges when the stored energy of one organism becomes the kinetic energy of another. In each energy transaction a loss occurs: each organism is consumed by another with resulting entropy of energy, a prediction of the second law of thermodynamics. More specific implications of these physical laws will become apparent later in this paper.

At this juncture one might demur by arguing that this line of reasoning is superfluous since man is a culture-bearing animal. Indeed anthropologists have devoted hundreds of pages to distinguishing the naked ape from other animals, and these differences are acknowledged. But what is accomplished by stressing these dissimilarities? To answer this question we may learn more about human behavior and the operation of human ecosystems if he is not excluded a priori from animal systems in general. By recognizing that man is a biological being with many similarities to other living populations, hypotheses pertaining to the maintenance and survival of human populations can be deduced from biological and ecological laws which would be otherwise inappropriate since we cannot make culture operational for similar analysis.

Embedding man in nature does not deny his distinctive means of behavior: culture. Culture can be viewed as part of the information coding, processing, and effecting component in an ecosystem. Man's behavior is guided by learned codes and interpretable experiences. But like other animals, man has a genetic endowment enabling him to learn

160

and interact with other populations. Like man, other animals also use culturelike means of adaptation. Granted, symbolizing is not essential to imitative behavior, but drawing a distinction is not always incisive. Margalef (1968:97–99) has recognized these similarities and has accorded an information status to burrows, trails, and nests, and goes so far as to distinguish a cultural channel as more important than genetics in the evolution of higher vertebrates. Symbolizing, if one accepts this idea, is a particular form of the cultural information channel that permits the efficient storage of a greater amount of information than was previously available and itself is a product of evolutionary processes. In these terms culture in a larger system, the ecosystem, is subject to more general laws than culturologists will admit. At the same time it is more than the extrasomatic means of survival for human populations; at the level of the ecosystem it may also function for maintaining stable relations between populations.

Ecological explanations are enhanced if man is treated as another biological population. The recognition of the human population as an important component is a departure from traditional cultural ecology studies, which rarely mention its needs. Yet like other populations, humans have food requirements to fulfill metabolic and other energy demands. How these are met is quite another matter. Inheritance rules, post-marital residency, and rituals, to name a few, may affect a population's food consumption, and are specific for each system. So, too, animals have idiosyncratic means for surviving, but these should not deter us into missing the similarities shared by all organisms. In these terms, human populations are not unique; they still consume energy derived through trophic exchanges with other populations. Human populations also can be quantified as variables according to numbers, age, sex cohorts, reproduction rates, and so forth, to facilitate ecosystemic analyses. Ecologically, the survival of man is a proper question only when phrased in empirically operational biological terms.

The ecosystem is similar to any living system. Its goal is to perpetuate itself; its subsystems work to this end. After it is disrupted, the ecosystem returns to its previous condition by various feedback mechanisms. It is hierarchically arranged both in structure and regulation. Parts of any lower level, including entire populations, may undergo change or even extinction for the survival of the more inclusive unit. And under a given set of environmental conditions, the ecosystem tends to achieve maximal organization, buffered against disruption until these conditions change.

By means of maintenance they are adaptable since they can modify behavior in the face of environmental flux.

Bounding ecosystems remains an analytical problem. Simple systems with few populations usually have a clear demarcation line, but with increasing complexity, the problem is more acute and often becomes a matter of scientific expediency. When we deal with truly dominant species, one or more that determine the structure and operation of the system, then the boundary problem is somewhat simplified because their range becomes conterminous with the system's edge.

The environment of the ecosystem is also problematical. Obviously the larger the geographical area, the greater the number of factors that may impinge: soils differ, slope angle and direction vary, and elevation may increase, to name a few. From the total environment it is necessary to distinguish and empirically examine the effective environment, that is, those extrasystemic factors that impinge directly upon the system. Partitioning the environment in this manner permits one to hold some variables constant (gravity, for example) if they are unimportant for explaining a variable within the ecosystem.

Regulatory mechanisms based on feedback loops within the biological and environmental components of ecosystems keep these systems from changing as well. However, exogenous stresses sometimes go uncorrected and a new ecosystem results. Natural selection is the critical process. The environment of an ecosystem is changing continuously but its effects are regularly counteracted. When they are not, the organization of the ecosystem is rearranged. Some pathways for the matter-energy-information circuits are blocked while new ones may emerge. Although it sometimes happens that new components are added, selection usually works on variables and structural relations already present in the system. Less complicated systems must adjust to pronounced physical environmental stresses, while complex systems must contend with competition from new populations or whole ecosystems. Evolution and devolution result from natural selection.

Devolution occurs when an ecosystem's complexity is reduced through either the simplification of food chains and information processing or the modification of regulatory hierarchies. Devolution may reproduce, but need not, a previous form of the ecosystem. Devolution is also a creative process that can lead to new ecosystems in geographical areas where they previously were unknown.

162

Evolution, our primary concern, results in greater complexity of organization. Selection produces a better organization, with more efficient linkages between the parts, to contend with an inimical environment. When these environmental pulses are large and occur at unpredictable intervals, several responses working in unison may emerge. But if the disturbances are small and frequent, simple feedback—with some controls responding to several different disturbances—can result. The reorganization and the responses reduce trial and error, an overly expensive means for coping, in favor of more resistant forms through increased specialization in a particular environment. As the ecosystem evolves it develops more components (progressive segregation), but each becomes more interdependent with a greater number of controls (progressive centralization). As the components lose independence through more efficient coupling, the ecosystem sacrifices its resilience to buffer radical changes in its environment. As the ecosystem evolves the amount of energy is not increasing at the same rate as its ability to process information about the environment. Human ecosystems illustrate this point very nicely.

Even though selection is continuous, and failure to counter it is the exception, nonetheless, the number of evolutionary processes and our comprehension of their functions are limited. Consequently, understanding of evolution is enhanced by examining it in the microcosmic perspective of succession. The general principles of succession as derived by ecologists give us a model for predicting changes in human ecosystems. From this comparative perspective we should better understand the place of human populations in nature and the role of culture in ecosystems.

Succession is the gradual replacement of one series of species by another until a stable ecosystem is achieved in a particular environment. It is best not to think about succession in definitional terms but rather as an evolutionary process. Each change is a modification of the physical environment by life-forms that establish conditions favorable for another set of organisms. As the environmental changes caused by the organisms accumulate, the impact of the physical environment is gradually modified. In the final stage the ecosystem is buffered against all but the most severe or unique environmental disturbances. The composition and structure of the biotic community then changes through time in a single and predictable direction—from a simple one composed of a few species to a complex and interdependent organization of many populations. If this trajectory is disrupted in the same environment, the process will start over and again proceed in unidirectional fashion; this is the living system's equivalent of the system theorist's goal-seeking.

The earliest stages of succession contain but a few species and those that are present are multiversant (Benninghoff 1968:72); that is, they are capable of enduring a wide latitude of physical environmental stresses. Each of these species has a high primary production and low standing biomass. Many of the plants are annuals. Energy-matter relations are simple with each species at various levels of the food chain having few alternative sources of energy. Minerals are imported into the system and information about the environment is very great since physical factors exercise such a pronounced control over the entire system.

The plants and animals gradually change the environment thorugh succeeding stages or seres. The plants in particular change the soil composition as organic matter accumulates and is decomposed in the detritis cycle. Trees replace grasses and herbs; their canopy and height change the ground surface temperature, light intensity, and speed and pattern of the wind. With these biological modifications of the physical environment additional species with less extreme tolerance can enter the ecosystem. Slowly the system becomes more complex, information content increases, and the physical environment is modified from homogeneous severity to a patchiness of increased variability.

Within the ecosystem the various populations can be viewed as special purpose systems that may or may not survive from start to climax. Some are replaced by others for which they actually created an environment. Some species that are minor components at the start may become dominant, while others, such as the grasses, may dominate early in the history of a particular ecosystem but soon lose importance. Odum (1971:251) characterizes the strategy of the ecosystem as survival through community control of environmental perturbations.

The final stage or end of the successional trajectory is a mature ecosystem characterized by the highest number of species and the greatest variety of plants and animals in the history of a particular successional sequence. As predicted by Ashby's Law of Requisite Variety, the ecosystem consists of numerous specialized parts and coherence between these parts dampens environmental changes. The populations occupying the various levels of the food chain are interrelated in weblike fashion with each herbivorous, omnivorous, or carnivorous species having a number of alternative food sources. Minerals now cycle within the

164

system. Information about the various states of the system is obviously high but can be processed more efficiently than in simpler, less efficient systems. New information is rarely introduced. The end result is that these pauciversant species (Benninghoff 1968:72) control the ecosystem to a degree that only major disruption will alter the dynamic stability of this organization.

This model has been criticized for being appropriate only in environments with regular and recurrent stress. The ecosystems in these settings are able to survive loss of populations because of their high redundancy and buffering. In environments where physical disturbance is random and the intensity of the stress is irregular the neat progression is not evidenced precisely because few species have evolved that can endure this environment (Sanders 1969). The amount of information needed to cope with this condition is very great, but must be handled by generalized controls.

Human populations also participate in ecosystems and are involved in their evolution. From my previous discussion we can deduce hypotheses that apply to human societies. First, if we start with the hypothesis that a human population is a special purpose system along with other populations with a role in an ecosystem, then we can better appreciate how structural relations are maintained. Too often man is assumed to be dominant in all ecosystems, but this assertion may retard our knowledge of man's actual role. We want to discover how culture operates not only for the survival of man but also to regulate other populations to the *advantage* of the ecosystem. How did hunters and gatherers in the deciduous forests in the central United States maintain relations between populations? We would expect extensive use of resources capable of rapid rebound from exploitation and mechanisms for limiting or dispersing human populations to prevent negative exploitation. If this hypothesis is affirmed one can then examine the impact of agriculture on the ecosystem. Was this the mechanism that led to anthropocentric ecosystems? Again this is another popular assumption—the revolutionary consequences of agriculture—that needs careful examination. With an agricultural economy other predictions are possible. Since agriculture simplifies the ecosystem but can be manipulated for increased production, we expect an elaboration of institutions to monitor the environment and to overcome the vicissitudes of the physical environment that are no longer buffered by a mature system. Since these disturbances are more random and irregular, we expect greater centralization and coordination of the structural components of the ecosystem. The information processing institutions should increase to the advantage of the survival of the promoted human population.

Finally, if man has not always been an ecological dominant what are the expected consequences of contact between the simplified anthropocentric ecosystem and a natural ecosystem? Based on our general theory the former system becomes an unpredictable and intense disruption that the latter is unprepared to regulate. In a competitive situation the system with the most potential for increasing yield and organizing for monitoring the environment will have the advantage. In a conquest situation we would expect the more complex system actually to maintain another system in a simplified form with the energy from that system being used to maintain the victor. Ecologically speaking, more mature systems move against less mature and derive energy from them to support the organization of the former; politically speaking, this is colonialism.

We now examine a more specific model in the form of a case study using pooled data from the middlewestern United States. This is an excellent area for generating hypotheses deduced from an evolutionary model because a detailed chronology and numerous excavated sites yielding paleoethnobotanical and paleoethnozoological remains make possible manipulations unavailable elsewhere. Despite these advantages we should recall that no substantiated settlement system incorporating seasonal and functional variability in occupations, despite decades of labor, has been published. For the time being this limits testing and necessitates the building of more specific models which can be expected to be revised often.

To monitor this evolutionary sequence we will use rough energy values derived from foods identified from the archaeological record. These are tabulated by converting the poundage from minimum individual counts to calories. The accumulating information of relative quantities of plant and animal remains from sites allows the construction of food chains or webs for various time periods. At the same time knowledge of these species permits the construction of models related to information about the prehistoric environment. Although I concur with Needham (1959) that much of the biological competition with the ecosystem is for minerals, our limiations are restrictive enough, and the study of geochemical cycles in prehistoric human ecosystems will have to await another opportunity.

*Paleo-Indian.* Theoretically we should commence with a detailed

166

discussion of Paleo-Indian hunters, but adequate data beyond obvious stylistic differences in some populations of fluted points are unavailable. One could hypothesize that these differences are not a result of long-time occupation in the area, as some investigators have suggested, but rather are material expressions of local variability in food procurement strategies. If this were the case, then we would expect groups were dependent upon game that was localized, nonmigratory, but nonetheless dispersed. Deer territorial behavior meets this prediction, and the Paleo-Indian ecosystem may not have differed appreciably from the Early Archaic. Figure 5.1 projects some of the speculated game and potential plants back into this period of earliest occupation in the east. Naturally a number of imponderables remain to be answered before the question marks can be removed.

The composition of the post-glacial landscape is a problem. In many areas traversed by Paleo-Indians, spruce occupied forests that are now purely deciduous. Many plants displaced to a mosaic of more southerly refuges were migrating northward into regions still dominated by more northern species to form communities unrecognizable today. How this configuration of mixed vegetation affected the distribution of Pleistocene and modern animals engenders only more guesses. The latitude of climatic fluctuations also must be considered before we assign mean values of precipitation and temperature not unlike those enjoyed today. Moreover, wide rivers carrying the cold discharge of melting glaciers may have affected the seasonal movements of animals. For early man the environment may have possessed enough instability to limit species abundance and to inhibit prolonged residency in any one area. Instead, frequent movement within a recognizable, delimited territory would produce the morphological variability in fluted points characteristic of forested areas. Whether the extinct fauna of more open habitats such as Domebo (Leonhardy 1966) or extant animals constituted their quarry, is also relevant. The human food chains, in the absence of extensive and varied edible plant resources, were limited to only a few alternative food resources and formed ecosystems not unlike the Early Archaic which followed.

*Early Archaic.* Early Archaic human populations as components in local ecosystems are envisioned, as predicted by the evolutionary model, to have a limited number of food chains. The vegetative environment about 7,000 B.C. in south central Illinois contained the floristic elements now typifying this region but perhaps in different proportions. In other

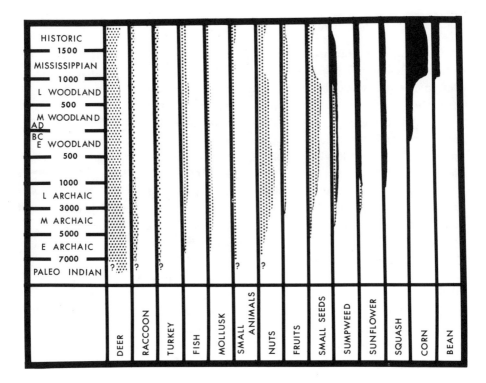

Figure 5.1 Hypothetical subsistence pattern changes in the Middle West. The stippled graphs represent wild plants and animals used for food by the Indians; the solid graphs are domesticated plants. The values are relative internally and many minor food categories are omitted.

words, the regional ecosystem may still have been somewhat immature and simplified with a tempered physical environment nevertheless an important influence. A careful examination of Figure 5.2 discloses that the simplicity of the biotic community and its predicted wide swings in potential annual yield offered man limited foods. Evidence from the Stanfield-Worley site (DeJarnette, Kurjack, and Cambron 1962; Parmalee 1962), the Allen site (Morse 1967), Modoc (Fowler 1959), and Graham Cave (Logan 1952; Klippel 1971a; 1971b) indicates that deer was the most important food source, followed by raccoon, while squirrel, turkey, aquatic resources, opossum (now shown), and rabbit (not shown) were much less so. Vegetative resources are not known but tool kits— mano, milling stone, and nutting stones (Graham Cave, Klippel 1971b and Modoc, Fowler 1959:49)—for processing certain plants, and nuts in

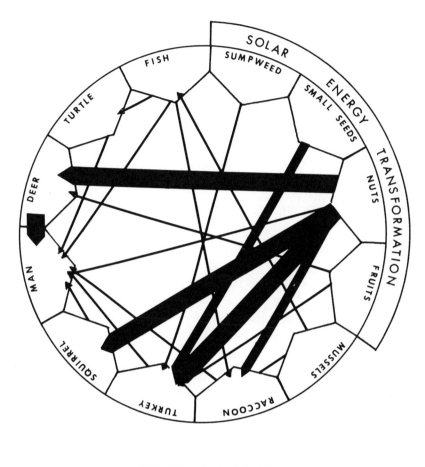

IMPORTANCE SCALE

| | |
|---|---|
| →  | 1 — 10 % |
| ► | 10 — 40 % |
| ► | 40 — 80 % |

Figure 5.2  Early Archaic anthropocentric food web. Figures 5.2–5.6 represent diagram-matic models of food webs from the perspective of the human population. They also show resources shared with animals.

169

particular, are rare. This implies that meat derived from the second trophic level and omnivorous animals was the primary source of protein, calories, and other nutrients. Implicit, but not proven, is the basic division of activities within the society: males hunt and females prepare the food.

Three ecologically significant points emerge. First, the human population was undoubtedly small. Second, the animal species that formed the basis of the human diet had to endure localized environmental fluctuations. Third, the information component behind the human procurement strategies was closely attuned to animal behavior or signs related to animal movements.

Since, along with other predators, man represents the highest trophic level in this ecosystem, getting proportionally less energy than species in the lower two levels, his population would be predictably small. Such populations being dependent upon the ability to pursue game at a certain level of success, movement itself may have been part of the regulatory hierarchy limiting the size of a mobile human population. Spontaneous abortions, nutritional stress, and male absenteeism could have contributed to physiological control of a lower birthrate. Infanticide, as a by-product of load carrying limits (Lee 1972), was a possible cultural regulation. Early Archaic period sites of limited number and duration of occupation support the idea of both small and mobile groups.

The animal populations hunted by Archaic people were able to rebound rapidly from predation and natural disasters. Deer were the single most important subsistence item. As a browsing animal, deer occupied a number of habitats of early successional seres along rivers, in clearings, or at the edges of prairies. Deer are capable of withstanding very heavy exploitation–to levels of fifty or sixty percent. At lower levels they may degrade their own ecosystem; at high levels their ability to rebound rapidly is reduced. Beside their high biological reproductive capacity their coloration, social patterns, and seminocturnal feeding habits render them more inconspicuous than their actual numbers suggest when their numbers are reduced. Therefore it is doubtful that Early Archaic hunters actually eliminated these animals from an area. Instead, with lower numbers, search time was increased relative to successful kill. This ratio probably was one triggering mechanism defined in cultural terms that contributed to a decision to move camp. While man was a predator in the deer's biotic environment, the physical environment affected numbers and dispersal from year to year. Unseasonable weather could affect fawns and food quality, especially the quantity of nuts, seeds, and fruits. As the deer adjusted to nature's whims, so did man.

Raccoons are nocturnal, fringing forest dwellers. Omnivorous in diet and with high reproductive potential, they too, can tolerate a high degree of predation. However, pursuing a raccoon with an atlatl in twilight, setting traps, or dislodging them from their tree-top dens may have consumed more time and effort than their kill-rate and food value warranted. Raccoons appear in much lower numbers in sites than their potential yield of ten to twelve per square mile per year.

Other animals such as turkeys, opossum, squirrels, and rabbits may have presented ethological defenses that Early Archaic technology was not prepared to overcome.

The availability of aquatic resources probably was different from today. The stabilization of rivers flow rate, particles in suspension, and composition of bottoms affected the development of mussel shoals, and their convenient accessibility to man. The same factors and others would determine the availability of fish. Drumfish, for example, were recovered from the Allen site (Morse 1967), but excluding long distance transport their presence was due to freshwater mollusks in that vicinity. This fish usually will not take a hook and may have been caught with a spear or net. However, when the river systems reached maturity is unanswered.

Central to our discussion was the structure of Early Archaic information processing. We have mentioned that when there is dependence upon a small number of foods, monitoring the important resources is of critical importance. The presence of deer at a level of expedient kill undoubtedly was paramount. By speculating we can imagine this was accomplished by watching simultaneously for several signs in nature—scats, browse, lairs, and so forth.

Our model and archaeological evidence suggest that Early Archaic man was not an ecological dominant, and that his populations were subject to physical and biological laws. Regulating these ecosystems was not a particularly difficult matter. Cultural rules of infanticide and exogamy may have helped to regulate numbers, while shamanistic practices related to hunting (analogous to those described by Moore [1957] for the Naskapi) could have increased kill rates by randomizing hunting patterns as well as reinforced other evidence that dictated when a group should move.

*Middle Archaic.* The plants and animals available to these Archaic populations probably were the same as today. Certainly the archaeobotanical plant evidence supports this (Asch, Ford, and Asch 1972). This is important because several archaeologists, most notably McMillan (1971) and Klippel (1971b), have argued that an altithermal had an effect on human food resources and settlement during this period. Our evidence from the Koster site and assessment of data from other sites leads to a conclusion that a climatic change may have affected annual yields of certain fruit and nut bearing trees but that basically the gallery forests along permanent streams and rivers where most sites are located could buffer this climatic episode, if it existed. The question is whether or not human food sources were diversified enough to counter variable production.

Again the plant evidence from Koster and the animals from Eva (Lewis and Lewis 1961) and other sites mentioned earlier indicates that the food base was expanding. Deer are still primary with all other animals secondary. Vegetable foods, especially nuts, are increasing with important consequences. Small seeds like sumpweed (*Iva annua*), knotweed, smartweed (*Polygonum* spp.), and lamb's quarters (*Chenopodium album*) were also gathered (Figure 5.3).

This system for human population is still subject to physical environmental stresses, since they were sustained by a restricted food base. However, if stresses occurred when several resources were plentiful their impact was dampened. Such a control was culturally regulated.

Flannery (1968) has argued for the role of scheduling in human resource procurement strategies. Evidence from the Middle Archaic suggests the beginning of a culturally defined pattern based on information capable of predicting future levels of availability that continued into historic times. Nuts were collected in the fall along with small seeds and some fruits. Fall and winter hunting of deer, raccoon, turkey, and squirrel followed. Spring witnessed the killing of migratory fowl and perhaps the collecting of young greens, from the same small seeded plants which would yield a fall harvest. Summer was a time for fish, turtles, mussels, and infrequent hunting of game. Water fowl returned from their northern nesting areas in the fall, and once again they became a seasonal food source.

These foods still demand a seasonal round with the periodic reoccupation of certain sites a frequent event. Even with a series of new biological feedback loops, deer remain important. However, the size of the territory exploited may have been reduced as a consequence of the local availability in great numbers of several vegetable foods. Two

172

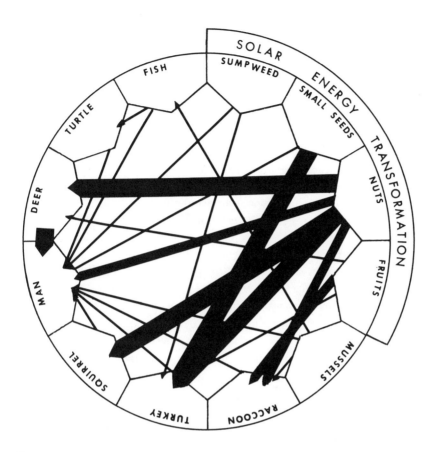

Figure 5.3 Middle Archaic anthropocentric food web. See Figure 5.2 for scale and explanation.

examples from the plant food base illustrate the potential basis for rearranging seasonal movements. Hickory masts from a single species are not locally available two consecutive years. After utilizing an area one year another will become the source the next. Despite being only several miles away, the exploitation territory for nuts must include these alternative nut tree groves. While these nut trees are part of the mature forest, useful seed plants are colonizers of disturbed habitats. These pioneer annuals grow in bare soil as multiversant species giving diversity to the developed ecosystem. Prodigious producers of seed, they may only yield for several years before their insect predators and floral competitors quickly eliminate them unless disturbance is renewed. In this case succession must be set back for man to continue to benefit from this resource.

The scheduled utilization of locally abundant resources may have become a selective mechanism for changing the Middle Archaic "population policy." The collecting of nuts, seeds, and mussels may have marked an important change in societal division of labor. If men continued to hunt, women may have become the collectors of these additional resources. As frequency of movements declined, children who could assist women in collecting and preparing food, were no longer a liability. I do not know if this is the proper cause-and-effect sequence, but a slight population increase is becoming evident during this period that may *not* relate to the presence of more food but rather reflect a change in the cultural practice of population regulation for processing alternative foods.

Cultural changes were not particularly rapid during the Middle Archaic, but those that did occur should not be automatically attributed to the natural environment. Granted, the human food web was not fully mature and heavy dependence upon deer was still a liability under unfavorable circumstances. Nonetheless, selective pressure emanating from relations between human groups now should be considered as potential sources of change.

*Late Archaic.* Figures 5.1 and 5.4 reveal an intensification of resources used in the Middle Archaic with several new, though seemingly insignificant, additions to this prepottery horizon. The introductions are cultivated squash (*Cucurbita pepo*), sunflower (*Helianthus annuus*) and sumpweed (*Iva annua* var. *macrocarpa*). The squash is an introduced tropical cultigen, while sunflower and sumpweed were domesticated in the Middle West.

Nuts increase in importance to human populations as do the small seeds with interesting implications. Hickory and walnuts are the best single vegetable source of protein and calories in the native plant environment; most other plant foods require combinations in order to complement deficient amino acid structures. These nut trees do have the disadvantage of not providing the same annual yield which requires access to a relatively large procurement territory. But if even slight population increases and budding established smaller territories and reduced accessibility to alternative sources, then small seeds were a logical alternative. They were easier to process though more were required to yield an equal amount of calories, and combinations were needed to provide an adequate vegetable protein. However, sustained yields of these seeds were possible with continuous disruption of succession. As Struever (1968) has argued, this is what the highly reliable annual flooding of major

Figure 5.4 Late Archaic anthropocentric food web. See Figure 5.2 for scale and explanation.

midwestern rivers did to the floodplain. Increased dependence on volunteer annuals may have led to their domestication.

If disturbance became the watchword of territorial constriction, then man solved the problem through domestication. Sunflowers produce an allotoxin that reduces the sunflower's viability and germination as it accumulates in the soil (Wilson and Rice 1968). Grown in unchurned soil sunflowers soon eliminate themselves. Late Archaic man was depending upon their achenes. In areas where soil disturbance was not regular, either man had to create it or lose an item in his food base. The deliberate intervention in the life cycle of the sunflower and part of the ecosystem led to domestication. Although the same biochemical phenomenon is not common to other edible seed plants of importance to Archaic people, annual availability was. Again, when nature failed, man may have guaranteed a habitat for these plants. In biological terms within the ecosystem energy moves from less mature to more mature systems. Annual seeds are the product of an immature part of a patchy ecosystem used to sustain human populations with their greater systemic complexity. This is not to say that man was an ecological dominant.

The effect of horticulture is difficult to assess but data from Koster (Asch, Ford, and Asch 1972), Newt Kash Hollow (Jones 1936), and Salts Cave (Yarnell 1969) support the idea that it provided harvestable commodities that helped to *stabilize* other fluctuations in the human ecosystem. There is no evidence for extensive land clearance or for storage of the cultivated plants. They probably were eaten in season. Cultivation might be viewed as a regulatory device that reduced potential friction over resources between neighboring human populations and that prevented the human population from overexploiting other populations. Its full significance—large, sustained yields—was not realized for several millennia!

Changes in the Late Archaic ecosystem probably were not caused by climate. By this time the human ecosystem was mature and had a complicated maze of alternative energy gates, including storage facilities, that could dampen all but the most disastrous environmental stresses. At the same time, though, long distance trade increased markedly over previous periods. This contact with other populations and the demand for exotic decorative and ceremonial items from distant sources may have contributed to a redeployment of resources and allocation of time. Intertribal trade may also have served to regulate the distribution of people between groups. In the regional ecosystem with the many human populations we are discussing, trade, cultivation, and probably ritual activities helped to sustain individual human population, and at the same time maintained the system-serving role of the human populations. It appears then that from the Late Archaic onward the sources of ecosystemic change in the Midwest originated outside the physical environment, regardless of recent modifications in climatic schemes.

*Early Woodland.* This period is another stage along the evolutionary sequence. Pottery is a new technological item that may have changed techniques of food preparation, but if quantities of fire-cracked rock, a by-product of hot stone boiling, is any indication, these vessels were merely a more durable material replacement for the perishable cooking utensils used in earlier periods. Corn is another new food item that did not dramatically alter the food web (Figure 5.1).

The archaeology of this period produces an increase in evidence of ceremonialism. Mounds covering persons interred with exotic grave goods are particularly notable. Domestic structures were larger and were used for seasonal if not year round inhabitation. Such a duration of occupation has potentially dire consequences for an ecosystem.

Since this settlement change does not appear to change the economic base of the human populations, information and regulatory processing became increasingly complex. The population had to "read" a number of different "signs in nature" to determine when to plant, which resources were available, in what quantity, and when. Scheduling strategies varied from year to year and between areas within the same year depending upon their interpretations. Ritual activity undoubtedly was linked to these interpretations. Derived from the shaman's rites of the Archaic, these may have become calendrical rites announcing a new seasonal activity or propitiating a beneficial spirit with offering of food to be shared by all. Some perhaps regulated exchange or the single or corporate movement of group members. The exploration of these and other ideas is critical for understanding the dynamics of Early Woodland life.

*Middle Woodland.* Hopewell, a term which attracts fanfare and curiosity, receives more attention than all other Woodland periods; yet many fundamental questions remain unanswered.

Site number and size increase over earlier periods, but Asch (1973) has studied the problem of Middle Woodland population size and does not think that it exceeded one person per square mile. If this is so, natural production in most river systems can sustain this number without supplementary horticulture. The dietary pattern (Figure 5.1) constructed with evidence from the Twin Mounds site near Cincinnati, Ohio (Ford, unpublished analysis), the Macoupin (Ford, unpublished analysis), Apple Creek (Parmalee, Paloumpis, and Wilson 1972), and Scovill sites (Munson, Parmalee, and Yarnell 1971) in the Illinois River Valley, to mention a few, indicate that the familiar consumption patterns of deer, raccoon, fish/nuts, and small seeds continued. In other words even with population expansion the energy base is not changing, while the information system is undergoing increasing elaboration.

Trade and burial ceremonialism receive further amplification within the context of an egalitarian society. The mounds could easily be the tumuli of ancestors formally endowed with "expensive" objects at

177

intervals by the decendants in thanks for usufruct rights to land and resources. These rituals could have served to disperse people according to sociological descent and prevent environmental degradation.

*Late Woodland.* This period culminates one evolutionary line in the mid-continental area of the United States (Figures 5.1 and 5.5). Natural, high-yielding resources were intensively exploited by more people occupying larger sites. The entire range of nut trees—walnut, butternut, hickory, oak, and hazel—were used. Hazel nuts, which increased in use in Middle Woodland times, continued into this period at an even higher level of exploitation. All the small seed plants were intensively collected in the late summer and fall, and evidence exists for increased consumption of fruits (although not necessarily on a per capita basis). This is a period of maximum redundancy within the food-chain, and even though evidence is lacking, I suspect that edible bulbs, roots, and greens as well had an important place in this system. Horticulture possibly witnessed an increase before A.D. 1000 but current evidence is noncommital. Sites similar to those in the Kaskaskia River Valley (Ford 1972a) show very little evidence of domesticated plants. Again, with sunflowers, sumpweed, squash, and corn being raised, their role, nonetheless, was supportive and a form of security. It is naturally occurring plant products that fill the early Late Woodland storage pits at Apple Creek and in the Kaskaskia area.

The Late Woodland cultures do reveal several technological and social changes of significance. The newly introduced bow-and-arrow replace the atlatl and become the major instruments for hunting and warfare. Hunting efficiency may have increased as a result of this change. Certainly social relations were affected, but probably for other reasons. Skeletons show arrow wounds as a cause of death, and burials are found in composite ossuaries indicative of increasing community solidarity. Warfare is yet another regulatory mechanism that can function to benefit the ecosystem by limiting the size of human populations residing in a particular area and thereby reducing pressure on plant and animal populations.

From the Early Archaic into the Late Woodland human populations were part of natural ecosystems. As man's numbers grew, social relations changed, and food exploiting territories were adjusted. The species of plants and animals that supported his needs increased in absolute number and were redeployed quantitatively relative to each other. There is no acceptable evidence that fire was used as a tool for altering the landscape or that any large-scale land clearance was undertaken. Culture regulated

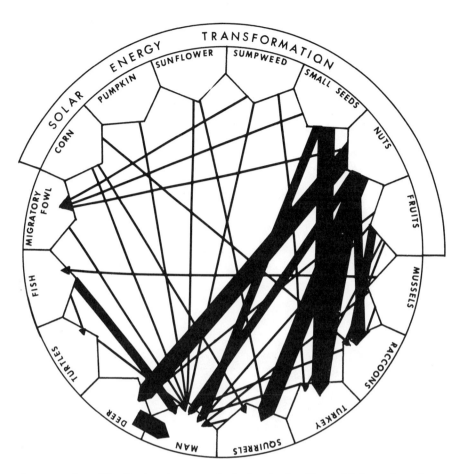

Figure 5.5 Late Woodland anthropocentric food web. See Figure 5.2 for scale and explanation.

human populations to the advantage of the natural ecosystem. Although cultures changed, the impact of climate as a source of change was stymied by an intertwined ecosystem with many optional energy gates before the bow-and-arrow, pottery, or horticulture were present. Many enticing cultural changes are manifested in exotic material remains attributed to past ritual and social activity, and hint at social interaction and the development or failure of information systems and controls as their raison d'être. Then, for still obscure but probably similar evolutionary reasons, in the environs of the lower Mississippi Valley a new culture evolved that changed man's role from a system-serving to a self-serving population.

*Mississippian.* The Mississippian ecosystem depended upon corn horticulture (Figures 5.1 and 5.6). The landscape became simplified once again as it had been following the melting of the glaciers. This time,

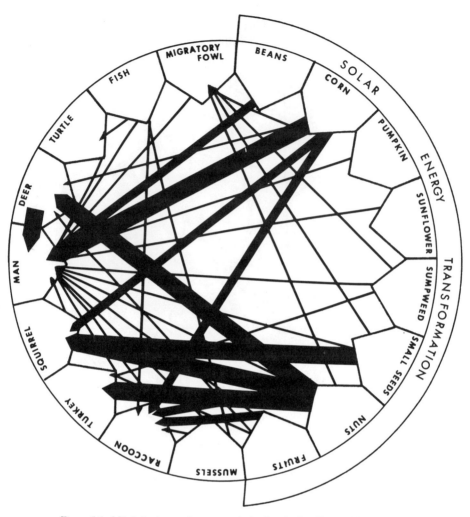

Figure 5.6 Mississippian anthropocentric food web. See Figure 5.2 for scale and explanation.

however, there is an important difference: a large human population is deliberately maintaining a simplified ecosystem for its own benefit.

Horticulturalists practicing large-scale land clearance, as Mississippian populations were, are ecological dominants. Their rules and actions determine which plants and animals will be present and which should be removed. Their goal is an immature system with a high productivity that can be increased if necessary. The result is very high yields in a restricted area, but there is a chance for climatic events once again to destabilize the system. Unlike the natural ecosystem containing Late Woodland populations in which natural yield could not be increased but climatic fluctuation could be buffered, the Mississippian anthropocentric eco-system can increase its yield but cannot control directly climatically induced disasters.

The solutions to this dilemma are limited. One is to continue to rely on a series of wild foods when crops are insufficient. Hunting and gathering varied in importance according to horticultural yields. Once the land is cleared, these natural resources may drop and be less reliable for an even larger population than they ever were for Woodland people. Only a few families could depend upon this option and not for a long period of time. The addition of common beans to the horticultural complex gave the Mississippians a vegetable protein and calorie source in a very restricted area when compared to the edible yield for humans in natural ecosystems.

Another is in the realm of social structure and ritual. Egalitarian societies have various impersonal means of extracting surpluses from households and redistributing them to those in need. Kinship rights, trade, and ritual are all used at some time. However, these may be inadequate for sustaining large populations living in a large area. If these are inegalitarian societies, they can use the political-ritual technique of redistribution by a central authority. Ritual continues to play a corrective role both in time dependent and variable dependent ways, but informa-tion processing permits accommodating individuals' needs that can go unaided in egalitarian societies.

Mississippian societies were undoubtedly inegalitarian and apparently conform to varieties within Service's (1962) chiefdom stages of social organization. In reducing the ecosystem to an immature stage they required an elaborate monitoring system to know the conditions of the growing crops. As this continued crop losses could be handled through rituals or through direct redistribution from a chief's storehouses. Egalitarian societies lack a common reference value and quick means of adjudicating discrepancies between two farmers' yields. Not so with bureaucratic systems. Here there is a reference value and farmers' crops can be compared with it. Disparities can be corrected rapidly and efficiency but at a cost. As the information and control hierarchies grow, so does the need to support them through taxes or donation ostensibly for gods or their earthly representatives. Mississippian populations wedded to the land could not move to new resources as their ancestors had; instead, when faced with crop failures the food had to be moved to them. It is not surprising that the Mississippian period is characterized by "cults" which must have evolved in several places and spread as part of the ritual means for maintaining a viable human population faced with uncontrollable crop losses through ceremonial redistribution of harvests.

Contact between Mississippian and Late Woodland societies posed an interesting ecological conflict. Late Woodland populations were still special purpose systems in a natural ecosystem. They probably had some rituals to assist the growing corn and other crops and even some to thank the spirits, but dependence upon nature's bounty left them unable to increase total energy without changing the system. Mississippian systems could easily conquer Late Woodland societies unable to regulate this unexpected stress in their social environment. To resist and to protect their populations, Late Woodland populations must have undergone some very rapid gyrations depending upon the nature of their contact. If it was steady and intense, they could resist by increasing their reliance on corn, thereby mimicking Mississippian societies, and following Romer's Rule to evolution. If the contact was periodic, they undoubtedly formed new sodalities designed to handle the threat and thereby maintain an egalitarian organization and the ecosystem. If they were conquered, they could have been amalgamated into the Mississippian chiefdom, had their system simplified, stripped of local controls, and used to support the larger system.

*Historic.* In historic times both the Mississippian and remaining Late Woodland populations underwent devolution. Contact with still another kind of system, European economic expansion, produced profound changes. The resulting indigenous ecosystems, however, were new forms of lower organization unlike any preceding prehistoric ecosystem examined in this paper.

Diseases accidently introduced by early explorers virtually decimated the susceptible human populations. Unable to muster the personnel required to maintain a chiefdom or to support materially its organization, Mississippian communities became egalitarian, anthropocentric ecosystems with a few social trappings revealing previous stratification. Late Woodland societies also suffered population losses though of a lower magnitude.

Direct contact brought both groups into the economic sphere of the foreigners. Demands for hides and furs led to unregulated hunting and trapping patterns. Supply and demand generated by an outside market was uncontrolled by native hunters. Diminution of animals led to conflict over trade routes and economic favors. Local demands for trade goods, steel traps, guns, and ammunition reoriented the focus of subsistence activities. It is possible that with men engaged in hunting for an external market and away trading, some Late Woodland populations may have increased their reliance on horticulture hoping to stabilize their subsistence base while actually rendering their lives more vulnerable to outside disturbances.

With trade relations providing the selective pressures, Mississippian societies discarded many of their local regulatory prohibitions toward other populations within their ecosystem, became simplified, dependent, and exploited by European trade empires. They never regained their former independence; the environment they degraded never recovered.

This analysis has proceeded from three basic assumptions: nature is intelligible to analysis; systems exist in nature; and the universe is a suprasystem composed of less inclusive but more coherent systems. The laws of the more inclusive systems apply to the lower levels, such as ecosystems. Consequently, models with increasing degrees of specificity can be built from a general explanatory foundation.

Three stages of theoretical and analytical analysis have been presented in an attempt to develop an ecological explanation. The first and most general explained the characteristics of a living system. The second was more specific and related these characteristics to the evolution of ecosystems. The third applied archaeological observations in the midcontinental area of the United States to the evolutionary model. In the final stage a model is generated consisting of a series of testable and partially tested hypotheses whose further validity can be pursued with more specific empirical evidence. Following this logical procedure, explanations of greater generality can account for more phenomena than do more disciplinary bound interpretations.

By giving variables biological meaning we are able to examine processes common to all living systems, and use laws appropriate to these systems. Anthropology has produced few, if any, lawlike statements; but the physical and biological sciences have. If we make our problem operational in terms appropriate to analysis of a more general theory such as synthetic evolutionary ecology, we can employ these principles and free ourselves from induction and tautology. The next step is to quantify the components we have presented and to pursue further deductive explanation.

We have discussed unregulated environmental stresses as the source of new cultural changes but these disturbances by themselves do not dictate the form of a system. This is based upon the previous organization and the structural position of the human population in a more inclusive system. The examples from the Midwest suggest that man was not an ecological dominant until about a thousand years ago and that cultural institutions viewed from an ecosystemic perspective helped to regulate relations between species. Moreover, we argued that the role of the physical environment as a cause of systemic change was mitigated by redundancy until Mississippian times when human populations, opting for an energy yield amenable to expansion, subjected their system to environmental vagaries. At the same time it was the expansion of agriculture that enabled this change in man/land relations; yet cultivation had proceeded for several thousand years as a supplement to an already complex foodweb. Its full potential was not realized until selective pressures favored its preference. The inception of a horticulturally based ecosystem with man as the dominant species had further implications for increased and economical information processing, regulatory mechanisms, and competition between ecosystems of two, and eventually three, incompatible organizations. The same ecological processes also produce political states and civilizations. Archaeologists finally have the methodology and theory to improve vastly our knowledge of human evolution.

## ACKNOWLEDGMENTS

I am indebted to the many midwestern archaeologists whose persistent inquiry into ecological questions aroused my curiosity and who will provide answers to many of the questions this chapter raises. I am particularly grateful to James B. Griffin for stimulating my ecological interests and for supporting my initial ideas with a research assistantship. Wenner-Gren Foundation grant No. 1433, on paleo-climates in North America financed that work and its assistance is deeply appreciated. This chapter has also benefited immensely from the helpful criticims of Roy A. Rappaport, Kent V. Flannery, and Karen C. Ford. Naturally, its deficiencies are my responsibility. George W. Stuber prepared the illustrations.

*6*

# Population Aggregation
# and Systemic Change:
# Examples from the American Southwest

## MICHAEL A. GLASSOW

*Department of Anthropology*
*University of California*
*Santa Barbara*

## STATEMENT OF THE PROBLEM

An archaeologist's task of determining the nature of extinct cultural systems and explaining the differences and similarities between them is frustrated by the fact that his observations are not of living cultural systems but instead of the material remains of extinct ones. These material remains exist in archaeological sites as spatial arrangements of objects having varying formal properties. In essence, the archaeologist is faced with the formidable task of translating information derived from these static patterns into information about cultural systems, the real topic of his interest as an anthropologist. This means that the archaeologist must devote a considerable portion of his effort to making these translations through essentially the same methods of hypothesis-testing that he uses in explaining differences and similarities in cultural systems.

From a systems perspective, the kinds of observations that the archaeologist would wish to make are those which reflect not only the nature of sociocultural components and their positions in matter-energy (or information) flow networks but also the kinds of matter and energy processed by the components. Based on this perspective, it would seem possible to specify at least some of the classes of observations that will yield particular kinds of information about these systemic features. For instance, the *shape* of a component would often reflect the *kind* of matter or energy processed through it, and the *size* of a particular component would generally reflect the processing *rate*. But for all the effort devoted to presenting such measurements of the formal properties of objects, only initial attempts have been made to relate them to the characteristics of cultural systems.

The other major category of observations, having to do with the patterns of spatial distributions of objects, has recently drawn nearly comparable interest among archaeologists primarily in the context of the study of settlement patterns (Chang 1958) and also, even more recently, in intracommunity studies (Hill 1966; and an earlier, somewhat isolated case, Clark 1954). The general assumption underlying this interest in spatial distributions is that relative proximity of objects reflects their articulation in matter-energy flow networks. It is the implications of this assumption that will be the topic of this chapter.

It is to be expected that patterns of spacing reflect patterns of matter-energy flow since cultural systems, like other living systems, attempt to economize matter-energy expenditures in their operations, and one of the ways of accomplishing this is to reduce the distance over which it must travel from one component to another. We would expect, therefore, that the components of cultural systems or subsystems will tend to "clump" or cluster, forming a unit that is separated by unoccupied space from parallel types of systems. The spacing between these clustered components would form a particular pattern, and the pattern should reflect the nature of the relationships between the components. In addition, what are clusters of components with distinctive distributional patterns on one level of organization hierarchy may form units on a higher level. In fact, because a cultural system would always have a series of hierarchical levels of organization, we would expect that each level would have a distinctive distributional pattern.

This chapter will focus on the patterning of aggregation of one particular type of cultural component: the residence unit of a nuclear or extended family. Being composed of a set of individuals, this component is, of course, not a minimal unit. Nevertheless, it represents, in a rough sense, the smallest number of individuals that cohabit with each other in social systems throughout the world. This aggregate of individuals, composed of at least a woman and her children and often her husband, appears to be largely concerned with the reproduction and nurture of offspring as well as with basic activities of subsistence (Murdock 1949:6 passim). The archaeologist is often able to identify this social unit by the fact that it almost invariably occupies some sort of shelter which frequently leaves distinctive remains after abandonment. In fact, it is this population unit which is most often the basic unit of the archaeological study of settlement patterns (Chang 1958; Beardsley et al. 1956).

The reader may notice that the following list of determinants of population aggregation is similar to the set of causes of aggregation among plants and animals first proposed by W. C. Allee (1931). Allee's principle, that a population with given intrinsic characteristics will have an optimum pattern of aggregation in a given environment, applies equally well to human populations. With human populations, however, we naturally have to consider cultural variability in determining optimum patterns of aggregation.

## CLASSES OF INTRACULTURAL (INTRINSIC) DETERMINANTS OF POPULATION AGGREGATION

*Characteristics of the economic goods which flow between population units:* If the frequency or rate of movement of certain economic goods such as foods, fuels, raw materials, and so forth, is relatively high, the distance between the components will be relatively short. Relatively large volumes and unit sizes of products, as well as relatively high degrees of perishability, will also tend to minimize the distance over which such economic goods would travel.

*Characteristics of activities which bring population units together:* If a number of population units must come together relatively frequently to carry out a cooperative activity such as the manufacture or maintenance of a facility, the participation in warfare (or defense), or the shift of membership to status positions of their social structure, then they will tend to minimize the distance over which they must travel to congregate. Also important, if the activity must be carried out relatively quickly in order to be effective, the participating population units will tend to be aggregated.

*Characteristics of communication between population units:* The type, frequency, and necessity of communication between population units may be more important in determining their aggregation than archaeologists and ethnologists have traditionally thought. This class of determinants is closely related to the first two classes, but in spite of this concomitance it nevertheless includes observationally different phenomena. Given that a particular type of communication between population units is necessary for their successful adaptation, the distance between them will tend to be relatively short if the frequency of communication or the quantity of information passed between the population units is relatively high. Moreover, the distance limits of a communication medium may impose relative degrees of aggregation. For instance, if verbal communication exists only in the medium of the spoken voice, distance between the participating population units must be relatively short. Finally, distance between population units will be relatively short if information must pass between them relatively quickly.

*Characteristics of stationary facilities:* It may be economical to make facilities large enough to serve more than one population unit or to make them in a contiguous series for the purpose of minimizing losses of economic goods processed through them. Houses and storage rooms, for instance, might be joined together to minimize construction costs or to maximize heat retention. In the case of contiguous houses, the population units occupying them would obviously be aggregated. If access to other kinds of communal facilities not used to shelter population units is relatively frequent, or if the volumes or rates of goods processed through facilities are relatively high, the distance from these of the population units using them will be relatively short.

*Demographic characteristics of populations:* A population of households obviously must be close enough to each other (in terms of available modes of transportation) so that mating arrangements may be made. However, this determinant would come into effect to produce aggregation only where population density is extremely low, such as among populations practicing Paleolithic or Paleo-Indian adaptations.

## ENVIRONMENTAL (EXTRINSIC) DETERMINANTS OF POPULATION AGGREGATION

A series of population units will tend to locate as close as practicable to those resources which require the greatest amounts of energy expenditure to exploit or transport. So to the extent that a series of population units obtain such resources from the same locality, they would tend to be aggregated near it. Generally, the previously mentioned characteristics of economic goods that flow between population units would be relevant to evaluating which environmental resources would tend to produce population aggregation if they were localized. The difference is that the goods are moving from their locations in nature to cultural components, rather than from one cultural component to another.

This admittedly cursory survey of the variables that would tend to produce aggregations of such population units as households helps to clarify an important point: a series of households may be forming a spatial aggregate—existing more closely to each other than to others—for any of a variety of different reasons. The degree of aggregation, measured on some sort of linear scale, does not by itself tell the archaeologist much about the organizational features of a cultural system. But if the archaeologist has ascertained that aggregation does in fact exist, he would have reason to look for the operation of any of the above organizational character-istics which determine aggregation. Most likely, all or nearly all of the determinants would be found to contribute in different ways to produce a particular pattern of household aggregation. In addition, certain of the determinants will be masked or superseded by others. To put it another way, not all the organizational properties of a cultural system which *could* be manifested in spatial patterns of aggregation will be so. On the other hand, the determinants may be operating against each other to produce only weak aggregation. This is particularly possible in cases where the distribution of environmental resources promotes dispersion while socio-economic determinants promote aggregation. In such cases, the observed distributional patterns would best be explained by using a model which expresses the optimum distribution expected when total costs of moving matter-energy are lowest (a model based on game theory, for instance).

## QUANTITATIVE EVALUATION OF DEGREE OF AGGREGATION

The identification of aggregations of households is quite an easy task when considering such obvious aggregates as some of the well-known archaeological sites in the American Southwest—for instance, Pueblo Bonito in Chaco Canyon or Cliff Palace at Mesa Verde. Each of these is composed of a series of contiguous dwellings with a very distinct community boundary. In fact, such sites probably represent hierarchical levels of aggregation beyond simple household aggregates. But the problem of identifying aggregates becomes more acute where households are distributed over the area of a region as individual sites, as in parts of the American Southwest around the time of Christ. For this reason considerable attention is devoted here to various quantitative measures of aggregation. Since anthropologists have devoted so little attention to such measures, I have turned to the work done by geographers. Even in this work, however, we do not have all the quantitative measures we would need, so I am forced to explore some supplementary techniques.

The first type of measurement is based on relative densities of loci (sites or households, in respect to our interests) within a series of partitions of the two-dimensional space in which we are interested. A grid pattern, for instance, may be superimposed over the area of interest and a tabulation may be made of the number of loci per grid unit. The proportional frequency distribution of loci may be compared to a Poisson distribution having a mean equal to the mean number of loci per grid. The Poisson distribution would represent the expected distribution if the loci were randomly distributed. Given that the variance of the Poisson distribution is always equal to its mean, if the variance of the observed distribution of proportions is significantly greater than this mean-variance then the distributon of loci is tending toward aggregation. If the observed variance is smaller, then the distribution of loci is tending toward regularity. Significance, of course, depends on the quantity of grids included in the analysis as well as the degree of sensitivity required by a particular research design. It may be determined by a goodness of fit test.

O. D. Duncan describes two other measures of spatial patterning, based on density figures which may be computed from areas of unequal size, instead of grids (1957:28–32). The two indices are concerned with differentiating between equally spaced or regular and aggregated or "concentrated" distributions of loci. They do not, however, differentiate between either of these two extremes in patterning and random patterns.

Any of these measures based on density information should be used with some caution. In the first place, the size of the grid units (or other types of area partitions) may influence the results by either over-emphasizing or underemphasizing the presence of aggregations (Duncan 1957:31–32). Moreover, if the grid dimensions transect an aggregate in either or both of its dimensions its presence will be greatly obscured. If one is willing to put forth the effort, however, both of these shortcomings can largely be eliminated. This is done by combining the results of several different grid sizes and several randomized placements of the grid frames, randomizing both the orientation of the grid dimensions and the positioning of grid corners.

The shortcomings of using measurements of grid densities of loci are not present in another approach to the problem which considers, instead, the relative spacing of loci in relation to each other. This technique, known as "nearest neighbor analysis," was originally developed in plant ecology to explicate distributional patterns in stands of plants. Since this work by Clark and Evans (1954), the geographers concerned with locational analysis have been applying it to human settlement patterns (Duncan 1957:32–34; Haggett 1965:231–33). Archaeologists are just now beginning to see the potential of this technique in discovering and explicating distributional patterns (Stickel 1968). The technique uses as basic data the direct linear distance from each locus to its closest neighboring locus. The statistical average in a distribution of these nearest neighbor distances, given the overall density of the loci in the total area under consideration, will have certain relationships with the average distance expected if the loci were randomly distributed, depending on whether the loci are, in fact, randomly distributed, uniformly distributed (equidistant spacing or "hexagonal distribution"), or clumped. This relationship between observed and expected means is given as an **R**-statistic (Clark and Evans 1954; Duncan 1957:33).

The latter result could tell us that a distribution of habitations does in fact have nonrandom aggregations, but, again, we have not identified exactly where these aggregations are. Moreover, it would be best to look at a graphic distribution of the nearest neighbor distances where the **R**-statistic indicates either a random or equidistant distribution. There could very well be some irregularities on the lower end of the distribution reflecting some aggregates obscured by the rest of the area's distribution pattern. Nevertheless, nearest neighbor analysis relieves the vagaries of the grid density technique and may, in the long run, be easier to compute.

Neither of these two approaches, as mentioned, tells us anything about aggregations beyond their existence. Each could be modified, however, to give us the additional information concerning membership, location, size, and density of each extant aggregate of the distribution. In the grid density approach, we might establish a pattern of equidistant reference points over the area of concern, giving each of the points an identification number. These points would be dispersed at distances no greater than the length of the grid sides of the pattern we plan to use for determining densities. As the grid pattern is successively superimposed over the area in different orientations, the grid densities *and* the identification numbers of the stationary reference points which appear in the grids are recorded. Statistical tests would then be run to identify which grids of each superimposition contained nonrandomly high densities of loci, given the specified level of significance. The same reference point numbers should occur in a significantly high proportion of these grids if an aggregation exists. Additional tests could be devised to determine contiguity of reference points associated with high grid unit densities where the aggregate covers a multi–grid-sized area. The density of loci in the aggregate could be obtained by averaging all the grid unit densities associated with the identifying set of reference points. So, in the end, we would have specified the location, size, and density of aggregates in a distribution of loci. The only difficulty remaining is that we would not have an accurate idea of the boundaries of the aggregates.

In expanding nearest neighbor analysis for our purposes we would begin by assigning an identification number to each locus in the area of interest. Then the distances to the nearest *and* the next-nearest neighbors would be measured. Based on the R-statistic computed from only the nearest neighbor measurements, those loci linked by nearest or next-near-est neighbor lines of significantly short lengths would be listed according to their reference numbers. Loci forming aggregates in the distribution would be reflected as a bounded series of overlapping identification number linkages. The next-nearest neighbor measurements are added, incidentally, to compensate for situations of weak aggregation or where there is a comparatively high number of "reflexive pairings" of loci—that is, where nearest neighbors are reciprocal between pairs of loci. Using additional gradings of nearness may be required in other situations where aggregates have internal structures. As with the previous technique, this form of nearest neighbor analysis gives us a means of determining the location, size, and, with a computation of average nearest neighbor distances, density of an aggregation of loci. What is more, the technique specifies exactly which loci are members of particular aggregates, a feat the other techniques would not necessarily accomplish.

As important as the identification of aggregates is to the objective of isolating the components of extinct cultural systems, interest must eventually advance toward explicating the structural relationships be-tween different kinds of components in networks of matter-energy flow.

In a study of settlement pattern, for instance, we would wish not only to identify the components of a settlement system but also to determine the pattern of flow of people, goods, services, and economic goods between the members of a community or between the communities which make up the system. This objective may be approached by observing the spatial relationships between different classes of loci, or between certain classes of loci and one- or two-dimensional phenomena. This type of search is based on the assumption previously mentioned: the distance between a series of different cultural components, or between cultural components and environmental features, tends to be minimized to the extent that total costs in the transfer of matter-energy between them is minimized. In this context, different classes of loci, lines, or areas would represent different classes of components in a cultural system or an ecosystem. The addition to the spatial analysis of this new dimension, or actually series of new dimensions, would obviously increase its complexity, and the different approaches to analysis could potentially be many. Nevertheless, these approaches could be classified into the same two major categories used in measurement of the degree of aggregation of a set of undifferentiated loci.

In the grid density approach a grid frame could be superimposed over a map of the region in question, and the frequencies of loci, lengths of lines, or sizes of areas for each of the classes in each grid would be computed. A regression-correlation analysis might then be performed to determine whether certain classes tend to covary with one another in geographic space. The distance measurement approach would involve direct distance measurements analogous to nearest neighbor measurements, and the analysis would consider whether these distances are nearer than would be expected if the distributions of each class were independent of each other. The statistical test used to determine the degree of spatial covariation of the classes with one another would depend upon the particular analytical problem. One particular problem of multivariate locational analysis, the measurement of the degree to which one class of loci tends to aggregate around members of another class of loci, will be given consideration later on. An excellent introduction to the techniques used by geographers in this type of locational analysis may be found in the text *Spatial Analysis*, edited by Berry and Marble (1964).

In concluding this section, I would like to point out that many descriptions of site distributional patterns do not require either the above-mentioned or other even more sophisticated statistical approaches.

Aggregations, for instance, may be so discrete and easily defined simply through visual observation that a quantitative definition is superfluous. Nevertheless, there are certainly many situations in which the patterns are not so obvious, and when we begin to compare different regions with respect to degree of aggregation or the degrees of spatial association between two or more patterns in the same region we are inevitably committed to the use of quantitative measures. Another point worth emphasizing is that statistical description of site distributions means nothing in itself and should never be undertaken without relating the descriptions to the explication of cultural systems or cultural change.

## DISCOVERING THE DETERMINANTS OF HOUSEHOLD AGGREGATION: AN EXAMPLE FROM NORTHEASTERN NEW MEXICO

My survey data from northeastern New Mexico may be used as an example of a problem of explaining patterns of household aggregation and the application of some simple quantitative techniques in seeking the determinants of the pattern. A series of sites dating around A.D. 1300, representing a Puebloan agricultural adaptation, have been located on the Ponil Creek near the town of Cimarron (see Map 6.1). This is a particularly interesting archaeological manifestation for our purposes as there is no evidence of the very obvious, bounded, "apartment-like" aggregates found elsewhere in the Southwest. The 800-year-plus sequence in the Cimarron District represents a series of adaptations beginning with an Early Basket Maker type (defined in the Cimarron District as the Vermejo Phase) and ending with an agricultural adaptation designated the Cimarron Phase (Glassow 1972). The site distribution of this phase is the topic of the following analysis. Throughout this sequence sites seem not to have been larger than about two households, reflected in both site area and, in many cases, visible portions of house foundations. Nevertheless, there is reason to suspect that some of these one- or two-house sites may have been grouped together into nonrandom clusters. Our first task, then, is to determine whether this is so. Following this, if nonrandom aggregates of sites are discovered, we will attempt to determine the extent to which these aggregates can be explained by the discontinuous distribution of arable land adjacent to these habitation aggregates on the one hand and socioeconomic interaction on the other.

Before proceeding with these aspects of the analysis, however, some

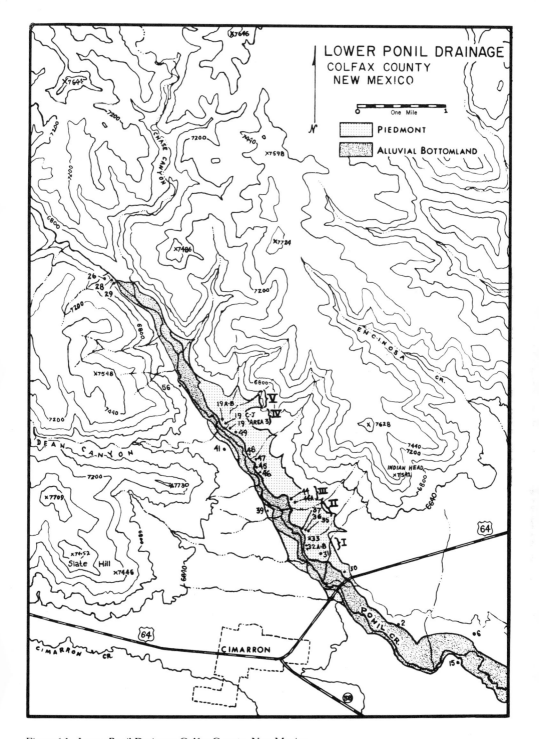

Figure 6.1   Lower Ponil Drainage. Colfax County, New Mexico.

consideration should be given to explaining why the sites of the Cimarron Phase are located in this portion of the Ponil drainage as opposed to other locations above or below. Actually, there are six other sites not shown on the accompanying map. One is located about a half-mile downstream from the area shown on the map; three are located near Ponil Camp about 11 miles upstream from Highway 64 on the Middle Ponil fork; and the other two, containing comparatively little occupational debris, are located on the North Ponil fork, also about 11 miles upstream from Highway 64. I will have some additional comments on these disparately located sites later on. The location of the main group of sites of the Cimarron Phase can be explained by reference to two variables: the location of firewood and a dependence on agriculture. The former variable operates to reduce the frequency of sites downstream where virtually no wooded land is present. The Cimarron Phase sites extend only about 2 miles out onto the High Plains which begin very abruptly along a southwest-northeast-trending line close to the route of Highway 64. In fact, Puebloan sites of any time period have never been found much beyond these limits in any of the drainages north or south of the Ponil. (However, the Cimarron Creek to the south and the Vermejo Creek to the north have analogous distributions.) Possible exceptions not seen by me may exist considerably farther to the east near Springer, New Mexico, where extensive wooded areas do occur.

The second variable appears to be the location of plots of arable land large enough to support a population primarily dependent on agriculture for sustenance. As reflected in numbers of sites per phase, population density was considerably less in times antedating the Cimarron Phase. This situation probably allowed proportionately more dependence on wild plant resources which are much more abundant in the northerly portions of the Ponil drainage. With increasing population density, however, agriculture would begin to replace wild seed gathering to the extent that wild seeds could no longer provide enough food per capita population. As dependence on agriculture increased through time, proportionately more arable land would be needed per capita population, and since the northerly portions of the Ponil drainage are relatively narrow, the population would shift to locations downstream where the canyon is considerably broader (the portion covered in the map). The breadth of the Ponil Canyon, in other words, is taken to be a rough measure of the amount of arable land per unit of canyon length.

Turning now to the site distribution covered in the area of the map, our first task is to discover nonrandom aggregations of sites. The steps in my procedure for testing the hypothesis stated above are as follows:

(1) *Plotting the sites and measurement of their nearest neighbors.* The sites in this region were located by me in reconnaissances carried out in the summers of 1967 and 1968. These reconnaissances were undertaken on foot and all ground within the canyon was covered with the exception of the upper portions of the piedmont slopes, which were only spot-checked. Terrace edges and other well-drained prominences of ground were given special attention, but not to the exclusion of landforms less likely to contain sites. The pattern of site distribution is fairly obvious from the information given on the map. All are located on the edge of the first terrace above the alluvial bottomlands, and nearly all are on the northeastern side of the creek.

For purposes of the test, I will not consider the sites on the southwestern side of the creek. While the measurements of their nearest neighbors could easily be taken, most would involve measuring across the creek, and the breadth of this unoccupiable bottomland would potentially bias the sample to an unknown degree. As shall be seen, the choice of the site group on only one side of the stream will be adequate for the purposes of this example. These sites were plotted on a USGS air photograph twice enlarged (18" x 18"), and distances were measured in centimeters to the nearest millimeter. The several habitations designated **LP**-19 **C** through **J** form what would seem to be an obvious cluster, and the distances were too small to measure accurately on the photograph. Consequently I arbitrarily assigned their nearest neighbor distances (mostly less than 100 feet) the value of 0.05 cm., which would not be far from the real distances and would not greatly affect the results. These distances are given in Table 6.1.

(2) The *Spatial Analysis.* The nearest neighbor statistic represents the difference between the *actual* mean distance between sites and their nearest neighbors and the mean distance *expected* if the population of sites were randomly distributed. The expected mean is calculated from the site density using a formula developed by Clark and Evans (1954), and the nearest neighbor statistic is computed by dividing the actual mean by the expected mean.

Determining the boundaries of the area in which sites occur, which is necessary for computing the site density, posed some major problems. As a general rule the boundaries should be placed so as to enclose all sites but very little beyond this. This is very important because if the area

# TABLE 6.1
## DISTANCES FROM PONIL CANYON SITES TO NEAREST, NEXT-NEAREST, AND THIRD-NEAREST NEIGHBORS

| Site | Nearest Neighbor | Distance | Next-nearest Neighbor | Distance | Third-nearest Neighbor | Distance |
|---|---|---|---|---|---|---|
| LP-6 | 2 | 6.8 cm | 30 | 13.9 cm | 31 | 17.0 cm |
| 2 | 6 | 6.8 cm | 30 | 7.1 cm | 31 | 10.2 cm |
| 30 | 31 | 3.1 cm | 32A | 3.9 cm | 32B | 4.0 cm |
| 31 | 32A | 0.9 cm | 32B | 1.0 cm | 33 | 2.1 cm |
| 32A | 32B | 0.1 cm* | 31 | 0.9 cm | 33 | 1.2 cm |
| 32B | 32A | 0.1 cm* | 31 | 1.0 cm | 33 | 1.1 cm |
| 33 | 35 | 1.0 cm | 32B | 1.1 cm | 32A | 1.2 cm |
| 35 | 36 | 0.3 cm* | 37 | 0.7 cm | 33 | 1.0 cm |
| 36 | 35 | 0.3 cm* | 37 | 0.4 cm* | 33 | 1.3 cm |
| 37 | 36 | 0.4 cm* | 35 | 0.7 cm | 44A | 1.4 cm |
| 44A | 44 | 0.3 cm* | 37 | 1.4 cm | 36 | 1.8 cm |
| 44 | 44A | 0.3 cm* | 37 | 1.7 cm | 36 | 2.1 cm |
| 46 | 45 | 0.7 cm | 47 | 1.3 cm | 48 | 2.5 cm |
| 45 | 46 | 0.7 cm | 47 | 0.8 cm | 48 | 2.0 cm |
| 47 | 45 | 0.8 cm | 48 | 1.2 cm | 46 | 1.3 cm |
| 48 | 47 | 1.3 cm | 45 | 2.1 cm | 49 | 2.2 cm |
| 49 | 19, Area 3 | 0.7 cm | 19J | 1.2 cm | 19I | ca. 1.25 cm |
| 19, Area 3 | 19J | 0.4 cm* | 19I | 0.4 cm* | 19H | ca. 0.45 cm |
| 19J | 19I | ca. 0.05 cm* | 19H | ca. 0.1 cm* | 19F | ca. 0.15 cm |
| 19I | 19H | ca. 0.05 cm* | 19F | ca. 0.1 cm* | 19G | ca. 0.15 cm |
| 19H | 19G | ca. 0.05 cm* | 19I | ca. 0.1 cm* | 19F | ca. 0.15 cm |
| 19G | 19H | ca. 0.05 cm* | 19F | ca. 0.1 cm* | 19E | ca. 0.15 cm |
| 19F | 19E | ca. 0.05 cm* | 19G | ca. 0.1 cm* | 19D | ca. 0.15 cm |
| 19E | 19D | ca. 0.05 cm* | 19F | ca. 0.1 cm* | 19G | ca. 0.15 cm |
| 19D | 19E | ca. 0.05 cm* | 19F | ca. 0.1 cm* | 19G | ca. 0.15 cm |
| 19C | 19E | ca. 0.05 cm* | 19D | ca. 0.1 cm* | 19G | ca. 0.15 cm |
| 19B | 19A | ca. 0.05 cm* | 19C | 0.6 cm* | 19G | ca. 0.65 cm |
| 19A | 19B | ca. 0.05 cm* | 19C | 0.6 cm* | 19G | ca. 0.65 cm |

*significant measurements for isolating aggregates
brackets indicate reflexive pairings

enclosing the sites is too generous the nearest neighbor statistic will indicate tendencies toward clustering which may not actually exist. For my purposes I defined the area in terms of the size of the type of landform upon which sites occur. As observable on the map this landform is simply the edge of the first terrace above the alluvial bottomlands, so the area was taken to equal the length of a line running along the length of the terrace where sites occur times a somewhat arbitrary breadth of 0.25 cm (as measured on the air photographs).

The computation of the nearest neighbor statistic resulted in a figure far beyond the range of possible values theoretically determined by Clark and Evans (1954:447). It became readily apparent that the one-dimensional or linear characteristic of the site distribution accounted for this discouraging result. In other words, nearest neighbor analysis as defined by Clark and Evans makes the assumption that site distributions and the area from which site density is computed occupy two dimensions with comparatively little tendency toward linearity.

In light of the inadequacy of Clark and Evans's nearest neighbor analysis for the data at hand, I turned to a somewhat simpler analysis which also uses nearest neighbor information but is applicable specifically to linear distributions. First described by Clark (1956) and applied by the geographer Dacy (in Haggett 1965:232–33), the analysis does not require knowledge of site density nor is it concerned with the actual distances to nearest neighbors. Instead, it uses the quantities of "reflexive pairings" among at least three orders of nearness. That is, the proportion of pairs of sites which reciprocate in nearest, next-nearest and third-nearest neighborliness are compared to theoretical expected proportions for each order of nearness if the distribution were random. Clark indicates that the theoretical proportion for a particular order is equal to two-thirds raised to a power equal to the number of the order (1, 2, and 3). If the observed proportion is less than the expected the distribution is defined as grouped or aggregated and if the proportion is greater the distribution is tending toward uniformity.

To carry out this analysis, third-nearest neighbors were computed and added to Table 6.1, and then the reflexive pairings were bracketed. Table 6.2 presents the results of the analysis.
These results indicate an unquestionable tendency toward site aggregation. We are now in a position to ask what is determining this aggregation.

(3) *Testing Alternative Hypotheses: Aggregations of Cimarron Phase*

TABLE 6.2
REFLEXIVE PAIRINGS IN NEAREST, NEXT-NEAREST, AND
THIRD-NEAREST NEIGHBORS AMONG PONIL CANYON SITES.

| Order | No. of Pairs | Observed Proportion | Expected Proportion | Description |
|---|---|---|---|---|
| 1 | 8 | 0.285 | 0.667 | aggregated |
| 2 | 4 | 0.142 | 0.444 | aggregated |
| 3 | 2 | 0.071 | 0.235 | aggregated |

*Sites Being Determined by Locations of Arable Land or by Socioeconomic Ties.* Map 6.1 shows two types of landforms in the Ponil Canyon: alluvial bottomland adjacent to the stream and alluvial fan or piedmont land above the stream. The bottomland is now entrenched by the stream to a depth of approximately eight feet. However this condition appears to be relatively recent as meanders in the stream course, although active, have not appreciably expanded the entrenchment laterally. Similarly, the piedmont is now entrenched in many places by side-canyon drainages, and the recency of this is even more obvious, it having lengthened considerably in the several summers I have worked in the area. Both the piedmont and the bottomland are now largely open and unwooded. The piedmont was probably in this condition prehistorically, but apparently much of the bottomland has been cleared for farming only during the historic period. Some patches where modern fields do not occur, particularly north of Highway 64, are covered with a thick brush vegetation which may have covered much more of the land prehistorically.

I originally thought that the bottomland would have been the major landform used for farming by the Puebloans living on the Ponil ca. A.D. 1300. Therefore, I suspected that the abundance of this land—that is, the breadth per unit length of the canyon—would have been the major determinant of site frequency. This is apparently not the case, however, since highest frequency of sites (the **LP**-19 series) occurs where the bottomland is narrowest. Furthermore, the broadest areas of alluvial bottomland have few or no sites next to them. Alternatively we could argue that the piedmont lands were those used since they may actually have been more accessible for farming than the bottomland, which very likely was covered with brush prehistorically. Additionally we can argue that aggregation of sites is determined by the distribution of piedmont land, particularly those portions which form the outwashes of the side canyons. But before testing this hypothesis, let us turn to the task of identifying the site aggregates.

From Table 6.1 we need to select those sites which are connected by nearest or next-nearest neighbor distances which are "significantly" short. Significance in this case refers to those distances shorter than the mean distance, 0.45 cm. That is, we shall consider all distances up to 0.4 cm. Conveniently, another criterion for determining significance coincides with this: an obvious gap exists between those distances 0.4 cm. and below and all the rest which are 0.7 cm. and above. So, in scanning Table 6.1, we have the following connections between sites.

TABLE 6.3
SITE CLUSTERS AMONG PONIL CANYON SITES

| Nearest Neighbor | Next-Nearest Neighbor | Aggregate No. |
|---|---|---|
| 32A | 32B | I |
| 32B | 32A | |
| 35 | 36 | |
| 36 | 35 · · · 37 | II |
| 37 | 36 | |
| 44A | 44 | III |
| 44 | 44A | |
| 19C through J and Area 3 | | IV |
| 19B | 19A | V |
| 19A | 19B | |

These five aggregates, as well as the others in the central group of sites, are all on the lower edge of piedmont land. Moreover, comparatively few sites are located in the Ponil drainage in areas lacking piedmont land. Piedmont land is nearly absent, for instance, on the southwestern side of the stream, and it is also sparse upstream and downstream from this main piedmont region.

If we argue that farming was the "akchin" type, the fields would be located in front of the mouths of the side canyons which come down off the plateau to the northeast, and the habitation sites would then be adjacent to the fields. The **LP**-19 series is obviously in such a location. The other clusters, including the **LP**-45 through 48 group not defined as an aggregate, all appear to be in the same type of situation. Except for **LP**-30, none of the sites included in the analysis are farther away than 1.5 cm from the modern extant washes, and the average distance is approximately 0.65 cm. If the sites are distributed independently of the locations of the washes, their average distance from the nearest wash would be approximately one-quarter the average distance between the washes. Since the distance between the washes averages 4.0 cm., the predicted average distance of sites from them, if sites are distributed independently of washes, would be 1.0 cm. Considering that the actual average distance of 0.65 cm. is only about two-thirds of this figure, we have reason to believe that sites tend to be aggregated around the mouths of washes, which suggests that aggregation is in fact determined by locations of arable land. (It should be mentioned here that these distances are difficult to measure due to alteration of the courses of side-canyon drainages by modern dams at their mouths and by a substantial modern irrigation canal running along the upper margin of the piedmont. Moreover, the courses have undoubtedly migrated back and forth across the piedmont many times since ca. A.D. 1300.)

In conclusion, on the basis of these associations we may accept the hypothesis that aggregations of sites are determined by the distribution of arable land. Even sites on the other side of the stream and those others upstream and downstream appear to be in similar situations, although this is not always evident from the data presented on the accompanying map. Some apparent exceptions do exist, however, and we should consider these. Otherwise, we may have grounds for rejecting the hypothesis. Sites **LP**-26, 28, and 29 are located upstream where the Ponil Canyon abruptly narrows. But in this location the bottomland is much sandier than that downstream and therefore may have been relatively more accessible for farming. Also, the outwash fan of Chase Canyon may have provided a broad tract of arable land. Three of the five sites located several miles upcanyon from these yielded very scanty evidence of occupation and are therefore probably very temporary. Two others, located on opposite sides of the Middle Ponil Fork near Ponil Camp, are substantial occupations. A large tract of verdant but unwooded alluvial bottomland near these two sites may have been the land farmed, depending, perhaps, directly on the higher rainfall in this region for a source of moisture. So the varying locations of these additional sites do not provide us with grounds for rejecting the hypothesis. Their disparate environmental situations may only reflect a population density slightly beyond the carrying capacity of ideal land for farming in this region as a whole.

The strong support for this hypothesis makes it difficult to assess the possible role of intracultural and socioeconomic factors in determining aggregation. Under these circumstances the easiest way to test this alternative hypothesis would be to look for features within the sites that form a cluster which would reflect higher rates of social or economic interchange between the sites within a cluster than between sites of different clusters. This type of study might follow the form of analysis carried out by Hill (1966) at Broken K Pueblo to determine household groupings. In lieu of the data necessary to carry out such an analysis, however, we might be able to demonstrate the operation of socioeconomic factors by observing characteristics of the site distributions within each cluster. For instance, an aggregate of sites located on only one side of the mouth of the wash instead of both may be reflecting aggregations for reasons beyond that of minimizing distances to arable land. Cimarron Phase aggregates tend to follow this pattern, but when the locations of the nonaggregated sites are included the pattern is not so obvious. In fact, it would appear that sites tend to be equally distributed on each side of their respective washes, the only exception being the **LP**-19**C**-**J** and Area 3 cluster. Excepting Area 3, these sites are very tightly aggregated on one side of the wash. Consequently, based on this distributional pattern, we would have reason to suspect that **LP**-19**C**-**J** represents a clustering for reasons in addition to the location of arable land. On the other hand, we still do not have good reason for suspecting the same in regard to the rest of the site clusters.

## ORGANIZATIONAL CHANGE AS REFLECTED IN CHANGING PATTERNS OF AGGREGATION OF HOUSEHOLDS

So far, this study has dealt only with the problems that arise in measuring aggregation, isolating aggregates, and differentiating between variables which could produce aggregation of households. These procedures must now be fitted into the objectives of discovering and explaining processes of organizational change. As an example of how this may be accomplished, we turn to a consideration of organizational change in the rise of agriculturally based societies in the northern Southwest.

The trend throughout this area from a period of time starting around A.D. 400 appears to have involved not only increasingly larger spatial aggregations of households but also the inclusion of these into hierarchies of increasingly higher levels of social organization, as outlined by Steward (1955a:151, 172). This type of growth began during what is generally known as the Basket Maker III period, arising out of the earlier Basket Maker II adaptations when no more than perhaps three or four households formed a community. In some cases the growth of aggregate size appears to be very abrupt, involving communities composed of several adjacent but spatially distinct clusters of households. Although archaeologists have reported the presence of considerable numbers of such Basket Maker communities in several districts of the northern Southwest, only a few of these have been investigated (Gladwin 1957:53).

Leaving aside any problems that might possibly exist in the measurement of Basket Maker aggregation—which are certainly minimal with regard to the distinct and well-bounded Basket Maker III aggregates—we might first ask what increasing aggregation reflects about changes in Basket Maker adaptations. This question is not easily answered using available data, but some hypotheses may nevertheless be suggested, all having to do with intrasystemic features of Basket Maker adaptations.

The first hypothesis asserts that Basket Maker household aggregation is a response to the initiation of methods of water control for agricultural purposes. This hypothesis is generated from statements made by Wittfogel (1955), Wittfogel and Goldfrank (1943), and Steward (1955b). While none of these scholars states such a hypothesis—they are more concerned with the relationship between water control and sociopolitical organization—it is implicit in much of their explication of the rise of a "hydraulic society." They speak of the development of "centralized control" and "managerial density" as concomitant with the development of hydraulic agriculture (Wittfogel 1955; Steward 1955b); and it could be argued, in formulating the hypothesis, that these aspects of sociopolitical organization necessitate aggregation of population into one community. This, in fact, would be one of our major assumptions covering this hypothesis. From a proletarian point of view, though, we could argue that an aggregated population would be necessary so that task-groups of sufficient size could be called together to build and maintain irrigation

204

works. The larger and more elaborate the works, the larger the task-group would have to be.

Looking more broadly at the prehistory of the American Southwest, there are increasing numbers of reports of fairly sophisticated irrigation works, many still unpublished. We do know, however, that such dense and aggregated settlements as those of the twelfth-century occupation of the Gila-Salt river drainage in southern Arizona are associated with elaborate irrigation works (Gladwin 1957:253–68). Water control systems not quite so extensive but obviously important are also known to have existed during the eleventh- and twelfth-century occupation at Chaco Canyon in northwestern New Mexico. These involve catchment basins, ditches (embankments?) for collecting sheet runoff from rains, and canals for guiding water over distances up to approximately one mile. Similar water control facilities are reported at Mesa Verde in southwestern Colorado (Rohn 1963, Lister 1966:65–66). These are all later manifestations, however, and water-control facilities appear not to have been of any great significance in the northern Southwest during Basket Maker III times. But this may only be a consequence of their obscurity and their neglect by southwestern archaeologists.

In light of this condition of the reported archaeological record, we might consider ethnographically known Pueblos in the Southwest. Here we find that the hypothesis has comparatively little to do with the explanation of modern Pueblo aggregation. The Hopi, for instance, glare out as a case where aggregated settlement is not associated with extensive water control. The small amount of irrigation practiced historically by the Hopi was devoted to springfed garden cropping of small plots on mesa slopes (Forde 1931:369; Hack 1942:34–36). The bulk of the agriculture was carried out on two classes of landforms: (1) floodplains which were located either on broad washes or at the mouths of arroyos, accounting for 73 percent of the field area, and (2) "dry" lands which derive moisture from ground water seeping from the mesas above the fields or from the rainfall efficiently captured by the sandy deposits of dunes (Hack 1942:26, 33–34). In either field situation irrigation is not reported to have been used traditionally. The Rio Grande Pueblos, on the other hand, apparently practiced irrigation prehistorically. Edward Dozier recognizes this contrast between the Hopi-Zuni and the Rio Grande Pueblos, and he points out that communal effort of the adults of a Rio Grande village is needed to use and maintain an irrigation system (1970:131–32). Taking

205

into consideration these ethnographic data, we may conclude that aggregation of households does not necessarily reflect the participation of a Basket Maker household aggregate in communal acitivities associated with water control; and in lieu of evidence of Basket Maker III irrigation practices, we might best consider other possibilities.

A more plausible hypothesis might be that Basket Maker aggregation arose as a result of the economic interdependence between households (and larger social segments) made necessary by variability in crop yields from year to year coming from a household's fields. This hypothesis would apply to situations where environmental variables, such as rainfall patterns, have diverse and unpredictable effects on crops from one year to another—effects which are of such a magnitude that a social unit the size of a family or even a clan may, on occasion, obtain unusually low crop yields. In such a situation this social unit would depend on another affiliated social unit which fared better that year for donations of food. In another year this donor may find itself having to be a recipient. It would be argued that these interdependent social units would maintain spatially close residence so that distribution between units could take place with a minimum of effort and so that these economic obligations could be reinforced through communication and group ritual.

The Hopi would appear to be a prime case in point. Apparently their rainfall-floodwater form of agriculture is not all that uniform in year-to-year production from one field to the next, and certain cultural adaptations exist which tend to minimize the effect of this variability, although they probably do not eliminate it. For instance, households and clans divide their landholdings into several plots located in a diversity of topographic situations (Forde 1931:368 passim). The vagaries of crop yields, in spite of this compensation, would have a great impact on a social unit the size of a household. So a larger unit, the clan, may exist not only to reallocate land as it becomes unproductive or as families increase or decrease in size, but also to insure that all households of the clan receive adequate sustenance. The same factors may operate to hold the clan together to form a village, although on this scale the interdependence of social units may come into effect only very occasionally. This may be reflected in the degree of durability of the association of the clans which make up a village. While these associations have lasted for long periods of time, quarrels between clans have ended in permanent splits such as Old Oraibi's disintegration at the beginning of this century (Titiev 1944:69–95).

Unfortunately the ethnographic data on the Hopi do not specify the degree to which economic interdependence between social units took place, so the perspectives I have developed in reference to the Hopi must remain somewhat circumstantial. We only have alluding comments such as Forde's: "Several statements suggest that the individual could not in practice refuse demands should occasion arise for a share in the crop from fellow clanswomen" (1931:371). Supplementing Forde's data, Don Talayesva (Sun Chief), an old inhabitant of the Hopi pueblo of Oraibi, told me in a recent conversation that any family of his village experiencing crop failure would obtain food from neighbors.

The hypothesis also obtains some support from the changes in the environmental locations of communities from Basket Maker II to Basket Maker III times. While Basket Maker II sites in several different districts of the northern Southwest tend to be in well-watered habitats, Basket Maker III sites, particularly those inhabited by larger aggregates of households, tend to be in drier regions. But to gain any real confidence in this hypothesis, we must know more about the hydrographic characteristics of arable landforms in the vicinity of Basket Maker III sites. It might also help to know more about economic reciprocity among the modern-day (or historic) Hopi and Zuni and the social and ideological correlates of this reciprocity.

The two hypotheses considered so far are related at least in part to a more basic "covering" hypothesis having to do with the relationship between, on the one hand, the rate and medium of information flow between social segments (households), and on the other hand, the spatial correlates of this rate and medium. Specifically, as the rate or quality of information flow between social segments increases, holding the information medium constant, the spacing between the segments decreases. Given that Basket Maker communication was primarily by word of mouth, the social interaction assumed to be associated with water control systems or economic reciprocity would have been greatly facilitated by the aggregation of the participating households. It should be pointed out, however, that our knowledge of the quality and rate of information flow necessary for social activities such as these is largely absent.

Another set of hypotheses may also be considered to have some possible relevance to the origin of Basket Maker aggregation, but more to the *form* of aggregation than to aggregation itself. By the end of the Basket Maker III period in many parts of the northern Southwest—Alkali Ridge being a good example (Brew 1946)—the population of a community was living in contiguous-roomed structures instead of a scatter of pithouses. Two factors may be involved in determining this form of aggregation. First, much less labor is expended on housebuilding if a new dwelling is built against the one or two walls of an adjacent building, and as Basket Maker populations began to devote more energy to obtaining an agricultural subsistence, this decreased labor expenditure in house-building may have been important. The second factor is derived from the insights of the animal ecologist, W. C. Allee, who observed that certain social insects aggregate their dwellings in cold weather to increase the efficiency of body heat retention (Allee 1931:70). The insulating qualities of contiguous dwellings and storage rooms would minimize the amount of heat lost in keeping a room warm. Considering that firewood would have been quickly cleared from the immediate vicinity of a Basket Maker community, any practice which tended to conserve it would have been favored. However, the real advantages of this practice would probably not be realized to any great extent until a large number of rooms were aggregated together, as in the case of large Pueblo III period communities.

Going on to a distinctively different hypothesis, it may be that Basket Maker populations aggregated together in response to belligerence between neighboring populations. It is assumed here that a population is much better able to defend itself and its property if it lives in a tight aggregate rather than in spatially dispersed units vulnerable to systematic attrition through warfare. But in applying this hypothesis to the rise of Basket Maker III adaptations, let alone any other segment of south-western prehistory, we have only shaky evidence of continual belliger-ence. In spite of this, many archaeologists have speculated that warfare not only caused population aggregation, but also caused regional aban-donments and long-distance population movements. Many of these state-ments are summarized by Jett (1964:290–96) and Davis (1965). Jett, in particular, has blamed the Southern Athabaskans (Apaches, Navajos) for belligerence against Puebloan peoples (1964:297–98), although as Davis has pointed out, present archaeological evidence indicates that the Athabaskans were not in the Southwest until sometime after A.D. 1500, much too late to account for most prehistoric aggregation (1965:353). Nevertheless, Davis suspects that the tight village aggregates appearing after ca. A.D. 1100 may have been in response to competition with drought-disrupted Shoshonean hunter-gatherers as well as Puebloan farmers. But the evidence for any type of warfare among Basket Maker

III populations is at best circumstantial, so we would have to conclude that this hypothesis would probably play only a minor role, if any role at all, in explaining Basket Maker aggregation.

Brief attention should be given to a few other hypotheses which have been considered by others in one context or another. Haury, in one of the most extensive considerations of the explanation of aggregation in southwestern archaeological literature, has offered a hypothesis which may be considered as an incomplete version of some of those which I have just presented. He says that southwestern populations may have aggregated under the requirements of social structure, although he does not explicitly specify why social structures encompassing larger population numbers came into existence other than mentioning general factors such as defense and environment (1956:5 passim). To a degree, he seems to be confusing the explanation of increases in the size of social units with explanation of increases in size of spatial aggregation. Nevertheless, he does say in passing that aggregation could have been brought about by "the requirements of the religious system in promoting rain-producing ceremonies." Consideration of this factor would have to assume either that such ceremonies did, in fact, cause rain, which is of course unlikely, or that religious systems involving large numbers of people arise independently of population aggregation. It is more likely, however, that dependence operated in the opposite direction: that is, such religious systems are dependent upon the existence of large social groups. Ideological behavior of this sort probably serves to *maintain* the integration of the elements in the aggregate, but it would not be responsible for the *creation* of the aggregate.

Another hypothesis which has seen some favor in southwestern archaeology is that aggregation is perhaps a result of "influences" or "diffusion" from neighboring aggregated populations (Reed 1956:17). This type of reasoning begs the question, however, since the knowledge of aggregation is no explanation of its acceptance by a recipient of that knowledge, even if we can demonstrate that this knowledge did originate elsewhere. We are still left with the basic question: why did people aggregate?

Having presented this series of alternative hypotheses, it may be concluded that many of them may play a role in accounting for the marked increase in aggregate size during Basket Maker III times. The question arises, then, as to how we would go about determining these varying roles. One way would be to test each hypothesis in turn, looking for the intrasystemic features which each hypothesis states is determining aggregation. A more powerful way, however, would be to start by developing a theory comprehensive enough to account for many aspects of the change from Basket Maker II to Basket Maker III adaptations —that is, a model of cultural change which could be predictively expanded to cover all those aspects of the cultural systems to which each of the aforementioned hypotheses pertains.

One such theory would consider the observed Basket Maker II to III changes to be a consequence of changes in the subsistence system involving the increased importance of maize agriculture. This shift in subsistence would be seen as a response to increasing population density in the northern Southwest. It is asserted that Basket Maker II subsistence involved the exploitation of a variety of natural resources, among which were various wild seeds and nuts that were stored over the winter months. Maize was planted and also stored for winter use, but its real importance in the annual subsistence cycle may have been to supplement wild plant foods during the summer. If maize were planted beginning in April, it would be available as "green corn" from July to October when wild seeds would become available. The portion of maize stored over the winter may have been primarily for the next spring's planting.

Assuming, then, that Basket Maker II populations were gradually increasing in size, or that foreign populations were expanding into the northern Southwest, the excess would eventually have been pushed into the portions of the northern Southwest marginal to those in which a successful Basket Maker adaptation could have been practiced. These marginal areas would have been the drier, less vegetated regions at lower altitudes—regions having lower densities of the plant foods upon which Basket Maker II population depended. In these new habitats maize-growing would have been increased to compensate for diminished natural food resources. Since maize seed is in many ways a kind of food differing from the wild seeds which were used by Basket Maker II populations, different kinds of storage and processing facilities would have been developed—for instance, larger granaries, trough metates, and pottery cooking containers. These changes in storage and processing facilities are, of course, the distinctive new "traits" of Basket Maker III adaptations.

More pertinent to the hypothesis-testing, however, are the changes which would have taken place in the nature of agricultural field facilities. Not only would fields have been larger in size per capita population, but

210

the types of landforms and their hydrographic characteristics would have been markedly different in the Basket Maker III habitats. Specifically, since rainfall is lower in these habitats, fields would have been located so as to take advantage of concentrations of runoff. These would have been alluvial fans normally receiving adequate but not destructively intensive flooding from the watersheds behind them. This flooding would not always have been optimal, however. In one year a field would experience flooding intensive enough to destroy a maize crop, while in another year the flooding may not have been enough. In addition, not all fields would be equally affected during any one year, not only due to spottiness of rainfall, but also due to variation in the size of the watersheds that provided the floods.

The Basket Maker III populations would have compensated for this unpredictable environmental variability with patterns of reciprocity between households. That is, if one household did not bring in enough maize in one year, it would depend upon a neighboring household which would have purposefully planted enough excess maize, knowing full well that the situation might be reversed in another year. Thus, the model as presented so far would favor that hypothesis which asserts that Basket Maker III aggregation was a result of the necessity of maintaining the social ties concomitant with economic reciprocity. In this context, reciprocity and its social and spatial correlates are viewed as arising in response to the unpredictability of subsistence inputs into households.

Perhaps more important, however, in promoting aggregation would have been the necessity of social mechanisms for revising the allocation of farmland as a scarce resource to the households using it. Considering that individual household sizes would increase or decrease every several years, adjustments in the amount of farmland allocated to a series of households would have been almost a continuous process. Farmland reallocation, incidentally, is one of the major functions of clan (sib) groupings among the Hopi (Forde 1931).

This theory of change from Basket Maker II to Basket Maker III adaptations requires considerably more empirical support than is presently available in order to serve properly as a vehicle to predict changes in patterns of aggregation. In addition, we should attempt to obtain more confidence in the major assumption of the theory: the assertion that both economic reciprocity and land allocation require aggregation of participating households into a community (at the subsistence-technological level of the Basket Makers). Assuming that the model does have this sort of support, we may proceed to consider how the model could be extended to account for other possible determinants of Basket Maker III aggregation, as well as the form which the aggregations take. For instance, it could be argued that warfare as a determinant would not be expected to exist, since the Basket Maker III adaptation, as a new systemic type, had considerable growth potential, and with this potential it had the capacity to radiate out into many other regions of the northern Southwest with comparatively little structural change and without the accumulation of competitive stress. We might also be able to account for certain characteristics of aggregate form. As an example, the economy obtained in building contiguous-roomed as opposed to single-roomed granaries may reflect the increasing proportion of human labor devoted to tending fields and grinding maize into a flour. It should be emphasized, however, that these examples are presented primarily to demonstrate the advantages of working with a theoretical model of a system rather than with a series of relatively unrelated alternative hypotheses. In the long run, this systems approach would result in considerably lower expenditures of research energy.

Reflecting back on data from the Cimarron District, it will be remembered that the determinants of household clustering appeared to be primarily the discontinuous locations of arable land rather than intrasystemic relationships of the households forming each of the clusters. Considering that the prehistory of agricultural adaptations in the Cimarron District spans several centuries starting about A.D. 500, it is curious that aggregation into communities did not occur as it did among the Basket Makers to the west within a span of time of perhaps less than 100 years. The reason for this difference appears to be the differences in the regions marginal to those where successful Basket Maker II-type adaptations could be carried out. While the Cimarron District and various districts farther west in the San Juan Basin all have the well-watered, pinyon-covered plateau country dissected by perennial streams (usually at altitudes around 7,000 feet), which is the kind of environment in which Basket Maker II adaptations flourished, the Cimarron District lacks the drier, lower-altitude, sandy washes which the Basket Maker III populations of the San Juan Basin probably used as agricultural fields. In the Cimarron District the lower-altitude country breaks abruptly to the east into the short-grass plains with river valleys containing perennial streams which are often marshy and are susceptible to intensive late-summer flash floods. As a consequence of this differing hydrography, while population density increased in the Cimarron District beginning about A.D. 500, it never expanded out onto the marginal areas on the plains. Instead, the population continued to reside in the comparatively well-watered canyons, apparently adding fields watered by high water tables as side-canyon alluvial fans became inadequate for the increasing population size. So crop yields were probably never as unpredictable as those of Basket Maker III populations to the west, and the individual households did not have to depend upon reciprocity to the extent that Basket Maker III populations probably did.

## SUMMARY

Archaeologists have just barely scratched the surface in using spatial or locational analysis to elucidate and explain variability in cultural systems. Utilizing a few of the analytical techniques of quantitative geography, this chapter has suggested directions in which this type of analysis might proceed. It was argued that the spacing of archaeological phenomena reflects organizational features of cultural systems. In particular, the nonrandom clustering or aggregating of cultural components was asserted to reflect their relatively closer articulation in matter-energy flow networks. At the very least, the presence of aggregation of such phenomena as archaeological sites provides a basis for proposing hypotheses which would be then tested against independent data.

Ideally, hypothesis-testing would take place in the context of testing a larger scale theory of the nature of cultural systems or cultural systemic change, which may be expanded to consider many different components and processes. As represented in the theory of change from Basket Maker II to Basket Maker III adaptations in the northern Southwest, an archaeologist might start building such a theory by considering changes in certain inputs or outputs of matter-energy into or out of the cultural systems in question, as well as the ecosystems of which the cultural systems are components. In the case of the Basket Maker changes, it was argued that population density began to increase in the San Juan Basin beyond that which could be supported by Basket Maker II types of adaptation. New adaptations of the Basket Maker III type arising in a different type of habitat of the San Juan Basin were based on higher per

213

capita inputs of maize. On the basis of these assertions, many different aspects of systemic change may be built into the theory, including those which have to do with changes in degree of household aggregation; for if changes in matter-energy inputs took place, many aspects of the system would have to make adjustments. On the other hand, the theory should also be able to indicate what kinds of changes would *not* be expected. As a result, by deriving hypotheses from theories of cultural systems and ecosystems, the archaeologist would find himself in a position in which he may formulate economical research programs. That is, he would be in a position to specify the spatial patterns of the archaeological record which would be expected if his theories are true representations of reality.

# Toward an Explanation of the Origin of the State

## HENRY T. WRIGHT

*Museum of Anthropology*
*University of Michigan*
*Ann Arbor*

The construction of research strategies for the investigation of state origins is complicated by two principal factors: the type of explanations required and the samples available to test them. Most proposed explanations, and no doubt those to be proposed in the future, involve the interaction of a number of variables, regardless of whether or not a proponent chooses to specify one such variable as critical. Faced with such interaction, the laboratory scientist can create experimental situations in which some variables can be controlled in order to observe the behavior of a few others. In contrast, field surveyors can obtain large samples which permit them to control statistically the behavior of most variables in order to consider the behavior of some others. Unfortunately these avenues are not easily followed by those who seek to explain state origins. States developed without direct articulation with existing states on perhaps as many as eight occasions many millennia ago. If neither experiment nor statistical control is feasible, how are multiple variable explanations to be tested? Before attempting to answer this question let us consider some proposed explanations relevant to the origin of the state.

## TRADITIONAL THEORIES OF STATE ORIGIN

Past explanatory theories are useful because they indicate both the classes of variables and types of variable linkage which have been, to some extent, concordant with the evidence. The typology of such efforts adopted below makes explicit the classes of variables which may be useful in the future. The examples chosen are predominantly recent, not because they are structurally better than those of the nineteenth century but because the empirical evaluation of such earlier explanations by recent workers has both increased and ordered our knowledge of early states. The later attempts of each type must account for this more comprehensive body of knowledge.

*Managerial theories* involve certain activities whose complexity or structure requires certain kinds of management in the common sense of the term. Such activities might include irrigation or trade. Changes in management might involve increasingly professional administrators or increasingly despotic rulers.

Karl Wittfogel's influential general theory of Oriental or hydraulic societies, those in which the ruling class and the managing bureaucracy are identical, was first proposed in the 1930s and finally given full explication in *Oriental Despotism* in 1957. His propositions relevant to the origin of the state, defined as a professional government (Wittfogel 1962:239), may be diagrammed as in Figure 7.1. In this and succeeding diagrams the numbers represent pages in the cited edition. Dotted lines indicate implicit connections. Such diagrams are admittedly my interpretation of the various authors' longer and far more subtle presentations.

*Internal conflict theories* involve the existence of differential access to wealth, conflict or threat of conflict, and the subseqeunt emergence of the state as a mediating and dominating institution.

As early example of this approach is that of Engels (1884). In 1957, I. M. Diakonov published an explanation specific to the formation of the state, defined as the administrative machinery of a class society, in Mesopotamia (Fig. 7.2) (Diakonov 1969:185). There is an implication that the increased wealth of the ruling classes is invested in the means of production.

216

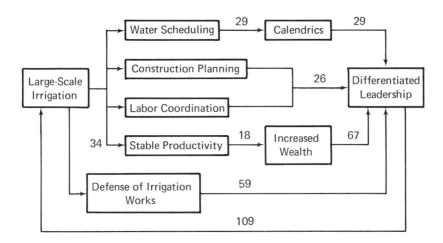

Figure 7.1  Flow diagram of Wittfogel's propositions.

Figure 7.2  Flow diagram of Diakonov's propositions.

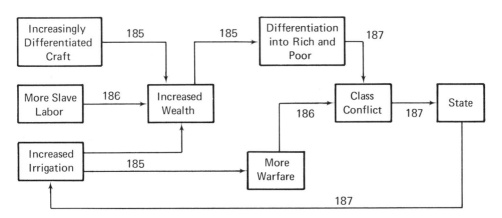

*External conflict theories* involve conditions which enable and require one society to dominate and control the means of production in another society. The institutions which permanently maintain this dominance constitute the state. Robert L. Carneiro has recently elaborated a general theory of this type (Fig. 7.3). He defines a state as an autonomous territorial and political unit having a central government with coercive power over men and wealth (Carneiro 1970:733). In this theory population growth is a prime mover. Each increment in population leads to increasingly larger and more centralized organizations. Once supralocal integration occurs the rise of states and empires follows inexorably.

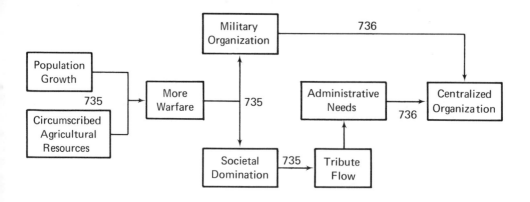

Figure 7.3   Flow diagram of Carneiro's propositions.

*Synthetic theories* involve the interrelated operation of several processes at once. A recent example of this type of theory is presented in the work of Robert McC. Adams. A specific theory of the development of the state in Mesopotamia can be extracted from his *Evolution of Urban Society* (Fig. 7.4). States are defined as hierarchically and territorially organized societies in which order is maintained with monopolized force (1966:14). A somewhat different diagram could be constructed for his analysis of Mesoamerica. Both managerial problems and external conflict are explicit factors here.

From these four seemingly different examples four useful generalizations can be drawn.

(1)   States are variously defined as either a kind of government (that is, specialized and hierarchical), or a kind of society with such a government. Some authors add that the state maintains a monopoly of force.

(2)   All examples of theories involve the interaction of a number of variables, even if one is specified as a prime mover.

(3)   All examples involve implicit or explicit positive feedback processes leading to growth, but none involve stabilizing negative feedback processes. Specifically, the government makes investments in irrigation in the constructs of Wittfogel, Diakonov, and Adams, and strengthens military capacity in the construct of Carneiro, thus leading to stronger government. However, the factors which limit the growth of prestate societies or primary states for periods of time or which lead to their decline have yet to be dealt with.

(4)   The connections between certain elements are neither specified nor obvious. For instance, how and why managerial needs or class conflict lead to specialized, hierarchical government are unclear.

Future general theories must involve carefully specified multiple

218

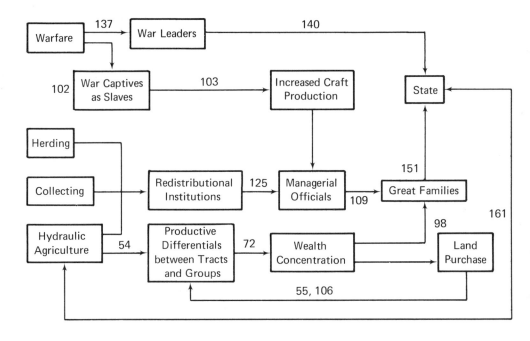

Figure 7.4 Flow diagram of Adams's propositions.

variable relationships governing both growth and stability. These relationships will express interrelations between management, internal conflict, external conflict, and other processes.

## EXPLANATION AND TEST

In this paper an explanation of a variable's behavior will be the place of that variable in a tested theory. We seek explanations of complex cultural processes such as state evolution for quite practical reasons: at present the ramifications of planned changes in the cultural systems in which we participate often cannot be predicted. The type of explanation which I seek should make specific prediction possible. Such explanation requires the building of a theory: a set of general assumptions, definitions of dimensions and variables, and statements of relationship between variables. Testable relationships extracted or deduced from such a theory are hypotheses. Many would consider the general statements of variable relationship in a tested theory to be "laws." Such a term has a definite "public relations" impact. However, it seems to me that the term connotes a search for "natural truths." Scientific endeavor produces theories for the moment confirmed, not "truths." Law aside, when a process has been expressed as one or more variables and the behavior of these has been shown to be a function of other variables, the process has been "explained."

How are testable consequences to be generated from a proposed theory involving variable interaction, given the limited data available on state origins? Such consequences can be generated with a theoretically based systemic model. By a model I mean a set of statements of dimension and variable definition and of variable relationship which represent a specific phenomenon, in our case a specific area of state development. Models need not be general and need not be theoretically based. Those which are so based can involve more than one theory. For instance, a model might involve tested theories drawn from plant ecology, geology, and communication science. A system is here considered a set of variables related in such a way that varying any one through its full range of values results in changes in all others. Note that a system is here defined as a type of formulation, not a phenomenon. Such a definition has a number of useful properties (Von Bertalanffy 1968:55–77). It enables one to show which variables operate in a given system, even in systems with hierarchical or specialized regulatory subsystems which operate only under extreme conditions. Once a theoretically based systemic model has been constructed, consequences can be generated by providing initial values for the variables and successively transforming the model given various input conditions. Such generation is simulation. The end product of a simulation or the variable changes during a simulation can be tested with data from appropriate phenomena. Repeated testings of different simulation models derived from a theory on different cases should lead to progressive improvements in the theory and to increasingly better explanations.

## STATES AS SOCIETIES AND STATES AS SYSTEMS

States have been defined in many ways. Some definitions, for instance those referring to legitimate force or property holding, deal with specific features sometimes found in societies far too simple to be considered states. The definition I am using refers to general features of social organization which necessitate other features considered definitional by others. For my purposes a state can be recognized as a society with specialized decision-making organizations receiving messages from many different sources, recoding these messages, supplementing them with previously stored data, making the actual decision, storing both the message and the decision, and conveying decisions back to other organizations. Such organizations are thus internally as well as externally specialized. Such societies contrast with those in which relations between the society's component organizations are mediated only by a generalized decision-maker and with those in which relations between component organizations are exclusively self-regulating. In contrast, a state can be conceptualized as a sociocultural system in which there is a differentiated, internally specialized decision-making subsystem which regulates varying exchanges between other subsystems and with other systems. Regulation definitionally involves information flow, even if such is expressed in flow of material items.

The conceptual definition has several implications of interest. First, information flow obeys the principle of channel capacity (Quastler 1956). For instance, individual people can only perceive, reason, and communicate accurately at a certain rate. Therefore if an administrator must handle information at a faster rate, either his organizations ceases to operate effectively or two administrators must carry the burden. If so, a higher-order administrator *may* be needed to coordinate these two. With increasing information flow, more levels of hierarchy may be added, with the higher-order administrators making only a few general decisions about lower-order specific decisions. (These points are developed in Wright 1969:1–6.) Traditional management theories such as those diagrammed in the first section of this paper may be subsumed under such a formulation. Second, information flow cannot exist by itself. It is conveyed in the form of materials or energy. For instance people, objects, food, and so on are needed to maintain specialized decision-making subsystems. Taxes, corvée, sinecured estates, and fines are all devices used in states for extracting such material support from other subsystems. Third and last, materials and human resources usually seem limited relative to the demands of the system. Therefore, decision-makers will usually engage in whatever competition and/or collusion possible without destroying the system in order best to maintain their segment of the hierarchy. Such political action will further define the internal structure of the decision-making subsystem. Traditional internal conflict theories may be subsumed under such a formulation.

Given these definitions and implications, it follows that if one wishes to test theories of state development one would have to define the subsystems operating in a given case of state development and to devise some means of measuring the major flows into, within, and between these subsystems during this period of development. With such measurements and a body of theory one could then attempt to predict changing patterns in the organization of the decision-making subsystem, and proceed to test these predictions.

Now let us consider the problems that have arisen and the progress achieved in pursuing such a general strategy in one single case of state development.

## SOUTHWEST IRAN AS AN EXAMPLE OF RESEARCH STRATEGY

Among all the areas where one could study early state development, Mesopotamia has a unique advantage. From earliest times, daily administrative records were kept on relatively durable clay tablets. This enables one to test efficiently many kinds of hypotheses about administrative organizations. In my first research project in Mesopotamia, under the guidance of Robert McC. Adams, I worked not with state origins but with the structure of a developed Early Dynastic state in southern Iraq using archaeological and textual data. Following the principle of channel capacity, this work demonstrated that the number of levels of administrative hierarchy in an organization was a function of the rate at which that organization would have to process information regarding the activities it conducted (Wright 1969). It seemed logical that higher-order state governmental institutions might also have arisen in response to such information processing problems. But what were the causes of such problems? Nearby southwestern Iran presented a practical natural laboratory for the study of the bases of state development.

Archaeologically attested state developments cover such vast areas and spans of time that it is difficult to investigate their organization in a season or two of fieldwork. For example, state development in southwestern Iran involved a number of interacting processes occurring during a period of almost ten centuries and in a diverse region covering more than 20,000 square kilometers. The work of Hole, Flannery, and Neely (1969) provided an understanding of prestate developments, and the work of the Délégation Archéologique Française en Iran (summarized in LeBreton 1957) and the general survey of Robert McC. Adams (1962) provided a basic framework for the period of state development between 4000 and 3000 B.C. However, when I began my work in the spring of 1968[1], I had little accurate evidence of the variables which might be considered

222

elements in subsystems of a systemic model. I conceived of my work with this case of state development as being composed of two stages, each involving a number of field projects.

In the first stage, each project would be directed at elucidating two or more potential subsystems and structured in terms of one or more traditional hypotheses explaining state development. The end result of this procedure should, in the first place, be a set of tested hypotheses, some rejected and some accepted. The confirmation of any of the traditional particularistic hypotheses, derived from proposals such as those discussed in the first section of this chapter, would not be conclusive given the standards set for useful explanation in the previous section of this chapter. Most of them demonstrably fail to explain at least one case of early state development. However, even if increased irrigation, population, or trade occurred in every case of state development, one would still have to demonstrate exactly how such changes determined the organization of decision-making. In the second place, there should be demonstration of the relative changes in and relations between key variables in the potential subsystems. We should have moved from a position in which we knew a potential subsystem existed, as we knew that rural population existed because there were small sites of the successive periods between 4000 and 3000 B.C., to a position in which we could demonstrate at least relative changes in key variables, such as aggregate population, average size of rural settlement, and the spacing of rural settlements. Furthermore we should be in a position to test hypotheses about the mechanics of these potential subsystems; for example, that decrease in rural population involved agglomeration into more central settlements rather than the uniform decline of all settlements. At the end of this first stage we could begin assembling the systemic models within whose context possible explanations could be tested. Let me emphasize that such possible explanations are not simply generated or suggested by the fieldwork. They are generated by constant attempts to make explict and question one's own assumptions in the light of the efforts of other workers on one's own and related fields. However, without the models, which can be constructed only with the aid of such fieldwork, there would be no way to provide exact tests of hypotheses dealing with such abstract concepts as channel capacity.

In the second stage each project would focus on the absolute measurement of one or more of the critical variables operating in the developed systemic model. In the case of certain variables such as those relating to population, the estimation of such measurements may require little or no additional data collection. In the case of others such as those relating to agricultural production, the estimation of such measurements may require the more extensive application of methods and research designs utilized in the first stage. In yet other cases such estimation might require the application of new methods and research designs. In this second stage of research there would be a shift from predominant concern with the productive subsystems to predominant concern with the decision-making subsystems and with regulatory links between them and the other subsystems. The end result would be one test of a synthetic theory of state development using a comprehensive systemic model of southwestern Iran between 4000 and 3000 B.C.

At the present moment three field projects contributing to the first stage have been completed, and one additional project has been planned. Direct evidence of the mechanics of population growth and decline, rural agriculture production, craft production and local exchange, and interregional exchange have been obtained. There is yet little direct evidence of transhumant herding, of higher-order decision-making, and of relations between various emerging states throughout Mesopotamia. Let me utilize aspects of the three field projects as examples of the strengths and problems of the approach outlined above.

In 1963, I planned an excavation project on a small town in the Deh Luran Plain, a valley marginal to the main area of state emergence on the Susiana Plain. I hoped to elucidate changing organization for warfare and for interregional exchange. The working model from which hypotheses were to be derived can be diagrammed as in Figure 7.5

I argued that because of the town's marginal location it would bear the brunt of any competition between states, and because of its location on the traditional trade route between southwest Iran and Iraq it would have evidence of changing flows of wood, stone, and other commodities being transported into lowland Mesopotamia. The specific hypotheses to be tested were: (1) that competition over agricultural land, perhaps dictated by increasing population and decreasing land quality, required fortified towns and specialists in military administration; and (2) that increased participation in interregional exchange, whose growth was perhaps dictated by the increasing population of Greater Mesopotamia, required specialists in economic administration both to organize local export production and to redistribute imports.

No positive evidence of military competition was recovered in the

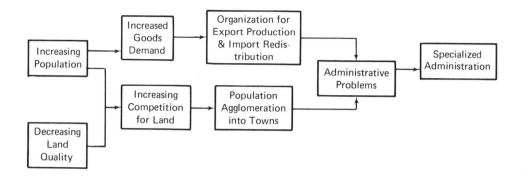

Figure 7.5   Flow diagram of Wright's 1968 working model.

excavations. Given the probably elementary level of warfare such negative evidence means little. Patterns of competition were monitored in 1971 with survey methods. The data relevant to interregional exchange were most useful (Wright 1972). The reorganization and growth of early trade beginning about 3200 B.C. followed the appearance of administrative specialists. Therefore trade did not cause administrative specialization and the second hypothesis could be rejected. Evidence from other sites throughout southwestern Iran made available since 1968 confirms this rejection. Furthermore there was a regular proportional relationship between changes in the relative values of imports and of exports. Some of the mechanisms of administered interregional trade were thus explicated. As is usually the case in archaeological research, some of the data not immediately relevant to our problem proved interesting. For instance, we improved the local ceramic sequence which would be useful for dating settlements in future surveys, and we added to the stock of subsistence remains which would some day be needed to attack the problems of agricultural and herding organization.

In the spring of 1969, I planned a brief general survey project to provide complete settlement pattern maps for most of the foothill valleys hithertofore unsurveyed. In that same season Frank Hole and James Neely were also conducting surveys. A portion of the working model was altered and is described in Figure 7.6. Thus in the light of the previous season, I had separated exchange and the state, and viewed increasing interregional trade and agglomeration into towns as changes occurring after state formation. I continued naively to assume population increase. The hypothesis that structured the season's work was that military

225

Figure 7.6 Alterations of the working model.

competition for the fruits of a complex interregional economy forced craftsmen and other workers into the towns about 3000 B.C.

The results of the various surveys were surprising for three reasons. First, the settlement data from three of the component plains of southwestern Iran showed no evidence of simple population increase. Population oscillated throughout the fourth and third millennia B.C. Second, the data indicated that towns grew up rather abruptly around 3500 B.C. and did not grow further until late in the third millennium B.C. Third, there seemed to be a regular pattern of smaller centers around the towns suggesting placement for transport efficiency. Thus, though there was little evidence of interregional exchange until after state emergence, there was perhaps a transformation of local exchange coincident with state emergence. Clearly a complete rethinking of my position was needed. I spent the autumn of 1969 evaluating my concept of explanation, my definition of the state, and the possible ways of explaining state development. I circulated several papers embodying these thoughts to various colleagues, and I profited immensely from their copious and often deservedly harsh comments.

In the autumn of 1970 I returned to southwestern Iran with a relatively large staff. We planned: (1) a resurvey of the settlements on the large and centrally located Susiana Plain; (2) a program of geological soundings around a sample of fourth millennium settlements; and (3) an excavation on a small rural site of about 3400 B.C. the period of state emergence. The completely restructured working models could be diagrammed as in Figure 7.7. This model expresses a situation similar to what Sanders (1968) has termed "economic symbiosis" in Mesoamerica. The separation of "administrative" from "political" problems results from the realization that internal competition could have been as important as information processing in the development of specialized administration. During the fieldwork we hoped to check the population estimates based on earlier surveys, and to test the specific hypotheses about local exchange derived from settlement spacing by comparing samples of craft manufactured goods from various sites. However, our

226

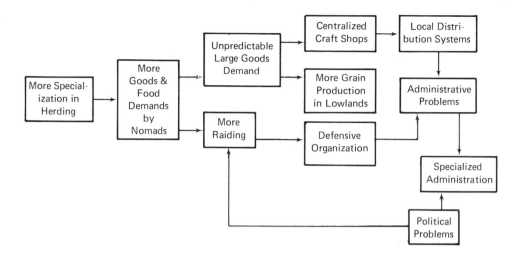

Figure 7.7  Flow diagram of Wright's 1970 working model.

primary objective was to elucidate the organization of rural agricultural production. The specific proposition which structured this aspect of the season's research was that if estimated grain production on the plain could be demonstrated increasingly to exceed rather than balance the estimated demand of the settled population, then the excess grain must be moving in intraregional or interregional exchange networks probably to fully transhumant herders who in this region cannot survive without external sources of grain and craft goods. Furthermore, the animals produced by such transhumants would be moving into lowland settlements. Such interaction would require the increasing specialization of administrative organizations for several reasons. Even at the present stage of analysis it is still not certain that useful direct estimates of grain production can be made. Such estimation will require more knowledge of the present habits of the flora and microfauna whose remains were found in our sampling units, and more samples of seeds from fourth millennium B.C. rural village sites. Thus the working proposition cannot be either accepted or rejected at the present time. However, the results of the detailed settlement survey conducted and analyzed by Gregory Johnson have far exceeded our expectations. Using a newly developed ceramic chronology, Johnson has been able to demonstrate changes in settlement size and density over relatively short periods of time. By studying minor stylistic variations on pottery vessels he has been able to isolate what are probably the products of a single workshop or closely related group of workshops. By mapping the distribution of these varieties he has been able to test specific hypotheses about the relations between specific

227

towns, small centers, and villages generated with settlement spacing data (Johnson 1973).

The results of the 1969 season were considerably amplified, and our knowledge of the mechanics of population change and local exchange were vastly improved. An unexpected but welcome result of Johnson's analysis was the isolation of settlement spacing changes both around 3800 B.C. and around 3200 B.C. which can best be explained as resulting from military competition. He has suggested some specific hypotheses about the causes of this competition and has pointed to the actual sites where these hypotheses might best be tested (Johnson 1973).

In the next field effort, I plan a general survey of certain upland valleys in an effort to elucidate the development of fully transhumant herders. The working model will be only slightly modified. Some further work on small rural settlements as noted above, and on towns may be needed to round out the first stage of research. In preparation for the second stage, first versions of computer simulations of interregional exchange and of agricultural production have been prepared. However the presentation of a comprehensive regional simulation model of southwestern Iran in the fourth millennium B.C. is several years in the future.

Even though research is not far advanced, some concept of the type of explanatory theory which will emerge is possible. The specific processes that are important in the models built for each case will probably not be important in the general theory. It is the type of interaction between these processes that will be important in such a theory. For instance, population growth and competition over land or water might be crucial in one case, while the interaction of economically specialized groups might be more critical in another. Both sets of specific processes would create similar problems of information processing and competition. Furthermore, it seems possible that the problems generated by a single process would not lead to the emergence of specialized administration, since the ranking decision-makers could accommodate by shifting their administrative resources around. Only when problems are generated in several areas would the decision-making apparatus be forced to change.

## SUMMARY

This chapter has briefly presented one archaeologist's approach to the development of a theory of state origins, one of the most complex transitions in the record of cultural evolution. I have discussed some recent attempts at explanation all of which I have attempted to rework and synthesize in the context of my understanding of the scientific process and of my own field experience. From these attempts has come the flexible research strategy which I am using in southwest Iran. Several points merit emphasis.

1. Research strategy depends upon what one wishes to explain. For instance, had I been interested in "urbanism" rathern than "states" when I turned from questions of trade and population in 1970, I probably would have focused on craft organization in towns rather than on rural production and local exchange.

2. Research strategy depends upon one's criteria of explanation. If I had felt that to specify a prime mover was an adequate explanation I would have begun my work with a study of population rather than a study of interregional exchange and competition. To have held such a view of explanation and to have demonstrated the complex variation in population in 1968 rather than almost two years later, would, I hope, have led me to an immediate questioning of my basic assumptions. Since I felt that the demonstration of many links in a system of variables was necessary to adequate explanation, with which links I began was a matter of practical, not theoretical, importance. In the second place if I had felt that to show general correlations between variables sufficed to demonstrate linkage, I would not have been concerned with such quantitative measures as numbers of people, or quantities of goods exchanged, or of areas of land used for different purposes. As a result my survey and excavation methods might have been quite different.

3. In planning and field research, formally phrased hypotheses, rather than a general problem or working model alone, are valuable. On the one hand they force one to try a variety of methods in efforts to produce satisfactory test data rather than to reapply blindly a traditional set of methods designed for other types of problems. On the other hand they force one to think carefully before diverting all his resources into interesting but unexpected phenomena which always appear in the midst of excavation or survey.

4. Any field project should have a number of such hypotheses, since field conditions usually prevent the measuring of one or more critical variables, and thus the testing of one or more of these hypotheses.

5. Models and simulations are best viewed as means for the construction of testable hypotheses about specific systems. They are not ends in themselves.

229

I hope that this chapter will provide others with useful insights into the practical problems of building explanatory theories. It should at least convey an understanding of the amounts of time and effort required. I myself am convinced that this investment has been, and will continue to be, worthwhile, and that in the foreseeable future we shall have extensively tested predictive theories of state development.

### NOTE

1. The fieldwork of 1968 and 1970 was sponsored by National Science Foundation Grants GS-1936 and GS-3147. The fieldwork of 1969 was sponsored by a Horace Rackham Faculty Research Grant. The later seasons benefited from the help of Ford Foundation Archaeological trainees.

# Resource Utilization and Political Evolution in the Teotihuacan Valley

## WILLIAM T. SANDERS

*Department of Anthropology*
*Pennsylvania State University*
*University Park*

## THE TEOTIHUACAN VALLEY AS A HUMAN HABITAT

The Teotihuacan Valley is a small topographic unit that forms a sub-area within the larger hydrographic basin referred to in the literature as the Valley or Basin of Mexico. The Teotihuacan Valley embraces an area of approximately 600 km² as compared to the 7,800 km² that make up the larger basin. The valley is a single hydrographic system with all streams draining into the Rio de San Juan which in turn empties into Lake Texcoco. To the south it is defined by a range of hills called the Patlachique Range, to the north by a string of isolated volcanic cones (Chiconautla, Maravillas, Malinalco, Cerro Gordo) separated by wide, low passes. The elevation of the valley floor varies from 2,240 meters near the lake shore to 2,260 at the upper end; the surrounding ranges reach a maximum height of 3,050 meters.

Because of this high elevation, the valley has a winter frost season—one of its critical climatic characteristics with respect to occupation by a farming population. None of the pre-Hispanic cultigens were adapted to growth during this season so the valley was essentially a one crop area. Frosts begin in October and last into March in normal years. The average annual precipitation is about 548 mms., but it has varied over the past 19 years from 378 to 792 mms. Perhaps 80 percent of the rain falls between June 1 and October 1. Rainfall when it does occur is explosive and has great erosive power.

In normal years, the climatic regime is favorable for the cultivation of maize, the Mesoamerican staple, but the wide variation in rainfall, frequent occurrence of internal droughts during the rainy season, and particularly, the combination of a late inception of the rainy season with an early inception of the frosts presents serious problems for cultivators and crop losses are frequent.

The altitude limits within which maize cultivation is feasible in the Basin of Mexico generally, range from 2,240 m. to approximately 2,700 m. above sea level. The frost season is so prolonged above 2,700 m. that maize cannot be grown. Within the zone of cultivation (2,240–2,700 m.) frosts are most frequent at the lowest elevations and the intermediate levels, that is, between 2,300 and 2,500 meters above sea level, are relatively free from them during the season from March 1 until November 1.

Most of the drainage of the valley today is seasonal and even during the rainy season, there is water in the numerous barrancas (seasonal streams) only for a few hours or days at a time. An exception to this rule are the springs at San Juan Teotihuacan midway up the valley. Approximately eighty springs provided an average flow of 588 liters per second in 1954. Drainage on the slopes is extremely destructive and both sheet and gully erosion are serious problems for cultivation.

Soils in the Teotihuacan Valley are generally fertile and capable of sustained cultivation without the addition of great quantities of fertilizers. Furthermore, the soils generally have excellent moisture retention qualities. They are, however, highly susceptible to erosion and the major soil characteristic that affects production is soil depth rather than nutrient balance.

Recent palynological studies by Kovar (1970) indicate that no major climatic changes have occurred in the valley over the past 3,000 years. There is evidence, however, from Gamio's 1922 study, that the output of water from the springs was 60 percent higher then than in 1954. Mooser's studies of the geology of the valley indicate that some of the barrancas in the middle section of the valley were permanent streams or at least had a much more extended flow of water during the rainy season. He also suggests that permanent water resources were found in other portions of the valley during the Early Classic Period and postulates the existence of springs within the area of the Classic City that had a flow of between 100 and 200 liters per second and provided much of the water supply for the city.

The reduction of quantity of surface water is undoubtedly correlated with, and was caused by, the destruction of the forests on the hillside and a process of steady continuous erosion during the pre-Hispanic periods. This later process was enormously accelerated after the Conquest by the drastic reduction of population during the sixteenth century, abandonment of marginal lands and their conversion to pasture lands for sheep and goats, introduced by the Spaniards.

In summary, the major problems of cultivation in the valley are frosts, combined with the low and variable precipitation, along with erosion on sloping terrain.

Aside from substantial agricultural land, the valley also has a number of critical raw materials for the maintenance of a pre-Hispanic peasantry. In several extensive areas, particularly within the Classic City, major superficial deposits of basalt are found that provided raw materials for grinding stones. A fairly extensive deposit of obsidian for chipped stone tools occurs east of Otumba at the upper edge of the valley; potter clays occur in the middle valley near San Sebastian; reeds for baskets were abundant in the area around the springs; and salt could be obtained from the immediate lakeshore. At least in the Formative times the nearby slopes were covered with pine forests, so that wood was in abundant supply. The only major deficiencies in the resources of the valley were lime for cooking and for construction, and aquatic protein foods (the portion of Lake Texcoco fronting on the valley was poor in lake food resources). During the Formative Period however, game was probably abundant throughout the valley.

As the population increased in size during Classic and Post Classic times, resources must either have been seriously depleted (such as game and wood) or no longer sufficed for the need of a greatly expanded population (such as obsidian and salt).

## THE AZTEC PERIOD–ECOLOGICAL CLIMAX

I will begin with the Aztec Period at the end of the pre-Hispanic sequence, for a number of reasons; the combination of ethnohistorical and archaeological sources provides us with a more complete picture than any preceding phase and furthermore, the archaeological data are less equivocal.

Sixteenth-century sources such as the *Relación de Tequisistlan* and the *Suma de Visitas* (1905) demonstrate that the alluvial plain between San Juan and the lake shore was irrigated by a master canal system based on the springs. In fact, the morphology of the system was virtually identical to that in use at present. The contemporary system provides 3,652 hectares of land with water; in Aztec times, the yield of water was at least 60 percent higher so that the irrigable area was minimally as high as 5,800 hectares. It may have been greater; the *Relación de Tequisistlan* states that in 1580 the irrigated area extended from San Juan all the way to the lake shore. Most of the land served by the system was owned by the town of Acolman and its dependent villages but the springs were owned by the ruler of Teotihuacan located up valley and the water was rented to the ruler of Acolman.

Canal irrigation today, and this was undoubtedly true in the Aztec Period as well, has two major functions. First, it permits a late spring planting prior to the inception of the rainy season, thus solving the problem of early frosts, and second, it provides water for an additional irrigation during the summer in cases of mid-season droughts. Based on studies conducted in connection with the Teotihuacan Valley Project, the 5,800 hectares postulated as under irrigation in the sixteenth century could have supported at least 46,000–52,000 people (calculating an average yield of 1,200–1,400 kg. per hectare and an average annual consumption, per capita, of 160 kgs.). The system was, therefore, a major component in the ecological system of the valley.

Today, much of the sloping terrain of the piedmont and the lower slopes of the surrounding hills are severely eroded and of marginal value for agriculture. Archaeological evidence indicates that in 1519 erosion was carefully controlled by means of a series of structures adapted to the variable angle of the slopes. Today farmers in the valley control erosion by two basic methods. On low gradients they enclose the field with low banks of earth planted with maguey; such fields are referred to as bancals. In areas of steeper gradient, more formal defensive walls of rock, earth,

234

and tepetate are used; we will refer to the technique as terracing. There is conclusive evidence of terracing in Aztec times and in all probability, the bancal technique was used as well.

The productivity of terraced lands is extremely variable, dependent on maintenance, soil depth, and the position of the terrace in relation to drainage from the slopes above. In some cases, particularly where the terrace systems are located near the bases of large, steep-sided, denuded hills, runoff drainage is abundant and is carefully funnelled by canals and embankments into the terrace system. In other areas, such runoff is minimal. In the former case, the dependability of crops is very high and average yields probably range around 800–1000 kgs. of maize per hectare. In the latter cases, this average over a long span of time, probably drops to as low as 400–500 kgs.

In the middle portions of the valley, above San Juan, today most of the piedmont and the lower slopes of the hills are virtually denuded of soil and are of marginal value for cultivation. Agriculture in this area focuses on the narrow, deep-soil alluvial plain situated between the two piedmonts and a system of flood water irrigation is used to raise the productivity of this land. Drainage from the denuded hills and piedmont flows into a series of large barrancas. These barrancas, both on the piedmont and in the plain, are provided with a series of dams that capture the floodwater and divert it into the fields in the alluvial plain and on the lower edge of the piedmont. The system is most highly developed in the alluvial plain between San Martin and Otumba. The development is undoubtedly a post-Conquest phenomenon since it is essentially the product of the colonial period erosion of nearby slopes. In Aztec times, most of the runoff and soil would have been trapped by the mentioned terrace systems and in effect the alluvial plain could have been described essentially as the lower tier of the terrace systems. Flood water irrigation was apparently of significance definitely only on the north piedmont of the valley between Cerros Chiconautla and Malinalco. This is an area characterized by gently sloping terrain without major hills or ranges to produce abundant runoff for terrace cultivation. Dams were constructed across the wide passes to trap soil and water for irrigation of land at the lower edge of the piedmont. The upper part of the Teotihuacan Valley around Otumba consists predominantly of terrain of this type and may have been another area of flood water irrigation.

One of the purposes of the Teotihuacan Valley Project was to reconstruct the population size and distribution at the time of contact.

These data have been published in detail in Volume 1 of the final report (Sanders et al. 1970). Here I will simply summarize it briefly. The total population of the valley in 1519 was approximately 130,000 people. At this time the valley was divided up into 6 polities: Chiconautla, Tepexpan, Tezoyuca, Acolman, all located in the lower part of the valley below the springs; Teotihuacan located at the springs; and Otumba in the upper portion of the valley. All of these polities paid tribute to Texcoco, located outside of the Teotihuacan Valley to the south. The capital of each consisted of a densely settled urban community with a population varying between 1,000 and 8,000 inhabitants and perhaps 12–22 percent of the total population resided in these central communities. The balance of the population was distributed into a great number of rural settlements that varied considerably in settlement pattern, variations that were closely linked to ecological patterns. Within and on the edge of the alluvial plain were compact, radially patterned villages comparable to those found in the alluvial plain today. The bulk of the rural population, however, was distributed in an almost continuous band along the piedmonts of the valley with houses integrated with terrace systems, a type of settlement I referred to in a previous study as a line village (Sanders 1965). This type of village is particularly common in the Texcocan piedmont today. The noted polities varied in total population from 4,000 to 35,000 people.

The political subdivisions of the valley must have resulted in striking imbalances in agricultural and nonagricultural resources. All of the obsidian, for example, was within the territory of Otumba, salt was found only within the jurisdictions of Tepexpan and Tezoyuca, and ceramic clays were restricted to the territory of Teotihuacan. Chiconautla and Tepexpan were both deficient in good, irrigable agricultural land and Otumba's agriculture holdings, although considerable in size, was located in what was essentially marginal agricultural land with respect to grain production. As today, much of the land there was probably given over to specialized production of maguey. Acolman on the other hand controlled most of the top quality agricultural land of the valley. This imbalance was a powerful stimulus toward local specialization and the development of markets. In 1519, the largest market was found at Teotihuacan in the center of the valley. Although the entire area was tributary to Texcoco outside of the Teotihuacan Valley, the position of the market plus the ownership of the springs and of some of the better agricultural land led to an informal political and economic dominance by

236

this one community. The town was also the largest community in size and we would argue that this was both the product and the cause of the ecological pattern. It should also be noted that the entire chinampa area around the springs, the most productive agricultural land in the valley, was owned by Teotihuacan. Although this area could not have exceeded 1,000 hectares, the yields were 50 to 100 percent higher than that of the permanently irrigated land within the jurisdiction of Acolman so that Teotihuacan actually had an agricultural base almost as productive as Acolman. This is particularly true when we consider that much of the middle valley of the alluvial plain was also under the control of Teotihuacan.

In the subtitle of this section, I have referred to the Aztec Period as one of ecological climax. I am borrowing this term from biological ecology and it refers to a situation where there is a maximum energy utilization of a given environment. This, in terms of the limitations of Mesoamerican technology, precisely describes the Aztec use of the valley and it was probably the only period in its history when this was the case.

The only portions of the valley not heavily utilized were those above the 2,400-meter contour. As shall be demonstrated in the following section, the avoidance of this area was undoubtedly the product of the severe erosion that took place during the Formative Period.

### ALTICA TO PATLACHIQUE—ECOLOGICAL SUCCESSION

The Formative occupation of the valley differs strikingly from that described for the Aztec Period. All Altica and Chiconautla phase settlements consisted of hamlets (rural communities with less than 100 inhabitants). All three known Altica settlements were in the Patlachique Range. Of the nine substantial Chiconautla sites, six were located within the same range, one on the upper piedmont of Cerro Gordo, one on the lake shore, and another on the upper piedmont, above Otumba. In summary, eight of the nine known sites were located in areas higher in elevation than the corresponding band of Aztec piedmont settlement, in areas of marginal agricultural use in Aztec times. The one exception, furthermore, on the basis of our ceramic analyses, was probably a salt making station.

The Cuanalan Phase was marked by some diversification of settlement types. Three sites were substantial villages, both located on the edge of the alluvial plain in locations comparable to Aztec villages in the same area. One of them was located near the springs at San Juan, two others at the southern edge of the lower valley near Cuanalan. One of the latter communities covered some 6 hectares and we estimate a population of several hundred people. The balance of the sites, twenty-one in all, were comparable in size and geographic location to the Altica and Chiconautla settlements.

Between the Cuanalan and Patlachique phases is a little known transitional phase we have referred to as Tezoyuca. All known sites (six in all) were small (4–9 hectares), densely settled villages located on the top of a chain of foothills of the Patlachique Range that face the lower section of the Teotihuacan Valley. One of them, the Tezoyuca type site, is on an isolated hill above the village of Cuanalan and it is tempting to see this shift of occupation from the alluvial plan to the hilltop as relating to an intensification of patterns of land competition. The low number of such sites, and their restricted geographic distribution within the valley, however, is puzzling. It was also during this phase that public buildings appeared for the first time and each site has a small civic-ceremonial precinct.

The overall picture that emerges from the Middle and Late Formative Period data is one of a small but increasing population of pioneer farmers living in small settlements with a striking preference for settlement at the higher elevations (2,400–2,600 ms.) and organized into societies probably integrated by kinship ties rather than the principle of ranking or stratification.

During the period in question, the higher elevations of the valley undoubtedly had a respectable soil cover (one can see remnants of the old soil cover in various places today). This plus the heavier rainfall and relative freedom from frosts would have made this portion of the valley ideal for settlement by a population in the early stages of its adaptation to the area.

The lack of evidence of terracing during the period and the small size of the settlements suggest extensive practices of cultivation—this is also indicated by the small total size of the population. Generally speaking, farmers tend to practice systems of cultivation that give the highest return per hour of work and extensive practices are generally more productive in this sense than intensive ones. In part of highland Mexico today, particularly in areas of hilly terrain, relatively high rainfall, and low population density, a type of swidden cultivation referred to as tlacolol is

238

practiced and we suspect that this was the system practiced by the pre-Patlachique population of the valley.

In an area like the Teotihuacan Valley, however, the practice of swidden agriculture on hillsides would have led to severe erosion and it is doubtful that a substantial population or a stable ecological system could be established based on this approach. The relatively early appearance of villages in the alluvial plain indicates that other alternatives were being tried some time after the initial occupation of the area.

During the first four phases of the Formative Period, there is a striking lack of correlation between population clustering and the position of nonagricultural resources. The population as a whole seems to have been well below even the level of full utilization of the hillier land with long cycling swidden agriculture and the implication from the settlement pattern data is that such resources were readily accessible to all settlements.

The Patlachique Phase, which follows, is perhaps the most critical one in the history of the valley and was truly a time of transition. The previous predilection for residence in the upper elevations seems to continue, if one simply makes a numerical count of sites. Fifty-seven sites, all hamlets or collections of hamlets, were located in the 2,300–2,600 meter band, indicating a sizable expansion of population in those areas during this phase, to perhaps two-and-one-half times that present in Cuanalan times.

Even more striking, however, is the enormous expansion of population in the vicinity of and within the alluvial plain. The hilltop community at Tezoyuca expanded into a large, sprawling community, covering 50 hectares, on the lower flanks of the same hill.

Even more imposing is the population concentration found at and near the Early Classic city. Millon (1966) estimates the community here as covering at least 4 square kilometers or 400 hectares, an enormous settlement compared to anything earlier or contemporary. He estimated the population at 5,000–10,000 people. (More recently Millon has revised this estimate to 600–800 hectares, or 20,000–40,000 people. See Millon 1973.)

It is difficult, of course, to present an accurate picture of population size and distribution from archaeological settlement pattern data alone and our survey was not complete. But what does stand out is the fact that no cluster of population in the valley in Patlachique times was remotely comparable with that found within and near the area of the Classic city.

239

None of the hillside settlements had populations exceeding 100 inhabitants so that the total population of the known sites, dispersed over a considerable area, was possibly no greater than that of the Teotihuacan site. In all probability, therefore, between one-third and one-half of the total population of the valley was concentrated at Teotihuacan. (If we use Millon's higher estimate for the population of the city, then 80,000–90,000 were living there.) There is also evidence that the valley population was politically unified under the leadership of the town since ceremonial construction is completely absent in the smaller sites.

This brings us to the question of the why and the how of this shift in population distribution and its political consequences. The location of the Teotihuacan community clearly indicates a new focus on cultivation of the alluvial plain. The location plus the large size of the population can most reasonably be explained by the inception of some form of intensive cultivation at this time. This postulation is given added support by the pollen graph presented in Figure 8.1. The core was taken by Anton Kovar from a place near Atlatongo called El Tular. Particularly significant in the graph is the behavior of a group of plants called cyperacea or sedges. These are plants that live under swampy conditions. In the lower levels of the graph (from 3 to 6 meters below the surface) cyperacea make up 30 percent of the pollen sample and sedges were undoubtedly the dominant plants all over the spring area prior to its drainage for irrigation. At the 3–2.5 meter level the percentage suddenly and dramatically drops to perhaps 7 percent of the total sample, then gradually declines to a low point of 3 percent in the uppermost level. The most likely explanation for this reduction is artificial drainage of the swamps. El Tular is a small spring located 2.5 kilometers downvalley from the main cluster of springs at San Juan, indicating that the drainage project had evolved to include land at least that far downvalley.

By a comparison of the pollen profile from El Tular with another one taken at Cuanalan, where it can be directly correlated with the Formative occupation there, we have been able to relate the El Tular graph to the history of settlement in the valley. It seems that the rapid reduction of sedge pollen at El Tular dates from the Patlachique Phase, thus strikingly agreeing with the history of settlement in the valley. Also supporting this explanation is the fact that maize pollen appears approximately or slightly before the time of the sudden reduction of the frequency of sedges.

In 1969, in a paper given at the AAAS symposium on Pre-Hispanic

240

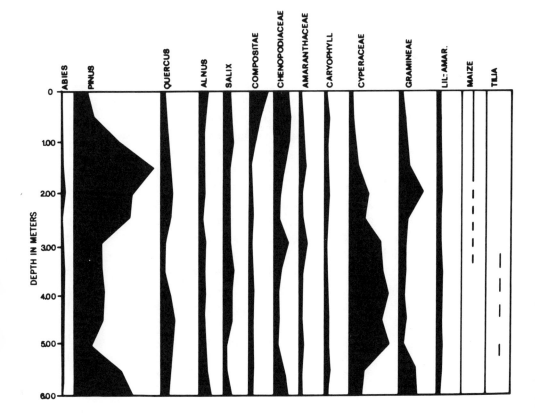

Figure 8.1   Pollen diagram 1, El Tular.

Land Use in Mesoamerica, Kent Flannery presented calculations of the
productivity of maize agriculture during the various phases of the
Formative Period in the Valley of Oaxaca. He noted the small size of the
ears of maize in Formative sites in the Tehuacan Valley. He then
established productivity figures based on a comparison of the ear size of
Formative, post Classic and contemporary maize and arrives at a figure
for Early Formative maize of perhaps only 20 percent of modern yields.
In his Valley of Oaxaca model for the Early Formative , he postulated
widely spaced sedentary hamlets and villages, the inhabitants of which
cultivated fields with a yield of as low as 200 kgs. per hectare. I doubt that
sedentary villages can be maintained with a yield that low. The problem I
feel revolves around the point as to whether a simple comparison of the
size of ears is adequate as a basis for estimating productivity figures. The
probabilities are great that the smaller Formative maize plants (since they
would have required less water and nutrients for growth) were either

planted closer together than the larger, more demanding varieties of modern maize, or as Mangelsdorf et al. point out, was a plant that produced several stalks with multiple ears (1964).

In summary, while I agree completely with the thesis that the large eared varieties of modern maize undoubtedly produce greater yields than Formative maize, I doubt that the difference in productivity was as extreme as Flannery argues. By Terminal Formative and Early Classic time, yields were more probably two-thirds that of modern varieties, and I would argue that Early Formative maize, in order to form the basis of a sedentary village economy, must have yielded minimally an average of 400–500 kgs. per hectare—the minimal level that modern cultivators feel a field is worth planting. (This figure is based upon my studies of contemporary agricultural practices, in Mexico [Sanders 1965; also see Allan 1965] for an account of peasant attitudes towards minimum productivity in Africa.)

My impression is that much of the irrigated land used in the Teotihuacan Valley at this time was probably similar in its morphology to the chinampas presently found near the springs of San Juan. Today, because of the overall desiccation of the valley, only 100 hectares of land can be cultivated in this manner, but at the end of the Formative the area of high water table could have been considerably greater.

Much of the area between Atlatongo and Santa Maria Coatlan was swamp during the Formative Period and the system of cultivation may have been in the neighborhood of 1,000 hectares. Considering the high productivity of this type of land and even considering the lower yield of Terminal Formative maize, the entire Patlachique town (assuming a population of 5,000–10,000) could have easily been supplied with its basic maize requirements from these lands and even have produced a substantial surplus. If Millon's more recent estimates of the population of the city are correct, then a sizable percentage of the lower valley would have had to be irrigated as well.

It would seem probable that the key nonagricultural resources of the valley were directly controlled by this central town or the ruling group of the town, but direct evidence of such a pattern is absent in the archaeological record and will be exceedingly difficult to come by. One major resource, good pottery clay, is found only within the vicinity of the town; another, basalt, is found in all areas of Patlachique settlement concentration. The lack of settlements near the obsidian and salt

242

producing zones we suggest indicates direct control of these resources from the central town.

What we have postulated for the Patlachique Phase is a polity involving the entire valley with a population of perhaps 20,000–50,000 people. This polity was integrated under the leadership of a town of 5,000–40,000 people whose demographic, and consequently political, dominance can best be understood in terms of their control of a key agricultural resource.

The Formative Period, in summary, was one of experimentation, in which a variety of approaches were used in the exploitation of the valley. The term ecological succession, used in the subtitle, is comparable in meaning to that in biology. In the latter field it refers to the process and steps by which a plant community reaches climax stage—or the most efficient utilization of the environment. The change in vegetation as a pond becomes a bog and ultimately a woodland is a classic example.

### THE TEOTIHUACAN PERIOD—ECOLOGICAL SELECTION

The period we refer to as the Teotihuacan Period covers the following phases in chronological order: Tzalqualli, Miccaotli, Tlamimilolpa, Xolalpan, and Metepec. This period is marked by a series of extraordinary events, some of which were local. Others far transcend events not only in the Basin of Mexico but throughout Mesoamerica.

In the Teotihuacan Valley there was a veritable population explosion in which the Patlachique town grew first (Tzaqualli Phase) into a city estimated by Millon (1966) to have at least 30,000 people (a 1973 estimate is 60,000) and ultimately to a metropolis (Late Xolalpan Phase) of 125,000 people.

During the same time, the city underwent a series of architectural transformations from an unplanned, relatively dispersed pattern to a much more densely settled rectangular grid pattern, from an essentially homogeneous agricultural community to one marked by increasing occupational specialization and social stratification.

With respect to events outside of the valley, Teotihuacan emerged first as the dominant polity of Central Mexico, ultimately of all of Mesoamerica, with an extensive network of ties, some involving trade relations, others, conquest, of areas as far afield as the Valley of Guatemala.

Quite obviously not all of these processes can be linked directly to local ecology, but some of them undoubtedly are the product, in part or in whole, of local ecological processes that began in the Patlachique Phase. Unfortunately we do not have direct data to demonstrate that the population growth during the first phases of the history of the city was closely related to the expansion of the permanent irrigation system but there are a variety of data that indirectly point to this conclusion. First, the pollen graph does show a further decline of sedges in those levels that must correlate with the Teotihuacan Period, indicating a continuous process of artificial drainage of the spring area. Second, the city itself was traversed by a number of major barrancas all of which were artificially straightened and altered—demonstrating the existence of a definite pattern of manipulation of drainage systems. Combined with this is evidence at the city of hydraulic construction in the form of a series of canals and reservoirs. Finally, we have evidence at marginal locations in the valley, of canals that are certainly pre-Aztec (that is, they run underneath Aztec-Contemporary systems); they occur in one of the few areas of heavy rural Teotihuacan Period occupation (on the north slope of Cerro Gordo). These canals were either of the flood water type or possibly based on permanent streams, but in either case this use of marginal hydraulic resources would strongly suggest full utilization of the primary sources.

Several researchers, both in conversation and in publication, have criticized my argument about the functional significance of the permanent irrigation system in the evolution of Teotihuacan as a state and city on the basis that the system was too small to have played the major functions I have suggested. The utility of my approach has already been demonstrated, at least in the emergence of the Proto-state and Proto-city during the Patlachique Phase. It now remains to discuss the continued significance of the system during the final evolution of the city. In his recent studies (1966, 1973) Millon estimates the population of the Tzaqualli city at 30,000–60,000. Thus, population greatly exceeded what could have been supported by the chinampa system of the spring area. He has also made the point that during this period Teotihuacan had already emerged as a city. If the permanent irrigation system, however, was used to the maximum extent, it could have provided most of the maize for the entire Tzaqualli city without the need of other agricultural land! Surpluses and other crops could have been provided from the

244

balance of the land of the valley or from outlying areas. Even if one argues that less productive varieties of maize were used, it is still obvious from the data that the majority of the food supply for the Tzaqualli city could have been derived from the irrigation system alone and all of its food supply from the total resources of the Teotihuacan Valley. We must also bear in mind the strong possibility of other sources of permanent water or an even greater flow from the San Juan springs as was the case in 1920.

As the city grew to a metropolis of 125,000 people, it obviously far outgrew the production of the permanent irrigation system. One more point, however, should be stressed here. We have estimated the average production at 1,400 kgs. per hectare, a figure derived from our study of contemporary cultivation. In fact, this is a conservative figure based on the fact that animal fertilizers are only sparingly utilized today by the population. If we consider the fact that the sewage of the city of 125,000 people discharged into the system, the average productivity could have been considerably above this figure and approximated that of lands today which are consistently fertilized (such lands probably yield on the average 1,800–2,000 kgs. of maize per hectare).

With respect to the Basin of Mexico as a whole, there is growing evidence that the system of farming and patterns of land use were not as intensive during the Teotihuacan Period as during Aztec times. We estimate the maximum population in Early Classic times at about a quarter that of the Aztec, perhaps 250,000 people. It could have been as low as 200,000. If we accept these figures and calculations, then in Teotihuacan times the irrigated plain, an area of 58 km², provided the basic food supply for 15–20 percent of the population of a total area of 7,800 km²—by any definition a critical resource.

In summary, the early phase of the evolution of the Teotihuacan city and state can be functionally understood as a response to irrigation agriculture, and even in its latest phases the irrigation system remained a critical resource in the economy of the city. The rapidly expanding population can in part be linked to the growth of this system.

There is evidence that this rise of population, however, was also the product of a process of massive migration into the city from the area south of the Teotihuacan Valley. Following Parsons (1971), the Formative history of the Texcoco piedmont region is one of a gradually expanding population, reaching a climax during the equivalent of our

Patlachique Phase. Following this there was a dramatic and drastic reduction of population which coincided very closely with the population explosion at Teotihuacan in Tzaqualli times documented by Millon. It is tempting to see all of these events as functionally correlated: the rise of a valley-wide state or chiefdom in Patlachique times, the subsequent conquest of the Texcoco piedmont settlements, the rapid and possibly planned movement of population to the city from that area and its integration into the political structure of the city, and finally, the sudden influx of manpower as relating to the final expansion of the irrigation system.

In this context the significance and value of Wittfogel's hydraulic agricultural hypothesis (1955) becomes particularly meaningful. The control of the springs was a factor in the emergence of Teotihuacan first as the Valley of Teotihuacan polity. The unification of the valley under Teotihuacan provided this polity with a competitive edge over nearby smaller ones on the Texcoco piedmont; the combination of these settlements and their nucleation into a single major population center (which to a great degree was made possible by the expansion of the canal system) in Tzaqualli times resulted in the nucleation of perhaps 80–90 percent of the entire population of the Basin of Mexico into a single physical settlement, thus assuring the ultimate control of the basin. In short, the significance of a key resource must be evaluated in terms of the contemporary demographic situation and in a context of a process of levels of competition related to levels of integration. The Teotihuacan irrigation system was not a critical resource in Aztec times—because of the relative size of the total population of the Basin of Mexico (estimated at 1,000,000 people) to the capacity of the canal system. Under the demographic conditions of Aztec times other, more productive systems of agriculture (see Armillas 1971) and the area in which they were found became the critical resource. The Aztec period was one of greater variation generally of intensive practices of land use which permitted a full use of the basin's agricultural resources. Hence our use of the term "ecological climax."

In the subtitle, the Teotihuacan Period was characterized as one of ecological selection. This term has no real counterpart in biological ecology but it seems a useful one in this context. What is implied by the term is that the period was one in which a relatively stable ecological system emerged, but also one in which there was not a maximal use of the

246

energy potential of the area, certainly not comparable to that characteristic of the Aztec Period. The picture we have of Teotihuacan ecology is
rather comparable to what is found today among the Hausa of northern
Nigeria. Each Hausa city or town is located within a small core area of
intensively cultivated land. The balance of the area is much less densely
settled, considerably larger in size, is cultivated using extensive practices
of farming, and is politically and economically dependent upon the core
(Buchanan and Pugh 1966).

In the case of Teotihuacan, in its early phases the Texcoco piedmont,
the upper Teotihuacan Valley and the northern edge of the valley,
played the role of the hinterland to the core; in its later phases the Basin
of Mexico became its hinterland. There were probably smaller local
patterns of core-hinterland relationships in the Central Mexican area in
Late Formative and Early Teotihuacan times; centered around Cui-
cuilco, Amalucan, Azcaputzalco, Cholula, and probably others.

This ecological selection was made possible in part because the total
population base was small, in part because the growth of Teotihuacan
political power outside of the basin occurred at a faster pace than the
population grew within it, thus making overall intensification of land use
unnecessary. Food and other resources could be drawn from a much wider
orbit. Problems of transportation, however, made it imperative that at
least a substantial percentage of the food supply be drawn from a nearby
source, hence the continuing function of the core. Millon in several
papers has demonstrated a definite increase of craft specialization as an
economic factor in the growth of the city (1966, 1967, 1970, 1973). This
process undoubtedly is linked with Teotihuacan's growing political power
and widening of its orbits of trade for its craft products, and concurrently
its geographic range of sources for food staples.

It may seem to many readers that I have taken an extreme position
when I argue that the rise of Teotihuacan as a city of 125,000 people and
as the center of a state of several million people with military colonies as
far afield as Kaminaljuyu was the product of the evolution of an irrigation
system that watered only 58 km$^2$ of land and could supply a maximum
food supply for a population of only 52,000 people; but the argument
must be understood in terms of historical processes operating in a context of rising levels of competition over a period of 1,000 years and it
must be viewed within the framework of the core-periphery concept.

With respect to resource use other than agriculture, the situation

247

during the Classic Period changes strikingly from the Formative. The requirements for such resources as obsidian, salt, lake foods, and lumber for a city of 125,000 people undoubtedly far exceeded the local resources of the Teotihuacan Valley. Although settlement pattern data from some portions of the Basin of Mexico are lacking, what we do have suggest that the Teotihuacanos treated this huge area as a sort of personal resource domain to maintain the life-style of the city. Obsidian processing became a major industry of the city (Millon [1967, 1970], for example, defines 500 definite craft specializing house compounds within the city of which the majority were obsidian workers) and the local obsidian resources were clearly unable to meet this demand. The huge Pachuca deposits north of the Teotihuacan Valley were under extensive exploitation at this time and Teotihuacan became the major obsidian supplier for Mesoamerica. Aside from this, most of the small sites that were reported by Parsons (1971a, b, 1973) in the Texcoco-Xochimilco-Chalco areas he feels were special activity sites for collecting specific resources. Such sites occur up near the base of the main mountain range where the remaining forest resources were located, on the piedmont, and along the lakeshore where the collection of salt and lakeshore products was probably the major stimulus for their location.

## TOLTEC PERIOD

To complete the picture of the history of land use patterns of the Teotihuacan Valley, we need now only to summarize the situation during the period from the end of Teotihuacan as a city and as a major political power and the Aztec period, the period referred to in the literature as the Toltec Period.

With the collapse of the city and the state it governed there was a rapid and major population decline in the Teotihuacan Valley. In the succeeding Xometla Phase the total population residing outside of the borders of the ancient Teotihuacan city probably did not exceed 10,000 people, of which at least two-thirds resided in compact villages and small towns on the edge of the irrigated plain. Until Millon's survey is published, we only have a vague idea of the size of the population that remained at Teotihuacan itself but from preliminary data it was at least equivalent and probably substantially larger in size than that of the outlying population. The Xometla pattern is highly suggestive that the rest of the valley was in fact of marginal value at the apogee of Teotihuacan. What we have apparently is a rapid movement of skilled craftsmen, merchants, and other specialized personnel to new political centers; the remainder of the population were probably descendants of the farming class of the Teotihuacan city. The pattern, therefore, is again one of ecological selection, that is, towards the irrigated core; it was made possible not because of the expanded political power of the central community but because of the total population decline of the valley.

The succeeding Mazapan Phase set the stage for the phase of ecological climax we have described for the Aztec Period and it witnessed a rapid expansion of settlements in virtually all areas of the valley that were occupied in 1519. The difference is essentially one of intensity and density of settlements rather than total pattern. In this sense, the Mazapan Phase could be considered one of ecological succession.

The following maps (Figures 8.2–8.9) attempt to reconstruct the history of settlement of the Valley of Teotihuacan during pre-Hispanic times. The reconstruction is imaginative in the sense that it goes considerably beyond the archaeological data.

This is particularly true where we have delineated tribal and provincial borders. With respect to the tribal borders drawn in Figures 8.3 and 8.4, our model is based on the pattern of territoriality commonly found among contemporary tribal societies with low population densities. Because of the needs of defense such societies tend to cluster their settlements within a relatively small core area, an area which furthermore is the scene of their most intensive subsistence activities. Territorial rights over this core are jealously guarded and defended. Tribes also claim large tracts of peripheral territories that are vaguely defined and extensively utilized; on the map in Figure 8.6 we have indicated the core territories based on hamlet and village spacing.

With respect to provincial borders, in Maps (Figures) 8.7 and 8.8 we have applied the principle of site ranking and spacing to define them, drawing particularly on the pattern in Map (Figure) 8.9 for the Conquest Period where the controls are good.

The reconstruction of patterns of land use and resource exploitation are intended as models which agree with the direct or indirect data cited in the paper but we freely admit their tentative nature and the possibilities of later revision as more data become available.

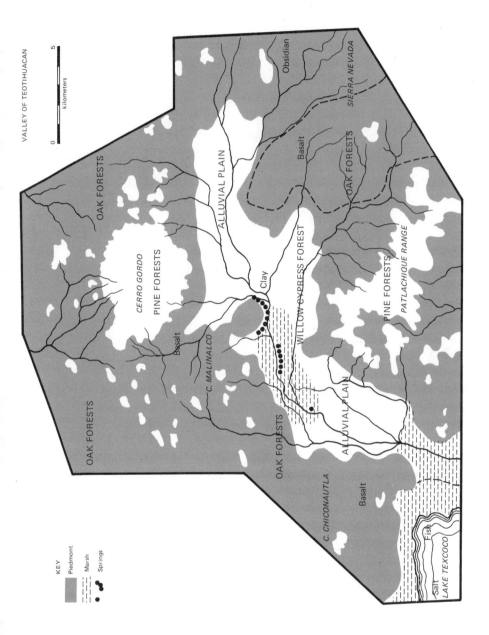

VALLEY OF TEOTIHUACAN

0 kilometers 5

KEY
Piedmont
Marsh
Springs

OAK FORESTS

CERRO GORDO
PINE FORESTS

Basalt

ALLUVIAL PLAIN

Clay

C. MALINALCO

OAK FORESTS

WILLOW-CYPRESS FOREST

ALLUVIAL PLAIN

OAK FORESTS

C. CHICONAUTLA

Basalt

Fish
Salt
LAKE TEXCOCO

Obsidian

Basalt

OAK FORESTS

SIERRA NEVADA

PINE FORESTS

PATLACHIQUE RANGE

Figure 8.2   Natural environment and key resources.

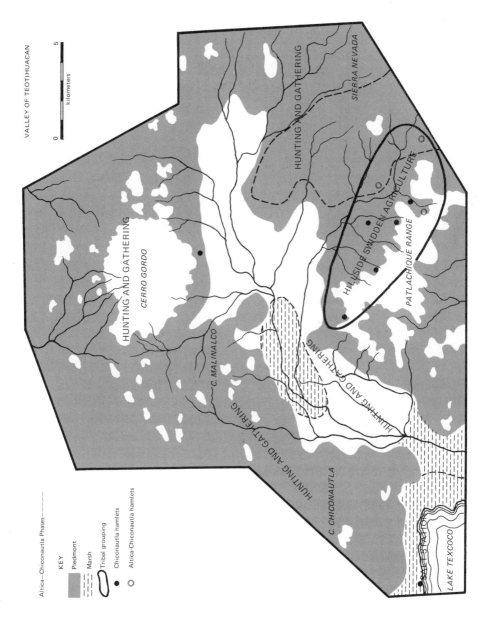

VALLEY OF TEOTIHUACAN

Altica–Chiconautla Phases ————

KEY

Piedmont

Marsh

Tribal grouping

• Chiconautla hamlets

◦ Altica-Chiconautla hamlets

HUNTING AND GATHERING

SIERRA NEVADA

HILLSIDE SWIDDEN AGRICULTURE

PATLACHIQUE RANGE

CERRO GORDO

HUNTING AND GATHERING

C. MALINALCO

HUNTING AND GATHERING

HUNTING AND GATHERING

C. CHICONAUTLA

LAKE TEXCOCO

kilometers

0        5

Figure 8.3   Altica-Chiconautla Phases.

Figure 8.4  Cuanalan Phase.

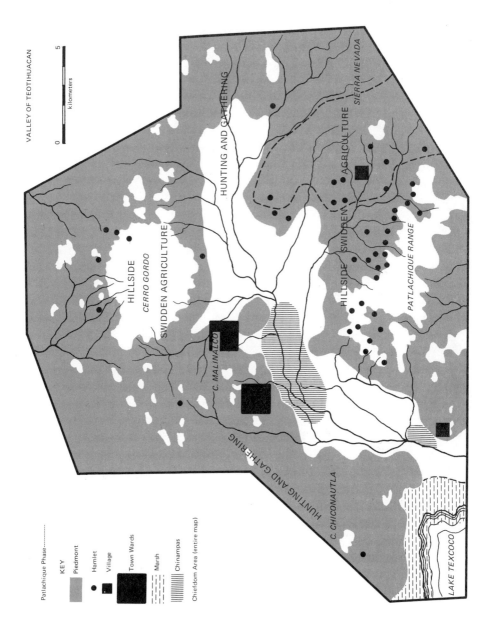

VALLEY OF TEOTIHUACAN

0   5

kilometers

HILLSIDE
*CERRO GORDO*
SWIDDEN AGRICULTURE

HUNTING AND GATHERING

*SIERRA NEVADA*

HILLSIDE SWIDDEM AGRICULTURE

*PATLACHIQUE RANGE*

*C. MALINALCO*

HUNTING AND GATHERING

*C. CHICONAUTLA*

*LAKE TEXCOCO*

Patlachique Phase..........

KEY

Piedmont

●   Hamlet

■   Village

Town Wards

Marsh

Chinampas

Chiefdom Area (entire map)

Figure 8.5   Patlachique Phase.

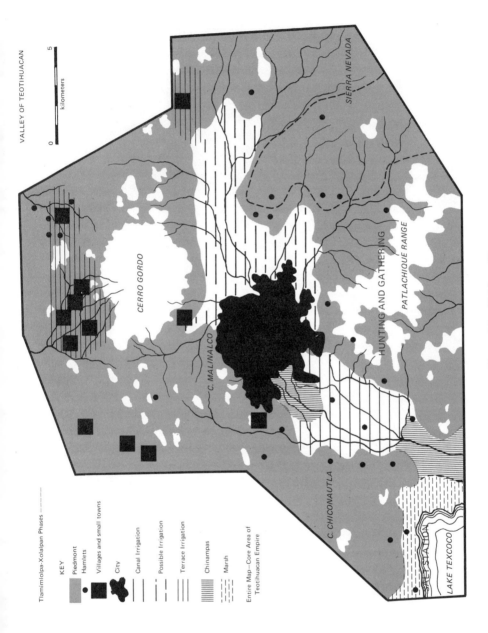

VALLEY OF TEOTIHUACAN

0    5

kilometers

Tlamimilolpa-Xolalpan Phases

KEY

Piedmont

Hamlets ·  ▪ ■

Villages and small towns

City

Canal Irrigation

Possible Irrigation

Terrace Irrigation

Chinampas

Marsh

Entire Map—Core Area of
Teotihuacan Empire

CERRO GORDO

C. MALINALCO

C. CHICONAUTLA

LAKE TEXCOCO

SIERRA NEVADA

HUNTING AND GATHERING

PATLACHIQUE RANGE

Figure 8.6  Tlamimilolpa-Xolalpan Phases.

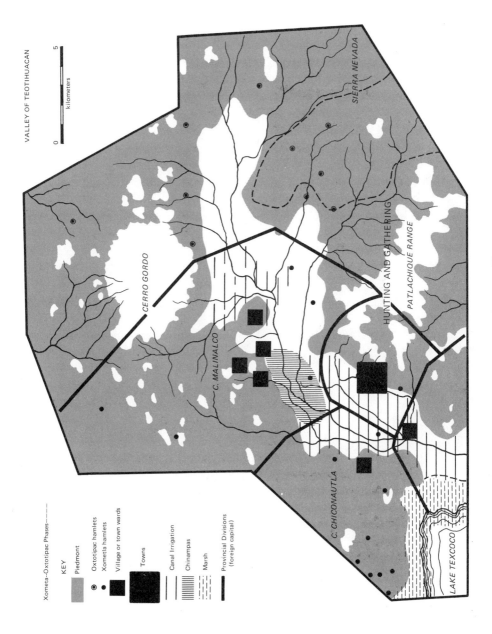

Figure 8.7  Xometla-Oxtotipac Phases.

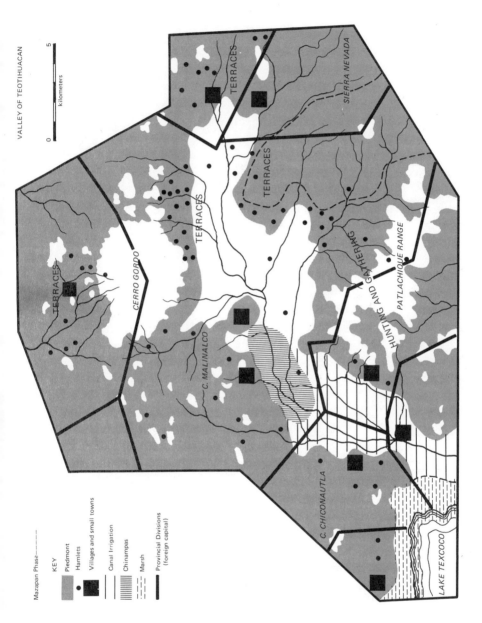

VALLEY OF TEOTIHUACAN

0 5
kilometers

KEY

Mazapan Phase
Piedmont
Hamlets
Villages and small towns
Canal Irrigation
Chinampas
Marsh
Provincial Divisions
(foreign capital)

TERRACES

CERRO GORDO

TERRACES

TERRACES

SIERRA NEVADA

TERRACES

C. MALINALCO

HUNTING AND GATHERING

PATLACHIQUE RANGE

C. CHICONAUTLA

LAKE TEXCOCO

Figure 8.8  Mazapan Phase.

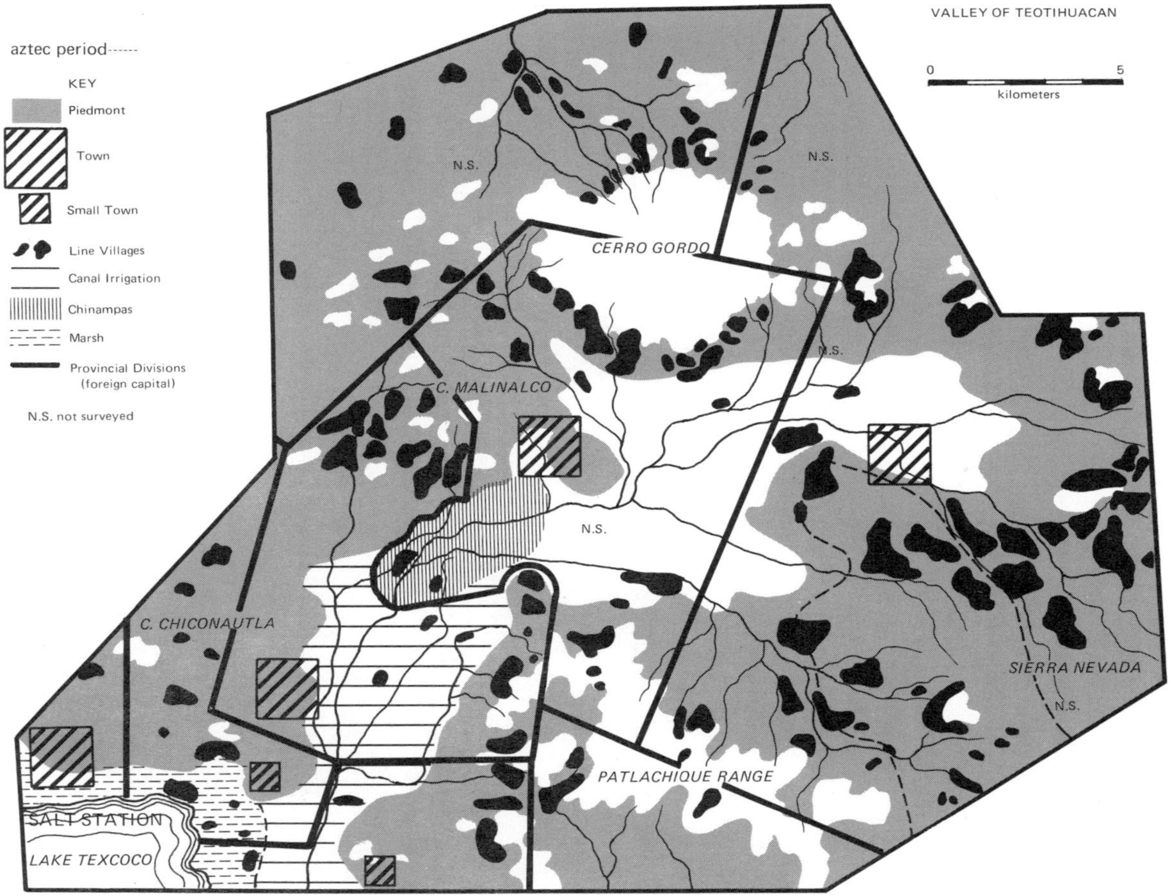

VALLEY OF TEOTIHUACAN

0 — kilometers — 5

KEY

aztec period ------

Piedmont

Town

Small Town

Line Villages

Canal Irrigation

Chinampas

Marsh

Provincial Divisions
(foreign capital)

N.S. not surveyed

CERRO GORDO

SIERRA NEVADA

PATLACHIQUE RANGE

C. MALINALCO

C. CHICONAUTLA

SALT STATION

LAKE TEXCOCO

N.S.

Figure 8.9  Aztec Period.

# Systems Theory and Simulation:
# The Case of Hawaiian Warfare
# and Redistribution

FRED PLOG

*Department of Anthropology*
*Arizona State University*
*Tempe*

One of the themes, if not the major theme, of the papers and discussions in the School for American Research seminar on prehistoric change has been systems theory. This focus is not at all surprising given the immense popularity of systems theory and systemic concepts in archaeology and, to a lesser extent, in anthropology as a whole. An equally evident theme is the disagreement among the seminar participants with respect to specific interpretations of systemic concepts and the systems literature, not to mention quite varied evaluations of the portions of that literature useful in anthropological studies. Again, I would argue, this disagreement rather accurately reflects a larger debate within archaeology and anthropology.

Near the end of the seminar, it seemed to the participants that a number of these issues might be better understood by all of us if we participated in a cooperative effort to use the systems literature in attempting to gain insight into a particular phenomenon. Before turning to that phenomenon, I want to review some of the issues and points of disagreement that underlay our initial decision to attempt a specific application of systems theory. Inevitably, my statement of a number of these issues will clearly betray my own position in regard to them. Finally, I do not wish to imply that our viewpoints on these issues were diametrically opposed.

## SUBSTANTIVE AND FORMAL SYSTEMS

At least two usages of the concept of system were evident in our discussions. On the one hand, the term was used to refer to on-the-ground or *substantive* systems—organized exchanges of matter and energy between individuals and groups and the resultant interdependency of those individuals and groups. On the other hand, the term was used in reference to systems of variables or *formal* systems. These describe not on-the-ground behavior and organization, but the causal connections that determine behavior and organization.

## USEFUL ASPECTS OF SYSTEMS THEORY

At least three interpretations of the utility of the systems literature were evident in our discussions. (1) Systems theory is a source of concepts. This position was taken by those who find utility in discussions of, for example, equifinality, homeostasis, and deviation amplification. Advocates of this position argue that a concern with such concepts provides a significant basis for the orientation of fieldwork and for the formulation of explanations. (2) Systems theory is a source of propositions or laws that govern or describe the behavior of systems. The proposition that deviation-amplifying processes must be triggered by exogenous events is an example. So are the many statements one can read that take the form: "Under conditions a . . . d, systems tend to. . . ." (3) Systems theory is primarily of analytical utility: it provides guidance in modeling a set of relationships, whether on-the-ground or causal. Simulation models and the literature describing their design are the best examples of this interpretation of systems theory.

260

## THE UTILITY OF SIMULATION MODELS

Among those who express some interest in the modeling component of systems theory, there are different viewpoints taken on the issue of the utility of such models. Some argue that such models are useful prior to undertaking fieldwork as a means of identifying data that must be collected in order to use the systems literature in its broader aspects. Another perspective is that simulation is the stage in systems research when one determines whether or not a particular systems model works—when the system is turned on does it perform in the same manner as the on-the-ground system? Finally, it is argued that simulation involving multiple computer runs of a model is necessary for probabalistic reasons. To wit, if a particular model predicts only a single possible outcome, it is not a system model but a functional description. If more than a single outcome is possible, then multiple "runs" of that model under varied conditions are necessary in order to understand the manner in which the system adjusts to varying environmental contingencies, and to understand the fit between the model and the on-the-ground system.

### HAWAIIAN WARFARE

It was the realization that these different perspectives were not mutually exclusive but in many ways complementary that led us to believe that we might better understand these issues by attempting a specific application of systems theory, constructing a model of a specific system. We chose to consider the case of evolution from chiefdom to state organization in Hawaii discussed by Saxe in this volume (chapter 4). This direction was chosen for two reasons. First, Saxe had brought to the seminar a paper which contained far more data than the others. Second, Saxe's paper raised a very fundamental issue, that of the relationship between homeostasis and morphogenesis. Specifically, he argued strongly that this evolutionary episode was triggered by an exogenous variable or "kicker," and that changes from one system form to another are inevitably so initiated. Some participants argued that this proposition should be treated as a testable hypothesis—that it should not be assumed but demonstrated. It was agreed that simulation would provide a useful means for testing Saxe's argument.

Our efforts focused on understanding the apparent stability of the cyclical rise and fall of dominant paramounts who came close to, but never quite succeeded in, establishing hegemony over the islands, and the factors which upset this apparently stable system leading to the appearance of the Hawaiian state. Specifically, we needed to determine whether the system was in fact stable. As an alternative, one could argue that the system never was stable, that, over time, paramounts came closer and closer to hegemony and total dominance was finally obtained. Given evidence of a stable system, we needed to determine whether only external variables could upset that stability or whether it could also be upset by internal changes.

Our efforts to understand this phenomenon focused on three separate questions: (1) What factors led to the recurrent efforts on the part of paramounts to conquer their neighbors? (2) How were opponents selected? (3) What factors determined the winner and the loser of a conflict? Question one is implicitly two questions since conflicts between paramounts were sometimes initiated by the paramounts themselves and other times by members of marginal clans who attempted to shift their allegiance from one paramount to another.

The simulation done in attempting to answer question two is trivial. A variety of solutions can be proposed to the question of how opponents are selected that do not differ substantially from one another. Answering question number three is anything but trivial. Had we successfully determined how wars were won and lost we would all have been hired by The Rand Corporation at salaries far higher than those we currently earn. It was our efforts to answer question one that offered the greatest insight into systems theory, simulation, and the evolution of the Hawaiian state.

Our efforts to understand the recurrent warfare in the Hawaiian islands focused on the economic organization of the islands, particularly the redistributive system. We went in this direction for three reasons. As a rule, the collection and redistribution of resources by the chief and his lineage made up the most basic organizational linkage in a chiefdom. Given the ubiquitous association of chiefdom organization and warfare, this central organizational linkage seemed a likely locus of the factors that led to warfare. Second, the data indicated that most warfare in the Hawaiian islands was economic warfare—it was fought not so much for killing (although deaths did occur), or for political dominance (although political domination did result), as for both immediate and long-term control of resources. Finally, the predominant cultural materialist bias

262

made an economic-ecological focus desirable because it was these phenomena that we were best equipped to discuss.

### THE SIMULATION MODEL

It should be understood that the participants in the seminar did not simulate Hawaiian warfare. Nor did we complete the simulation model in either a substantive or a formal sense. We did, however, sketch the substantive and formal linkages that lie at the core of such a model, and in the process gained considerable insight into the operation and organization of Hawaiian chiefdoms.

Our efforts to build a model of the operation of the redistributive system that links individual ramages to a paramount ramage focused on the relationship between the paramount ramage and one other ramage in the paramountcy. That is, we assumed that the relationship of the paramount ramage to any one ramage was governed by rules that were structurally homologous to the rules governing the relationship of the paramount ramage to all other ramages. Such a proposition does not therefore, exclude the possibility of ranked clans.

Figure 9.1 shows the system which we ultimately defined. I have used the conventions shown in the key to that figure in illustrating the system.

1.  The paramount ramage and each other ramage possess a stock of resources (1), (2).
2.  The primary linkage between the paramount ramage and any other ramage is the flow of resources between their two stocks via collection and redistribution (3), (4).
3.  Other resources enter and leave the resource stock of any given ramage through production and consumption (5), (6).
4.  The paramount ramage acquires and expends resources through production and consumption (7), (8).
5.  The paramount ramage resource stock is also dependent on the flow of resources from all other ramages (9), (10), and on the quantity of resources won and lost in warfare (11), (12). The resource set of the paramount lineage is larger and has a greater variety of inputs and outputs than that of any other ramage.
6.  Each of the flows described above is regulated by some combination of cultural and natural variables.

To this point I have described the structure of the system. Let us now

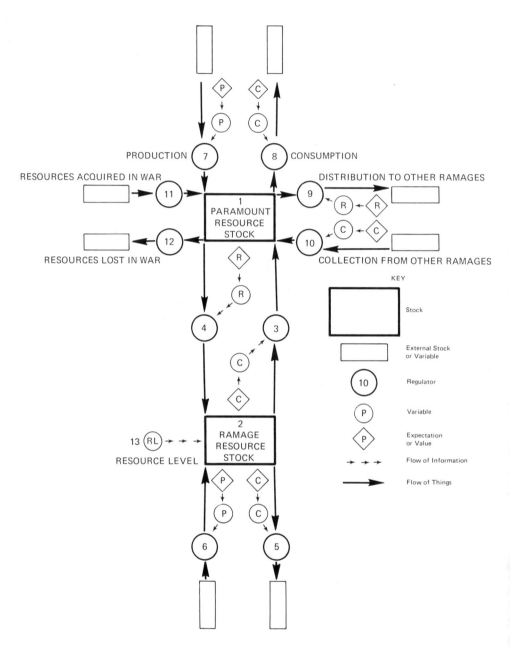

Figure 9.1 Systems model of flows between a paramount resource stock and that of a ramage.

turn to the question of the factors that regulate the flows of resources between the two stocks.

First, for every ramage, there is a resource level (13) which must be maintained in order to insure that the ramage has the resources required for the survival of its members. Normally, a ramage will have a resource set larger than this minimum that is employed for both consumption and redistribution. What is critical for the analysis, is simply that some minimum resource level, below which the members of the ramage will begin to die off, is identified. Ordinarily, the major source of the resources held by a ramage will be its own production. Ethnographic data suggest that a lesser quantity of goods is redistributed to a ramage than is collected from it. In other words, the redistributive network is not a normal source of production above consumption for the ramage. Therefore, the relation between production and consumption is a critical one. Should production fall below consumption, and resources subsequently fall below the allowable minimum, then the ramage is creating a problem for the paramount. He must (a) forego collecting resources from the ramage, or (b) increase redistribution to the ramage, or (c) allow the members of that ramage to begin to starve, in which case it will likely attempt to ally with another paramount.

Let us assume a case in which as a result of some factor, the resource stock of a ramage has in fact fallen below the resource level. What are the options available to the paramount? First he can determine whether the production of the ramage is below the expected minimum or the consumption above some expected maximum. If either is the case, then the "blame" for the resource imbalance lies with the ramage; the paramount will presumably resolve the difficulty by motivating ramage members to modify their consumption and/or production practices. Second, he can examine the relationship of his own collection from and redistribution to the ramage to the expected balance of that ratio. If this relationship is out of balance, it can be adjusted.

Let us assume that a paramount has determined that a ramage is both producing and consuming as expected and that his redistribution to and collection from the ramage is at the expected levels. Either he must choose to refuse to alleviate the resource problem of the ramage, thereby risking an attempted defection and resulting warfare, or he must either increase redistribution or decrease collection to alleviate the problem, thereby creating a deficit which he must make up from some other source of goods.

What sources are open to a paramount for making up this deficit? First, he can resolve the resource deficit by increasing collection from or decreasing redistribution to other ramages. Whether or not he will choose to do so depends on the size of the deficit to be made up and the expected limits within which he is allowed to operate without risking attempts on the part of other ramages to ally with another paramount. It is important to recognize that no argument is made here that redistribution and collection must be equal for all ramages or for any one of them. The argument is that there is an expected relationship between redistribution and collection as well as expected limits to how far a paramount can go in modifying that relationship without risking attempts on the part of the members of one or more ramages to leave the paramountcy.

Second, the chief could conceivably respond to the resource deficit by modifying the consumption/production relationship within his own ramage. Such a modification could take one of two forms. He might attempt either to motivate members of his lineage to greater production or to decrease their consumption. Decreasing consumption might mean decreasing either day-to-day consumption or sumptuary consumption. The important role which sumptuary behavior seems to play in chiefdoms may well indicate that this behavior is the most typical source of resources for meeting deficits. The risk of this course of action is, however, great. Assassination or, less typically, removal from office by close kinsmen is a relatively common event in the Hawaiian chiefdoms. This threat places a powerful limit on the ability of paramounts to resolve a resource deficit in this manner.

The third and final option available to the paramount is warfare. The calculation of the desirability of taking this course of action must involve estimating the quantity of resources that will be expended in warfare, the quantity of resources that might be obtained through the war, and the probability of success in the war.

The success of this or any other simulation model would rest in large part on successfully determining the order in which different alternatives are considered. What is intriguing about this model is the suggestion that while warfare is in many respects a winner-take-all situation—the paramount either wins the war and remedies that resources difficulty or ends up in worse shape than at the outset—it may be a more desirable solution than acquiring the additional resources via his own ramage and thereby risking his own assassination or overthrow, or overtaking the resources from other ramages and risking loss of those ramages. At least, it is apparent that there are conditions under which warfare would be the only alternative as well as conditions under which it would be the most desirable alternative. Moreover, not only does it minimize internal friction, but it may also overcome or ameliorate dissension as the paramount mobilizes ideological, affective, and organizational ties for warfare.

It should be apparent that we have to this point constructed an as-if model. We are trying to determine how and why tendencies toward warfare might be inherent in the organization of a chiefdom. There are alternative models.

It should also be clear that this is a very deterministic model. For the sake of clarity, I have discussed the model from the perspective of the paramount. But even from this perspective the behavior of the paramount is absolutely constrained by cultural expectations and environmental contingencies. The advantage of the model is that it has been constructed in such a way that it can be programmed for computer simulation and one could then examine the fit between the model and the ethnographic data describing the events that are available to us. Clearly, more work would be required before such an effort could be made. For example, it would be necessary that the "let's assume a resource problem exists" be replaced by statements that specify when, where, why, and to what magnitude such problems do occur. Before discussing the relationship of this model to the systems issues identified at the outset of this chapter, I want to describe briefly the next stage that would need to occur in carrying this systems model toward a computer simulation.

## TOWARD A COMPUTER SIMULATION

The following section summarizes the kinds of logical statements that are required in order to put a model like this one on a computer and run it. The statements are not a final simulation model in any sense, but simply illustrate how data pertinent to the relationship between the paramount and any one ramage would be handled in a simulation model. Throughout, it is assumed that the situation for the entire paramountcy can be determined by summing relevant data for each ramage. What I shall describe is a single cycle of a simulation model. Ethnographically, a cycle might be equivalent to a year, several years, or a fraction of a year.

1.  Read resource level (13). This statement is a simple instruction to check the stock of resources held by the ramage. This datum is stored at some locus in the computer.

2.  If the resource level is less than X, read production and consumption. This statement is based upon the earlier argument that there is a level below which resources cannot fall if the ramage is to survive. It is further based upon the assumption that any resource deficit will first be made up by attempting to modify production and consumption by the ramage.

3.  If production is less than Y or consumption greater than Z, increase the former to Y or decrease the latter to Z. This statement asserts that for every ramage there is an expected level of production and consumption to which actual production and consumption may be raised in attempting to offset the resource deficit.

4.  Read resource level. This statement is a simple instruction to check the resource level to determine whether the deficit has been offset.

5.  If resource level is less than X, read redistribution and collection. This statement asserts that given a failure to offset the resource deficit by modifying production and consumption, a consideration of improving the situation via redistribution and collection is the next step.

6.  If redistribution is less than A, or collection greater than B, increase redistribution to A or decrease collection to B. This statement asserts that there are limits beyond which a paramount will not go attempting to resolve a resource deficit, but that he is obligated to go at least as far as those limits.

7.  Read resource level. This statement is a simple instruction to check the resource level to determine whether the deficit has been offset.

8.  If resource level is less than X, increase probability of warfare. This statement asserts that if a paramount has not increased redistribution or decreased collection to a point where the resource deficit is offset that the probability of a war is increased.

9.  If redistribution is increased or collection decreased, record an increment. This statement asserts that if redistribution has been increased or collection decreased, resources to offset those that have now been given to the ramage to offset its deficit must be found.

10. Read collection from other ramages and redistribution to other ramages. This statement asserts that a paramount will first attempt to handle this increment by modifying his relationships with other ramages.

11. If collection from other ramages is less than M or redistribution to

other ramages is greater than N, increase collection or decrease redistribution. This statement asserts that there are limits to which a paramount will go, but beyond which he will not go in adjusting relationships with other ramages to obtain the needed increment.

12. Read increment. This is a simple instruction to determine whether the increment has been offset.

13. If increment is greater than zero, read paramount production and paramount consumption. (At this point all of the kinds of statements have been defined at least once. Therefore, I will assume that the interpretation of each of the statements is clear.)

14. If paramount production is less than J or consumption is greater than L, increase production or decrease consumption.

15. Read increment.

16. If increment is greater than zero, read probability of winning a war, resources expended in a war, potential resources acquired by warfare.

## CONCLUSIONS

The discussion of the simulation model was not carried farther than this stage in the process. However, I would like to argue that there are advantages of carrying an analysis to a point like this one, even if a full-fledged simulation is not intended. These advantages can be stated in terms of the issues identified at the outset of the chapter.

### SUBSTANTIVE AND FORMAL SYSTEMS

In the context of this analysis the relationship between substantive and formal systems has been clarified. On the one hand, we have "mapped" the relationship between actual groups of people and the resources they possess created by exchanges of those resources. On the other hand, we have begun to identify the cultural rules and natural laws that regulate the relationship. Even if we cannot specify the rules or laws, we are able to suggest that they must exist in some ideological or organizational form.

### CONCEPTS, PROPOSITIONS, AND SIMULATION

All three of these components of the systems literature have been relevant to the analysis. We set out to test a proposition derived from the literature. Some of the concepts guided us in setting up the model, and, carried to its final conclusion, a simulation would permit a test of the model.

## THE USES OF SIMULATION

I would suggest that a powerful case can be made for the utility of simulation in at least two contexts. First, an exercise such as this one can be of great utility in identifying the kinds of information that must be collected in the field if a particular model is to be carried beyond the exercise stage. All of the behavior that we have imputed to paramounts, the cultural rules that have thereby been specified are covered by this thought. Second, again carried to its conclusion, the simulation would provide a means of testing a proposition about the evolution from chiefdom to state for which archaeological data are inadequate and ethnographic data are unobtainable in principle as well as in fact. That is, the kinds of data that are necessary to understand an evolutionary episode such as this one simply do not exist in the archaeological record. Not only are similar situations nonexistent ethnographically, but the reality of the field situation would not permit the collection of a set of data that would describe everything which we have proposed to simulate. On the other hand sufficient data could be collected to permit the simulation to proceed on an empirically sound base, and sufficient data could be collected to determine whether any given simulation was succeeding or failing.

# 10
# Discussion

This chapter consists of edited portions of the taped seminar discussion, with a few brief editorial insertions. The aim is to present a reasonably coherent picture of some of the major issues and arguments, agreements, and disagreements. As would be expected, the individual contributions do not, for the most part, accomplish this. While there were indeed large areas of general agreement, there were also some fundamental areas of disagreement—some of these are endemic to the social sciences, and will probably continue to be debated for years to come.

My initial intent was to present much of the discussion verbatim. This would have been too lengthy, however, so I have severely edited it. I have not only deleted many interesting ideas that were presented, but also most of the supporting data, detailed arguments, and examples adduced by the participants. In the interest of brevity I have, in fact, been forced to rephrase some of the material into a more economical form. Nonetheless, I do not believe I have distorted any of the original meaning, stated or implied; the issues are clearly revealed. Copies of the original tapes are on file at the School of American Research.

The discussion is arranged by topic or issue, roughly in the chronological order of their occurrence at the seminar. Several of the topics kept recurring throughout the proceedings, however, and I have collated these discussions and placed them together under their appropriate headings. Needless to say, the headings are my own; the original discussion was by no means so well organized. There is, in fact, no reason to regard these discretely organized topics as mutually exclusive.

## RELATIVITY OF THE DATA BASE

The following discussion concerns the idea that in explaining change the nature of our explanations will be the same, whether we use prehistoric, historic, or contemporary data—the temporal loci of the data are irrelevant.

STUART: Social anthropologists find their data among living peoples; archaeologists find their data in the ground.

HILL: I'm assuming that an explanation of change is an explanation of change, whether we're dealing with prehistoric societies or not.

FORD: The only reason we've phrased it in terms of prehistory is that we're a bunch of prehistorians.

WRIGHT: As Fred [Plog] said in his paper, the same kinds of laws will be applicable to both prehistoric and modern situations. I don't think anybody would disagree with that.

GLASSOW: Yes, but we are using prehistoric data, and therefore we do have to make our research operational differently.

SANDERS: I don't see any difference in whether we make our models operational with archaeological or ethnographic data. The archaeological problems are methodological; that is, we obtain our data by different means. But that's something else; I don't see why the archaeological problems are any different from a theoretical point of view.

GLASSOW: No; I agree. But I'm saying that we ought to be considering the problems of how we're going to be measuring our variables, and we should choose variables in terms of the data archaeologists deal with.

SANDERS: If we're interested in how and why societies change, we can't decide not to use certain variables if we find that we can't measure them with archaeological data. Such variables may be important; and if we can't find them in our data, then we can't do evolutionary studies—it's that simple. But I can't imagine that we can't find some kinds of evidence for any one of the variables we might think is important.

PERLMAN: Right; and using ethnographic data in building a general model to account for change is perfectly acceptable. In fact, this will help us get ideas that are of importance to such a model.

STUART: Yes. In the process of building the variables into a general explanatory model, the sources for our data are irrelevant. In testing it, however, we will have to measure our variables in terms of the data we find in the ground. But that's a different issue.

## WHAT IS AN EXPLANATION?

The first really major issue encountered involved the question of what formal, logical model of explanation we should use. The discussion arose out of consideration of Plog's paper, in which he espoused the necessity for employing the Hempel-Oppenheim model (Hempel and Oppenheim 1948; Hempel 1966). While most of us agreed that something like this should be our goal, and that some form of the logico-deductive approach is necessary, Perlman did not agree. He began by pointing out that Hempel emphasizes the necessity for prediction, and prediction is not the same thing as explanation

PLOG: What is understanding? Hempel says that in prediction we are able to predict; in explanation we understand why the prediction works.

WRIGHT: But you can have prediction for the wrong reasons.

PLOG: I agree. And when we reach the point of being able to recognize this we will have some justification for referring to ourselves as scientists. This will be the case when we have a number of predictive models that all predict equally well, and we have to figure out which one is predicting for the right reasons.

PERLMAN: You believe that the priority is to seek predictions first, and worry about explanation later; I do not.

PLOG: Unless you can build us a definition of explanation that does not include prediction, I don't see how you can say that what we really have to do is explain and not predict.

STUART: Mel [Perlman], what is your alternative definition of explanation?

PERLMAN: There are two types of validity. One is the Hempel-Oppenheim model, which requires that propositions be deduced strictly from laws; all propositions must be logically deducible. This model emphasizes logic and prediction, and maintains that there are certain kinds of criteria one must have for a valid explanation.

PLOG: Then you would say that there are two kinds of formal models of explanation.

PERLMAN: There is a continuum, of which Hempel has taken only the strongest, most rigorous part. I'm saying that propositions do not always have to be deduced from one another; this is too restrictive. Science is open-ended inquiry, where we neither prove nor disprove.

HILL: But this doesn't conflict with the Hempel kind of formulation.

PERLMAN: I'm saying I do not want to limit scientific activity by asking my colleagues to follow Hempel's paradigm. Other philosophers of science do not insist on logical deducibility among propositions; they allow more latitude in the nature of the logic. They use terms like "inference" and "implication"; this is looser logic.

HILL: Then you're saying that the general Hempel-Oppenheim model is OK, except that you don't want to use it in the strictly deductive-nomological sense; you don't want the logical deducibility to be that tight.

PERLMAN: No, I'm talking about a much looser relationship among propositions. I think the relationship should be logical to some degree; we all want to move toward the more rigorous end of the explanatory continuum. I do not, however, want to restrict myself at the beginning by saying that this is how I must start doing research.

STUART: You want to begin by developing an "explanation sketch," right?

PLOG: Mel [Perlman], I think you're saying that if we become too concerned with meeting rigorous standards we will become paralyzed and unable to do research.

SANDERS: Yes; it would lead us into working on little insignificant problems.

PLOG: That may be true, but I think we should at least set high standards; we should not just give up.

PERLMAN: I'm not suggesting that. I'm agreeing that logical deduction and prediction are our long-term goals. But I'm talking about effective research procedures. I think we should use looser logic, and develop explanations before worrying a great deal about predictability.

SAXE: Mel [Perlman], you're not criticizing the Hempel model as a goal, but rather in terms of the tactics of arriving at the goal, right? Tactically, you have a good point; there is a distinction between the goals of science and the actual ways in which people go about *doing* science. So you're keeping the Hempel-Oppenheim model as a goal, and talking about the practical operational considerations too, right?

PERLMAN: I'm not so sure.

STUART: Then what do you suggest as your "looser" model of explanation that will give us more comprehensive vision?

PERLMAN: Well, I currently have a path analysis going that has a dozen variables, yet I can only explain 15 percent of the variability. I need to be able to control for many other variables, and so must maintain a high degree of flexibility.

SANDERS: Flexible methodologies provide the great theories, not the rigorous methodologies.

PLOG: Yes, but I'm assuming that most of us are not Darwins.

GLASSOW: If we use rigorous methods we might increase our Darwin-like activity.

SANDERS: Provided that you can design tests that can solve the big problems—that is the difficulty.

PERLMAN: That's what I question. Rigorous methods may serve as blinders, preventing us from developing theory. I'm arguing for greater openness and tolerance.

PLOG: Or, are you opting for a different set of blinders?

HILL: I think we agree that we're not trying to restrict the use of imagination. This might happen to certain people who use rigorous methods, but it need not.

PERLMAN: Consider this. A theory is a set of interrelated propositions or laws; and if you say these laws must be logically deducible from one another, you are quickly going to limit the numbers of propositions that you can put into a theory. As soon as you build a hierarchy of propositions, with each being deducible from the last one, you quickly decrease the possibilities for the entire system of propositions; so by the time you predict at the empirical level you've got very little left. If, however, we accept the idea that the logical relationships among propositions can be ones of implication or inference, rather than deduction only, it increases vastly the number of propositions we can put into the system. And further, we can in part support our theories by the fact that the set of propositions is interrelated; that is, one proposition gains support from the others, even if it's on the same level and not hierarchically related.

GLASSOW: You're posing an imaginary problem.

SANDERS: No, it is important because it involves research strategy.

PERLMAN: In a logico-deductive system there is a rigid hierarchy of logically deduced propositions. A *systems* type of explanation is better because it is more flexible. The propositions in the system are interrelated by inference and implication, and new propositions can be added at any time new variables are thought to be important to the explanation. Many such new variables are at first unknown, and cannot be deduced from an original covering law. Therefore, to place a great emphasis on the covering law may hinder the goal of explaining the largest amount of variance we possibly can. A covering law is an axiom that is accepted as a matter of faith. We don't have to do that in a systems type of explanation; in a system, each of the propositions helps to support the other ones.

BINFORD: That's the method of science. That's the strength of a covering law; you have a whole series of partially independent domains for testing the law.

PERLMAN: The problem is that you have to accept the covering law as an axiom.

BINFORD: Yes, but only during the process of deduction. I think you are simply saying that you don't want to be harnessed with a particular rigid structure of thought, and that we all exercise what we might call "intuition." I think this is true; but once we have a series of ideas, regardless of how they are obtained, we want to depart from loose, intuitive thinking. The strategy is to begin to build the deductive consequences of the truth or falsity of our propositions; it must necessarily be a logico-deductive strategy. I'm not saying we must always *think* in this way; that may not be the way we get ideas in many cases.

PERLMAN: I agree; but it doesn't get at the question of how much variance we can explain in any given situation. Using your method we might be able to pick out the most critical variables, and be able to explain a certain percentage of the variation, but it wouldn't be exhaustive because we would leave out a number of important variables not yet discovered. We need to account for as much of the variation as possible—which means that we must search for additional variables.

BINFORD: I think you're talking about two different things—explanation on the one hand, and correlation on the other. You're using explanation in the statistical sense when you refer to variance. Let's say that I do a correlation analysis and find that 30 percent of the variation in the length of women's dresses can be "explained" by the activity of sunspots. This is not an explanation in any sense of the word; it is a search technique. Correlation analysis is good as a search technique, but correlations are not explanations; they provide us with relationships that

276

are then in need of explanation. The explanation comes when you can relate observed correlations in terms of a general set of propositions. At that point, we're right back to the logico-deductive framework. No matter how much correlation you do, you have not explained anything unless it can be integrated into a general logico-deductive set of propositions.

PERLMAN: I agree that we do need that kind of logical hierarchy; but I see it as a continuum of logic.

STUART: No, Mel [Perlman]. Logic is . . . you either are or you aren't; it's like being pregnant or not.

PERLMAN: I guess it's just my hang-up; the logico-deductive thing inhibits me in my search for ways to construct a theory.

BINFORD: It shouldn't; it should never be an inhibitor. It's only after you've carried out your search techniques and discovered relationships that you are in a position to ask questions that lead to explanations. Then, once you generate an explanatory proposition, you may be able to deduce the consequences of it for other sets of data which you didn't search. So there's feedback going on. Part of what I'm saying is that search techniques are necessary, in that they help us ask questions; but the methods and techniques we use to guide us to ask good questions are often quite different from the techniques and procedures we follow to get good answers.

[EDITOR:] It should be noted that while Perlman remained largely unconvinced by these arguments, most of the participants agreed that anything that is to be explained can only be explained by putting it into a logico-deductive context. This does not necessarily mean, however, that any of us would subscribe to the Hempel-Oppenheim "deductive-nomo-logical" (D-N) model as being useful. This model requires that we already have adequately tested and confirmed laws, which we do not have. It also assumes that such laws constitute truth, and we agree that a priori truths are not prerequisite to hypothesis testing and theory building—in fact, they have no place in science at all. If we ignore these stringent requirements, however, the general logico-deductive model presented by Hempel and Oppenheim is indeed useful.

## THE NATURE OF SOCIETAL SYSTEMS

The following discussion is divided into three subsections. The first deals with systemic structure, function, and process. It concerns the questions, "What is a system?" "How are societal systems structured?" "How should we conceive of subsystems, components, and suprasystems in dealing with societies?" "What are the meanings of the concepts 'function' and 'process'?" In short, "How must we describe societal systems such that we can adequately explain stability and change?" The systems concepts proposed by James G. Miller (1965 a-c) are critically examined.

The second subsection focuses on a more rigorous concept of "system"—that is, a system as a set of variables articulated by relationships which can be described as a set of mathematical equations (and ultimately simulated). It deals with the questions, "How do we define a system for purposes of analysis?" "What are the requirements for such a system?" "How are system boundaries isolated?"

The third subsection focuses on the concept of "information." "What is it?" "What are its various meanings?" "What is the place of information in a societal system?" This concept is discussed in relation to the concepts of matter and energy.

### Structure, Function, and Process

Discussion begins with a consideration of Miller's conception of systems and subsystems (1965 a-c). After defining a system as "a set of units with relationships among them" (1965a:200), Miller suggests that "subsystems" are systems in their own right, and each subsystem carries out one or more "functions" or operations for the system—and each contains "components."

SAXE: Miller defines "subsystem" on the basis of "functions"—that is, you have a "deciding function," a "transducing function," and so on. You look at all the things in a society that engage in transducing operations, you put them all together, and there's your subsystem. There's no way in the world, however, that you can find time-space elements for components systemically articulated that go together into anything called a transducing *system*. Every subsystem must be isolable as a system in its own right, and Miller's subsystems are not of this nature.

HILL: In other words, if we look at all the things that carry on transducing *system*. Every subsystem must be isolable as a system in its subsystem; it would be a diffuse sort of thing made up of many different kinds of organizations, components, and so on, each carrying on different kinds of transducing activities. It would not be a system in its own right.

278

# Discussion

SAXE: Yes; I can give an example. One of the contributions of substantive economics in anthropology is that there is no separate economic system. Economic relations are carried on in certain situations by virtue of being part of *other* ongoing activities—they are embedded in other activities.

HILL: And these activities are not linked together as a subsystem—or they are so loosely linked that the linkage is irrelevant.

SAXE: Right. The problem is that Miller uses the concept "function" in a naive way; he uses it in the sense of "What does it do?" You know, the function of a piece of chalk is to write. But there's another way to use "function"—it can be used in the mathematical sense. For example, something acts as a function of 2 *ab* squared over *y* prime, etc. In this case you have a set of functional relations among elements in the system; when one varies, the values of one or more of the others will vary. This is a very different kind of system (or subsystem) than that used by Miller. And further, Miller's use of function to mean "What does it do?" leads us into all sorts of ethnocentric hang-ups. We find ourselves being able to talk about things like dysfunction, purpose, etc; and this permits value judgments to sneak into our systems. There is great ambiguity over the concept of "function" in anthropology.

SAXE: Another problem involves the question of what a "component" of a system is. You [Hill] say that each subsystem contains components; I assume you mean that. But do you mean that things like marbles on a floor are components? Can components be systems in themselves, or are they something different?

HILL: To me, a component is a real matter-energy thing, like a projectile point, a person, etc. Miller would say, for example, that the heart is a component of the circulatory system, and I would agree.

STUART: OK, but a component can be a system in itself as well.

GLASSOW: Agreed. But we must also consider the meaning of the concepts of "structure" and "process." Miller defines structure simply as the spatial relationships among various kinds of things within a system. And "process," to him, is change in the loci of these things within the system, or the fluctuations of matter or energy through time. "Process" is how a system operates.

SAXE: I think Miller uses the term "structure" to refer to the configuration of a system at a specific point in time—a snapshot view.

GLASSOW: Let me quote from Miller: "The structure of a system is the arrangement of its subsystems and its components in three dimensional space at a given point of time" (1965b). That's the snapshot view. Then he discusses "process:" "All changes over time of matter, energy or information in a system is process" (1965b).

HILL: We cannot view structure as a snapshot, because we want to include alterations in a system's *state* as part of its structure; the structure is not static, it is dynamic. And "process" is involved in both state changes and true systemic change.

STUART: Yes. A system in equilibrium can have various changes in state, such that the matter-energy elements in it are positioned differently at different times; you'd get a different snapshot at each time, even though it maintains the same structure. In short, "structure" is defined by mathematical relational statements that determine how and where things will be distributed in a system. It is relationship statements that are critical. We are dealing with multistate systems; they cycle in some fashion according to their mapping on environmental parameters. "Structure" is thus a dynamic rather than a static description. Miller takes his snapshot view because he's thinking of systems as organisms, where one can imagine something very close to a single-state system. In sociocultural systems, however, we have many states. For example, in hunter-gatherer groups the components of the system may be aggregated or dispersed in different seasons of the year; but it is all the same system, and a description of the structure of the system involves describing all of its states and how they interrelate.

[EDITOR:] The subject shifts here to the taxonomy of systems—notably the question of the usefulness of systems "types" and "levels" as presented by Miller (1965) and K. E. Boulding (1956). Miller, for example, proposes a series of hierarchically nested system levels (p. 212), beginning at the "atomic level" and proceeding through the more encompassing levels of cell, organ, organism, group, society, and so on. The question is, is there some existential or phenomenological set of system types or levels that we should be concerned about?

SAXE: This business of "levels" of systems is just crap.

HILL: Miller is assuming that there are only certain ways in which we can appropriately classify systems, and that the investigator has little or nothing to do with defining systems according to the attributes he is interested in. His levels are defined in terms of degrees of complexity, openness, amount of information processed, etc.

SAXE: Here again the problem is that Miller thinks of a system as an organism rather than as a population. When he talks about living

# Discussion

systems, he's got a bounded pussycat in mind; he fails to deal with populations. He can be faulted for this, because he could presumably deal with populations of pussycats, mice, rats, or human beings.

STUART: And the important thing is that populations evolve, and organisms don't.

SAXE: Yes, but let me give an example to illustrate my point. Let's say we want to know how Hitler's personality got to be the way it was. We can't look at his psychology only; we must also look at his position in society. So what we do is isolate a system that includes *both* the psychological level and the sociological level. We would have a cross-level system, and it's perfectly valid.

GLASSOW: Whenever we deal with a system and its environment we are crossing levels.

FORD: In systems *analysis* the concept of levels is unimportant; a system is composed of any relevant variables, regardless of whether or not some people might call them environmental variables (or variables from different "levels").

HILL: There are virtually an infinite number of ways in which we can isolate levels, right?

SAXE: Yes. And you can call any valid isolation of a system a "level" if you want to. The whole business of types and levels of systems is meaningless to me.

### A More Rigorous Concept of System

This discussion deals with the distinction between substantive and formal (mathematical) systems, and the necessity of using the latter in analysis.

WRIGHT: The implication of all this is that we will probably not be dealing with systemically organized natural phenomena. Systems are sets of propositions about relationships existing in natural phenomena. A system is a set of interrelated propositions described by equations—this is the mathematical concept of system.

PLOG: Yes, we haven't talked about this definition of system. It does not refer to *the* sociocultural system.

STUART: Why not?

PLOG: Because it doesn't refer to the actual parts of a substantive system, such as task groups, artifacts, etc. A mathematical system is composed of variables, and a task group is not itself a variable. In

Wright's and my terms, the components of a system are variables or measures of some kind; and we're talking about the relationships among these. This is opposed to the ideas of Miller (1965) and Buckley (1967), in which components are organizations, groups, and so on. The size and composition of a group are variables, but not the group itself.

WRIGHT: Here's an example. Let's take one thing and look at it from the points of view of both a substantive and a formal system. In an early Mesopotamian urban system (in the natural system sense) you would see agricultural work groups, herding organizations, and so on, as subsystems; and there would also be administrators processing information and coordinating activities. That's the standard viewpoint. But the formal, mathematical system is different. Here we might be dealing with the amount of information that is being handled or processed by the various groups, and how it relates to the number of levels in the administrative hierarchy. My two variables in this case are "rate of information flow" and "number of levels in the hierarchy"; and the system is the relationship, not the task groups.

PERLMAN: Yes. Each variable is one of the components of the system, and these variables are related to one another in specifiable ways.

STUART: It seems to me that we deal with *both* kinds of system—the on-the-ground systems and the formal ones. We are interested in relationships going on in substantive systems, and we specify certain characteristics or dimensions of them, which are the variables we're interested in. The interrelationships among these variables become the analytical system. We don't really know what a task group is anyway; we're always interested in certain dimensions of it.

SANDERS: But can't we analyze a task group itself?

STUART: Not in systems terms. We would instead want to deal with some characteristics of such a group—say the structure of its personnel, the number of people in it, the rate at which it produces certain things, and so on. These are the kinds of variables used in systems analysis.

HILL: So our system descriptions will be sets of equations relating the variables, such as "$x$ is a function of $y$," or "$x$ is some particular function of $y$"—or something more complex.

FORD: We agree then?

SAXE: That's right, troublemaker!

WRIGHT: I'm willing to speak in the two different idioms, but I'll always keep them separate. I see people slipping into the traditional meanings of "system" and "function" without realizing it. I've just become hard line on this.

[EDITOR:] The following deals with two questions: (1) What are the boundaries of a formal system? (2) What should be included in it?

FORD: Something else should be mentioned here. There are always many potential variables that could be measured in a given systems analysis, but they are not because they are not terribly important to the specific analytical system of interest—such things as amount of rainfall, temperature variation, and lots of other things.

STUART: Such things can be called "variety"; they exist in the substantive situation, but are not related systemically. But it may happen that over time some of these things become critical to the operation of the system, and must therefore become part of our analytical system as well.

FORD: I think we always have to be aware of variety in a system, however, because when the selective pressures on the system change, it is this variety that is acted on by selection.

GLASSOW: What you include in a system depends on how general a system you want to deal with. You can set up a model dealing only with very gross aspects of systems, or you can refine it by breaking down the gross variables into more refined ones. It just depends on what your intent is to begin with.

SAXE: I want to remind you that even though we're dealing with analytical systems, this does not mean that there are not real systems out there. It is not all in our heads; real systems exist.

STUART: Yes, we agreed on that; but our choice of the kind of systemic isolate we're going to study is important. For some purposes a given system may be regarded as a subsystem, while for others it is the system of interest itself; it's relative to the system isolate one is interested in.

SAXE: Sure; the universe is an interlocked system of subsystems. To me, there lies the linkage between individuals, sociocultural systems, ecosystems, and so forth.

[EDITOR:] In the following, the point is made that sets of variables that have interrelationships cannot be considered "systems" unless their relationships are homeostatically regulated. Stuart alluded to this idea in previous discussion. Variables that are not part of an analytical system may at some point become systemically involved—this would constitute systemic *change*. But such variables are considered not to be involved in the system until their values are systemically regulated within the system.

STUART: I think we have a confusion here. Sets of variables that have values and relationships with one another are not necessarily systems. They have to be homeostatically regulated; this is the only way we can know we're really dealing with a system.

WRIGHT: Really?

STUART: Yes, if we're talking about living systems. You have to account for something external which triggers homeostats.

WRIGHT: Sure; it's a necessity of logic. And this is why I separate formal from substantive systems—because otherwise we don't know what is internal and what is external to a given system.

STUART: The one thing we must keep constantly in mind is this distinction between formal and substantive system. We may have lots of variables we want to consider, but only some of them are systemically interrelated at any given time. Later, of course, we may have a new variable come in, and homeostatic mechanisms to maintain it.


### Information

The nature of "information" in systems is briefly discussed here.

STUART: Matter, energy, and information are not three different kinds of things. Statements about the character of matter and energy in a system are what we mean by information.

SAXE: Information, then, is interchangeable with matter and energy.

STUART: We have to realize that information as "communication" among people is a different kind of thing. The trouble is that many people use the two meanings interchangeably; this leads to a lot of strife in dealing with systems theory.

PLOG: We need to recognize two kinds of information. One is information flowing in a substantive system (communication, etc.); the other is information we as investigators are using in dealing with systems.

WRIGHT: Yes, there are two things involved. There's the actual communication going on inside a substantive system; but there's also our system of equations relating variables. The latter is *our* information.

HILL: I thought there were three kinds of information. One is matter-energy flows, or the patterning or structure of constraints in a system; another is communication or regulatory signals in the substantive system; and the third is our own information as represented by equations.

284

WRIGHT: You can subdivide indefinitely.

STUART: It's a very broad usage of "information" to say that any structuring is information. My suggestion is that we use "information" only to refer to communication or regulatory signals in the substantive system, and call it "meaning" or "understanding" when we're talking about information *we* get about systems. This will be the convention.

[EDITOR:] This was agreed upon.


## THE NATURE OF SYSTEMIC CHANGE

This discussion concerns what change *is* in societal systems, as well as what it is *not*. It considers the questions, "How do we know when a change has occurred?" "How do we recognize it?" and "What are the processes involved in systemic change?" The focus is on the processes of change within the context of general systems theory; further discussion of change processes can be found in subsequent sections.

SAXE: What does "change" mean to you, Fred [Plog]? You define it in your paper as longitudinal variability.

PLOG: I'm saying that when we find some cultural thing that varies between Time-1 and Time-2, that is change.

STUART: I think you're confusing things. It is true that we have to plot things in time and space, but we're really interested in knowing when some type of *organization* has changed from one thing to another. The term "morphogenesis" has been used in this regard.

SAXE: Is "change" synonymous with "morphogenesis?"

GLASSOW: Or does it simply mean variability that occurs through time?

STUART: Systems theory is presumably going to allow us to distinguish between fluctuations in system *states* and real systemic change.

SAXE: Yes; we want to be able to deal with how a system *got to be* the way it is (evolution). This is quite different from simply describing how a system operates. I don't think a "functional" description of a society is going to be enough to allow us to explain change. I would say that stable systems can be described in "functional" terms; but when the functional relations change, in the mathematical sense, I think we have morphogenesis.

STUART: First, let's say something about homeostasis; there's a problem here. Buckley's (1967) idea that homeostasis applies only to organisms, and not to his so-called "complex adaptive systems" (or societies) is nonsense.

GLASSOW: Right. Homeostasis has to do with the way a system operates; and if we want to understand what happens when change starts taking place in societies, the concept is crucial.

STUART: Yes; it applies to all living systems.

GLASSOW: Wait; I'm confused by something Jim [Hill] said in his paper. He made a distinction between rapid change and slow, accretionary change.

HILL: Yes; I felt that morphogenesis (evolution) can either involve very rapid, major changes, or it can be very slow and accretionary; the latter would occur as stress on a system gradually increases. The way I see it, this kind of change need not result from positive feedback processes; it can also result from negative feedback processes. I visualize it as a situation in which there is long-term stress impinging on a system; as the stress continues, the system makes small negative feedback kinds of responses which result in gradual change. It just responds each time; there's no deviation-amplification (runaway feedback). There's just a change in the environment, and a concomitant change in the system in order to adapt.

STUART: You are confused. The point is, any time a system responds in a different way than it had previously, positive feedback is involved (by definition). It isn't necessarily runaway feedback; that occurs only when the system is unable to develop satisfactory new homeostatic homeostatic mechanisms.

SAXE: Can I take a stab at this? Negative feedback processes are, by definition, those that result in homeostasis. Positive feedback processes are those that result in a moving away from homeostasis (change). So anytime you have change, however small or gradual, negative feedback processes are being replaced by positive feedback processes.

STUART: By the way, we're getting at something we touched on earlier. That is, we're talking about multistate systems. A system may have a number of states it cycles through in equilibrium—and as long as this organization is maintained we have homeostasis.

HILL: But I'm still not sure when a system has changed.

GLASSOW: This was my question. How do we distinguish change from the normal alteration of states within a stable system? I would postulate that whenever we have negative feedback types of adjustments we're talking about the normal operation of the multistate system; and when we have positive feedback loops operating, we're talking about change—it will involve a whole reorganization of the system.

## Discussion

SANDERS: You probably can't tell which you've got until you have a fairly long time span to deal with.

STUART: Exactly.

SAXE: And this is why it's so crucial for archaeologists to get hip to this stuff. Archaeologists are in the best position to deal with change.

[EDITOR:] The nature and processes of change are further considered in the context of discussing the evolution of social stratification in Hawaii.

WRIGHT: Let's give an example. Let's say that the first people to inhabit the Hawaiian Islands had a chiefly ranking system, but organized for a very small population. Then we had changes in demography and productivity which resulted in increasing complexity of the ranking system. Now, are those simply alterations in system state, or is the later system in fact a different system?

SAXE: I would see it as a different system; change occurred. In order to describe the operation of the second system you mentioned, you would have to rewrite the set of equations describing the system. This would also be the case after the arrival of Captain Cook, when the state developed. This would be the third system, and would also require rewriting the equations.

PERLMAN: But at what point can you say a new system emerges? Is it one kind of system on one day, and another the next?

WRIGHT: The system has changed whenever a new element (variable) is brought into the system. The relationships in the system are changed, in the mathematical sense, when you have to introduce new variables or transformations into the systemic equation.

STUART: Effectively, we find that when we need to introduce another variable or change the mathematical statement in order to make the system work (simulate), we have a change.

WRIGHT: Yes; and change occurs when certain thresholds are reached.

PLOG: You are saying that if a system exceeds a certain point in terms of the values of one or another of the variables in it, then it must change—or if a critical variable gets below a certain value, change will also occur. It cannot maintain homeostasis using the previous homeostats, so it must change at this point.

SANDERS: I see it a different way. I believe there is *always* evolutionary change unless something stops it from proceeding. There is always continuous progress unless a powerful force operates to stop it.

SAXE: Do you mean "progress' or "change?"

SANDERS: I'm saying change *is* progress. Societies move toward increasing complexity; this is a unilinear principle that operates everywhere. Of course, the environment can prohibit progress in many cases.

STUART: Let me have a try. Let's take Rappaport's Tsembaga Maring example (1967). He has described a system. Now there are lots of *other* things going on in the real, substantive society there; but none of these things is necessary for understanding the operation of his system. These other things are not systemic variables for him, but rather constitute the variability that living systems generate; they are just there. When and if it is necessary to consider *another* one of these variables, the system has changed. This is because one would have to write a new function, in the mathematical sense.

HILL: Let's take the shift from hunting and gathering to agriculture. We can describe the hunter-gatherer subsistence system as a set of equations relating the important variables. But at some point, because of stress on the system, a threshold is reached. At this point, the old homeostats fail to maintain equilibrium, and something else (say maize) is selected for in order to prevent the system from collapsing. This is a change, since a new component or variable must now be added to the mathematical system, and we must rewrite the equations. That's how I understand it.

STUART: Exactly. And it accords with the hard-line definition of "system" as functional statements in the mathematical sense. We all seem to agree.

## THE SOURCES OF CHANGE

Is systemic change caused by factors *internal* to a given system, or by factors impinging on the system from *outside*, or both? The following discussion begins and ends with the argument that systems in equilibrium cannot change themselves, and that it is a logical necessity that they can only change as a result of external factors. There was general agreement.

Some of the confusion in this discussion resulted from the fact that the participants were at times confusing the formal, mathematical kind of system with the substantive, on-the-ground kind. This should be kept in mind while reading it.

Discussion begins with the question of whether or not the precontact Hawaiian system could have evolved into a "state" level of organization in the absence of external inputs.

## Discussion

SANDERS: Don't you think population growth in Hawaii would have eventually forced a change in the organization necessary to integrate it? Would this not have led to the evolution of the state? Or would this only happen with pressure from an outside group?

SAXE: My assertion is that it would require extrasystemic inputs.

STUART: And the reason is that the precontact chiefdoms were stable for 200 years or more. They expanded and contracted, but no chief could get a monopoly on all of the resources until the gun was introduced; thus the state would probably not have developed without something like this happening.

HILL: But you [Saxe] said there was some morphogenesis prior to contact. How could this happen? Surely you don't always need to have new peoples coming into a system to get change.

SAXE: No, but you have to have something to create instability in the ongoing system.

WRIGHT: There could have been a major environmental change.

SANDERS: I think all you'd need is increasing intensification of agriculture, which would result from population growth. This is a local process, if Boserup's ideas are correct (1965). It would have led to ranking.

HILL: Do you regard population growth and intensification as external or internal factors?

SAXE: External. The concept "external" doesn't necessarily mean in the spatial sense. I used the example of a cancerous cell developing in a body. Yes, it's getting sustenance from the body, but the source of this is external to the cell. The input must come from the larger system. It can be from either a suprasystem, as in this case, or from another external system. But it is logical that the input must come from outside the system we're interested in. It is interesting to note that where this external system is the suprasystem, the change in the subsystem we are looking at could result from inputs that are actually part of normal homeostatic fluctuations that go on in the larger system.

FORD: This is like Hawaii. If you look at a single chiefdom, the other chiefdoms in conflict with it are external to it. However, if you look at all the chiefdoms together as a single system, the warfare becomes a regulatory mechanism in that larger stable system.

SAXE: Exactly.

STUART: Of course. For example, many subsystems in Polynesia are tribally organized; but the functional statement that relates them all is chiefly.

SAXE: While I feel sure that the source of change is always extrasystemic, I'm not sure it always comes from a suprasystem. At one and the same time I look at the universe as a hierarchical system of subsystems, and also as an *interlocked* system of subsystems, with no necessary hierarchy. I think it's safest to simply say "extrasystemic" rather than "superordinate."

STUART: Some may be adjacent systems; others may be superordinate systems.

SAXE: And when I say we must look outside a given system for sources of change, I don't mean spatially; I mean this in a relational sense—outside the system of interacting variables that describe the system.

SANDERS: Is population growth external to a system?

PERLMAN: There's confusion here between the two different definitions of "system." Sanders is suggesting that population is internal to the system, and thus an internal source of change. This may be the case in the substantive definition of "system"; but if the system is a set of variables and equations, population can very often be external.

WRIGHT: This is why I separate formal from substantive systems.

## VARIETY, SELECTION, ADAPTATION

In this section, consideration is given to the nature of systemic response, given that a system has undergone stress to the point at which its homeostats cease to regulate it adequately. In other words, what happens when an exogenous source of stress forces a system to change? What is "adaptation?" What is "selection?" Are the processes of selection conscious or unconscious on the parts of the participants involved? What is the importance of intrasystemic "variety" in the selection process?

PLOG: The two critical problems we're trying to deal with in the context of explaining change are: (1) making a statement about the *variety* in a particular system at $T_1$ and $T_2$; and (2) understanding the nature of the selective processes that are operating on that variety between $T_1$ and $T_2$. One of the most successful and operational attempts to do this is by Richard Levins (1968). His approach focuses on providing an operational means for describing systemic and environmental variability, and attempting to predict what an optimal adaptation would be in

290

given situations. So the aim is to be able to predict how systems will adapt to different environmental situations.

SAXE: What does the term "adaptation" mean? My understanding is that it doesn't always have to be a beneficial response. Lots of things are "adaptive behavior" that don't necessarily serve to maintain the society —the behavior of revolutionaries, for example. This is adaptive behavior in a sense. So I think we have to be careful not to confuse adaptation with system maintenance devices.

PERLMAN: I agree. "Adaptation" can include both system maintenance devices and change.

STUART: Adaptation is the fitting of homeostatic devices to the environment.

GLASSOW: But change can be adaptive also.

SAXE: Sure, but we do want to guard against using "adaptation" to be synonymous with "beneficial" or "functional."

STUART: I agree. There's also the problem of creeping anthropocentrism. We don't want to regard system responses as necessarily involving conscious or purposeful decision-making, as may be implied in Hill's paper.

HILL: But this is not to say that conscious decision-making doesn't sometimes occur.

STUART: No; but what happens is that a system has a lot of variety in it, much of it not systemically related. As Boserup says (1965), much of this variety has been in the cultural system for a long time—some of it just starts paying off under certain circumstances (for example, under stress).

SAXE: The idea that variety must be consciously produced is a complete negation of the concept of natural selection. In natural selection there's a pool of variability that arises in a population that environmental conditions either favor or don't favor. It's anthropomorphizing to say that societies "select for" new forms of organization, and so forth when faced with stress.

GLASSOW: Yes, it's irrelevant whether or not populations make conscious decisons; it would not affect our explanations.

STUART: I would just say that populations *do* things when under stress; they respond. I call these "adaptation gambits." These are the things that are selected for or against. In terms of selection, they either can be sustained or they cannot.

[EDITOR:] All agreed at this point, in spite of the arguments below.

## IDEALISM VS. MATERIALISM:
## INDIVIDUALS VS. POPULATIONS

A major argument arose over the importance of ideological factors in explaining change. That is, can we explain and predict change by reference solely to the material circumstances to which a system is (or was) responding, or are ideological things (such as choice, goals, norms) also important to take into account as determinants of change?

Second, and related to this, was the question of whether our analyses must take account of the behavior and psychologies of individuals, or whether change can be explained at the population level without concern for the individual.

These issues were inextricably intertwined during the discussion, so I have not tried to separate them or put them into any particular order.

PERLMAN: You speak of "optimal adaptations." Do people choose these? Where are we on the question of rational choice?

PLOG: I'm assuming that people are rational, and that they make choices.

SAXE: But this is irrelevant to our explanation.

HILL: We're assuming that decision-making takes place, but we don't need to worry about it if we can predict behavior without worrying about it.

PERLMAN: If we're going to understand the processes of change, we need psychological data. I'm studying the evolution of marriage among the Toro [Africa], and there's a great deal of freedom of choice there.

SANDERS: You don't need psychological variables. I assume that psychologies can themselves be explained by ecological and sociological variables.

PERLMAN: Social structure doesn't determine personality type; I don't believe that.

SANDERS: How do you explain the personality of the individual?

PERLMAN: You have to look at his particular history.

SANDERS: I know; but his "history" is the product of the operation of all these social and cultural variables.

PERLMAN: But you can't sum them; he's an individual who can choose. Choice is important in explaining changing divorce rates.

SAXE: No. We don't have to deal with each individual; we're talking about individuals as populations.

PERLMAN: I want to get at norms. Norms are shared in varying degrees, and they change.

292

# Discussion

WRIGHT: If I said that archaeologists have demonstrated an .80 correlation between volume of information flow in an organization and its hierarchical structure, would you tell me I'm crazy?

PERLMAN: No; maybe you can do this in archaeology. You're dealing with simple societies where the freedom of choice is limited. This is not true for modern societies. The more complex a society gets, the more freedom of choice individuals have.

GLASSOW: I doubt that; it may even be the reverse.

SAXE: If we can predict behavior at a populational level, as Wright suggested, why deal with individual actors?

PERLMAN: Change takes place through individuals. At some point in time, a Mr. Smith starts something, which leads to change. We need to know where he got the idea—and why he didn't follow the norm. Perhaps it was a stress of some kind. We must look for the source of why he made a decision that was new, and which led to change.

GLASSOW: No; the patent files in Washington, D.C., are full of little ideas that Mr. Smith had—but how many of them every get put into operation? In explaining change, we don't care why some person came up with his idea; instead we ask why that idea was put into effect by the cultural system.

STUART: A similar problem comes up in genetics. For most purposes we're not interested in explaining how a particular mutation happened, but rather why it became pervasive or not.

PERLMAN: I would say that the thing Mr. Smith started was found to be adaptive by a large portion of the individuals in the population; and they adopted it because they shared his goals.

GLASSOW: No system changes because of some internal property of it; it changes because of stresses from the environment. I think there are various kinds of natural circumstances that make a particular "choice" the most effective "choice" to make; and these are for you to discover.

STUART: Individuals do think things up. But then we're not even half-way home; the next question is so what? We want to know how an innovation becomes pervasive in a society.

PLOG: Mel [Perlman], you're reading variety out of the picture. You're saying it's simply mutation or innovation, and we don't have to worry about variety. For example, in a given society some people may be hunting and gathering while others are practicing agriculture; this variability is itself adaptive—forget about the norms.

SAXE: I think you can inject variability on a structural basis without going to individuals. I think our ideas, perceptions, and the whole society can be accounted for on a structural level.

HILL: Yes. I think we often inappropriately mix our systemic levels. We can explain variability and change in any given system in terms of variables relevant to that kind of system level.

GLASSOW: Mel [Perlman], the things you are considering to be psychological variables are in fact cultural variables, when you look at it from the point of view of what is producing those psychological sets. You can exclude individual psychologies, and simply use as your variables the things that are determining those psychologies.

SANDERS: Right. Would you [Perlman] be satisfied without explaining the psychological characteristics? Why do your people have a psychological attitude that affects divorce rates?

PERLMAN: I'd like to know.

WRIGHT: I think that the principles operating at the psychological, variety-creating level are different from those operating at the socio-cultural level. The same types of explanations will not work at both levels; the laws are going to be different.

STUART: The critical distinction is not between sociological and psychological factors, but rather between populational and organism analysis. Organisms do not evolve—populations do. So this is the level we're working at.

SAXE: Some things just can't be explained psychologistically.

[EDITOR:] The discussion continued again later, but in a different context.

PERLMAN: I still think choice is important. Some of you are saying that we can determine the direction of change from the kind of stress that is put on a society, but I think there's more to it. We need to know what the people decided about the alternatives. We can't predict the direction of change from knowing about the stress situations alone.

STUART: No, we can still predict. We can say something about the range of those responses that would be suitable for coping with a stress in a given situation; we can predict that there will be selection for certain things and not others.

PERLMAN: Presumably there's a range of choice in the ways in which people can deal with their problems.

GLASSOW: I don't think there's as much choice as you think there is. In fact, if I know the characteristics of a stress situation, as well as those of the population prior to stress, I can probably predict what the adaptation will be.

PERLMAN: But there is probably more than one alternative. Mike [Glasgow] is saying that a population *must* do certain things.

STUART: No—only the ones who are going to make it!

PLOG: According to Levins (1968), there is more than one optimal solution for any given environment.

STUART: But there is a determinant range of responses that will be viable.

PERLMAN: OK, but you're assuming that humans are rational and will choose the optimal solution; I don't buy that offhand.

SAXE: I presume they will approximate optimality if they are going to survive in the long run.

PERLMAN: Well, archaeologists deal with long time spans; I don't.

SANDERS: But the point is, this is no different from natural selection generally.

GLASSOW: If there are as many "choices" as you imply, Mel [Perlman], there really wouldn't be any systems!

PLOG: Miller (1965c) proposes that the least costly alternative will be tried first, and so on down the line.

GLASSOW: Sure; so there's not much choice after all.

SANDERS: And it ought to be possible to explain virtually all choices that are made.

GLASSOW: Yes, but Mel [Perlman] has a different conception of "choice"; to him they are equally viable.

STUART: The point is that not all populations make optimal responses; in both biological and cultural evolution, some didn't adapt. So the determinism is not so much that we can say that a given population will respond in a specific way; it is that we know that if it doesn't optimize (within a determinant range of alternatives), it is not going to make it. So there's not a wide range of choice.

HILL: Obviously. If there were freedom of choice, we probably couldn't predict anything at all.

SAXE: Why is there so much resistance here? I think it's because archaeologists don't deal with short-run things. The situation may be different for social anthropologists; that's a fact of life.

[EDITOR:] The question then arose as to whether or not societal systems have goals.

PERLMAN: I was suggesting that societies have several goals beyond survival; and as we move toward the modern era, and away from the strict need for survival, there is more freedom to add more goals.

SAXE: I agree that when *any* society is faced with survival, its choices are limited; but it's not correct to say that the more complex a society is, the more choice people have. That requires testing.

HILL: I think he means by "goals" that the system is coping with stress situations.

PERLMAN: Yes; they have "needs." They choose alternatives that will permit them to optimize.

GLASSOW: It is difficult to know what kinds of choices a population would have, given that certain kinds of decisions *must* be made. The business of goals is teleological and unproductive.

WRIGHT: Looking at ethnography, the "goals" I see involve optimizing such that a population can survive.

[EDITOR: The question of the importance of norms came up at this point.]

SAXE: Norms are unimportant for our purposes. There's a great deal of discensus in societies. And besides, I don't know how you'd ever measure what percentage of normative consensus there was. Norms are only knowable indirectly (through questionnaires, and so on); I wouldn't want to build a systemic model with them.

HILL: I think, however, that there's a place for "stored information" in a system.

GLASSOW: Norms are part of the information a system uses in its maintenance; they help maintain it in a particular state. And I agree that they can act to impede change. But explaining a time lag in adaptation is a different problem than the one we're dealing with.

PERLMAN: Not necessarily. Norms and ideologies create stress themselves. In my case, there's a strong norm requiring the payment of bridewealth; and this causes extreme stress during rinderpest epidemics, when there are large losses of cattle. So here we have two stresses.

GLASSOW: Yes; norms have a conservative effect; their existence can affect new kinds of adaptations that are formulated.

HILL: I just want to know if we need to take account of stored information or norms in explaining change.

WRIGHT: Norms are observations made by the people in a society; they're not terribly relevant to action in many cases, and they don't explain it.

SAXE: An attribute of norms is that they are breached. How else would we find out about them? That's important to keep in mind.

STUART: Yes; they become important in the breach precisely because they are boundary-maintaining mechanisms.

HILL: I agree that norms are only differentially shared, but I think there's a place for information as a part of the system. Under stress, societies draw on past experience in the process of coping. This experience is stored information. Now, do we archaeologists have to measure it?

WRIGHT: We have to talk about it. The problem is that archaeologists can only measure it indirectly.

STUART: Using ethnographic analogy we know that certain kinds of information systems or ideologies are associated with particular kinds of organizational structures; these things can be used. But we don't have to measure prehistoric information bits, communication, and so on.

HILL: You all seem to agree that we will be measuring the *results* of decision-making processes, but not the actual prehistoric decision-making processes or information. And we also agree that structure translates as information for us.

SAXE: Right.

[EDITOR: In a discussion of the Plains Indians, there was consideration of the effects of *past* systemic structure on charge.]

FORD: A guy by the name of Oliver points out that on the Plains different kinds of organizational change occurred even though the different societies involved were in the same kinds of environments. This is because these groups were structually different from one another before change occurred (before the horse). The point is, the structure of a society prior to change will be a factor determining the kind of change that occurs.

HILL: Yes; there are prior structural constraints. Some of this may also involve information storage or "memory." But in any event, this kind of thing is important and does have to be considered.

## STRATEGY FOR RESEARCH

The discussion thus far has considered, either directly or indirectly, some aspects of research strategy, though it has focused on the broader issues. But we also dealt with more specific ideas about how we might actually go about doing research to explain change.

The first of two subsections that follow is concerned with hypothesis testing. Since there was general agreement that our explanations will involve multivariate determinants, there was a question about whether we should test hypotheses one at a time, or whether we should use systems of hypotheses that would integrate all recognized determinants into a single complex hypothesis. And as a part of this there was discussion of how we know when we have discovered all of the relevant determinants.

The second subsection is devoted to measurement, especially the kind of measurement scale that should be used in quantifying variables and measuring change.

### Hypothesis Testing

PERLMAN: You are all implying that we should be testing one hypothesis at a time, or looking at two variables at a time. This is the classic model of analytical procedure in science. The whole equals the sum of its parts.

WRIGHT: You're doing it variable by variable, Fred [Plog], without concern for interactions among the variables. There are serious mathematical problems in handling interactions.

PLOG: I agree; but we can begin on a bivariate basis. We can then use partial correlation path analysis, which ultimately deals with variable interaction.

PERLMAN: But that assumes that you're talking about linear functions.

PLOG: OK, some of you are saying we can't look at variables a couple at a time.

PERLMAN: The problem comes in our inability to control for all of the other variables that are inevitably interacting on the two we are looking at by themselves.

HILL: I see no reason that one cannot begin by looking at two variables at a time. Later in the analysis, however, one should begin to suspect interactions, and come up with hypotheses relating several variables at a time.

SANDERS: I prefer to work with two at a time. I take the "prime-mover" approach. For example, I am proposing that the volume of trade is the prime mover in the evolution of markets; when the volume reaches a certain point, the development of a market becomes automatic in order

298

to regulate flow. If you throw in all the other possible variables, you're in trouble.

PLOG: I think we're beginning to decide we must do it systemically.

GLASSOW: But when it's done bivariately, it's not as if one is not being systemic; it's just that only a small portion of the system is being considered.

WRIGHT: The real question is, how do we test a complex systemic hypothesis? We have to do this, since the reason we're working with systems theory is that we're unhappy with the quality of explanation that the classical strategy and logic imply. I can't predict when a state will appear in that way. We wouldn't use systems theory if we were not forced to do it.

SANDERS: I agree that the systems approach is best in the long run, but it may be forty or fifty years before we can really do it.

PLOG: But if you can measure the variables you already claim to be able to measure, it's not a question of waiting; it's a question of sitting down and designing the model.

SANDERS: But, again, I work with the prime-mover idea. Some factors, like population growth, are prime movers. We can understand a great deal about the growth of complex societies by just using prime movers, although they are not totally sufficient of course.

FORD: We need to construct systems of hypotheses much as Rappaport does (1967). All of his variables can be measured—calories, number of pigs, amount of land in cultivation, amount of work done by women, and so on. We're dealing with ranges of values in all these variables—and they all affect one another in certain specified and quantifiable ways. It can even be simulated. We have to learn to do this.

PLOG: Yes; and we can build such models prior to collecting the data. We can then gather data with some knowledge of the kinds of measurements needed.

HILL: It seems to me that all of the examples of morphogenesis we've talked about begin by a single input, such as guns in the Hawaiian case.

WRIGHT: That is a fundamental error. You have multiple causes at any time A and B in some combination result in C. It's a multivariate system.

SAXE: Right. In Hawaii, one could say that the state developed from a single cause—European contact. But that covers up a lot of variables, such as the number of ships involved in trading, the number of guns acquired, the number of chiefs involved, and so on.

299

HILL: And rates in these things.

SAXE: Right. So even though we can summarize it by saying "European contact," it's not just one thing.

PERLMAN: OK; but once we have a system of hypotheses specified, can we test them one at a time?

GLASSOW: Sure; you could test one, two, three, or more hypotheses, depending on what you want to do. Or, you can test your system as a whole.

WRIGHT: Mike [Glassow], it seems to me that in your paper you could relate all of your hypotheses into a single system. I don't think I can do it in my research; I have to test them one at a time (that is, two variables at a time).

GLASSOW: I tested them one at a time simply to show which variables might be operative in explaining "aggregation." But I agree that they could be put together into a multivariate explanation.

SANDERS: This is a good point. You would not have a high degree of correlation with any *single* pair of variables, so you have to deal with all of them. For example, let's say we want to explain "nucleation" in an area. This might be promoted by warfare, localized irrigation requiring communal labor, and other things—but none of these things is sufficient in itself to produce nucleation. So I don't see how we can accomplish our task by analyzing them separately.

GLASSOW: I agree with you a hundred percent.

HILL: I think we generally agree; but I still think it's OK to test hypotheses one at a time in the initial stages of research. This may be how we determine which variables should ultimately be included in a larger set of systemically related hypotheses.

### Measurement

GLASSOW: How do we measure change in systems? I think there are sometimes relatively gradual changes, and sometimes major and rapid changes. The rates of change vary, and this needs to be measured.

SANDERS: I use Service's typology (1962, 1963); but I think we need a more specific typology of chiefdoms, states, and so on; it needs to be more refined. Then we could discuss the processes of evolution from one type of chiefdom to another, and from chiefdom to state.

HILL: The problem is that there are so many ways to classify these things; we would never agree.

300

# Discussion

SANDERS: Granted, but we have to do it.

GLASSOW: We can classify in terms of attributes of the systems that are relevant to any given piece of research.

PLOG: No. We have to work in terms of *continuous* variability. We can't ever make predictions about systems if we continue to organize the world in terms of discrete categories.

SANDERS: We don't have to use discrete categories; we can measure change in terms of specific variables we're interested in. For example, I can easily get a quantitative measure of change in specialization. But I use the Service typology because it's hard even to talk about these things unless we give them labels. How can we even discuss continuous change?

GLASSOW: A taxonomic model is not good, however.

WRIGHT: I don't think Service's typology represents arbitrary breaks in a continuum; these are real, discrete stages.

SANDERS: Yes, but there are whole ranges of kinds of chiefdoms and states.

BINFORD: We can say, for purposes of analysis, that a state exists when certain characteristics are present. But we're really talking about how we measure these characteristics. I think we want a continuous instrument of measure, even though the actual way in which concrete cases are clustered may not be continuous. With regard to the state, for example, we might want to measure changes in "power." There might be gradual and continuous increases in power, or there may be thresholds where there are big jumps; in the latter case we would find discrete clusters with regard to power. But we have to discover such clusters before we can explain them; and it takes an interval scale measurement procedure to do this. This is better than taking some formal property, and saying that this property differentiates $x$ from $y$, and then trying to explain how $x$ got to be $y$.

SAXE: In the case of the state, we have a continuous growth of power, but with a major structural break occurring at a certain point.

BINFORD: But if we measure power on an interval scale, we can see the distributions of concrete cases on that scale, and can identify when thresholds occur. The same goes for specialization, and so on. This allows us to see where on the scale the changes actually occur, and we then have something real to explain.

WRIGHT: I don't think that the method of science is to look at concrete cases and then generalize.

BINFORD: That's not what I'm saying. I'm asking first, "What is the distribution?" If we have concrete cases continuously distributed, in which there are no clusterings, then we have no basis for setting up discrete or ordinal categories; instead, we have continuous variability to explain. On the other hand, if we have clusters in the distribution, we have real discrete or ordinal scale breaks to explain. I'm saying that before we worry about the *definiens* for inclusion or exclusion in the ordinal category "state," we should examine the distirbution of concrete cases with respect to an interval scale.

WRIGHT: But you're throwing out useful typological thought that has gone into the definitions of "chiefdom" and state."

HILL: It might be helpful to recall, Henry [Wright], that you decided not to explain "civilization" or "urbanism" because they are too complicated and ill-defined to deal with. Then you got more specific and talked about explaining the "state." And now you're getting even more specific and trying to explain increasing "administrative specialization," but you're dealing with discrete typological categories.

WRIGHT: "Administrative specialization" can be defined as a continuous variable.

BINFORD: If you want to use that as an index of power, fine.

HILL: I don't think we even want to explain the "state"; who really cares? Actually, we want to explain each of the various kinds of behavior that make up what we call the "state." For example, we want to explain increasing centralization of power, increasing craft specialization, increasing status differences, and so on. And sometimes we may want to explain why some of these things occur together. But terms like "state" or "chiefdom" are not empirically established entities; they are lump labels for a number of aspects of behavior, each of which we are interested in explaining.

SANDERS: You want to explain process.

HILL: Right. You see, there are lots of kinds of things we mean when we say "state"—there are increases in monopology of force, craft specialization, administrative specialization, and many other things. Each of these is a conceptually different variable and can be measured on a continuous scale. And if we do this we might find those thresholds that Lew [Binford] is talking about, and then explain them. There is no a priori reason to believe that all of these different variables are congruent with one another, and that all change together at the same time. We have to measure them separately, on a continuous scale, and *find out* to what degree they vary together, and to what degree they cluster into meaningful discrete categories.

## Discussion

BINFORD: Yes. I think there's always confusion between the character of the instrument for measure one uses and the pattern of the distribution of the values one gets when applying that instrument. I can take a ruler, which is a continuous instrument, and measure all of the pieces of paper in this room. I will find that they are all 8½ x 11 inches—so there is no continuous variability in the external world in this case, even though I'm using a continuous instrument for measure. In any situation, the clustering one observes may turn out to be in fact a series of points clustered on a scatter diagram, with big gaps between clusters. In that case, we have demonstrably discrete variability; and we can then give labels to the clusters if we wish.

PLOG: Yes, but is the clustering going to be all that neat?

BINFORD: That's not something to speculate about; it's something to *do*—that's the point. If there's justification for a distinction between chiefdom and state, then there should be some kind of clustering. But if we have continuous variability between the two, for example with regard to managerial specialization and so on, then there is no justification for the distinction; we don't have discrete differences to explain.

PLOG: Of course; I agree.

[EDITOR:] There was general agreement that we should measure all variables on an interval scale whenever possible. But there was also discussion of precisely how we can make operational the measurement of specific variables using archaeological data. I will not present any of this discussion here, but simply point to our conclusion that it is currently possible to get reasonably adequate measures of most or all of the variables we might want to use in explanatory models. We considered most specifically the variables of degree of craft specialization, centralization of power, degree of complexity, population size, amount of warfare, and amounts of different kinds of food resources consumed. The conclusion was that while measuring some of these things may often be difficult, there are often indirect ways to do it that are at least adequate for our purposes; and a number of examples were given in support of this contention. Furthermore, it was agreed that archaeology is continually developing better and better techniques for measuring variables more precisely, and that this will continue. But perhaps the most important conclusion related to this was that team research, involving experts from various fields (and different kinds of archaeologists as well), will be mandatory if we are to develop and test models purporting to explain change (see Struever 1971).

## EVOLUTION OF THE STATE

The following discussion focuses on the evolution of complex societies, especially the "state." Much of the discussion at the seminar used this problem as a vehicle for considering the nature and processes of change. Unfortunately, I have had to cut out most of this interesting discussion, but have preserved a few of the most enlightening parts in greatly abbreviated form. This section could have been entitled, "Miscellaneous Observations on the Origin of the State."

The discussion deals with three questions primarily: (1) What is the state? (2) What are its determinants? (3) Is there a general explanation that would apply in all cases? These are not, however, presented in any systematic order, since to do so would destroy the logic and continuity of thought.

It is notable that some of the discussion involves the evolution of "chiefdoms"; this is because the participants agreed that some of the important attributes of the state are also present in chiefdoms, though to a lesser degree. Many of the basic processes involved in the evolution of complex societies are presumed to be operative in both the evolution of chiefdoms and states.

SAXE: The chiefdom organization existed in Hawaii during at least 200 years before the arrival of Captain Cook; it appears to have been a stable system. The interesting thing is that by understanding the nature of the North Atlantic societies and western capitalism, one could have predicted not only contact, but also that some form of state would develop; this happened throughout the Polynesian area. The situation was that the Europeans needed island products; and in order to get what they needed, they never rested until they had internal administrations in these societies that could result in the extraction of these products. That resulted in the development of statelike organizations.

SANDERS: There are some beautiful parallels to this process in West Africa.

STUART: And the Dahomey thing.

SANDERS: Yes; and the Buganda states resulted from the same thing. The procuring of European weapons gave an advantage to the leaders, and increased their power. In some cases this resulted in changing a chiefdom into a state, and in others it simply strengthened the power of an already extant state. Changes in land tenure and other things went along with this, of course.

# Discussion

SAXE: There's also British Central Africa, where you had egalitarian groups, and the development of the state was a complete European overlay.

SANDERS: I think this same process applies also to the relationship between the Olmec and Highland groups in Mexico, and probably to many other prehistoric cases of state development.

SAXE: I think the model would be appropriate anywhere, though the particulars would vary in each case.

STUART: This relates to Sahlins's Big Man, Poor Man paper (1963), in which he talks about the dramatic constraints operating on the activities of the chiefs prior to contact. Chiefs had power, but there was a definite limit to it. But after they got European guns, they could get away with extracting as many resources from their people as they wanted. Under these conditions it took only about 20 years for the state to develop.

SANDERS: And all of the chiefly apparatus, such as the tabu system, was abolished. It was no longer functional. With guns and a standing army, there was no need for these chiefly sumptuary rules for maintaining a power base.

WRIGHT: I think this explanation for the state is limited to cases where ranked polities are drawn into trade networks. And if guns are so important, this explanation won't work until we have the Iron Age in human history.

SANDERS: But don't you think it may possibly work in any case where trade networks are opened between societies of greatly different complexity?

WRIGHT: In some cases, yes; but this may be a very special case. In most of the cases we study, it is pressure on the means of *production* that leads to the development of specialized managers or administrators, and thus to the state; but here we're talking about direct pressure on the administrative element as being important, and there may be no change in the means of production.

SAXE: I think my explanation has more relevance for explaining the evolution of the state in Mesopotamia and Mesoamerica than you are willing to admit.

WRIGHT: It seems to me that even though the specific variables involved in any specific case may vary, the *general* explanation will always be the same—that is, it will relate administration to production. Specialized administrators evolve to manage production problems of some kind.

SANDERS: I agree; that's excellent. But they could also evolve to manage competition and warfare, as Ford indicated.

PLOG: But warfare does put pressures on the production subsystem, since more must be produced to sustain warfare.

SANDERS: Yes, I think it all relates to managing the production system. In Mesopotamia it might have been managment of irrigation.

WRIGHT: No, that probably didn't become important until late in the sequence. But thre were many other kinds of production problems that could have required management.

SANDERS: Could the regulation of trade have been important?

WRIGHT: There was not enough volume of trade in Mesopotamia, but it might work in Mesoamerica. We can get quantitative measures of trade volume in many cases; I'm talking about long-distance trade.

SANDERS: I was thinking of local trade. For long-distance trade I think the volume was too low to require changes in administration.

WRIGHT: There's a problem here. That is, chiefdoms can handle the local trade; you don't need a state. In fact, this is one of the raisons d'être for chiefdoms.

SANDERS: I still think it's important, especially when we get very large population increases. Under this condition, the number of specialists increases, and the coordination of local trade would require specialized administration.

WRIGHT: I think we have to decide precisely what we're trying to explain. Morton Fried says that the state follows automatically from social stratification. I don't agree. I've also rejected the idea of explaining "civilization" or "urbanism," since these things are too complicated and vague to deal with; so I decided on explaining the state. What is the state? It has a variety of features, but I focus on what I think is the fundamental and general characteristic of all states—specialization of administration. It is specialized with regard to other activities, and it is specialized internally as well. It makes decisions about decisions.

SAXE: OK; and you say that the management of irrigation was not important. But what about the idea that some people had the power to cut people's water off?

WRIGHT: This might work for Sanders, but not for me. Nobody was capable of controlling the big rivers in Mesopotamia; and if someone cuts your canal water off, you can always dig another one. In any event, irrigation simply wasn't a factor this early. Long-distance trade wasn't very important either. But I'm speculating that craft specialization and local exchange were very important. The argument is that you had two kinds of societies in the area—full-time cultivators and full-time transhumant herders—and exchange between them led to the necessity for full-time, specialized administration. But leaving aside the particulars of this case for the moment, I'm convinced that it is possible to develop a general formulation that would account for the origin of the state anywhere and at any time; and I'm working on this. But I don't know how I'm going to handle the "political" as opposed to the "administrative-managerial" factors.

SAXE: What do you mean?

WRIGHT: I'm making a distinction between managerial decisions, which are regular, bureaucratic, day-to-day administrative decisions, and political decisions, which involve power and conflict relations.

STUART: M. G. Smith calls it "political" and "administrative" I think. This might be important. You might want to discover the circumstances under which you begin to get this functional distinction between the political decision-makers who make the rules, and the administrators who simply carry out the rules. This would give us an empirical instrument of measure for the beginnings of the state.

BINFORD: You're saying that administrators have derived authority, while there are other roles in which real power is vested.

SAXE: You can't use the concept "power" without lots of argument.

SANDERS: I don't know why you can't measure it. You can measure it in terms of the amount to which people or local groups are being circumscribed in their behavior—for example, the degree to which they are forced to pay taxes, or carry their disputes to a central authority, and so on. I think there are a whole series of such measures of power that we can get at archaeologically.

SAXE: Power is the ability to impell the behavior of groups. But this means that both administrators and politicos exercise power.

STUART: Yes; and given our past discussion, we can agree to use measures of administrative specialization as an index of power. And power is distributed differentially in different kinds of states; sometimes it is centralized, and sometimes it is rather diffuse—yet the people at the bottom are equally circumscribed in their behavior. We have a state, then, whenever there is a specialized organization at the top that makes the rules.

SAXE: Yes; and this is a monopoly of force. Furthermore, it can occur in some states that are organizationally simpler than some chiefdoms. So the real problem is explaining how we get a monopoly of force.

WRIGHT: I don't think we can measure that. I'm measuring relative degrees of specialization in administration. This seems to be the thing that exhibits clustering on a continuous scale

BINFORD: Why? Managerial statuses always *derive* from and are made legitimate by a power source.

STUART: There's a question here over the degree to which monopoly of force must be present in order to have a state organization. I think it varies a great deal. Actually, a feudal system is a state, since it has a monopoly of force with regard to many things.

BINFORD: Right. I don't think you [Wright] can deny the existence of a power source and talk about managers at the same time. Managers imply the existence of power roles, since their authority is always derived or legitimized. And power is always going to be related to differential access or control of critical resources. Let me give an example from coastal Virginia. In the Chesapeake Bay area there are four major environmental zones: (1) the coastal zone, with salt water and tides; (2) a brackish water zone, with tides; (3) a fresh water zone, with tides; and (4) a riparian zone, further inland. The distribution of population in these zones is fascinating. The coastal villages were about 15 miles apart; in the transition area it was about 1.5 miles between settlements; and up in the riparian zone it goes up to 3.5 miles. Now, it is in the transition zone [Fall Line area] that the river water is shallow enough to use impounding weirs for fishing; so there is efficient access to both marine and anadromous fish in this area. Now, the period of migration of anadromous fish in these rivers is in April, and this is also the lean period of the year for other food resources. So these fish were critical resources for subsistence in the area. And where do you think the paramount chiefs were located? Right there in the transition zone! Chiefdoms evolved there because of a localized critical resource that the people in that zone had a monopoly on. Since the people in the other zones also needed this resource, the chief in the transition zone became a redistributor with tremendous power. Primogeniture even developed, since it was necessary to have formal rules to establish who was to regulate these resources. It is in this kind of situation, where we have localized critical resources, that chiefdoms develop as opposed to Big Man systems; and I think states probably arise in the same context. They arise because of the potential for power; and power may be exercised by coercion, such as the threat of cutting off the critical resources, or it may involve military action as was the case with Kamehameha in Hawaii. But power is *always* related to differential access or control of critical resources.

SANDERS: You just duplicated my argument for the Teotihuacan Valley situation.

WRIGHT: Yes; and you can use the same argument in other areas.

BINFORD: If we want a mimimal definition of "critical resource," it is a resource that relates to *security* rather than *efficiency*. For example intensified agriculture and irrigation generally result from population pressure and the resultant need for efficiency; but the need for security is different, and involves the distribution of resources relative to population. When there is a nonrandom distribution of essential resources, those people who control them are going to have power (because other people need the resources for subsistence security, and so forth).

WRIGHT: It is possible that this type of explanation can explain the state.

STUART: Yes; and if enough localized power is gained, the people in the hinterlands have no choice but to submit. The chief doesn't even have to make alliances anymore; he has monopoly of force—which means we have a state. Kamehameha got it through differential access to guns and ships.

WRIGHT: The problem is that I see no evidence in the Near East for any change in the technology of coercion.

BINFORD: Coercion can be accomplished in lots of ways other than using guns. For example, Mesopotamia is an area of very low subsistence security. As you get population growth and sedentism related to intensive exploitation of a limited number of resources, the more marginal populations will begin to depend on the main centers of production; and they can be coerced by the simple threat of cutting them off. You don't even need an army. In areas of high subsistence security, on the other hand, force may be needed, since groups are not as dependent on a localized area of production; they are more economically independent.

SANDERS: I think this is why the Mayan organization differed so greatly from the one in central Mexico. People were more economically autonomous in the Maya area, and their political system was consequently less tightly integrated. But consider Teotihuacan. There, the critical resource was the springs; a large population grew rapidly there, and the outlying people became dependent on them—or at least they were able to be dominated.

STUART: Yes; and as cities grow, a number of innovations occur in the cities. These may at first be "efficiency" kinds of innovations; but if the city has control over these innovations, it can gain "security" control over the hinterlands. We have modern cases of this; in fact, this is probably why peasant societies are controlled by the cities. And in any case, the "security" resources involved need not be subsistence resources; they could be many things, such as means for defense, control of ports of trade, and so on.

SANDERS: Control of trade was certainly important in Mesoamerica; but we still have to explain why the trade centers grew up precisely where they did. You had to have large population concentrations in these areas; this is why the springs at Teotihuacan were so important.

STUART: Another case is in the Trobriands. The greatest hegemony was always located in a specific area there. Why? I think it was because the technology of storage was the critical resource. Yams have to be dried; and I'll wager that it is in the drier areas that we find the centers developing.

SANDERS: Malinowski says that the highest ranking chiefdoms were in the areas of highest productivity, so there are other factors as well.

STUART: What do you think are the critical security resources in Mesopotamia that led to the state, Henry [Wright]?

WRIGHT: To give a facetious answer, Adams says it's orchards. There were optimal areas for orchards, usually along the river. However, we haven't found remains of orchard crops. I think there must have been a multiplicity of critical resources involved. But the interesting thing to me is that we begin to get specialized herding groups at this time. How would you [Binford] work this into your security-coercion idea?

BINFORD: Well, if you've got herders who depend on the products of the agriculturalists, these herders can be coerced by the threat of cutting them off.

WRIGHT: But the herders could also coerce the agriculturalists. After all, the agriculturalists needed the herders' sheep.

SANDERS: I don't think they needed the sheep as much as the herders needed the grain.

WRIGHT: Well, in any event, if power need not be exercised by the

310

actual employment of force, then I can see solutions to my difficulties with using power as a measure of the emerging state.

SAXE: It seems to me that with specialized herders and city folk you have the makings of a morphogenic system. Can you [Wright] specify the extrasystemic positive feedback networks involved?

WRIGHT: Maybe, in part at least. For one thing, agriculture becomes more specialized and is carried out on a very large scale at this time (ca. 4000 B.C.); there was evidently redistribution of grain. And this growth in production may have been in part a response to the herders' demand for grain. But the herders also needed craft products, especially water jars to replace their broken ones. My argument is that the sudden appearance of the herders in the spring placed an incredible demand on craft production in the settled communities; and in order to meet the demand, the communities had to reorganize by developing major craft guilds or workshops—this would be a craft version of Boserup's model of intensification (1965). This then creates distributional problems that have to be administered by increasingly full-time administrators.

SAXE: Beautiful! Now, could these feedback loops have existed prior to this kind of craft specialization?

WRIGHT: I don't think so.

SAXE: OK. This is much like Binford's security situation in the Chesapeake Bay area; this specialization leads to a security function. But let's go back a bit; what sets this all off?

WRIGHT: Probably greatly accelerated population growth; we have evidence for it at this time.

SANDERS: I certainly think population growth was the prime mover in Mesoamerica. I think this resulted in intensification of agriculture (Boserup 1965), which in turn led to changes in the social and economic institutions. I also think that sheer population size and density were important. In other words, when you get 100,000 people in an area, they can't be organized in the same way that 1,000 or 10,000 people can be organized. In order to integrate a large population, there have to be changes in the means of communication, transportation, exchange, and so on. Beyond this, I think competition was involved in stimulating them to integrate; this is important.

HILL: By what processes would competition lead to the integration of small groups into large units?

SANDERS: Well, in a competitive situation, the groups that are more highly organized have a competitive advantage; I tend to think of this in terms of military organization. As population grows, there is increasing conflict over resources, and this leads to warfare and a concomitant increase in the scale of integration.

HILL: But as Binford pointed out, there may not have to be any actual use of force—just the threat of it may be sufficient. And also, you seem to be ignoring the fact that there may have been a differential distribution of critical resources.

SANDERS: No, that is involved too. That's how I explain why the state developed first in specific areas in Mesoamerica and not in others.

GLASSOW: In your paper you talk about the springs and canal systems at Teotihuacan. How were those a factor in the emergence of the state?

SANDERS: Let me summarize the argument. There was a concentration of springs in one place, and the canals have to start at these springs. Around 200 B.C., a large community began to develop there; it was probably like a Service type of chiefdom, with 4,000–5,000 people [Taqualli Phase]. I think this community dominated the surrounding ones and integrated them into one large unit. By A.D. 100, Teotihuacan became a city of 40,000–50,000 people.

STUART: But why should they have extended their hegemony over the outlying areas?

SANDERS: Well, there's a great deal of environmental and resource diversity in the area. So different products are in different places, and they must have needed an organization for redistributing these resources. The chiefdom model fits nicely here. And the security function they played for the surrounding areas was probably that of providing for their defense. But it's more than that; the redistribution system was beneficial to everybody. The real question is why do I think the springs were so important in initiating this whole thing. My view is that there were important managerial requirements involved. Let's look at the situation today. There is an elaborate central council that meets at Acolman every month, and the purpose is to organize water distribution. They decide which village gets water when; and after that, each village has to decide which farmers get it when. But irrigation is crucial, and is only done once, just before the rainy season. And the point is, there's a limited span of time in which irrigation can be useful; it must occur between January 1 and June 1. So there's a lot of pressure on timing, and most farmers want to irrigate in April or May. There is a lot of conflict over this, since they can't all have it when they want it; and the competition is both between and within villages. There is a definite need for policing the water distribution too. All of this produces a need for centralized integration. The big problem arises, of course, because the water is coming from just one point, the springs.

WRIGHT: I had never realized that medium-sized irrigation systems might require managerial control.

SANDERS: Another example is in the coastal valleys of Peru. In some of these valleys there's plenty of water but a scarcity of land, and in others it is the reverse. So the conflicts occur over land in some cases and water in others. We really have to investigate each local situation separately. I'm not saying that the necessity for managing water distribution is why Teotihuacan emerged when and where it did; but I do think this would have given the people localized around the springs an added dimension of power. It must have been *one* of the factors that led to the evolution of social stratification and centralization of political power. This does not mean that all other Mesoamerican states arose in response to managing irrigation systems, of course.

HILL: There must be one or more covering laws we might derive from all this. I think we can relate Henry's [Wright's] material and your material under one statement if we wish. It would be a broad statement having to do with the necessity for coordination or control of critical resources that are distributed in some kind of nonrandom manner. The resources might also have to be scarce, such that competition is involved.

### SYSTEMS SIMULATION

This final section of discussion deals with the nature of computer simulation and how it might be useful in explaining organizational change. There was some argument over its usefulness in studying *change*, since simulations ordinarily replicate the operations of systems in equilibrium.

During the discussion, references are made to Saxe's Hawaiian data (chapter 4), since we had decided to make a preliminary attempt to set up simulation procedures for the Hawaiian case. There was also discussion of Rappaport's Tsembaga Maring data (1967) and Barth's Basseri data (1961).

This section is brief, given the lengthy discussion of simulation at the seminar. I have deleted most of the complicated technical aspects because it is impossible to present them economically here. Also this work was exploratory only, and was left unfinished.

PLOG: Up to this point we have been discussing systems *theory* primarily; we should now start getting into systems *analysis*. We ought to take the variables that Saxe considers to be critical in the Hawaiian case, build a model that is composed of these variables, turn the thing on, and see whether or not it does in fact produce the kind of system that needs extrasystemic inputs in order to get morphogenesis. In other words, we need to simulate the system and see if it works as a system; then we can decide to modify it if necessary.

SAXE: Didn't I do that in my paper?

PLOG: Yes, in a sense; this is the right direction. But systems analysts don't stop at the level of saying "This is how I think it works"; they specify the variables and go out and measure them. Then they specify a series of if-then statements, write a program, and run the thing to see if it works. We can't complete such a thing here and now, but we can get a start at it.

SAXE: How do we start?

PLOG: There's a systemic model underlying what you have written. But it needs to be spelled out in terms of the variables involved and the relationships among these variables.

SANDERS: This is one reason I'm not sure how far we can go in applying systems theory. We have not yet learned how to quantify these variables, weight them, and so on. I don't see how it can be done.

SAXE: I think we can do it if we have good data; but in the Hawaiian case I'm not sure we do. For example, I have no way of knowing at what point the redistributive network becomes sufficiently imbalanced for the natives to get restless.

STUART: Well, we certainly can measure such things as population density, boundaries between chiefdoms, percentage of chiefly skim-off, and so on. We might be able to do it.

SANDERS: I don't see how. I don't think we have sufficiently good quantitative data for any research problems that I know of. We simply haven't reached that stage yet. I grant you that we could do it if we did have good quantitative data.

PLOG: I think we can construct it before getting the data.

FORD: That's the direction Henry [Wright] is going in his own research.

SAXE: Can we simulate Rappaport's *Pigs for the Ancestors* (1967)?

314

PLOG: Yes, I don't see why not. Rappaport has already worked out what the variables and their relationships are. We've got at least three critical *level* variables—population, pigs, and land; and we've got a series of *rate* variables that determine these—death, killing, birth, and so on. We would need to specify all of the possible routes by which an individual can get either into or out of the population stock, if we're talking about the human population part of it. We would also have to specify all the ways that pigs get into or out of the pig stock, and all the ways that land gets into or out of cultivation. Then we would start with an initial stock of population, pigs, and land, and simulate to find out whether in fact our system develops problems every 15 to 20 years that are resolved by the homeostats discussed by Rappaport. I can't sit down and do it instantly; it has taken me and six students about 10 weeks to put together a reasonable simulation of the Basseri data (Barth 1961). It's not an easy thing to do.

FORD: Rappaport's work has already been simulated. The I.B.M. engineers did it for him, and it works. He is able to test hypotheses in terms of this kind of system. In other words, he can predict that when certain thresholds are reached—with regard to the size of the pig herd, etc.—certain rituals will be held. And I think it is very important that this kind of system is amenable to hypothesis testing. But there is also something it doesn't do. In simualtion analysis we cannot deal with the *origin* of the system of variables within it; we cannot talk about what brought the system into existence. All we can do is understand how the system works.

PLOG: No, this approach will answer both "how" and "why" questions. For example, it will answer the question, "Why does this particular group seem to have a stable population of about size X?" Yes, we are asking "how" all of our variables are related to one another, and "how" the system operates. But one might start with a question like, "Why is population size what it is?" and end up having to generate a model like this in order to answer the question. I don't see that it's limited to "how" kinds of questions.

SAXE: You may be right. Remember that I pointed out earlier that systemic changes in a subsystem may be part of the regular homeostatic (nonchange) variations in the larger system of which it is a part. Now what you just said is that when you ask "why" about the subsystem "population," you are really asking "how" it is part of the larger or superordinate system.

GLASSOW: In other words, all of our explanations of *why* are really oriented toward explicating *how* in fact systems operate.

SAXE: Yes—how they operate with regard to a superordinate system.

FORD: But we can also ask questions as to how the systems originated; that's what we're after in this seminar.

PLOG: I think we're saying that "how" and "why" questions are ultimately not terribly different.

SAXE: No. If that's what you're saying, there's a fundamental point being missed. We do want to know how a system came into being. This is why it seems to me that my own approach seems so high powered; the "how" and "why" are specifically linked. My approach tells you where to look for the "why"—that is, outside the system of interest.

PLOG: OK; if you want to know how a system came to be the way it is, the procedure is relatively simple. You essentially begin playing games with your model. You introduce some kind of an exogenous factor that creates an abnormal value for one or more of your variables; and then you see whether or not the system is able to work itself back to normal, or whether you just get a stoppage in your program because you've got a value so high or so low that the computer can't cope with it, given the instructions you've given it.

SAXE: This bothers me. If I were to give instructions to a computer on ranges for my variables, I would not be able to tell it the points at which the tolerance limits had been exceeded.

PLOG: You can tell it that.

SAXE: Well, I can't know it in the ongoing system. For example, if I tell the computer, "When certain variables reach a certain point, become a state," it's not really simulating.

PLOG: You're saying that one can build a model for which there is no possible outcome other than the one that you want.

SAXE: Yes; this is why a functionalist model is inadequate. For example, let's say you introduce a big increase in population into your simulated system. This is going to trigger negative feedback responses, such as warfare, infanticide, or whatever—and this will readjust the system. But what if you introduce a population density that exceeds the tolerance limits given to the computer? What's going to happen if you haven't told the computer what to do about it? Is it just going to shut down?

PLOG: OK. The program can handle the siutation by instituting one of

316

the homeostats—increase land in cultivation, slaughter of pigs, or whatever. Or, you might have to set some limits. For example, you might instruct the program that when population gets too big for the amount of available land, it should institute infanticide, fall apart, or whatever you want it to do.

HILL: But I don't see how this handles morphogenesis. I see that you can simulate the operation of a system, and you can change the values on the variables in terms of amounts and rates. But if in fact the tolerance limits you set are exceeded, I would think the only thing the computer can do is terminate calculations. I don't see how you can get any change occurring in the system; it can't evolve.

SAXE: Right, since you programmed the computer. But tell me this. What if you took the whole region of New Guinea and included the Maring as a subsystem within it? Might we then have morphogenesis possible in a simulation study?

PLOG: Yes. The way to do it is to take a system such as that, and have a number of possible interference points where exogenous variability can be introduced. That is, you could have a random generator that every now and then pops up a bit of interference—and you could then see if the system can handle it. This is the problem we face with the Basseri model. We know that frosts occur on the average of once every four years; but we can't build into the model that it must have a frost every fourth year. We have to set up a random generator such that in the long run we get frosts in one out of every four years; but we can also get them three years in a row on occasion. And the sheep are going to be decimated if that occurs. So what we want to know is, does the system recover from this, or does everybody sedentize?

SAXE: That's a regular functional alternative within the system—it's not a change.

HILL: Right. You can alter values on the variables that are already in your system and see what happens; and as long as the homeostats work, the system will adjust and there will be no change. But if some external input is so strong that the values on one or more of the variables are forced beyond the tolerance limits you set, it creates a situation in which you would expect morphogenesis to occur—but this cannot happen in a simulation; it can't tell you what kind of change will occur because that's not programmed into the ongoing simulation. All the program can do is terminate.

WRIGHT: Dump!

PERLMAN: The question is, can such a model ever help us in predicting the direction of change?

SAXE: Now we're back to where we were before. My suggestion is that we need to isolate the particular system we're interested in as one element in a larger system. Then we can simulate the whole thing and see what changes occur in the system of interest.

STUART: I don't think we're going to be able to predict for any given substantive system which elements of its internal variety are going to be selected for in setting up new homeostats when the old ones break down under stress. But we can predict the range of kinds of changes that *would* serve to cope with the situation. As we said before, there are presumably only a limited number of changes that would work.

GLASSOW: What you would be doing is developing another set of hypotheses, and a new simulation model.

HILL: OK; and Art [Saxe] is saying that we can think up those hypotheses by looking at the extrasystemic factors that are affecting the system. We would also have to take account of the past structure of the system, since it would further limit the number of possible changes that can be made.

STUART: And it is probably the case that only one or two of the so-called possible alternative changes will in fact work in sustaining the system.

HILL: Also, it should be possible to predict which of these "alternatives" will be selected for, perhaps as some kind of "least cost" or "optimization" function.

# 11

# Comments on Explanation, and on Stability and Change*

## MELVIN L. PERLMAN

*Department of Sociology*
*Brock University*
*St. Catharines, Ontario*

I consider it a privilege to have been asked to participate in this seminar and to comment on the papers. I have learned a great deal from what has been a vital experience extending long after the original five-day seminar. Fundamental issues were posed, confronted, fought over, and—if not resolved to the satisfaction of all—new light was brought to bear on them, and new questions emerged for future research. The seminar participants are to be congratulated on having posed and seriously grappled with many of the thorniest questions on explanation and on change. To have assembled in one book (especially in the Discussion Section) a large number of significant questions about the explanation of organizational change is in itself an important achievement. Moreover,

*For critical comments I am grateful to Trevor Denton, John Mayer, Luis Pardo, and Wayne Thompson.

both the original papers and the Discussion Section contain insights that constitute important contributions to the search for adequate answers to these complex questions.

In a short review it is not possible to comment on all these questions. I shall concentrate, therefore, on two questions and associated premises that I consider the most important. First, I comment on some aspects of the fundamental question: what is a useful kind of model of explanation to account for variation in complex phenomena such as human populations? Second, I comment on some aspects of the equally fundamental problem of how to account for both the stability and change of systems. One feels some trepidation in attempting to deal with such fundamental issues, and thus I hasten to add that my comments are not meant as an attempt at synthesis, but are only my reactions to the preceding chapters. Although I am in agreement with much of what is said in this volume, and especially with the general approach represented by the book, in the short space available to me I have emphasized mainly some controversial issues, as, in the long run, these may be more useful than comments on points of agreement.

In this first section I will argue that the deductive syllogisms have definite limitations in the social sciences; that the covering law, or deductive-nomological model of explanation, is inadequate for the explanation of dynamic, complex phenomena such as prehistoric populations; that it is not useful to attempt to combine the deductive-nomological model of explanation (Hempel's model) with a feedback model incorporating multiple variables. Finally I recommend the pattern model of explanation which is consistent with the use of tendency statements and factor theories, as well as systems theory and cybernetic explanation.

Any discussion of explanation necessarily entails logic. Plog, in his chapter (2) on explaining change, mentions this only very briefly, and then refers the reader—for the formal rules of explanation—to "any logic book." His brief discussion refers to denying the antecedent or affirming the consequent, and thus he seems to be using the conventional logic of classes or the classical syllogism. Although there are other logics or modes of derivation, it is often assumed that the only one is the Aristotelian syllogism. But that mode is largely alien to the advanced sciences (Brodbeck 1962:240), and has definite limitations in the social sciences (Gibbs 1972:197, 223). For example, given the importance of incorporating feedback mechanisms in explanations of change, it is clear that we can no longer rely on the adequacy of the restricted word order rules of the syllogism.

The explanatory model proposed by Plog is the Hempel-Oppenheim, covering law, or deductive-nomological model. As the battle over the usefulness of this model continues, I can only reaffirm the basic position that I took in the original discussion, namely, my opposition to it as a model likely to lead to adequate explanations of living, dynamic, complex phenomena, such as prehistoric populations. A number of others have recently expressed similar views. For example, the Hempel model, or at least the way it is applied, is seen as "precisely the physical-science approach that von Bertalanffy rejected in the 1920s as being inadequate in dealing with biological phenomena" (Flannery 1973:51). Longacre comments that "the so-called covering law paradigm does not hold for the physical sciences today any more than it does for anthropology" (1973:334). And Renfrew states that "the logical structure of a system model . . . differs fundamentally from that of a hypothetico-deductive explanation" (1973:1929). And Tuggle, Townsend, and Riley (1972) have expressed serious reservations about the deductive-nomological model of explanation.

In this volume, Wright sees no necessity for using covering laws as part of his formal model of explanation, and this appears to be the opposite of the views expressed by Plog at the beginning of his chapter on explaining change. However, Plog has elsewhere (1973a:194) stated that we are unlikely to find simple chains of causality, and in the latter part of his chapter (2) in this volume he has provided a number of models incorporating multiple variables and feedback mechanisms. He then goes on to say that "the models can be used in deriving both lawlike propositions and test implications." It is no doubt with these "lawlike propositions" that Plog brings in the Hempel-Oppenheim model. If we were to use Wright's terminology, these "lawlike propositions" would be called *hypotheses*, in which case I suspect the whole procedure would be both more understandable and more acceptable. As Wright points out, many would consider the general statements of relationships between variables in a tested theory or theoretical model to be "laws," although Wright himself would not use this term. Plog probably would accept this formulation which seems not inconsistent with his reference elsewhere to "systems of laws" which he distinguishes, significantly, from "individual laws" which "would not . . . prove useful by themselves in predicting outcome" (1973b:660–61). It is also noteworthy that Plog specifies further what kinds of laws he thinks are needed, namely, "laws of process" which are "statements of tendency, not of outcome" (1973b:656).

The above comments put us in a position to reexamine the degree to which it is possible or useful to attempt to combine Hempel's model of explanation, and a feedback model incorporating multiple variables. For one thing, Hempel (1966) discusses universalistic laws and probabilistic laws (which assert that under certain conditions, a certain outcome will occur), but says nothing about tendency statements (which specify what would always happen in the absence of interfering conditions). This is not surprising, and is fully consistent with Hempel's model of explanation, which is essentially a deterministic model. The use of tendency statements, by contrast, reveals a less deterministic view of the world, more in keeping with the modern systems view of the world (for example, Laszlo 1972, 1973; Gray 1972). Second, we must ask whether it is possible for tendency statements to operate alone, and Gibson provides a clear statement:

> no single tendency statement is of any use when taken by itself. . . . If we are to resort to tendency statements, then we *must* have a theory. We can only work by taking a number of such statements together, each of them stating the effect of some given factor in a situation, and arguing from these to what will happen in their combined presence. (1960:144)

It is precisely the pulling together of a number of such statements that is typical of a feedback model with multiple variables, examples of which have been provided by Plog himself in chapter 2. Hempel, however, provides numerous examples of the usefulness of individual or single laws, as all his examples are universalistic or probabilistic laws. Furthermore, Hempel's view of theory (1966:chapter 6) is that it comes after the laws have been developed, and is quite different from the laws. This is in marked contrast to the type of theory mentioned above by Gibson which he refers to as a "factor theory" and which is constituted essentially by the interrelated set of tendency statements (1960:144–55). Such a factor theory is an example of what Kaplan calls a "concatenated theory." The instance he cites is the theory of evolution (1964:298). Kaplan associates this type of theory with what he calls the pattern model of explanation, a model which seems fully consistent with what has been referred to here as a feedback or systems model (1964:332ff). He contrasts concatenated theory and the pattern model of explanation, on the one hand, with hierarchical theory and the deductive model, on the other (1964:298).

The latter, as developed by Hempel and Oppenheim, is based on the analytic method, which has given rise to enormously successful developments in the physical sciences. However, as others have pointed out (Rapoport 1968:xvii; von Bertalanffy 1968:18–19), the analytic method may not be adequate for dealing with the complexities of biological and social processes; it may perhaps ultimately be unequal even to the tasks posed by microphysics. To handle these, systems theory is being developed, proposing its own characteristic mode of explanation, a major feature of which is a number of interrelated tendency statements.

Rapoport has expressed the view that in the biological and social sciences we are not going to have "laws" that are analogous to the major laws in the physical sciences; at most, he says, there will be *models* of specific biological and social phenomena (1972:24). Ashby, in a rather similar vein, while not wishing to deny that there may be great "laws" yet to be discovered, nevertheless says that much of the work in the behavioral sciences will have to be on constructions of narrower range and much more complex structure (1970:111). These views are not surprising when seen in the light of Gibson's penetrating analysis of the limited usefulness for social inquiries of both universalistic or straightforward laws and probabilistic laws or chance-statements (1960:chapters 11 and 12). There are those who also refer to tendency statements as "laws" and this includes Gibson who calls them "theoretical laws" (1960:144). Thus, the heart of the matter is not a terminological debate over how best to use the term "law," but is concerned with the recognition of at least three different kinds of statements or laws, and with the implications and consequences of using the differing kinds.

Probably the least well-known is the tendency statement or theoretical law, which is a statement "about what would always happen in the absence of interfering conditions" (Gibson 1960:140). Such a tendency statement sets no limits to the number of exceptions which are to be admitted (as does a chance-statement; Gibson 1960:144). A major implication of using tendency statements, therefore, is the recognition that they are not deterministic, which is contradictory to the positivist tradition as represented by Hempel. In Hempel's tradition, phenomena not yet demonstrated to be fully determined are considered to be *effectively* stochastic entities, which means a belief that as soon as enough research has been done, they will become deterministic. The opposing side believes no amount of research will ever make an *inherently* stochastic process into a deterministic one (Sutherland 1973:147, 201).

Another consequence of using tendency statements is that they will be more useful for providing explanations than predictions (Gibson 1960:149–50). This again is inconsistent with Hempel's view of the symmetry of explanation and prediction, a view which—although it appears sound for classical physics—has been questioned by Hanson as regards living, growing sciences (1963:33). Both Scriven (1965, 1968) and Kaplan (1964:347–51) recognize a separation between explanation and prediction. Another consequence of using tendency statements is, as mentioned above, that they are of little use alone, and must be combined. But there is no simple way to combine them. This leads us to construct increasingly complex models, as we strive to explain such phenomena as prehistoric organizational change.

If Rapoport and Ashby are right in directing us to the construction of complex models of specific biological and social phenomena, then we may ask: what broad kind of model will be most useful? We may be sure that there is no such thing as an "all-purpose model" (Levins 1968). Nevertheless, I venture to suggest a basic model, based on Kaplan's distinction between the deductive model and the pattern model (1964:chapter 9). In particular, I see consistencies between the already mentioned tendency statements and factor theories, the pattern model of explanation, and systems theory and cybernetic explanation. That is, I believe those sympathetic to general systems theory would find the pattern model useful, especially for the explanation of complex phenomena such as organizational change.

Some idea of the pattern model of explanation can be obtained from the following quotations:

> According to the pattern model, then, something is explained when it is so related to a set of other elements that together they constitute a unified system. We understand something by identifying it as a specific part in an organized whole. . . . relationships are fundamental, as well as some notion of closure: wholeness, unity, or integration. . . . The particular relations that hold constitute a pattern, and an element is explained by being shown to occupy the place that it does occupy in the pattern. . . . For the pattern model, objectivity consists essentially in this, that the pattern can be indefinitely filled in and extended: as we obtain more and more knowledge it continues to fall into place in this pattern, and the pattern itself has a place in a larger whole. (Kaplan 1964:333–35)

The final point about a pattern having a place in a larger whole is specifically relevant to hierarchical systems with more than one level,

324

prime examples of which are human populations, prehistoric or otherwise. In general, these ideas show the clear similarity between the pattern model of explanation and systems theory, and the same ideas are related to cybernetic explanation. Bateson in his discussion of cybernetic explanation (1972; orig. 1967) uses "pattern" as one of his basic concepts; he too (like Kaplan for the pattern model) uses the theory of evolution as a classic example of cybernetic explanation. Bateson emphasizes that cybernetic explanation is always negative; that is, restraints are shown to be operating in such a way that many of the abstractly possible alternatives were not followed, and thus a particular event was one of the few that could, in fact, occur. This reveals an indeterminancy similar to that mentioned above in the discussion of tendency statements, which here may be related to restraints. Such negative cybernetic explanations are contrasted by Bateson to positive causal explanations. The latter are typical of the Hempel model of explanation. Similarly, as already mentioned, Kaplan contrasts the pattern model of explanation with the deductive model of explanation.

It is worth mentioning further that the notion of causality (as used by Hempel 1966:53) is not conducive to understanding phenomena conceptualized from a cybernetic and systems-theoretic point of view. To understand and explain such phenomena, especially if they involve change, we may find enlightenment—in combination with the procedures already recommended—through the application of the method and logic of the dialectic (for example, see Sorokin 1966:chapter 14; von Wright 1971:159–60; and Sjoberg and Nett 1968:67). In any case, these comments represent reflections on the kind of model that may be useful in explaining complex phenomena such as organizational change.

I turn now to the second question: how to account for both the stability and change of systems? In this section I will argue that the relatively restrictive definitions of the concept system used in this volume may have limited the range of problems investigated, including the basic issue of how to account for both change and stability at any time and place; that an adequate description and explanation of both change and stability in human behavior requires a multilevel approach; that the integration of a system (especially human populations) is a matter of degree; that the usefulness of organization can only be judged in relation to a given goal, and thus goals must be taken into account; that goals are not always selected in terms of a "least-cost" solution; that the intervening variable of ideology has not received sufficient attention in this volume; and finally I briefly outline a model to account for both the stability and change of systems.

Let me begin with the concept of a system. Most of the definitions of a system in this volume are consistent in that essentially they refer to an interrelated set of variables such that a change in one results in a change in all (or, in Hill's version, at least one) other variables, a definition that emphasizes 100-percent wholeness or coherence (Hall and Fagen 1968:85), a point to which I will return later.

Definitions of concepts serve particular purposes, and these definitions are no exception. One purpose, apparently, was to facilitate computer simulation, consistent with an emphasis at the seminar on quantification. While such an emphasis has its advantages, it also has some limitations. For example, mathematical systems theory has been brought to such a state of purity in its descriptive formalisms that it "emphasizes holistic, single-level descriptions, avoidance of instabilities, optimization under fixed constraints and artificial isolation of adjacent levels" (Pattee 1973:149). The approximations and limitations inherent in any single-level description have been emphasized by Simon, no matter whether the system is physical, chemical, biological, social, or artificial (1973). Moreover, "the very concept of stability loses its clarity as the systems grow in complexity" (e.g., complexity such as is evident in human, including prehistoric, populations); thus, rather than avoiding instabilities, what we need is to develop "the theory of organization through instabilities" and then "distinguish those instabilities that are simply disintegrative from those that reintegrate the elements into new levels of organization" (Pattee 1973:147, 151). As it seems unlikely that early advances in our understanding of these important problems (that is, formulation of theories to describe at least two levels at a time, which will allow interactions between alternative levels, and development of a theory of organization through instabilities) will be "found in quantitative mathematical models or in new formalisms" (Pattee 1973:148), some archaeologists and others may find the real challenge at the present time, paradoxically, in the use of *qualitative* models (e.g., see Reynolds 1974).

Another possible purpose of the definitions was to facilitate the analysis of relatively abrupt change, as opposed to relatively gradual change, as the former may be what is most feasible using archaeological data. For example, a definition of a system which implies a close

326

interrelationship between variables (such that a change in one results in a change in another or all others) would be very difficult to use, if one's purpose were to analyze gradual change where, let us say, variables change one at a time. Ashby, for instance, discusses the extremely common and very important category of systems having a multiplicity of equilibrial states, whose variables behave largely as part functions, and which are able to adapt progressively (1962:275–76; reprinted in Buckley 1968). Furthermore, natural systems commonly form an interlocking pattern of adjusted, partly-adjusted, and poorly-adjusted subsystems, so clearly a change in one variable does not always, or even usually, result in changes in all the others (Chorley and Kennedy 1971:16; see also Jonas 1974:91).

There is nothing wrong with formulating definitions for particular purposes; all scientists do it, albeit, some more consciously than others. What may be less well recognized, I think, is that any particular definition, while it illuminates the matter of interest, must necessarily leave something else in shadow (Kaplan 1964:66). Having achieved a high level of agreement on what is a fairly restrictive definition may mean that the seminar participants have not investigated a broad range of problems in what is clearly an extremely general field of inquiry. In addition to the topics mentioned above whose investigation has been virtually excluded by the nature of the definitions, another problem of central importance remained largely in shadow, namely, the basic issue of how to account for *both* change and stability at any time and place. To have confronted this issue squarely would have required a less restrictive definition of a system.

Other aspects of systems, in addition to definitions per se, also warrant some comment, if our aim is to explain both change and stability in systems. For example, systems can be usefully conceptualized as having levels, or the parts of a system as interacting between hierarchically ordered levels. An adequate description and explanation of both change and stability in human behavior requires a multilevel approach (see Simon 1973), and at a minimum, in my view, this would involve the individual, the social or cultural, and the ecological levels. It may be that a team project involving a social anthropologist and an archaeologist would be more likely to provide an adequate explanation than that provided by either specialist alone.

Organization and integration are other important dimensions of systems which must be taken into account in explaining their change and stability. Ashby points out that "the modern theory, based on the logic of communication, regards organization as a restriction or constraint," which is a *relation* between observer and thing, such that organization "is partly in the eye of the beholder" (1962:257–58). Any particular constraint will depend on both the real phenomenon and the observer. This view highlights the significant degree to which what we see is influenced by what we were trained to look for, and this includes the kinds of concepts we use and the definitions we give them.

This point can be illustrated by reference once again to the definition of a system, quoted earlier, used by most of the authors in this volume. What it trains its users to look for essentially is 100-percent wholeness which is the same as 0-percent independence (Hall and Fagen 1968:85). This means presumably that any system (by another's definition) which is not 100-percent integrated must be regarded by these authors as a nonsystem. Now let us ask: how does their position square with the kind of evidence one would require in attempting to explain, for example, the evolution of the state—a major concern of the seminar. For a state to emerge, in the prestate stage, presumably, one or some combination of the parts must assert some degree of independence, must establish itself as preeminent over the others. Indeed, it is precisely by asserting such independence, by breaking away from what might have been a 100-percent integrated system that a new and changed system gets established. Thus, far from increasing our understanding of the process of the evolution of the state, it could be argued that these authors' definition of a system makes it even more difficult to "see" the kind of organizational change (including some decrease in the 100-percent integration, at least for a time) that must have transpired in conjunction with the emergence of the state.

Not only for the state, but for other populations as well, much of the dynamics of change over time is to be found in the relationship between the parts and the whole. For instance, under conditions of stress one of the parts may tend to escape the restraining controls of the whole, and vice versa, the whole may exercise an overstrict control of the parts, making them lose their individuality, and either situation could result in organizational change (Koestler 1973:113). One current example in western cultures is that we foster individuality with the result that we undermine the cohesion of our social groups (Jonas 1974:91). At any rate, the integration of a system (especially human populations) is a matter of degree, and at certain times the influence of the whole over the parts may be stronger, whereas at other times, it may be the reverse (see Menninger 1967:94). Thus, it behooves us to use concepts and find other ways of "seeing" organization that will facilitate analyzing change as well as stability. This and related problems are not confined to the seminar participants or archaeologists alone, but pertain to the discipline as a whole.

The usefulness of organization can only be judged in relation to a given goal, as an organization that is good for one goal or in one context may be bad in another (Ashby 1962:263). Thus, goals must be taken into account, even if they are not pursued consciously, although some are consciously pursued. However, I do not believe, as Hill seems to, that goals are always selected in terms of a "least-cost" solution. While it is true that prehistoric populations had much less choice, as we move toward the present, options for survival increase, leading to greater opportunities for conscious choice among alternatives, and more control over the environment. But even in prehistoric times, some populations have been willing to "pay more" (work harder, dispense more energy) to obtain a particularly desirable goal—let us say, a great religious ceremonial pertaining to fertility. A different population might not consider the energy and food expended on the ceremonial to be a "least-cost" solution; however, for the population in question, it may be that in the days and weeks following the ceremonial, rains came which preserved the community in life. Thus, given the strong influence of beliefs and values on human behavior, each population may define differently what it considers a "least-cost" solution.

Even if we assume survival as a superordinate goal, there is no reason to believe that populations will always or necessarily select the same "least-cost" solutions—even in the same or similar environments—in their attempts to survive, especially given the importance of the already mentioned belief systems (see Reynolds 1973:471, 478). Such belief systems and related values constitute an intervening variable between environmental forces and the response of a human population. This intervening variable, in my view, has not received sufficient attention in this volume, although Ford emphasizes the importance of ideology. He points out that ritual or ideology may serve as regulatory mechanisms, and may also be sources of different kinds of organizational change, even though different societies are in basically the same kind of environment.

Ideology may be conceptualized as being in memory or memory

storage, and this leads me to comment briefly on the concept of information. One of the concerns at the seminar was whether it is necessary for archaeologists to take into consideration the meaning of information. At one level, in the above discussion on ideology we have already answered in the affirmative. I would like to suggest, further, that to explain organizational change, we must take into consideration variety, which is kind of information or new information; in turn, variety cannot be understood apart from the meanings that it has for some individual or population. Certain plants which we consider good to eat, for example, have been rejected by some native peoples because of the meaning they attach to this variety. During the discussion Richard Ford gave examples of Pueblo food practices which elucidate this point. Other peoples would attach a different meaning to exactly the same plants, and this could launch a great deal of change.

Having mentioned a few important preliminary points, I come now to some brief comments on the topic per se of how to account for both the stability and change of systems. Is it possible within the framework of a single model to deal with what seem to be opposites? To answer such a question let me begin by asking whether these so-called opposites can be conceptualized in any other way? A somewhat different view can be formulated by reference to the work of Whitehead who, basing himself on Einstein's theory of relativity, proposed an ontological principle of universal relativity (Whitehead 1969:34, 62, 65; orig. 1929). A similar view is expressed by von Bertalanffy who saw ultimate reality as "a unity of opposites," noted that "the contrast between structure and process breaks down in the atom as well as in the living organism," and held that "the popular antithesis between motion and rest becomes meaningless in the theory of relativity" (1955:262; reprinted 1968). From this perspective, then, the distinction between stability and change is only relative. For instance, depending on our point of view, we could discern both structure and process as well as both rest and motion in any system.

One way to illustrate this idea would be to take a term such as movement, and ask what quantities and qualities of movement there are in a given system. The kind of movement of greatest interest here would be movement toward order, organization, or negentropy to counteract the tendency of all nature, according to the Second Law of Thermodynamics, toward disorder. Many factors influence the amount and kind of order in a system. For present purposes I merely want to suggest that even

330

in what we would typically refer to as a stable system, there will be—given a long enough time span—some minimal amount of movement away from the existing order; similarly, in a so-called changing system there will still be some movement toward the preservation of the preexisting order. Some systems will be halfway between these two extremes, and they will exhibit movement in both directions. My point is simply that no system is either completely stable or completely in a state of change, and that both maintenance and change are typically going on simultaneously in any system, although at any given time one may be dominant, or our interests or habits may determine that we focus preeminently on one rather than the other.

A model incorporating three time periods would seem the minimum necessary to explain both organizational change and stability. This view is based on the assumption that a period of relative stability exhibiting dominantly negative feedback will—given a sufficiently long time span —be followed by a period of relative instability exhibiting dominantly positive feedback which will finally (if the system survives) return to a state of relative stability and dominantly negative feedback. Following my earlier comments, and recognizing that stability and instability are relative terms, stability here implies the existence of a steady-state condition in which the variables in a feedback loop remain essentially constant or very close to characteristic values, whereas instability (the other end of this single continuum) implies the existence of large self-sustained oscillations of the variables in a feedback loop, in the absence of changing disturbances (Powers 1973:284–85; 287). The basic process in either situation is one of goal-seeking (whether consciously or not), of seeking to eliminate disturbances. Minor disturbances involve only routine activity, unlikely to lead to much organizational change. Major disturbances (whether originating in imagination or in the environment), however, would typically lead to a great deal of rapid activity, and this could result in the system moving from dominantly negative to dominantly positive feedback, and then to considerable organizational change.

An interesting question, therefore, is: how does a system move from dominantly negative to dominantly positive feedback, and eventually back again—all the while pursuing the one basic process of seeking to eliminate disturbances? I assume that any complex system, certainly a human population, will simultaneously contain both negative and positive feedback loops, and that at any one point in time either one or the other will be dominant. A great deal of rapid activity in and of itself will not necessarily lead a system into dominantly positive feedback. A complex system and its parts are constantly attempting to eliminate disturbances through corrective action, but often this is not a very smooth process, especially if the system is busily engaged in rapid activity. The corrective action consists of a series of pulls and pushes which may either overdo or underdo the job. That is, while the corrective process is going on, there may be an overshooting or undershooting of the mark (Menninger 1967:87–88; see also Chorley and Kennedy 1971:16–17; 353).

Overshooting and undershooting may occur first in only one of the parts of a system. Further corrective action may indeed restore the system to equilibrium. Often, however, the corrective process acquires an autonomy which leads only to further deviation. Such autonomy can lead the part or subsystem to exhibit strong independent or self-assertive tendencies, which might otherwise have remained more closely integrated with other parts of the system. The independent activities of one subsystem inevitably affect other subsystems which, lacking their customary inputs, must adjust, and readjust until finally the governor or dominant subsystem attempts to assert control and reintegrate the whole. Such attempts at reintegration may have taken place all along the way, but if none of them succeeded, we may say that the system moves into a state of instability where positive feedback dominates—enhancing the possibilities for substantial organizational change.

The next question is: how does the system get back again to a dominantly negative feedback state of stability, though typically at a higher level of organizational complexity? One way in which this can happen, at least in human populations, is that one of the subsystems—either the formerly dominant one or another one—gains preeminance, often through superior information or power. Other subsystems are convinced, either through might or right, to mitigate their self-assertive tendencies and to engage in more integrative behavior.

These two tendencies—the self-assertive and the integrative—seem to be ubiquitous phenomena in all domains of life, and under stable conditions the two are in dynamic equilibrium (Koestler 1973:112–13). In various ways one or the other of these tendencies may take precedence and lead the system into a state of instability. I have briefly sketched one way in which this may happen, but it is clearly not the only way, nor is it the only way in which organizational change may take place. For instance, even under relatively stable conditions a great deal of organizational change takes place which we usually call growth. Thus, organizational change may take place gradually or abruptly, and through many different routes. Nevertheless there seems to be one fundamental process underlying all these changes, and this is the very same process which operates to maintain a system under, relatively speaking, stable conditions. This process is one of goal-seeking, whether conscious or not, of seeking to remove disturbances. While engaged in this one basic process, the outcome can be either that the disturbance is eliminated, resulting in system maintenance, or, for instance, overshooting or undershooting the mark, which can lead to system change.

# References

ACKOFF, RUSSELL L.
1964 "General Systems Theory and Systems Research: Contrasting Conceptions of Systems Science," in *Views on General Systems Theory*, ed. M. D. Mesarovic (New York: John Wiley and Sons, Inc.).

ACKOFF, RUSSELL L., AND FRED E. EMERY
1972 *On Purposeful Systems* (Chicago: Aldine Publishing Company).

ADAMS, ROBERT McC.
1962 "Agriculture and Urban Development in Early Southwestern Iran," *Science* 136:109–22.

1966 *The Evolution of Urban Society* (Chicago: Aldine Publishing Company).

ALEXANDER, WILLIAM DEWITT
1891 *A Brief History of the Hawaiian People* (New York: American Book Company).

ALLAN, WILLIAM
1965 *The African Husbandman* (New York: Barnes and Noble).

ALLAND, ALEXANDER, JR.
1967 *Evolution and Human Behavior* (Garden City, New York: The Natural History Press).

ALLEE, W. C.
1931 *Animal Aggregations, A Study in General Sociology* (Chicago: University of Chicago Press).

ARGYRIS, CHRIS
1959 "Understanding Organizational Change," *General Systems* 4:123–35.

ARMILLAS, PEDRO
1971 "Gardens on Swamps," *Science* 174:653–66.

ASCH, DAVID
1973 "A Middle Woodland Population Estimate for the Lower Illinois Valley" (preliminary examination paper, University of Michigan).

ASCH, NANCY B., RICHARD I. FORD, AND DAVID L. ASCH
1972 *Paleoethnobotany of the Koster Site: The Archaic Horizons*, Illinois State Museum Reports of Investigations, no. 24 (Springfield: Illinois State Museum).

ASHBY, W. ROSS
1960 *Design for a Brain*, 2d ed. (London: John Wiley and Sons, Inc.).
1962 "Principles of the Self-Organizing System," in *Principles of Self-Organization*, eds. Heinz von Foerster and George W. Zopf (New York: Pergamon Press).
1965a "General Systems Theory as a New Discipline," *General Systems* 3:1–17.
1965b *An Introduction to Cybernetics* (New York: John Wiley and Sons, Inc.).
1970 "Analysis of the System to be Modeled," in *The Process of Model-Building in the Behavioral Sciences*, ed. Ralph M. Stogdill (New York: W. W. Norton and Company).

BARTH, FREDRIK
1961 *Nomads of South Persia* (Boston: Little, Brown and Company).

BATESON, GREGORY
1972 "Cybernetic Explanation," in *Steps to an Ecology of Mind*, by Gregory Bateson (New York: Ballantine Books). (Originally published in April 1967, *American Behavioral Scientist* 10:29–32).

BEARDSLEY, RICHARD K., ET AL.
1956 "Functional and Evolutionary Implications of Community Patterning," in *Seminars in Archaeology: 1955*, ed. Robert Wauchope. Memoirs of the Society for American Archaeology, no. 11 (Salt Lake City: The Society for American Archaeology).

BECKWITH, MARTHA W. (ED.)
1932 *Kepelino's Traditions of Hawaii*, Bernice Pahua Bishop Museum Bulletin, no. 95 (Honolulu: Bernice Pahua Bishop Museum).

BENNETT, WENDELL CLARK
1931 *Archaeology of Kauai*, Bernice Pahua Bishop Museum Bulletin, no. 80 (Honolulu: Bernice Pahua Bishop Museum).

BENNIGHOFF, WILLIAM S.
1968 "Biological Consequences of Quaternary Glaciations in the Illinois Region," in *The Quaternary of Illinois*, ed. Robert E. Bergstrom. University of Illinois College of Agriculture Special Publication, no. 14 (Urbana: University of Illinois Press).

BERELSON, BERNARD, AND GARY A. STEINER
1964 *Human Behavior: An Inventory of Scientific Findings* (New York: Harcourt, Brace, and World).

BERRY, B. J. L., AND DUANE F. MARBLE (EDS.)
1964 *Spatial Analysis: A Reader in Statistical Geography* (Englewood Cliffs, N.J.: Prentice-Hall, Inc.)

BERTALANFFY, LUDWIG VON
1950 "Outline of General System Theory," *British Journal of Philosophy of Science* 1:134–65.
1951 "Problems of General System Theory," *Human Biology* 23:302–12.
1955 "An Essay on the Relativity of Categories," *Philosophy of Science* 22:243–63. (Reprinted in Bertalanffy 1968.)
1956 "General Systems Theory," *General Systems* 1:1–10.
1962 "General Systems Theory—A Critical Review," *General Systems* 7:1–20.
1968 *General System Theory* (New York: George Braziller, Inc.).

BINFORD, LEWIS R.
1962 "Archaeology as Anthropology," *American Antiquity* 28:217–25.

# References

1963 "Red Ocher Caches From the Michigan Area: A Possible Case of Cultural Drift," *Southwestern Journal of Anthropology* 19:89–108.

1968a "Some Comments of Historical Versus Processual Archaeology," *Southwestern Journal of Anthropology* 24:267–75.

1968b "Archeological Perspectives," in *New Perspectives in Archeology*, eds. S. R. Binford and L. R. Binford (Chicago: Aldine Publishing Company).

1972 *An Archaeological Perspective* (New York: Seminar Press).

BLACK, GORDON, DREXEL COCHRAN, AND ARTHUR SAXE

1959 "The Origins of the State: The Hawaiian Islands," unpublished manuscript.

BOHANNAN, PAUL J.

1958 "Extra-processual Events in Tiv Political Institutions," *American Anthropologist* 60:1–12.

BOHANNAN, PAUL J., AND FRED PLOG

1968 *Beyond the Frontier* (New York: The Natural History Press).

BOSERUP, ESTHER

1965 *The Conditions of Agricultural Growth: The Economics of Agrarian Change Under Population Pressure* (Chicago: Aldine Publishing Company).

BOULDING, KENNETH E.

1956 "General Systems Theory—The Skeleton of Science," *General Systems* 1:13–17. (Reprinted from *Management Science* 2:197–208.)

1968 *The Image* (Ann Arbor: University of Michigan Press).

BRADLEY, H. W.

1942 *The American Frontier in Hawaii: The Pioneers, 1789–1843* (Stanford: Stanford University Press).

BREW, JOHN OTIS

1946 *Archaeology of Alkali Ridge, Southeastern Utah*, Papers of the Peabody Museum of American Archaeology and Ethnology, Harvard University, vol. 21 (Cambridge, Mass.: Harvard University).

BRODBECK, MAY

1962 "Explanation, Prediction, and 'Imperfect' Knowledge," in *Scientific Explanation, Space, and Time*, eds. Herbert Feigl and Grover Maxwell. Minnesota Studies in the Philosophy of Science, vol. 3 (Minneapolis: University of Minnesota Press).

BROOM, L., B. J. SIEGEL, AND J. B. WATSON

1953 "Acculturation: An Explanatory Formulation," *American Anthropologist* 56:973–1000.

BRYAN, EDWIN H., JR.

1950 *Ancient Hawaiian Life* (Honolulu: Advertiser Publishing Company, reprint 1950).

BRYAN, WILLIAM ALANSON

1915 *Natural History of Hawaii* (Honolulu: Hawaiian Gazette Company).

BUCHANAN, K. M., AND J. C. PUGH

1966 *Land and People in Nigeria* (London: University of London Press).

BUCHLER, IRA R., AND HENRY A. SELBY

1968 *Kinship and Social Organization: An Introduction to Theory and Method* (New York: The Macmillan Company).

BUCKLEY, WALTER

1967 *Sociology and Modern Systems Theory* (Englewood Cliffs, N.J.: Prentice-Hall, Inc.).

BUCKLEY, WALTER (ED.)
1968a *Modern Systems Research for the Behavioral Scientist* (Chicago: Aldine Publishing Company).
1968b "Society as a Complex Adaptive System," in *Modern Systems Research for the Behavioral Scientist* (Chicago: Aldine Publishing Company).

CADWALLADER, MERVYN L.
1959 "The Cybernetic Analysis of Change in Complex Social Organizations," *American Journal of Sociology* 65:154–57.

CANNON, WALTER
1932 *The Wisdom of the Body* (New York: W. W. Norton and Company).

CARNEIRO, ROBERT L.
1970 "A Theory of the Origin of the State," *Science* 169:733–38.

CHANG, K. C.
1958 "Study of the Neolithic Social Grouping: Examples from the New World," *American Anthropologist* 60:298–334.

CHORLEY, RICHARD J., AND BARBARA A. KENNEDY
1971 *Physical Geography: A Systems Approach* (London: Prentice-Hall International, Inc.).

CLARK, J. G. D.
1954 *Excavations at Star Carr* (Cambridge: Cambridge University Press).

CLARK, PHILLIP J.
1956 "Grouping in Spatial Distributions," *Science* 123:373–74.

CLARK, PHILIP J., AND FRANCIS C. EVANS
1954 "Distance to Nearest Neighbor as a Measure of Spatial Relationships in Populations," *Ecology* 35:445–53.

CLARKE, DAVID L.
1968 *Analytical Archaeology* (London: Methuen and Company, Ltd.).

COE, MICHAEL D., AND KENT V. FLANNERY
1964 Microenvironments and Mesoamercian Prehistory," *Science* 143:650–54.

COHEN, RONALD
1964 "Conflict and Change in a Northern Nigerian Emirate," in *Explorations in Social Change*, eds. George K. Zollschan and Walter Hirsch (Boston: Houghton, Mifflin Company).

DAVIS, EMMA LOU
1965 "Small Pressures and Cultural Drift as Explanations for Abandonment of the San Juan Area, New Mexico and Arizona," *American Antiquity* 30:353–55.

DEJARNETTE, DAVID L., EDWARD B. KURJACK, AND JAMES W. CAMBRON
1962 "Stanfield-Worley Bluff Shelter Excavations," *Journal of Alabama Archaeology* 8:1–111.

DEUTSCH, K. W.
1948–49 "Toward a Cybernetic Model of Man and Society," *Synthese* 7:506–23.

DIAKONOV, I. M. (ED.)
1969 *Ancient Mesopotamia* (Moscow: Nauka Press).

DOLE, SANFORD B.
1892 "Evolution of Hawaiian Land Tenure," *Hawaiian Historical Society Papers*, vol. 3 (Honolulu: The Hawaiian Historical Society).

338

# References

DOZIER, EDWARD P.
1970    *The Pueblo Indians of North America* (New York: Holt, Rinehart, and Winston).

DUNCAN, OTIS D.
1957    "The Measurement of Population Distribution," *Population Studies* 11:27–45.

EASTON, DAVID
1956    *A Systems Analysis of Political Life* (New York: John Wiley and Sons, Inc.). (Reprinted in Buckley 1968a:428–36.)

EGGAN, FRED
1954    "Social Anthropology and the Comparative Method," *American Anthropologist* 56:743–63.

ELLIS, WILLIAM E.
1825    *A Journal of A Tour Around Hawaii* (Boston: Crocker and Brewster).

EMERSON, N. B.
1895    "The Bird-Hunters of Ancient Hawaii," *Hawaiian Annual* 21:101–11.

EMORY, KENNETH P.
1933    "Warfare," in *Ancient Hawaiian Civilization*, ed. E. S. Craighill Handy (Honolulu: Kamehameha Schools).

ENGELS, KARL F.
1884    *The Origin of the Family, Private Property, and the State* (New York: International Publishing Company, 1940 English ed.).

FLANNERY, KENT V.
1967    "Culture History v. Culture Process: A Debate in American Archaeology," *Scientific American* 217:199–222.
1968    "Archaeological Systems Theory and Early Mesoamerica," in *Anthropological Archeology in the Americas*, ed. Betty J. Meggers (Washington, D.C.: Anthropological Society of Washington).
1969    "Land Use and Settlement Patterns in the Valley of Oaxaca," paper presented at the American Association for the Advancement of Science meetings, Boston.
1972    "The Cultural Evolution of Civilizations," *Annual Review of Ecology and Systematics* 3:399–426.
1973    Archeology with a Capital 'S,' " in *Research and Theory in Current Archeology*, ed. Charles L. Redman (New York: John Wiley and Sons, Inc.).

FORD, RICHARD I.
1968    "An Ecological Analysis Involving the Population of San Juan Pueblo, New Mexico" (Ph.D. diss., University of Michigan).
1972a   "Floral Identifications," in *Late Woodland and Mississippian Settlement Systems in the Lower Kaskaskia River Valley*, ed. L. Carl Kuttruff (Carbondale: Southern Illinois University Press).
1972b   "An Ecological Perspective on the Eastern Pueblos," in *New Perspectives on the Pueblos*, ed. Alfonso Ortiz (Albuquerque: University of New Mexico Press, School of American Research Advanced Seminar Series).

FORDE, C. DARYELL
1931    "Hopi Agriculture and Land Ownership," *Journal of the Royal Anthropological Institute of Great Britain and Ireland* 61:357–405.

FORNANDER, ABRAHAM
1880    *An Account of the Polynesian Race, Its Origin and Migrations and the Ancient History of the Hawaiian People to the Times of Kamehameha*, vol. 1 (London: Kegan, Paul, Trench, Trübner, and Co., Ltd.).

FOWLER, MELVIN L.
1959   *Modoc Rock Shelter, A Summary and Analysis of Four Seasons of Excavation*, Illinois State Museum Reports of Investigations, no. 8 (Springfield: Illinois State Museum).

FRITZ, JOHN M., AND FRED T. PLOG
1970   "The Nature of Archaeological Explanation," *American Antiquity* 35:405–12.

GAMIO, MANUEL, ET AL.
1922   *La Población del Valle de Teotihuacan*, 3 vols. (Mexico: Secretaria de Agricultura e Fomento).

GEERTZ, CLIFFORD
1963   *Agricultural Involution* (Berkeley: University of California Press).

GERARD, RALPH W.
1957   "Unit and Concepts of Biology," *Science* 125:429–33.

GIBBS, JACK P.
1972   *Sociological Theory Construction* (Hinsdale, Illinois: The Dryden Press, Inc.).

GIBSON, QUENTIN
1960   *The Logic of Social Enquiry* (London: Routledge and Kegan Paul).

GLADWIN, HAROLD S.
1957   *A History of the Ancient Southwest* (Portland, Maine: The Bond Wheelwright Company).

GLASSOW, MICHAEL A.·
1972   "The Evolution of Early Agricultural Facilities Systems in the Northern Southwest" (Ph.D. diss., University of California, Los Angeles).

GRAVES, THEODORE
1966   "Alternative Models for the Study of Urban Migration," *Human Organization* 25:295–99.
1967   "Psychological Acculturation in a Tri-ethnic Community," *Southwestern Journal of Anthropology* 23:337–50.
1970   "The Personal Adjustment of Navajo Indian Migrants to Denver, Colorado," *American Anthropologist* 72:337–52.

GRAY, WILLIAM
1972   "Bertalanffian Principles as a Basis for Humanistic Psychiatry," in *The Relevance of General Systems Theory*, ed. Ervin Laszlo (New York: George Braziller, Inc.).

HABERSTROH, CHADWICK J.
1960   "Control as an Organizational Process," *Management Science* 6:165–71.

HACK, JOHN T.
1942   *The Changing Physical Environment of the Hopi Indians of Arizona*, Papers of the Peabody Museum of American Archaeology and Ethnology, vol. 35, no. 1 (Cambridge: Harvard University).

HAGGETT, PETER
1965   *Locational Analysis in Human Geography* (London: Edward Arnold, Ltd.).

HALL, A. D., AND R. E. FAGEN
1956   "Definition of System" *General Systems* 1:18–28.
1968   "Definition of System," in *Modern Systems Research for the Behavioral Scientist*, ed. Walter Buckley (Chicago: Aldine Publishing Company).

HANDY, E. S. CRAIGHILL (ED.)
1933a  *Ancient Hawaiian Civilization* (Honolulu: Kamehameha Schools).

340

# References

1933b "Government and Society," in *Ancient Hawaiian Civilization*, ed. E. S. Craighill Handy (Honolulu: Kamehameha Schools).

1933c "Feasts and Holidays," in *Ancient Hawaiian Civilization*, ed. E. S. Craighill Handy (Honolulu: Kamehameha Schools).

1933d "Religion and Education," in *Ancient Hawaiian Civilization*, ed. E. S. Craighill Handy (Honolulu: Kamehameha Schools).

1933e "Houses and Villages," in *Ancient Hawaiian Civilization*, ed. E. S. Craighill Handy (Honolulu: Kamehameha Schools).

1940 *The Hawaiian Planter*, Bernice Pahua Bishop Museum Bulletin, no. 161 (Honolulu: Bernice Pahua Bishop Museum).

HANDY, E. S. CRAIGHILL, AND M. PUKUI

1950 "The Hawaiian Family System," *Journal of the Polynesian Society* 59:170–90; 232–40.

1951 "The Hawaiian Family System," *Journal of the Polynesian Society* 60:66–79; 187–222.

1952 "The Hawaiian Family System," *Journal of the Polynesian Society* 61:243–82.

HANSON, NORWOOD R.

1963 *The Concept of the Positron* (Cambridge: Cambridge University Press).

1965 *Patterns of Discovery* (Cambridge: Cambridge University Press).

HARDIN, GARRETT

1963 "The Cybernetics of Competition: A Biologist's View of Society," *Perspectives in Biology and Medicine* 7:61–84.

HARRIS, MARVIN

1964 *The Nature of Cultural Things* (New York: Random House).

1968 *The Rise of Anthropological Theory* (New York: Thomas Y. Crowell Company).

HAURY, EMIL W.

1956 "Speculations on Prehistoric Settlement Patterns in the Southwest," in *Prehistoric Settlement Patterns in the New World*, ed. G. R. Willey. Viking Fund Publications in Anthropology, no. 23 (New York: Wenner-Gren Foundation for Anthropological Research, Inc.).

HEMPEL, CARL G.

1966 *Philosophy of Natural Science* (Englewood Cliffs N.J.: Prentice-Hall, Inc.).

HEMPEL, CARL G., AND PAUL OPPENHEIM

1948 "Studies in the Logic of Explanation," *Philosophy of Science* 15:135–78.

HILL, JAMES N.

1966 "A Prehistoric Community in Eastern Arizona," *Southwestern Journal of Anthropology* 22:9–30.

1972 "The Methodological Debate in Contemporary Archaeology: A Model," in *Models in Archaeology*, ed. David L. Clarke (London: Methuen and Company, Ltd.).

HOBBS, JEAN

1931 "The Land Title in Hawaii," *Hawaiian Historical Society Annual Report* 40:26–33.

HOCKETT, CHARLES F., AND ROBERT ASCHER

1964 The Human Revolution," *Current Anthropology* 5:135–68.

HOLE, FRANK, KENT V. FLANNERY, AND J. A. NEELY

1969 *Prehistoric Human Ecology of the Deh Luran Plain*, Memoirs of the Museum of Anthropology, University of Michigan, no. 1 (Ann Arbor: Museum of Anthropology).

HOLE, FRANK, AND ROBERT F. HEIZER
1969   *An Introduction to Prehistoric Archeology* (New York: Holt, Rinehart, and Winston).

HOMANS, GEORGE C.
1967   *The Nature of Social Science* (New York: Harcourt, Brace, and World).

HUTCHINSON, G. E.
1948   "Circular Causal Systems in Ecology," *New York Academy of Science Annual* 50:221–46.

JETT, STEPHEN C.
1964   "Pueblo Indian Migrations: An Evaluation of the Possible Physical and Cultural Determinants," *American Antiquity* 29:281–300.

JOHNSON, GREGORY A.
1973   "Local Exchange and Early State Development in Southwestern Iran," Anthropological Papers of the University of Michigan, no. 51 (Ann Arbor: Museum of Anthropology).

JONAS, DORIS F.
1974   "On Darwinian Psychological Anthropology," *Current Anthropology* 15:91.

JONES, VOLNEY H.
1936   "The Vegetal Remains of Newt Kash Hollow Shelter," in *Rock Shelters in Menifee County, Kentucky*, W. S. Webb and W. D. Funkhouser. Publications of the Department of Anthropology and Archaeology, University of Kentucky (Lexington: University of Kentucky).

KAMAKAU, SAMUEL MANAIAKALANI
1961   *Ruling Chiefs of Hawaii* (Honolulu: Kamehameha Schools Press).

KAPLAN, ABRAHAM
1964   *The Conduct of Inquiry: Methodology for Behavioral Science* (San Francisco: Chandler Publishing Company).

KHAILOV, K. M.
1954   "The Problems of Systematic Organization in Theoretical Biology," *General Systems* 9:151–57 (1964). (Reprinted in Buckley 1968a:45–50).

KLIPPEL, WALTER E.
1971a  "Prehistory and Environmental Change Along the Southern Border of the Prairie Peninsula During the Archaic Period" (Ph.D. diss., University of Missouri).
1971b  "Graham Cave Revisited, A Reevaluation of its Cultural Position During the Archaic Period," Memoir of the Missouri Archaeological Society, no. 9 (Columbia: Missouri Archaeological Society).

KOESTLER, ARTHUR
1973   *The Roots of Coincidence* (New York: Vintage Books).

KOVAR, ANTON
1970   "The Physical and Biological Environment of the Basin of Mexico," *The Teotihuacan Valley Project Final Report*, vol. 1. Occasional Papers in Anthropology, no. 1 (University Park: The Pennsylvania State University).

KROEBER, A. L.
1917   "The Superorganic," *American Anthropologist* 19:163–213.

KUHN, THOMAS S.
1962   *The Structure of Scientific Revolutions* (Chicago: University of Chicago Press).

KUYKENDALL, R. S.
1947   *The Hawaiian Kingdom, 1778–1845* (Honolulu: University of Hawaii Press).

# References

KUYKENDALL, RALPH SIMPSON, AND A. GROVE DAY
1948   *Hawaii: A History from Polynesian Kingdom to American State* (Englewood Cliffs, N.J.: Prentice-Hall, Inc.).

LASZLO, ERVIN
1972   *The Systems View of the World: The Natural Philosophy of the New Developments in the Sciences* (New York: George Braziller, Inc.).
1973   *Introduction to Systems Philosophy: Toward a New Paradigm of Contemporary Thought* (New York: Harper and Row).

LE BRETON, LOUIS
1957   "The Early Periods at Susa," *Iraq* 19:79–114.

LEE, RICHARD B.
1972   "Population Growth and the Beginnings of Sedentary Life Among the !Kung Bushmen," in *Population Growth: Anthropological Implications*, ed. Brian Spooner (Cambridge: M.I.T. Press).

LEEDS, ANTHONY
1963   "The Functions of War," in *Violence and War: With Clinical Studies*, ed. J. Masserman (New York: Grune and Stratton).
1965   "Reindeer Herding and Chukchi Social Institutions," in *Man, Culture and Animals: The Role of Animals in Human Ecological Adjustments*, eds. Anthony Leeds and Andrew P. Vayda. American Association for the Advancement of Science, Publication no. 78 (Washington: American Association for the Advancement of Science).

LEONHARDY, FRANK C.
1966   *Domebo: A Paleo-Indian Mammoth Kill in the Prairie-Plains.* Contributions of the Museum of the Great Plains, no. 1 (Lawton, Okla.: Museum of the Great Plains).

LEVINS, RICHARD
1968   *Evolution in Changing Environments.* Monographs in Population Biology, no. 2 (Princeton: Princeton University Press).

LEWIN, KURT
1935   *A Dynamic Theory of Personality* (New York: McGraw-Hill).
1947   "Frontiers in Group Dynamics, Part II-B," *Human Relations* 1:147–53. (Reprinted in Buckley 1968a:441–44, as "Feedback Problems of Social Diagnosis and Action.")

LEWIS, OSCAR
1951   *Life in a Mexican Village: Tepoztlan Restudied* (Urbana: University of Illinois Press).

LEWIS, T. M. N., AND MADELINE KNEBERG LEWIS
1961   *Eva, An Archaic Site* (Knoxville: University of Tennessee Press).

LISTER, ROBERT H.
1966   *Contributions to Mesa Verde Archaeology: III, Site 866, and the Cultural Sequence at Four Villages in the Far View Group, Mesa Verde National Park, Colorado,* University of Colorado Studies, Series in Anthropology, no. 12 (Boulder: University of Colorado Press).

LOGAN, WILFRED D.
1952   *Graham Cave, An Archaic Site in Montgomery County, Missouri,* Memoir of the Missouri Archaeological Society, no. 2 (Columbia: Missouri Archaeological Society).

LONGACRE, WILLIAM A.
1973 "Comment," in *Research and Theory in Current Archeology*, ed. Charles L. Redman (New York: John Wiley and Sons, Inc.).

MACARTHUR, J., AND M. CONNELL
1966 *Biology of Populations* (New York: John Wiley and Sons, Inc.).

MALO, DAVIDA
1903 *Hawaiian Antiquities* (Moolelo Hawaii), trans. in 1898 by N. B. Emerson (Honolulu: Hawaiian Gazette Company).
1951 *Hawaiian Antiquities*, Bernice Pahua Bishop Museum Special Publication, no. 2, 2d ed. (Honolulu: Bernice Pahua Bishop Museum).

MANGELSDORF, PAUL C., RICHARD S. MACNEISH, AND WALTON C. GALINOT
1964 "Domestication of Corn," *Science* 143:538–45.

MARGALEF, RAMÓN
1968 *Perspectives in Ecological Theory* (Chicago: University of Chicago Press).

MARNEY, M. C., AND N. M. SMITH
1964 "The Domain of Adaptive Systems: A Rudimentary Taxonomy," *General Systems* 9:107–33.

MARUYAMA, MAGOROH
1963 "The Second Cybernetics: Deviation Amplifying Mutual Causal Processes," *American Scientist* 51:164–79. (Reprinted in Buckley 1968a:304–13.)

MCMILLAN, ROBERT BRUCE
1971 "Biophysical Change and Cultural Adaptation at Rodgers Shelter, Missouri" (Ph.D. diss., University of Colorado).

MEAD, MARGARET
1956 *New Lives for Old* (New York: Mentor).

MEGGITT, MERVIN
1965 *The Lineage System of the Mae-Enga of New Guinea* (New York: Barnes and Noble).

MENNINGER, KARL
1967 *The Vital Balance: The Life Process in Mental Health and Illness* (New York: Viking Press).

MESAROVIC, MIHAJLO D. (ED.)
1963 *Views on General Systems Theory* (New York: John Wiley and Sons, Inc.).

MILLER, GEORGE A.
1963 "What is Information Measurement?", *American Psychologist* 8:3–11.

MILLER, JAMES G.
1965a "Living Systems: Basic Concepts," *Behavioral Science* 10:193–237.
1965b "Living Systems: Structure and Process," *Behavioral Science* 10:337–79.
1965c "Living Systems: Cross-Level Hypotheses," *Behavioral Science* 10:380–411.

MILLON, RENE
1966 "Extensión y Población de la Cuidad de Teotihuacan en sus diferentes periodos: un calculo provisional," paper presented at the Teotihuacan: Onceava Mesa Redonda, Sociedad Mexicana de Antropologia, Mexico.
1967 "Teotihuacan," *Scientific American* 216(6):38–48.
1970 "Teotihuacan: Completion of Map of Giant Ancient City in the Valley of Mexico," *Science* 170:1077–82.

344

# References

MILLON, RENE (ED.)

1973    *Urbanization at Teotihuacan, Mexico*, vol. 1, parts 1, 2: *Teotihuacan Map* (Austin: University of Texas Press).

MOORE, OMAR KHAYYAM

1957    "Divination—A New Perspective," *American Anthropologist* 59:69–74.

MOOSER, FEDERICO

1968    "Geología, Naturaleza y Desarollo del Valle de Teotihuacan," Materiales para la Arqueologia de Teotihuacan, INAH Serie Investigaciones, no. 17 (Mexico: INAH).

MORGAN, LEWIS H.

1870    *Systems of Consanguinity and Affinity of the Human Family* (Washington: Smithsonian Institution).

1877    *Ancient Society* (New York: World Publishing).

MORSE, DAN FRANKLIN

1967    "The Robinson Site and Shell Mound Archaic Culture in the Middle South" (Ph.D. diss., University of Michigan).

MUNSON, PATRICK J., PAUL W. PARMALEE, AND RICHARD A. YARNELL

1971    "Subsistence Ecology of Scoville, A Terminal Middle Woodland Village," *American Antiquity* 36:410–31.

MURDOCK, GEORGE P.

1949    *Social Structure* (New York: The Macmillan Company).

NADEL, S. F.

1953    "Social Control and Self-regulation," *Social Forces* 31:265–73.

NAKUINA, EMMA M.

1894    "Ancient Hawaiian Water Rights and Some of the Customs Pertaining to Them,"*Hawaiian Annual* 20:79–84.

NEEDHAM, A. E.

1959    "The Orgination of Life," *Quarterly Review of Biology* 34:189–209.

NOTTERMAN, JOSEPH M., AND RICHARD TRUMBULL

1950    "Note on Self-Regulating Systems and Stress," *Behavioral Science* 4:324–27.

ODUM, EUGENE P.

1971    *Fundamentals of Ecology*, 3d ed. (Philadelphia: W. B. Saunders Company).

PARMALEE, PAUL W.

1962    "Faunal Remains from the Stanfield-Worley Bluff Shelter, Colbert County, Alabama," *Journal of Alabama Archaeology* 8:112–14.

PARMALEE, PAUL W., ANDREAS A. PALOUMPIS, AND NANCY WILSON

1972    *Animals Utilized by Woodland Peoples Occupying the Apple Creek Site, Illinois*, Illinois State Museum Reports of Investigations, no. 23 (Springfield: Illinois State Musuem.

PARSONS, JEFFREY R.

1968    "Teotihuacan, Mexico, and its Impact on Regional Demography," *Science* 162:872–77.

1971a   *Prehistoric Settlement Patterns in the Texcoco Region, Mexico*, University of Michigan Museum of Anthropology, Memoirs, no. 3 (Ann Arbor: Museum of Anthropology).

1971b   *Prehispanic Settlement Patterns in the Chalco Region, Mexico, 1969 Season.* Manuscript.

1973 *Reconocimiento Superficial en el Sur del Valle de México, Temporada, 1972.* Manuscript.

PATTEE, HOWARD H.
1973 "Unsolved Problems and Potential Applications of Hierarchy Theory," in *Hierarchy Theory: The Challenge of Complex Systems*, ed. Howard H. Pattee (New York: George Braziller, Inc.).

PERLMAN, MELVIN L.
n.d. *A Systems Theory of Structural Change and Stability: The Evolution of Marriage Among the Toro*, unpublished ms., Brock University, St. Catharine's, Ontario, Canada.

PERRY, ANTONIO
1913 "Hawaiian Water Rights," *Hawaiian Annual* 39:90–99.

PLOG, FRED
1969 "An Approach to the Study of Prehistoric Change" (Ph.D. diss., University of Chicago).
1973a "Diachronic Anthropology," in *Research and Theory in Current Archeology*, ed. Charles L. Redman (New York: John Wiley and Sons, Inc.).
1973b "Laws, Systems of Law, and the Explanation of Observed Variation," in *The Explanation of Culture Change: Models in Prehistory*, ed. Colin Renfrew (London: Duckworth).

POWERS, WILLIAM T.
1973 *Behavior: The Control of Perception* (Chicago: Aldine Publishing Company).

PRINGLE, J. W. S.
1951 "On the Parallel Between Learning and Evolution," *Behavior* 3:174–215.

PUKUI, M. K.
1939 "The Canoe Making Profession of Ancient Times," *Hawaiian Historical Society Papers* 20:27–37.

QUASTLER, HENRY
1956 "Studies of Human Channel Capacity," in *Information Theory*, ed. Colin Cherry (London: Butterworth's Scientific Publications).

RAPOPORT, ANATOL
1956 "The Promise and Pitfalls of Information Theory," *Behavioral Science* 1:303–9.
1968 "Forward," in *Modern Systems Research for the Behavioral Scientist*, ed. Walter Buckley (Chicago: Aldine Publishing Company).
1972 "The Search for Simplicity," in *The Relevance of General Systems Theory*, ed Ervin Laszlo (New York: George Braziller, Inc.).

RAPOPORT, ANATOL, AND WILLIAM J. HORVATH
1959 "Thoughts on Organization Theory," *General Systems* 4:87–91.

RAPPAPORT, ROY A.
1967 *Pigs for the Ancestors: Ritual in the Ecology of a New Guinea People* (New Haven: Yale University Press).
1969 "Sanctity and Adaptation," *Wenner-Gren Symposium, The Moral and Esthetic Structure of Human Adaptation* (New York: Wenner-Gren Foundation for Anthropological Research).
1971a "Nature, Culture, and Ecology Anthropology," in *Man, Culture and Society*, ed. Harry Shapiro, rev. ed. (New York: Oxford University Press).
1971b "The Sacred in Human Evolution," in *Annual Review of Ecology and Semantics*, ed. Richard F. Johnson (Palo Alto: Annual Reviews, Inc.).

# References

REDFIELD, ROBERT
1930    *Tepoztlan, A Mexican Village* (Chicago: University of Chicago Press).

REED, ERIK K.
1956    "Types of Village-Plan Layouts in the Southwest," in *Prehistoric Settlement Patterns in the New World*, ed. Gordon R. Willey. Viking Fund Publications in Anthropology, no. 23 (New York: Wenner-Gren Foundation for Anthropological Research, Inc.).

RELACION DE TECCIZTLAN Y SU PARTIDO
1905    In *Papeles de Nueva España*, vols. 6–7, ed. Francisco del Paso y Troncoso (Madrid: np).

RENFREW, COLIN
1973    "Review of *Explanation in Archaeology: An Explicitly Scientific Approach*, by Patty Jo Watson, Steven A. LeBlanc, and Charles L. Redman," *American Anthropologist* 75:1928–30.

REYNOLDS, VERNON
1973    Ethnology of Social Change," in *The Explanation of Culture Change: Models in Prehistory*, ed. Colin Renfrew (London: Duckworth).

REYNOLDS, WILLIAM E.
1974    "The Analysis of Complex Behavior: A Qualitative Systems Approach," *General Systems Yearbook* 19:73–89.

RODGERS, WILLIAM B.
1966    "Development and Specialization: A Case From the Bahamas," *Ethnology* 5:409–14.
1967    "Changing Gratification Orientations," *Human Organization* 26:200–205.
1969    "Developmental Exposure and Changing Vocational Preferences in the Out Island Bahamas," *Human Organization* 28:270–78.
1971    "Incipient Development and Vocational Evolution in Dominica," *Human Organization* 30:239–54.

ROGERS, EVERETT
1969    *Modernization Among Peasants* (New York: Holt, Rinehart, and Winston).

ROHN, ARTHUR H.
1963    "Prehistoric Soil and Water Conservation on Chapin Mesa, Southwestern Colorado," *American Antiquity* 28:441–55.

RUSSELL, WILLIAM M. S.
1959    "Evolutionary Concepts in Behavioral Science II: Organic Evolution and the Genetical Theory of Natural Selection," *General Systems* 4:45–73.

SAHLINS, MARSHALL D.
1958    *Social Stratification in Polynesia* (Seattle: University of Washington Press).
1961    "The Segmentary Lineage: An Organization of Predatory Expansion," *American Anthropologist* 63:322–45.
1963    "Poor Man, Rich Man, Big Man, Chief: Political Types in Melanesia and Polynesia," *Comparative Studies in Society and History* 5:285–303.

SAHLINS, MARSHALL D., AND ELMAN SERVICE
1960    *Evolution and Culture* (Ann Arbor: University of Michigan Press).

SANDERS, HOWARD L.
1969 "Benthic Marine Diversity and the Stability-Time Hypothesis," *Report of the Brookhaven Symposium in Biology, Diversity and Stability in Ecological Systems* (Upton, N.Y.: Brookhaven National Laboratory).

SANDERS, WILLIAM T.
1965 *Cultural Ecology of the Teotihuacan Valley* (University Park: Pennsylvania State University, Dept. of Sociology and Anthropology).
1968 "Hydraulic Agriculture, Economic Symbiosis and the Evolution of States in Central Mexico," in *Anthropological Archeology in the Americas*, ed. Betty J. Meggers (Washington: Anthropological Society of Washington).

SANDERS, WILLIAM T., ANTON KOVAR, THOMAS CHARLETON, AND RICHARD A. DIEHL
1970 *The Teotihuacan Valley Project, Final Report*, vol. 1. *The Natural Environment, Contemporary Occupation and 16th Century Population of the Valley.* Occasional Papers in Anthropology, no. 3 (University Park, Pa.: Department of Anthropology, Pennsylvania State University.

SAXE, ARTHUR A.
1962 *A General Systems Model in Linguistics-English Noun Forms*, Papers of the Michigan Academy of Science, Arts and Letters, vol. 47 (Ann Arbor: University of Michigan Press).

SCRIVEN, MICHAEL
1965 "An Essential Unpredictability in Human Behavior," in *Scientific Psychology*, eds. B. B. Wolman and E. Nagel (New York: Basic Books).
1968 "The Philosophy of Science," in *The International Encyclopedia of the Social Sciences*, vol. 14 (New York: The Macmillan Company).

SECORD, PAUL F., AND CARL W. BACKMAN
1961 "Personality Theory and the Problem of Stability and Change in Individual Behavior: An Interpersonal Approach," *Psychological Review* 68:21–32.

SERVICE, ELMAN R.
1962 *Primitive Social Organization, An Evolutionary Perspective* (New York: Random House).
1963 *Profiles in Ethnology* (New York: Harper and Row).
1971 *Cultural Evolutionism* (New York: Holt, Rinehart, and Winston).

SIMON HERBERT A.
1965 "The Architecture of Complexity," *General Systems* 10:63–74.
1973 "The Organization of Complex Systems," in *Hierarchy Theory: The Challenge of Complex Systems*, ed. Howard H. Pattee (New York: George Braziller, Inc.).

SJOBERG, GIDEON, AND ROGER NETT
1968 *A Methodology for Social Research* (New York: Harper and Row).

SOMMERHOF, G.
1950 *Analytical Biology* (London: Oxford University Press). (Reprinted in Buckley 1968a:281–95, as "Purpose, Adaptation and 'Directive Correlation.' ")

SOROKIN, PITIRIM A.
1966 *Sociological Theories of Today* (New York: Harper and Row).

STEINEN, DIETHER VON DEN
1926 "Das Stande-wesen der Polynesier in seiner wirtshaftlichen Bedeutung," *Zeitschrift für vergleichende Rechtswissenschaft* 42:146–94.

348

# References

STEWARD JULIAN H.

1937 "Ecological Aspects of Southwestern Society," *Anthropos* 32:87–104.

1949 "Cultural Causality and Law: A Trial Formulation of the Development of Early Civilizations," *American Anthropologist* 51:1–27.

1955a *Theory of Culture Change* (Urbana: University of Illinois Press).

1955b "Some Implications of the Symposium," *Irrigation Civilization: A Comparative Study, Social Science Monographs*, no. 1 (Washington, D.C.: Social Science Section, Dept. of Cultural Affairs, Pan American Union).

STICKEL E. GARY

1968 "Status Differentiation at the Rincon Site," *Archaeological Survey Annual Report* 10 (Los Angeles: University of California, Dept. of Anthropology).

STRAUSS, ANSELM, ET AL.

1963 "The Hospital and its Negotiated Order," in *The Hospital in Modern Society*, ed. Eliot Freidson (New York: The Free Press).

STRUEVER, STUART

1968 "Woodland Subsistence-Settlement Systems in the Lower Illinois Valley," in *New Perspectives in Archeology*, eds. Sally R. Binford and Lewis R. Binford (Chicago: Aldine Publishing Company).

1971 "Comments on Archaeological Data Requirements and Research Strategy," *American Antiquity* 36:9–19.

SUMA DE VISITAS

1905 In *Papeles de Nueva España*, vol. 1, ed. Francisco del Paso y Troncoso (Madrid: np).

SUTHERLAND, JOHN W.

1973 *A General Systems Philosophy for the Social and Behavioral Sciences* (New York: George Braziller, Inc.).

TITIEV, MISCHA

1944 *Old Oraibi: A Study of the Hopi Indians of Third Mesa*, Papers of the Peabody Museum of American Archaeology and Ethnology, vol. 22, no. 1 (Cambridge, Mass.: Harvard University).

TUGGLE, H. DAVID, ALEX H. TOWNSEND, AND THOMAS J. RILEY

1972 "Laws, Systems, and Research Designs: A Discussion of Explanation in Archaeology," *American Antiquity* 37:3–12.

TURNER, RALPH H.

1962 "Role-Taking: Process Versus Conformity," in *Human Behavior and Social Processes*, ed. Arnold M. Rose (Boston: Houghton Mifflin).

TYLOR, EDWARD B.

1871 *Primitive Culture: Researches into the Development of Mythology, Philosophy, Religion, Language, Art and Custom* (London: J. Murray).

1889 "On a Method of Investigating the Development of Institutions; Applied to Laws of Marriage and Descent," *Journal of the Royal Anthropological Institute* 18:245–69.

1899 *Anthropology: An Introduction to the Study of Man and Civilization* (New York: D. Appleton; original 1881).

VAYDA, ANDREW P.

1961a "Expansion and Warfare Among Swidden Agriculturalists," *American Anthropologist* 63:346–58.

1961b "A Re-examination of Northwest Coast Economic Systems," *Transactions of the New York Academy of Science, II* 23:618–24.

VAYDA, ANDREW P., ANTHONY LEEDS, AND D. B. SMITH
1961 "The Place of Pigs in Melanesian Subsistence," Proceedings of the 1961 Annual Spring Meeting, American Ethnological Society (Seattle: University of Washington Press).

VICKERS, GOEFFREY
1959a "The Concept of Stress in Relation to the Disorganization of Human Behavior," in *Stress and Psychiatric Disorder*, ed. J. M. Tanner (Oxford: Blackwell Scientific Publications, Ltd.). (Reprinted in Buckley 1968a:354–58.)
1959b "Is Adaptability Enough?," *Behavioral Science* 4:219–34.

WATSON, PATTY JO, STEVEN A. LEBLANC, AND CHARLES L. REDMAN
1971 *Explanation in Archeology: An Explicitly Scientific Approach* (New York: Columbia University Press).

WEINGARTNER, RUDOLPH H.
1968 "The Quarrel About Historical Explanation," in *Readings in the Philosophy of the Social Sciences*, ed. May Brodbeck (New York: The Macmillan Company).

WHITE, LESLIE A.
1943 "Energy and the Evolution of Culture," *American Anthropologist* 45:355–56.
1945 "History, Evolutionism, and Functionalism: Three Types of Interpretation of Culture," *Southwestern Journal of Anthropology* 1:221–48.
1954 "Reviews of *The Nature of Culture*, by A. L. Kroeber and *Culture: A Critical Review of Concepts and Definitions*, by A. L. Kroeber and Clyde Kluckhohn," *American Anthropologist* 56:461–68.
1959 *The Evolution of Culture* (New York: McGraw-Hill).

WHITEHEAD, ALFRED NORTH
1969 *Process and Reality: An Essay in Cosmology* (New York: The Free Press). (Originally published in 1929).

WIENER, NORBERT
1954 "Cybernetics in History," in *The Human Use of Human Beings: Cybernetics and Society* (New York: Doubleday and Company, Inc.).

WILSON, R. E. AND E. L. RICE
1968 "Allelopathy as expressed by Helianthus annuus and its role in old-field succession," *Bulletin of the Torrey Botanical Club* 95:432–48.

WISE, JOHN H.
1933 "The History of Land Ownership in Hawaii," in *Ancient Hawaiian Civilization*, ed. E. S. C. Handy (Honolulu: Kamehameha Schools).

WITTFOGEL, KARL A.
1955 "Developmental Aspects of Hydraulic Societies," Irrigation Civilization: A Comparative Study, Social Science Monographs, no. 1 (Washington, D.C.: Social Science Section, Dept of Cultural Affairs, Pan American Union).
1957 *Oriental Despotism: A Comparative Study of Total Power* (New Haven: Yale University Press).

WRIGHT, GEORGE HENRIK VON
1971 *Explanation and Understanding* (Ithaca: Cornell University Press).

WRIGHT, HENRY T.
1969 *The Administration of Rural Production in an Early Mesopotamian Town*, Anthropological Papers of the Museum of Anthropology, University of Michigan, no. 38 (Ann Arbor: Museum of Anthropology).

# References

1972    "A Consideration of Inter-regional Exchange in Greater Mesopotamia: 4000–3000 B.C.," in *Social Exchange and Interaction*, ed. Edwin N. Wilmsen. Anthropological Papers of the Museum of Anthropology, University of Michigan, no. 46 (Ann Arbor: Museum of Anthropology).

YARNELL, RICHARD A.
1969    "Contents of Human Paleofeces," in *The Prehistory of Salts Cave, Kentucky*, ed. Patty Jo Watson, Illinois State Museum Reports of Investigations, no. 16 (Springfield: Illinois State Museum).

YOUNG, O. R.
1964    "A Survey of General Systems Theory," *General Systems* 9:61–80.

# Index

acculturation, 25, 26, 28–29
Ackoff, Russell L., 61, 156
Adams, Robert McC., 25, 218, 222
adaptation, 290–291; societal, 97
aggregations. *See* population aggregations
*Agricultural Involution* (Geertz), 25
agriculture, 12
Alexander, William Dewitt, 124
Alland, Alexander, Jr., 61
Allee, W. C., 187, 208
arguments, construction of, 18–20
Argyris, Chris, 60, 61
Armillas, Pedro, 246
Asch, David L., 172, 176, 177
Asch, Nancy B., 172, 176
Ascher, Robert, 159
Ashby, W. Ross, 60, 61, 62, 102, 156, 164, 323, 324, 327–28, 329

Backman, Carl W., 74
Barth, Fredrik, 313, 315
Basket Maker culture, 13–14; household aggregation patterns in, 194–214
Bateson, Gregory, 325
Beardsley, Richard K., 187
Beckwith, Martha W., 131, 132, 133, 136
*Behavioral Science*, 61
behaviorism, 25, 26, 29–30, 39–41
Bennett, Wendell Clark, 132
Benninghoff, William S., 164, 165
Berelson, Bernard, 19
Berry, B. J. L., 193
Bertalanffy, Ludwig von, 60, 61, 62, 117, 155, 156, 220, 321, 323, 330
*Beyond the Frontier* (Bohannan and Plog), 26
Binford, Lewis R., 6, 59, 98, 276–318 passim

biological ecology, 7
Black, Gordon, 137
Bohannan, Paul J., 26, 112
Boulding, Kenneth E., 37, 61, 280
Brew, John Otis, 207
Brodbeck, May, 320
Broom, L., 28
Bryan, Edwin H., Jr., 130–31, 136
Buchanan, K. M., 247
Buckley, Walter, 6, 60, 62, 63, 64, 70–78, 79, 80, 81, 82, 97, 98, 102, 111, 114, 118, 119–20, 282, 285, 327

Cadwallader, Mervyn L., 61, 62, 98
Cambron, James W., 168
Cannon, Walter, 62
Carneiro, Robert L., 25, 33, 217
Chang, K. C., 186, 187
change, 325–33; models in study of, 44–57; nonsystemic, 112–13; organizational, 24–43, 203–13; sources of, 288–90; systemic, 89–97, 113–15, 116–19
Chorley, Richard J., 327, 332
Clark, Phillip J., 186, 191, 197, 199
Clarke, David L., 61
Cochran, Drexel, 137
Coe, Michael D., 61
Cohen, Ronald, 61, 77
communication, 98–99
Complex Adaptive System Model, 70, 120
computer simulation, 14, 94, 259–70, 313–18. *See also* models
Connell, M., 52
Cook, James, 105, 106, 122, 126, 137–38
cultural ecology, 25, 26, 27–28. *See also* specific evolutionism
culture, 160–61

353

Darwin, Charles, 2
data base, relativity of, 272–73
Davis, Emma Lou, 208
definitions, 326–27
DeJarnette, David L., 168
Délégation Archéologique Française en Iran, 222
Deutsch, K. W., 63, 98
devolution, 162
Diakonov, I. M., 216, 218
differentiation, as behavioral dimension, 53, 54
dimension, defined, 44
Dole, Sanford B., 131
Dozier, Edward, 205
Duncan, O. D., 190, 191

Easton, David, 61
ecology: biological, 7; cultural, 25, 26, 27–28; evolutionary, 153–84
ecosystems, 153–84
Eggan, Fred, 37
Ellis, William E., 132, 133, 134, 135, 136
Emerson, N. B., 136
Emery, Fred E., 156
Emory, Kenneth P., 136
energy, as behavioral dimension, 53, 54, 55
Engels, Karl F., 216
Evans, Francis E., 191, 197, 199
evolution, 6, 7; political, 231–57
The Evolution of Urban Society (Adams), 25, 218
evolutionary ecology, 153–84
evolutionism, 2–5, 25, 26–27, 111–12
experimentation, 49
explanation, nature of, 15, 17–24, 273–77, 320–25

Fagen, R. E., 61, 326, 328
feedback, 23–24, 79–82, 86, 322, 331–32. See also self-regulation
Flannery, Kent V., 6, 61, 97, 158, 159, 172, 184, 222, 241, 321
Ford, Karen C., 184
Ford, Richard I., 11, 14, 153–84, 272–318 passim, 329
Forde, C. Daryell, 205, 206, 207, 211
formal systems, 260, 269
Fornander, Abraham, 135
Fowler, Melvin L., 168
Fritz, John M., 59
function, defined, 113
functionalism, 63, 111, 112

Gamio, Manuel, 232–33
Geertz, Clifford, 5, 25, 61
General Systems, 61

general systems theory, 7, 59–103. See also systems theory
Gerard, Ralph, 62, 98
Gibbs, Jack P., 320
Gibson, Quentin, 322, 323, 324
Gladwin, Harold S., 204, 205
Glassow, Michael A., 11–12, 14, 185–214, 272–318 passim
Graves, Ted, 26
Gray, William, 322
Griffin, James B., 184

Haberstroh, Chadwick J., 63
Hack, John T., 205
Haggett, Peter, 191, 199
Hall, A. D., 61, 326, 328
Handy, E. S. Craighill, 132, 134, 135, 136
Hanson, Norwood, 20, 324
Hardin, Garrett, 63
Harris, Marvin, 5, 15, 25, 31, 40
Haury, Emil W., 209
Hawaiian Antiquities (Malo), 129
Hawaiian Islands, 261–67; aboriginal social organization in, 130–36. See also Sandwich Islands
Heizer, Robert F., 61
Hempel, Carl G., 19, 77, 322, 323, 324
Hill, James N., 1–16, 59–103, 155, 186, 203, 272–318 passim, 326, 329
Hobbs, Jean, 136
Hockett, Charles F., 159
Hole, Frank, 61, 222, 225
Homans, George C., 46
homeostatic mechanisms, 62–64, 86–87, 88–89
Horvath, William J., 61
household aggregation patterns, 194–214
Human Behavior: An Inventory of Scientific Findings (Berelson and Steiner), 19
Hutchinson, G. E., 79
hypothesis testing, 298–300

ideology, 329–30
information, nature of, 284–85, 330
integration, 327–29; as behavioral dimension, 53, 54–55
Iran, state development in, 222–28

Jett, Stephen C., 208
Johnson, Gregory, 227–28
Jonas, Doris F., 327, 328
Jones, Volney H., 176

Kamakau, Samuel Manaiakalani, 124
Kaplan, Abraham, 322, 324, 325, 327
Kennedy, Barbara A., 327, 332

# Index

Khailov, K. M., 62, 98
Klippel, Walter E., 168, 172
Koestler, Arthur, 328, 332
Kovar, Anton, 232
Kuhn, Thomas, 21, 25, 60
Kurjack, Edward B., 168
Kuykendall, R. S., 125, 127, 137, 139, 142, 143, 144, 146, 148, 149

Laszlo, Ervin, 322
laws, 19–20, 30, 43, 323
LeBlanc, Steven A., 59
LeBreton, Louis, 222
Lee, Richard B., 170
Leeds, Anthony, 5, 61, 63
Leonhardy, Frank, C., 167
Levins, Richard, 290, 324
Lewin, Kurt, 39, 97
Lewis, Madeline Kneberg, 172
Lewis, Oscar, 38
Lewis, T. M. N., 172
Lister, Robert H., 205
"Living Systems: Cross-Level Hypotheses" (Miller), 19
"Living Systems: Structure and Process" (Miller), 65
locational analysis, 7
Logan, Wilfred D., 168
Longacre, William A., 321

MacArthur, J., 52
McMillan, Robert Bruce, 172
Makahiki, 122
Malo, Davida, 124, 126, 129, 130, 131, 132, 133, 134, 135, 136, 143
Mangelsdorf, Paul C., 242
Marble, Duane F., 193
Margalef, Ramón, 161
Marney, M. C., 97
Maruyama, Magoroh, 64, 78–83, 119, 120–21, 127
Mead, Margaret, 38
measurement, problems of, 97–101, 300–303
Mechanical Equilibrium Model, 70
Menninger, Karl, 329, 332
Mesarovic, Mihajlo D., 60
Miller, G. A., 98
Miller, James G., 19, 60, 61, 62, 63, 64–70, 75, 97, 98, 102, 156, 278, 280, 282
Millon, Rene, 239, 240, 244, 247, 248
models, 44–57, 111. See also computer simulation
Modernization Among Peasants (Rogers), 26
Moore, Omar Khayyam, 171
Mooser, Federico, 233

Morgan, Lewis H., 2, 25
morphogenesis, 119, 120–21. See also systemic change
morphostasis, 119
Morse, Dan Franklin, 168, 171
multilinear evolutionism, 3–5
Munson, Patrick J., 177
Murdock, George P., 187

Nadel, S. F., 67
Nakuina, Emma M., 132
The Nature of Cultural Things (Harris), 40
Needham, A. E., 166
Neely, J. A., 222, 225
neo-evolutionism. See specific evolutionism
Nett, Roger, 325
New Mexico, household aggregation patterns in, 194–214
Notterman, Joseph M., 95

Odum, Eugene P., 164
Organismic Homeostasis Model, 70
organization, 8, 24, 327–30
Oriental Despotism (Wittfogel), 216

Paloumpis, Andreas A., 177
paradigms, 21, 25
Parmalee, Paul W., 168, 177
Parsons, Jeffrey R., 245, 248
Pattee, Howard H., 326
Perlman, Melvin L., 15, 60, 61, 102, 273–318 passim, 319–33
Perry, Antonio, 131, 132, 134, 135
Pigs for the Ancestors (Rappaport), 87, 314–15
Plog, Fred, 2, 6, 8, 9, 14–15, 17–57, 59, 155, 259–70, 273–318 passim, 320, 321–22
political evolution, 231–57
population, as behavioral dimension, 53, 54
population aggregations, variability and change in, 184–214
population growth, 13–14, 231–57 passim
Powers, William T., 331
Pringle, J. W. S., 97
Pugh, J. C, 247
Pukui, M. K., 136

Quastler, Henry, 221

racial differences, 2–3
Rapoport, Anatol, 324
Rappaport, Roy, 5, 61, 63, 84, 87, 88, 89, 97, 99, 155, 157, 158, 184, 313, 314–15, 323
Redfield, Robert, 38
Redman, Charles L., 59
Reed, Erik K., 209

*Relación de Tequisistlan*, 234
Renfrew, Colin, 321
research strategies, 297–303; nature of,
    215–16, 229; Southwest Iran as example,
    222–28
resource utilization, political evolution
    and, 231–57 passim
Reynolds, William E., 326, 329
Rice, E. L., 175
Riley, Thomas J., 59, 321
*The Rise of Anthropological Theory*
    (Harris), 25
Rodgers, William B., 26, 37
Rohn, Arthur H., 205
Russell, William M. S., 97

Sahlins, Marshall, 5, 6, 25, 46, 47, 61, 62,
    63, 122, 123, 125, 130–36
Sanders, William T., 13–14, 165, 226,
    231–57, 272–318 passim
Sandwich Islands, 105–6, 121–50. *See also*
    Hawaiian Islands
Saxe, Arthur A., 8, 10, 11, 14, 76, 80, 105–
    31, 137, 261, 274–318 passim
Scriven, Michael, 324
Secord, Paul F., 74
selection, 46–47, 96, 290–91
self-regulation, of living systems, 62–64
Service, Elman R., 5, 6, 25, 26, 27, 46, 47,
    61, 62, 181
Siegel, B. J., 28
Simon, Herbert A., 62, 327
simulation. *See* computer simulation
Sjoberg, Gideon, 325
Smith, D. B., 61, 63
Smith, N. M., 97
societal systems, nature of, 277–85
Sommerhof, G., 97
Sorokin, Pitirim A., 325
*Spatial Analysis* (Berry and Marble, eds.),
    193
spatial distributions, 11, 186
specific evolutionism, 5–6
stability, 325–33
state, 12–13, 121–30, 215–30, 304–13
Steinen, Diether von den, 134
Steiner, Gary A., 19
Steward, Julian, 3–4, 25, 27–28, 204
Stickel, E. Gary, 191
strategy, defined, 44
Strauss, Anselm, 74
stress, 52, 62

Struever, Stuart, 174
Stuber, George W., 184
substantive systems, 260, 269
*Suma de Visitas*, 234
Sutherland, John W., 323
systemic change: nature of, 15, 285–88;
    population aggregation and, 185–214
systems, 116, 117, 326, 328; defined, 44, 61,
    106–9; societal, 277–85
systems theory, 7, 59–103; computer
    simulation and, 259–70

tendency statements, 323–24
Teotihuacan Valley, evolution of state in,
    231–57
*Theory of Culture Change* (Steward), 4, 25
Titiev, Mischa, 206
Tiv, 112
Townsend, Alex H., 59, 321
Trumbull, Richard, 95
Tsembaga, 84, 87, 89
Tuggle, H. David, 59, 321
Turner, Ralph H., 74
Tylor, Edward B., 2, 25

unilineal evolutionism, 2–3

variability, accounting for, 20–21, 43
variety, 290–91
variety generation, 45–46, 47
Vayda, Andrew, 5, 61, 63
Vickers, Geoffrey, 63, 97

Wallace, Alfred Russell, 2
warfare, computer simulation and, 261–69
Watson, J. B., 28
Watson, Patty Jo, 59
Weingartner, Rudolph H., 59
White, Leslie A., 3, 25, 26–27, 100, 111, 112
Whitehead, Alfred North, 330
Wiener, Norbert, 63
Wilson, Nancy, 177
Wilson, R. E., 175
Wise, John H., 131
Wittfogel, Karl A., 13, 204, 216, 218, 246
Wright, George Henrik von, 325
Wright, Henry T., 8, 12–13, 14, 155, 215–
    30, 272–318 passim, 321

Yarnell, Richard A., 176, 177
Young, O. R., 60